Jonathan
Behind Blue Eyes

Mike Dacy

BALBOA
PRESS
A DIVISION OF HAY HOUSE

Copyright © 2012 Mike Dacy.

All rights reserved. No part of this book may be used or reproduced by any means, graphic, electronic, or mechanical, including photocopying, recording, taping or by any information storage retrieval system without the written permission of the publisher except in the case of brief quotations embodied in critical articles and reviews.

ISBN: 978-1-4525-5676-5 (sc)
ISBN: 978-1-4525-5677-2 (hc)
ISBN: 978-1-4525-5675-8 (e)

Library of Congress Control Number: 2012914558

Balboa Press books may be ordered through booksellers or by contacting:

Balboa Press
A Division of Hay House
1663 Liberty Drive
Bloomington, IN 47403
www.balboapress.com
1-(877) 407-4847

Because of the dynamic nature of the Internet, any web addresses or links contained in this book may have changed since publication and may no longer be valid. The views expressed in this work are solely those of the author and do not necessarily reflect the views of the publisher, and the publisher hereby disclaims any responsibility for them.

Cover Photograph: Tiffany Godwin Dacy

The author of this book does not dispense medical advice or prescribe the use of any technique as a form of treatment for physical, emotional, or medical problems without the advice of a physician, either directly or indirectly. The intent of the author is only to offer information of a general nature to help you in your quest for emotional and spiritual well-being. In the event you use any of the information in this book for yourself, which is your constitutional right, the author and the publisher assume no responsibility for your actions.

Any people depicted in stock imagery provided by Thinkstock are models, and such images are being used for illustrative purposes only.
Certain stock imagery © Thinkstock.

Printed in the United States of America

Balboa Press rev. date: 10/02/2012

Table of Contents

Introduction
About the Author(s) 1
Gifts 7
The Alpha and Omega 15

Jonathan's Life in a Nutshell
The Early Years 23
The Move to Paulding County 43
Adulthood 57

Behind Blue Eyes
Introduction 63
The Dark Side 67
His Truest Essence 103
    Chris 103
    Remy 108
    Jonathan and Tiffany: A Love Story 115
    The Teachings of Jonathan 132

The Rollercoaster
Introduction 151
September 157
October 177
November to Early December 199
December to The Facility 215
The Facility 239
Post Rehab 277
February 295
March 313

April 347
The Search 373
You Are At Peace 399
The Funeral 401

The Aftermath
Healing 409
Facts, Thoughts and Thanks 433

Appendix
A Mother's Everlasting Love and Inspirations 445
References 465

Acknowledgements

There are so many people to thank who not only helped with Jonathan Behind Blue Eyes, but also traveled with Jonathan down his path. To recognize everyone who impacted Jonathan's life would amount to a chapter in itself, and this needs to be concise. To all of Jonathan's aunts, uncles, cousins and friends not mentioned in these pages, my love and thanks go to each one of you.

First, I want to thank Jonathan's mother, Terri, for your dedication to completing this book. Our brainstorming and your recollections, written contributions, and eye for detail have been a major contribution to this legacy to our son. Although not all of your writings are included in the book, the appendix, "A Mothers Everlasting Love and Inspirations" includes your work and exemplifies the beautiful and loving soul that you are. Thank you.

To all of my "kids"; whether you are blood, step, in-law, or have naturally become a member of our family, thank you for sharing your memories about Jonathan with me. Michael and Cherie Dacy, Matthew and Kristin Andrews, Ashley Johnson and Ben Turcotte, Matt Lee, Chris Lee, Tiffany Dacy, and my grandson, Remy Dacy, I love each of you and thank you for all of your help.

Michael, additional thanks for all of your editing work and help with the keynote and additional work needed to complete the book.

Tiffany, special thanks for sharing the story of your life with Jonathan and for the many wonderful pictures you have provided for this book.

Remy, thank you for your innocence. (See, 2 weeks are up!!!!)

To my brother, Joe Dacy, I thank you for your help with editing and your enthusiastic assistance with the Blue Eyes chapter of the book. More importantly, thanks for being a loving brother.

Alicia Spurling, thank you for your help with recalling life in the late

80's and early 90's and being there for Jonathan as he grew up and always opening your door to him whenever he needed you. Your continued kindness is appreciated and I will always cherish our friendship.

To Jonathan's grandparents, Bill Maxey and David and Frances Dean, and Jonathan's uncle, Scott Maxey: thank you for all of your caring and for helping Jonathan with whatever was needed at the time.

To my extended family at American Breast Care, who also happens to be my employer, I give more thanks to you than you can possibly realize. From the daily management of David Hensley, Dean Benton, and Robert Halley, to the executive leadership of Jolly Rechenberg and Jay Markowitz, you have created a culture many claim to have, but few actually achieve. Many companies profess to be "family" and make statements like "our employees and our customers come first." I assure you that my 40 years work experience have presented me with comparable slogans but not heartfelt execution. The reflection of this culture was never as obvious as it was during "The Rollercoaster", "The Search", and "The Aftermath" time periods, and it continues to this day. Thank you. To the people I deal with every day who work in customer service, manufacturing, development, accounting, sales, marketing, and warehousing: I thank you from the bottom of my heart for your hugs, your compassion, your sharing of similar stories, your counsel and advice.

Special thanks to two of those family members, Larry Prosser and Susan Short. Thank you for editing and all of your valuable feedback. This book would not be what it is if it wasn't for you.

To another extended family member, I thank vocalist Aquarius Statham for agreeing, on very short notice, to sing at Jonathan's funeral service. You touched our hearts singing The Lord's Prayer. Your beautiful rendition of Amazing Grace as Jonathan was being laid to rest, brought goose bumps to our flesh and tears to our eyes. Follow your dream; you have a beautiful heart, soul, and voice.

Cindy Kloch, my Birthday Buddy, thank you. When I asked you to edit the book, you told me that you would be perfectly honest. If the book wasn't good, you would let me know. You never did say that, but you did offer invaluable insight to the final edition. Thank you very much and, at the latest, I'll see you next April.

The title of the book and one of its chapters is based on the lyrics of the classic song Behind Blue Eyes. To the members of The Who, particularly to Pete Townsend for these words and to Roger Daltry for the incomparable vocals, thank you, not only for providing me with the inspiration to write this book, but for sharing your music with the world.

A note of thanks to the members of Limp Bizkit who not only performed a remake of Behind Blue Eyes, but added a stanza that is used in the book to describe a portion of Jonathan's life. Thanks to you.

I want to thank Ariadne Romano and her late husband, Francis, for the major impact you had on Jonathan's life. When he stayed with you for 3 weeks in 2004, you opened his eyes to the world of spirit and taught him how to look at his problems from a different perspective. He took the lessons you presented to him and carried them in his heart for the rest of his life.

During "The Rollercoaster", the last 8 months of Jonathan's life, he found himself in trouble with the law on numerous occasions. Jonathan and his family dealt with 7 different local and county police departments. There was one group that stood out with the way they communicated with Jonathan. The officers that he met recognized that Jonathan was gentle and troubled, and they responded with kindness, compassion, and non-judgment. I tip my hat to Chief of Police Gary Yandura and the officers of the Hiram, Georgia Police Department for displaying the actions that truly describe civil service. Thank you.

Throughout Jonathan's life, he was never without friends. Wherever we lived, he would strike up friendships and he maintained many of these friendships as he moved from place to place. He had a group of friends, despite the difficult period toward the end of his life, who stuck with him through thick and thin. Zach Price, Dustin Murphy, Josh Kidd, Derek and Molly Padgett, and Derek Griffin, thank you for your love and for always being there to lend a helping hand.

I also want to recognize a best friend of Jonathan who would have undoubtedly been there for him. The late Darin Settle, who gave his life for our country, is with Jonathan again as they have renewed the spiritual bond and friendship they shared together on earth.

Additionally, I want to thank the members of the publishing team at Balboa Press, for not only providing a service for first time authors, but for backing this service up with people who guided, supported, and encouraged me as I walked this path. Your help is truly appreciated.

Finally, to my wife Laura; you have always supported and encouraged me as I pursued my life goals. From the corporate management positions I've held, to my home inspection company, to following my spiritual path, and to the non-profit animal hospice care venture, you never said a negative word. As I obsessed with completing this book about the life of Jonathan, you were always there to listen and share ideas, and support whatever I needed to do to complete this work. I love and respect you more than you can possibly know.

Foreword

This heart wrenching account of Jonathan's life story brings forth the raw truths, memories, and emotions in the hearts of our family. While both difficult to write and also to read, it is a very important story, written to honor our son, his legacy, and his hopes and dreams of making a positive difference in the lives of others.

While his dreams of telling his story personally did not come to fruition, it is my sincere hope that, if sharing his story with the world can bestow the gifts of peace, love, and hope to even one individual or family, we can, through his inspiration, help him to complete and fulfill his greatest accomplishment.

This journey is one of sometimes nightmarish, seemingly insurmountable proportions; a story of immense love, heartache, and frustration, in a never ending attempt to save our son's life.

Terri Dacy

Introduction
About the Author(s)

My name is Mike Dacy and I'm the father of Jonathan. In some ways I knew him better than others, yet not as well as some people in other areas of his life. His mother and I divorced when he was 7, and after a year of being separated from me, he wanted to move from Tampa to live with me in Atlanta. We lived together much of the time during the next 21 years, though he did move out on several occasions, sometimes not coming back to my home for over a year. But even when he didn't live under the same roof with me, we would talk regularly to review what was happening in each other's lives.

This book is from Jonathan, written through me. Much of the work is his, and what isn't, comes from input that the rest of the family and friends shared with me. It is written from my perspective with some information coming from journals I kept. It's like a movie – Jonathan produced it, I'm the director, and the following people are the main characters in his life.

Tiffany – his wife and spiritual soul mate
Remy – his son
Ashley – his earlier love and mother of Remy
Terri – his mother
Michael and Cherie – his brother and sister-in-law
Kristin and Matthew – his sister and brother-in-law
Laura – his step-mother and my wife
Chris – his step-brother and Laura's son
Matt – his step-brother and Laura's son
Alicia – his former step-mother
Tiff – his earlier love
Molly – his earlier love

After his funeral service when friends and family had returned home, I took most of the next week off of work and began going through all of his belongings. I separated and sorted his things; and he had A LOT of things. A 10X12 storage unit was filled with files, keepsakes, military and outdoor gear, furniture, thousands of pictures, and journals of his life. His room was stuffed with additional like items. I made piles of his possessions to be given to family members, charity, or discarded. I looked through the pictures he had and began reading some of the journals he kept. I created a memorial wall for him in my workshop that displays some pictures of his life and the positive affirmations he wrote.

As I opened one of the boxes containing many of his journals, I came across a note left on top of the contents of the box. It read:

> "If you are going through this box, you better be f*@ing family and I better be f*@ing dead!!"

I'm assuming he left that note for me and that Jonathan wanted me to share his life's story with you. We'll also honor his passing, as conventional thinking and evidence point to the direction of suicide, yet a spiritual perception points to another. After he passed away, the family members looked for "answers" in a variety of different ways. Each of those stories is told. Finally, the family gives thanks to Jonathan for the gifts he brought into each of our lives.

Here is his gift to all of us.

Kristin and Matthew's Wedding
From left: Matt, Tiff, Remy, Jonathan, Laura, Mike,
Kristin, Matthew, Terri, Michael, Chris

Laura, Mike, Jonathan and Tiffany – Summer weekend cookout

Michael, Mike, Jonathan, Kristin and Alicia

Jonathan and Cherie

Jonathan and Ashley

Jonathan, Terri and Michael

Front – Chris, Kristin and Matt   Back – Jonathan and Michael

Jonathan Dalmond Dacy: February 7, 2004

Dear Opiate,

    I know I haven't seen you in a few days. I'm writing to you to let you know where I'm at and what's going on with me. But first, I want to thank you. I remember when we first met. You were always there for me. Whenever I started to get a headache you were willing to take away my pain. Do you remember? I'll never forget that. I started having migraines all the time, and so you were there with me all the time. Before I knew it, we were best friends. I wanted to have you around all the time. And you were. Not only would you take away my pain, but you gave me confidence, you made me feel so good. Before I knew it, you were the only reason I wanted to get up in the morning. I appreciate your willingness to make me happy. But just one thing, where the f*^#k are you now? Why did you take all my money? Oh, it's OK, I only have a son to raise. I only had car payments and rent payments. But you didn't seem to care about that. Oh, it's no big f*^#king deal. I'm only in a hospital now because of you. You wonder where I've been lately? I've been f*^#king miserable.....

Jonathan Dalmond Dacy: August 16, 2009

When God puts a dream in your heart, when he brings opportunities across your path, step out BOLDLY IN FAITH, EXPECT THE BEST, move FORWARD with CONFIDENCE, KNOWING that you are WELL ABLE to do what God wants you to do. If you are stepping outside your comfort zone it's a great thing – it allows God to show you his miraculous nature, assuming you are ALWAYS in a loving and forgiving mindset. All other emotions prohibit God from staying active inside your heart. When your heart is filled with hate, anger, judgment, fear, and grudges then there is no room for love, and therefore no room for God."

Gifts

Gifts We Give

Each of us enters the world with gifts to offer to others. As an infant, we give to our parents the gift of unconditional love and bless them with a sense of joy they never previously experienced. From the "terrible twos" through our teenage years we present them with ample opportunities to learn tolerance and patience.

They return gifts to us. They teach us to be honest, and with that honesty, the gift of trust. They show us how to be generous, and that it is better to give than to receive. They demonstrate and teach us the art of gentleness as our younger siblings come into the world. They point out how the young ones are defenseless, and how they depend on us to provide, care, and love them.

Our parents give to us a belief system. Whether it's organized religion, atheism, or something in between, they remind us to be faithful to those beliefs.

We remember those lessons, or gifts, that we received as we grow and attempt to be generous and honest to others. Our parents, in the meantime, continue to learn tolerance and patience as we present them with the scenarios of our life's chronicles that can exceed the limits of their trust.

Finally, as we reach adulthood, we are able to present to each other the gift of open-mindedness. Through our life experiences we've developed beliefs that don't necessarily agree with our parents. We may debate, argue, or completely disagree. Despite the assortment of viewpoints, as long as the original gift of unconditional love is remembered and received, all differences can be resolved.

Perception of Gifts

Gifts are received in many forms and are always being presented to us. They can be easy to receive or hard to comprehend.

The easiest gifts to perceive are those we receive as we sit under the

Christmas tree or celebrate our birthdays. These material items are easily recognizable and are generally "things" we want, or are given to us with a loving thought about us behind it.

We treat ourselves to material gifts as well. We complete a home improvement project and take our spouse out for a special dinner. Many of us work 45-50 weeks a year and during those weeks off from work, we give ourselves the gift of vacation. Whether it's just sitting around the house and vegetating, driving to the mountains, or taking a trip to Europe; we have earned these gifts.

Then there is the gift not of the material world, but the gifts received by our minds. These gifts may not be easy to identify, and, in fact, we may not acknowledge these as gifts at all. The simple reality of our being is a gift to others, as their being is a gift to us. As we go through our day, we are aware of the gestures people make, their facial expressions, the things they say or do. We read the newspaper and watch television. Anything we witness throughout the day can stir an emotion in us; from extreme hate to unconditional love and every feeling in between.

This is the most beneficial gift we can receive. It is how we learn to develop those virtues that we hold dear to our hearts. As we construe the gifts that we exchange with each other throughout the day as positive or negative, one thing is certain.

The gift of love, whether received or given, is the gift that offers the most joy to us; the joy of inner peace.

Gifts from Jonathan

Like all of us, Jonathan presents his gifts in many forms. The first of these are the thoughts that came from his mind that he wrote onto paper. His lessons to us consist of many quotations; the first two in the opening of the book as well as the last line in the conclusion. The chapter Behind Blue Eyes: His Truest Essence, centers on his notes. Any quotes you read within this book, unless otherwise noted, are from Jonathan's hand. Renowned philosophers, psychologists, and spiritual leaders are quoted. There are quotes from the Bible, poets and other writers who had an impact on his thoughts and belief system. Also, Jonathan's personal work is cited. He spent the spiritual portion of the last six years of his life studying, reading, and writing with the purpose of finding his way to God. He was meticulous at copying quotes, making sure they were "quoted" and then identifying the author of those quotes. If something is misquoted in this book, I apologize.

He didn't limit himself to one belief system. He loved the Bible and the contemporary teachings of Joel Osteen. He had almost all of Wayne Dyer's books and CDs, and would listen to his CDs while driving. He was intrigued by Taoism and its focus on the mind rather than the outside world. He enjoyed discussing A Course In Miracles principles with me.

He had a meditation shrine set up in his bedroom in my home, and another set up in his home with his wife, Tiffany. Each one focused on self-improvement, loving statements, and quotes from various religions and belief systems. There were also pictures of his loved ones, and positive affirmations placed to remind him as to what he was trying to achieve and what was ultimately important.

One of his favorite affirmations that he kept on the forefront of his meditation and prayer shrines was this verse.

The light of God surrounds me
The love of God enfolds me
The power of God protects me
The presence of God watches over me
Wherever I am, God is.

Jonathan loved to give gifts, and he cherished any gift from the heart which he received. Sweaters, pants, and the like were usually returned. Books, pictures, or anything created from someone's hand or heart were cherished. I have gone through what he retained in storage and he had every picture his son, Remy, has drawn for him; love letters and cards from years gone by; and other things that came from the heart.

The book is an honest look at Jonathan's life, and like most of us, his life had its ups and downs. He was addicted to narcotic medicines that were meant to help him through life. He was prescribed blood pressure meds, anti-depressants, anti-anxiety meds, and pain killers. His emotions would peak and valley; on many occasions things were either "great" or quite to the contrary, "it was the worst day of my life." He had his "skeletons" hiding in his closet. At times he had trouble controlling his anger.

On the other hand, Jonathan was one of the kindest, most loving persons you could know. He had a wonderful sense of humor. His love for his son, wife, friends and family saw the wonderful man he, at his purest essence, was.

You may wonder how a book could be written capturing so many of the details that made up his life. Jonathan kept journals. He started journaling when he was 10, documenting the daily activities of his Spy Club. He continued writing chronologically about his life until he was 23 with periods of time, sometimes up to a year, missing. After that, the tone of his writing changed. Not only did he write about his life, he wrote some beautiful poetry, positive affirmations, and lessons to live by. He made extensive to-do lists identifying short term tasks and long term goals. He listed the steps he needed to take in order to become educated or certified so that he might help others.

From the time Jonathan was 6 until his passing at the age of 29, he wanted to serve his fellow man. Until he was in his late teens his service goal was to honor and protect his country in the military. He had lofty goals of becoming a member of an elite force; and he trained and played war games as often as he could get his friends to participate. He had a library of books about Viet Nam, World War II, and general military strategic and tactical maneuvers. His aptitude for military operations was outstanding. He was quick to think on his feet, and in speaking with his friends, he was always the leader and the one with the ideas. Over the years he collected an arsenal of weapons and obtained official military gear. He spent countless hours in military surplus stores adding to his collection. He also received many gifts from his Grandpa Spurling, a retired Sergeant Major in the Calvary; not to mention that for the rest of us the Holiday Season was easy as he would provide a list of the supplies he "needed", and Santa would do the rest. He enjoyed the outdoors, loved to camp, go repelling, and play paintball. He was proud to be an American and he was preparing for a life in the military.

Something changed along the way. In his early teens he began suffering severe migraines and was diagnosed with Adolescent Migraine Disease. We were told not to worry as these would subside and eventually pass as he got older. In the meantime, we filled the prescriptions and experimented with different medicines to help ease his throbbing headaches. Most medicines didn't seem to help as much as he liked until he came across Oxycontin at the age of 18. It was also during this time that we visited a doctor who informed us that the cause of the headaches could be due to a deformity in his ear. Surgery was required and any hopes of being in the military were shattered as they couldn't accept him with this defect.

Despite having the surgery to correct the defect, the pain continued. He continued to seek medicines to relieve the pain and feel normal. He shelved his plans for the military and dropped out of high school. For the next 10 years he continued to provide service in the restaurant industry. He took great pride in his work, was promoted regularly into management positions, and focused on servicing the customer as well as his employer, always looking for ways to improve restaurant operations. He managed restaurant kitchens and took great pride in his work and the food he served. He also had responsibility in a few positions for front end management, and took that same pride in making sure the customer was served. Inevitably, what had become an addiction to prescription medicines got in the way, and he would lose a job. This happened for a number of reasons. He might lose his temper with his boss and get fired. He might blame others for the lousy work conditions and walk out. On a couple of occasions he was caught stealing (or borrowing as he would justify it to me) and get fired. Other times he might not show up for days and this resulted in his termination.

In 2004, during his stay at his 5th rehab clinic, he was introduced to a new method of treatment. Rather than the typical 12 step programs, and hanging out and waiting to go to, as he referred to them, "bull shit meetings," the approach was holistic in nature. Meditation, yoga, prayer, New Age thinking, were some of the daily routine, as well as accountability for the chores he was assigned. The pastors also performed a numerology test and a past life regression was conducted. Although this approach didn't solve his future problems, it opened his eyes to a new world of thinking. He began applying some of the ideas presented to him and dug deeper into alternative ways of thinking and perceiving. His journaling began to change. Rather than solely write about his life in chronological order, he began documenting his thoughts and ideas that might better serve himself or humankind.

One night in February 2010 after he finished working, Jonathan came into my workshop to discuss things. On this night he told me, "Dad, I want to get rid of all my addiction problems so that I can help people. I have so much I can teach them by sharing my life story and offering advice. I want to be a counselor or a teacher, and show them where I screwed up so that others don't make the same mistakes I did. I want to change the way society looks at people with addiction problems."

It's important to recognize that there was one constant goal in Jonathan's life: he wanted to serve and help others. The method he used to provide this service changed throughout the years, but nonetheless this thought was deep inside him. After he realized he wouldn't be able to serve in the military, he changed his focus to the hospitality industry. During the last couple of years of his life, he spoke with many fire departments to receive the guidance he needed to serve as a fireman. He also visited funeral homes in the area to see if he could assist with grieving families. Finally, as he shared with me on that February evening, his goal was to help people with addiction problems and change the way these people were perceived by mainstream society.

The final gift Jonathan brings to us comes in sharing moments of his life story even though he isn't here to present these in person.

Perhaps you are having addiction problems of your own. There may be a situation described in this book that will help you down your chosen path. A situation he was in and how he responded may remind you of something you have done in the past or may face in the future. He wanted to share the results of his decisions.

Maybe you know a loved one or family member who is experiencing addiction issues. There may be a scenario described that will help you decide how to pursue help for your loved one. Certainly our family was confronted with many situations regarding Jonathan, particularly during his last eight months. Decisions we made or didn't make affected how this period of time played out. Whether it is to follow our experiences or doing the complete opposite, it doesn't matter. If it ultimately brings more peace and resolution to your situation, then his gift has been received.

After reading this book, you might find something in your heart that gives you a better understanding of the nature of the disease. You may find that you show a little more compassion, patience, or understanding to a person struggling with addiction; less quickly to judge and more apt to reach out and support that person.

This is by no means a "how to" book. The end result is that Jonathan passed away, and obviously nobody wanted that. It will reveal his family's feelings, experiences, fears, anger, frustrations; yet more importantly the faith, hope, and love that we all shared. If you recognize something in Jonathan's story that will help, directly or indirectly, and bring inner peace into your life, then he will accomplish what he wanted to do with his life.

Some people may find this book disturbing. As Jonathan followed his life's journey he wasn't proud of everything he did. In trying to help in any way we could his family would intervene at times using both conventional and unconventional methods. He'd been exorcised a couple of times, he had a past life regression conducted, he was institutionalized in conventional 12 steps curriculum as well as holistic programs. To help with finding him after he had disappeared, we enlisted the help of a renowned psychic, who happened to provide valuable guidance for us.

Medicines are available to help with the sicknesses from which many of us suffer. New and improved medicines are presented regularly to better remedy these ailments. Yet each one has a list of side effects, some of them worsening the condition they were originally intended to help. Don't misunderstand me. Many of my loved ones are helped and are still alive because of these medicines. If we didn't have them, we might still be using leeches to suck the poisons out of our bodies. The point is that some of these medicines are addictive and can be very dangerous.

Perhaps Jonathan's life was served to provide the gift of "awareness."

Perhaps his greatest gift to all of us was to create enough cause and effect situations that put us in a mindset: "What do I do?" "How do I respond?" "How can I prevent?"

And maybe the answer lies in his favorite verse from the Bible. "And now these three remain: faith, hope and love. But the greatest of these is love." I Corinthians 13:13

Or as Jonathan wrote on September 19, 2007:

"Where there is life, there should also be love."

One of Jonathan's meditation shrines at home

Mike Dacy

Jonathan's office at Mike and Laura's house

Positive affirmations to live by

The Alpha and Omega

The Birth of Jonathan and His Siblings

Jonathan's big brother, Michael, was born at 6:54 PM on January 14, 1977. He came into this world a healthy, 8 pound 2 ½ ounce baby boy. I've heard that baby's eyes are always blue when they are born. Michael's eyes were brownish-black and we knew he would be one of a kind. As it turned out, he is and he is loved and admired by the many people who know him.

Kristin, Jonathan's little sister, was born at 7:00 PM on November 2, 1983. Her little 7 pound 4 ½ ounce body entered the world with very serious health conditions. Despite the life threatening operations she has faced, her sunny outlook on life is an inspiration to others as she gives love and shows compassion to everyone she meets. As Jonathan always described her, she truly is an angel.

As Terri prepared to give birth to our middle child, we hadn't come up with a first name. His middle name would be Dalmond; named after her little brother who had passed away at the age of 3 from leukemia, and her paternal grandfather. But we were having trouble deciding on a first name. As Terri entered the last trimester of her pregnancy, she spent much of her time reading. She recalled reading Jonathan Livingston Seagull while she was in high school and remembered how much she enjoyed this book. She bought a new copy and read it just before going into labor. She found that she loved the spirit and the unique character that God created the seagull to be. She felt in her heart that this baby would be mirrored in that spirituality and uniqueness. He would be one of a kind, just as Jonathan Livingston Seagull was!!

Jonathan Dalmond Dacy would enter this world at 9:54 PM on March 27, 1981; a healthy 10 pound beautiful baby boy.

Immediately after Jonathan was born, Terri experienced afterbirth complications. A nurse asked me if I could take Jonathan while they centered their attention on Terri. I whole heartedly agreed and she handed me a 2 minute old baby who was screaming his head off. I walked around with him, telling him everything will be all right, and eventually his crying stopped. He just stared at me with his angelic eyes as if to say "I trust you Dad."

Truly a moment I will never forget.

The Passing of Jonathan

It is said that one of the most difficult situations a person can experience is to bury their own child. I've witnessed this twice in my family.

The first occurred in 1969 when my father's twin brother, John, passed away. As the casket door was closed for the last time on the eve of the funeral, I remember my grandparents sobbing and my grandfather saying "This just isn't right." Uncle John was standing on a street corner in Chicago when a sudden heart attack hit. The coroner said he was dead before he hit the ground.

The second time happened in 2000 as I watched Jonathan grieve for his infant son. Cullen was born with trisomy disease and only lived 2 weeks. Jonathan was thoroughly distraught as he wept over the tiny coffin and then over his tiny grave.

What can you say to parents in times like these? It's not fair; the natural progression of life should be the child burying the parent.

Saturday May 8, 2010

At 11:00AM, our family gathered at the funeral home to set up the pictures and memorabilia we had gathered over the past three days to prepare for the guests who would gather to celebrate Jonathan's life. His close friends and family had collected hundreds of pictures and a variety of the many positive affirmations Jonathan tried to live by. It was a heartfelt tribute to his life and the man he had become and continued to strive to be.

A few days earlier, on May 4, 2010, Jonathan's body was discovered along some railroad tracks in Rome, GA. According to the coroner he had passed away several days before, so a closed casket service was performed.

So many friends and family made arrangements to travel from out of town in order to offer support to Jonathan's mother, brothers, sister, stepmother, son, wife and me. Yet, as I made the rounds and talked with so many of his friends and visited with relatives, I found that so many of them needed support for themselves. It's not easy to comprehend and accept a 29 year old man's life ending.

Visitation ended at 3:00PM and the service began. The Reverend Frank B. conducted the ceremony. The Reverend spoke about how he hadn't known Jonathan personally, but had become familiar with him through other ministers at his church and the family members he had spoken with over the past few days. He spoke beautifully about Jonathan and how our loving God has welcomed him into the Kingdom of Heaven. He emphasized this despite initial evidence that Jonathan may have committed suicide.

After the Reverend had finished Tiffany and I presented our eulogies. We were followed by Kristin and Terri.

It was then Michael's turn to speak. He so eloquently summarized the life of Jonathan during the next fifteen minutes. He spoke from his heart, with wisdom and understanding that only could have been taught to him by Jonathan's passing.

Michael's Eulogy

"My little brother, Jonathan Dalmond Dacy, lived a duality, a dichotomous life sometimes gleaming with extraordinary light and another of occasional deep, bitter darkness. He could be the kindest and most thoughtful friend, or a furious and spiteful enemy. With Jonathan, there was often little in between. He was a living exaggeration. He was a gentle warrior. Many of you never had the good fortune to know Jonathan well. I will now attempt to honor him with some of my fondest memories and most heartfelt thoughts.

Jonathan was often misunderstood. He once walked and lived with a confidence and poise that was awe inspiring, but it was also intimidating to some. To others it was scary. Jonathan was the epitome of a tough guy. He was the guy other men wanted to be and who women wanted to be with. He demanded respect and courtesy, and was intolerant for those who lacked similar character traits. Jonathan wanted to battle, not for the simple sake of a fight, but to embarrass those who cared for little beyond themselves. But let me be perfectly clear so his legacy is never mistaken or tarnished... while still a young man, he stopped looking for a fight, and began seeing the light of man. He learned to forgive; and beyond his armor, at the center of Jonathan's heart lived a combination of pureness, innocence, and love that no one I have ever known can match. He was sentimental to a fault, skin like tissue paper. Above all things...ALL THINGS...Jonathan loved his family, most especially his son, Remy. He and I would talk several times per year about getting our entire family together...grandparents, aunts, uncles, cousins, 2nd generation, 3rd generation, everyone! A reunion such as this would have been the most special gift he could have been given. It hurts and saddens me terribly that this never happened for him. Though we're not all here, if Jonathans peering down upon us today, I promise you he is honored and touched that you cared enough to make it here to bid him farewell. I sincerely thank you for that.

Jonathan was an artist, and his mind never ceased to create another abstract thought. As a child he used to talk about the two of us building a compound, of sorts. In his mind it would be a place large enough to house our entire family and all our friends…every single person in this room and more. It's funny, at least if you know Jonathan it is. He wanted it to be impervious to attack, yet beautiful and conducive to raising a family. He wanted it to be self-sustaining…produce, livestock, water, and energy. He imagined a bomb shelter and more weapons than our own military could probably afford. In these memories, I know he aspired to be a protector and provider. His ideology was innocent, without flaw, and mature well beyond his years.

Jonathan's frequent bouts of self-indulgence may lead some to believe he was selfish and incapable or uninterested in giving. Nothing could be further from the truth. Even as a child who did not understand the emotional relevancies of gifts or even the joy of giving, he was amazing. When I was a little boy, perhaps 8 years old (which made Jonathan 4 years old), I loved wildlife, but most especially insects. One year Grandpa Dacy made both of us insect boxes to house those we caught, for each of us among our favorite all time gifts. Jonathan and I would catch and release for hours, and Jonathan seemed to innately understand the joy this brought me. Jonathan was still too young to go to school, and was waiting for me at my bus stop, several blocks from home, when I came home from school one day. He was beaming with excitement. He said, "Michael, look what I caught for you!" Then he held up the insect box which he was hiding behind his back. Inside was a massive praying mantis, at the time the most interesting and terrifying living thing I had ever seen, let alone insect. The claws! The jaws! I couldn't believe his bravery, and it changed my life forever! It was at that very moment, even at that young age, that Jonathan established residence in my heart forever and became a hero of mine. An unforgettable moment for me. I think about it often and recall it vividly like it was yesterday, always have.

Another time when Jonathan was a young teenager, he spent hours carefully drawing a beautiful sword for me. It's one of the greatest pencil drawings I've ever seen, even to this day. I have it in my office at home. It wasn't my birthday or a holiday. Jonathan just loved me, and he found great joy in giving. He wrote me a book when he was five. It was only 4 pages, and it could be read in less than 30 seconds, but it stirred my soul.

Jonathan would often give to me his time. When I started making a decent salary, I was excited to spend my money doing fun things with Jonathan. I surprised him with a gift certificate to go skydiving. He came along rather unenthusiastically...he almost seemed bored. But he did it anyway. Another time when Jonathan turned 21, I took him to Las Vegas. We had a good time, but I don't think he really came home all that impressed. Another time I took him for a biplane adventure, and he was almost reluctant to fly. I think he only agreed to go because it was another opportunity to give back to me. In retrospect Jonathans perhaps the most giving man I've ever known. I truly mean that. He had very little materially, and never had a dime in his pocket that he didn't owe someone else, but Jonathan would give the shirt off his back if a man simply asked for it.

In Mark 12:41-44, Jesus sat down opposite the place where the offerings were put and watched the crowd putting their money into the temple treasury. Many rich people threw in large amounts. But a poor widow came and put in two very small copper coins, worth only a fraction of a penny. Calling his disciples to him, Jesus said, "I tell you the truth, this poor widow has put more into the treasury than all the others. They gave out of their wealth; but she, out of her poverty, put in <u>everything</u> - all she had to live on." The poor widow could have been Jonathan. Without judgment or prejudice, but with a heart of pure gold, he gave graciously and lovingly, if not abundantly. I have no doubt Jesus smiled kindly upon Jonathan for walking like Him. Who among us can say the same of ourselves?

Despite his unrelenting torment in recent times, I don't believe Jonathan ever truly wanted to leave this world. Conversely I believe he desired to live so perfectly well and flawlessly in the eyes of those he loved that he could not bear witness to himself or forgive himself of his own sins and misgivings in life. His anguish and self-loathing were seemingly tangible. It could affect an entire room. He knew this, and it further sickened him with guilt and grief. His sorrow was genuine and self-destructive. Jonathan maintained an often unattainably high standard for himself, and ultimately it contributed towards his anxiety, depression, and untimely death. I know this because of many reasons, but mostly because in recent years Jonathan would study and focus so completely on self-improvement and spiritual health that he would sacrifice everything else only to gain clearer perspective on whatever it was he was studying at the moment. As a result he experienced spiritual growth and enlightenment many of us will only ever read about. Unfortunately for all his new wisdom and understanding, he had to sacrifice in almost all other life arenas. That said, I believe it is not only possible, but likely, that Jonathan was searching for grace in those woods. Scripture says in regards to Jesus Christ, "But as many as received him, to them he gave power to become the sons of God, even to them that believe on his name." (John 1:12) This statement confirms to us Jonathan is in Heaven because not only did Jonathan believe in Jesus, but he tried harder than any man I know to live like Him. I only pray his remaining moments in this world were filled with the light of Heaven, and that it shone irresistibly and perfectly through Jonathan's soul.

Those who have worked with Jonathan can attest to his willpower and strive for perfection as well. They will tell you he would exhaust himself with work, spend endless nights contriving ideas to work better, get promoted, get promoted again, but eventually he'd lose interest when his coworkers or bosses didn't share his passion. While living with Cherie and me for a brief period a few years back, Jonathan work for a well-established and renowned restaurant with several locations in the Atlanta area. Jonathan was offered the opportunity to preside over the kitchen at a brand new location which was to complete construction within months. These are multi-million dollar restaurants, the position was the equivalent of an executive chef at a 4 or 5 star restaurant, and Jonathan had only been with the company for several months! He never even finished high school, but his perfection driven work ethic was exemplary, and he had proven most worthy of the promotion. Jonathan declined the position because it wasn't good enough...it wasn't perfect.

With absolute resolve, Jonathan sought this uncompromising perfection in all he did and all he was. The tattoo he proudly displayed on his forearm read INTEGRITY, and though he struggled to live up to the strictest definition of the word, he never stopped trying. This fact rings loud and true in his quest for true love. Jonathan loved, and was loved by, many girls and women in his brief life. Like he did with himself, he created a standard higher and so specific to his own needs that most women could never achieve it. And none did until Tiffany Godwin entered his life. Tiffany was able to humble and tame Jonathan unlike any person I had ever seen. Jonathan was a new man, a tremendously happy man. His joy was saturating and I was proud of him. Within weeks he asked her to marry him, she accepted, and he asked me to be his best man at the wedding. Of course I accepted as any brother would, but I was shocked, and behind closed doors I was judgmental and, I suppose, prideful. I didn't understand how he could be marrying this woman who he had known for approximately a month. I could never get beyond it. In my arrogance I later had a conversation with him about it, and attempted to change his mind. He wouldn't. He knew. He was unyielding, and I was selfish and mad about it. Through a couple of failed attempts to set a wedding, Jonathan and Tiffany were married only weeks ago. Of course, predictably, I was not his best man. Indeed he never even told me about the marriage. And I didn't deserve to know. However I now understand it to have been among Jonathan's sweetest days of his life. He and Tiffany spent a beautiful, glorious night together as man and wife, and I believe Jonathan was probably never happier than that singular moment.

I am ashamed. In our search for Jonathan over the previous week, I have seen glimpses of EXACTLY what Jonathan saw in Tiffany from the outset. Tiffany is a shining example of precisely the kind of love our world needs... the kind of love Jonathan needed desperately. Tiffany, you are my sister, and you are my family, and I love you as much as any person in this room. Thank you for your presence in Jonathan's life, however brief it may have been. I am convinced that Jonathan waited his entire lifetime to find you, his undeniable soul mate. You are the culmination of Jonathan's quest for uncompromising perfection.

Some of you have already heard this from me, but Jonathan and I shared a bond many brothers never experience. Our love for one another was 100% without compromise and unconditional. In 29 years I cannot recall a single day either of us fought, not one; but I can recall hundreds of days that our love, brotherhood, and friendship shined like the most brilliant of sunrises. I experienced almost every possible emotion with Jonathan, and I'm thankful for it all. His loss is excruciating, and with it, a piece of my heart will be forever absent. Over the previous several days, as a result of Jonathan's passing, I have reached many conclusions about my own life. If you don't hear anything else I say today, hear this. The greatest regret I have, and probably ever will have, is that I didn't maintain a close relationship with Jonathan in recent years. There still existed a kinship and bond that I suppose all brothers have, but we slowly grew apart. We rarely spoke. Our interests and our spirituality divided us, and my pride and arrogance further drove a wall between us. I failed to know and bond with Jonathan, the man, as well as I would have liked or should have, and I can confidently tell you he felt the same way. Please remember this. Learn a lesson from me, and apply it to your own lives. I'm speaking to anyone else who has let pride stand in the way of love. As Jonathan so correctly and thoroughly believed with all his heart and soul, "And now abide faith, hope, love, these three; but the greatest of these is love." (1 Corinthians 13:13)

The last time I saw Jonathan was April 24th, 2010, Dad's birthday, precisely 2 weeks ago. We were visiting together, exchanging gifts, and having a great time...Jonathan, Dad, Tiffany, Laura, Matt, Cherie, and myself. I hadn't seen Jonathan that happy in years. He was married now, and for the first time in a great while his smile inspired and motivated me; and I actually commented about it to Cherie as we drove home that evening. She saw it, too. I am immensely thankful for that moment with Jonathan. It is how I'll fondly remember my sweet, precious little brother, the man who, through his life and also his death, has given me more love than any one person deserves.

Because Jonathan desired nothing more than to give back to humanity, to pay respects in perhaps the greatest possible way, I want to ask for your charity, the same as Jonathan would have given you if only he could have. I am going to set a container on a table near the exit of this building. When you leave, if you find it in your heart, please give whatever you can afford. In Jonathan's name, I will donate the proceeds to an organization he believed in, one that I will select with the help of Tiffany and Dad.

Thank you."

Jonathan and Michael

Jonathan's Life in a Nutshell
The Early Years

He was a happy baby. I would give him "tummy blows" while changing his diaper, and he would laugh with delight. When we would have his picture taken, Terri would tickle his ribs and say "Teeth!!!" and Jonathan would smile from ear to ear with his baby teeth flashing. At the age of 4, Jonathan experimented with self-medicating for the first time. Kristin was in a hospital located a couple of miles from Terri's father's home. Michael, Jonathan, and I were there visiting with Terri's Dad and his elderly mother, who was taking heart medications. I picked Terri up from the hospital so she could spend a few hours with her family while Kristin napped.

"Teeth!"

Terri's grandmother would leave her medicines on the kitchen counter with the caps off, as the bottles were not only child proof but grandmother proof as well. After dinner, Jonathan quietly got down from his seat and went into the kitchen. Terri noticed the "quiet" that occurs when a child is into something that he shouldn't be into. She walked into the kitchen and found him taking his great-grandmother's medicine. Terri rushed over and stuck her fingers into his mouth. Out came a mouthful of pills. We rushed him to the hospital where they pumped his stomach, and kept him overnight for observation. We arranged to have him stay in the same room as Kristin. After Jonathan settled into his bed, I returned to Terri's Dad's house, picked up Michael, and returned to the hospital with him so we could all spend the night together.

From the time he was 5 or 6, he wanted to be in the military. He was fascinated with the military lifestyle. He possessed a high aptitude for military theory, strategic and tactical planning, and execution of the plan. He was the leader of the pack. As a youngster, he and his friends might "pick an enemy", for instance, me mowing the grass, and surround me and put themselves in a position for an all-out attack. They would all at once charge and shoot me and yell "We got you Dad!!" After Laura and I married and moved into our home, we would play flashlight tag. Jonathan (now 16) and his friends hid themselves in the dense brush in back of our house, and would sneak up toward the deck. Laura and I stood on the deck with flashlights, with the object being to shine the light on them before they could touch the deck.

The year before Laura and I married, Jonathan, Michael and I lived on the other side of town in Lawrenceville, GA. It was late August of 1996. Kristin stayed with me for some of the summer while Michael and Jonathan spent time with Terri in Florida. Michael was beginning his second year of college with his focus on culinary arts while he worked part time delivering pizza. Jonathan was working part time at a local department store as he prepared to begin his sophomore year in high school.

During his first week of school he was given an assignment to write 5 papers to describe himself and his interests. The first of these is titled "Best Friend."

"My best friend is Jimmy. We've been friends since 7th grade. I guess we are such good friends because he, as do I, likes the military, and he, too, wants to be in it. For this reason we obviously get along very well. We go most places together. Last summer we went to Florida to visit my mom together. We stayed for 2 weeks. The summer before last we went to Lake Lanier together a lot. We quite frequently spend the night at each other's house.

He is also the one I play paintball with. We both have the same paintball guns. We both have the same basic equipment.

I think and hope Jimmy and I will be best friends forever."

The second assignment was to write about the books he enjoyed reading.

"I have five favorite books. All of them are written by Richard Marcinko, a former Navy SEAL. The names of his five books (in order) are Rogue Warrior, Rogue Warrior Two – Red Cell, Green Team – Rogue Warrior Three, Task Force Blue – Rogue Warrior Four, and Leadership Secrets of the Rogue Warrior.

I probably like Rogue Warrior the best. It explains his experiences in Vietnam. It also talks about his life as a kid up through high school. It goes on to talk about joining the Navy and how he didn't like it until he found out about the Navy SEALs. He explains one of his operations and the equipment he used in the beginning. I found that very interesting.

Red Cell is very interesting too. The main issue I liked in this book was that he tried to train some of his, well, employees I guess, about the wilderness and tactics in jungle warfare for a paintball was he has been challenged to. Basically that took up the majority of the book. But, a little past halfway through the book he was called back to active duty in the Navy for security. His job was to hire some SEALs and plan ways to break into highly secured Navy buildings to prove that security there is not as good as they think it is. I find this book very interesting also.

In Green Team things get a little confusing, the terminology at least, so I didn't read the whole thing. But, the parts I did read were pretty good.

I'm not quite through with Task Force Blue yet. So far it is alright. He and his SEALs had to take control of a hijacked 747 plane.

And finally, Leadership Secrets of the Rogue Warrior. It is very good. It isn't a war book by any means. It tries to show you how to be a good leader. He states his thoughts about it and backs them up with real life situations, in business and in war."

For his next assignment he was asked to describe his favorite activities.

"My favorite hobbies and activities are paintball, shooting, riding my bike long distances, and, this may sound stupid to you so don't laugh, spying.

Paintball. I think by now if you have read my other pages you know what paintball is, so I won't explain.

Shooting. My friends and I like to get all of our guns and shoot; the only thing is that they are pellet guns, but it is still fun. Sometimes we shoot at cans and sometimes we hunt. We practice combat shooting and CQB (Close Quarters Battles) entering. You practice CQB by having someone set up targets and cans in your "kill" house and enter as a group from separate positions shooting all targets in a matter of seconds.

Riding bikes long distances. My friends and I do that a lot. We all get our bikes and ride the whole day, going everywhere. We stop somewhere and eat lunch, but we've been known to ride up to 50 miles a day.

Spying. Except for my friends, I don't know too many people who do this, and if they do, they don't take it as seriously as I. We all dress up in full combat gear, which usually averages out to about 40 extra pounds each. We carry canteens, first aid kits, survival equipment, night vision binoculars, and you can imagine the rest. We all wear woodland camouflage, also with combat boots. When we do this, we don't really break any laws or cause trouble; we just like to sneak right up on people without them knowing.

I guess that is basically all I do other than eat and sleep, but you don't want to know about that, right?"

He was then asked to define his life goals.

"I have many life goals. Some of them may seem unrealistic but I believe it will work. First of all, my friend Jimmy and I are planning on hiking the Appalachian Trail. It will take approximately 3 to 3 ½ months but we both find it worth the time. A few months after the hike I am going to join the military. I'm not exactly sure which branch of the military I want to join yet, but I know the basic area of work I want there, SPECWAR or Special Warfare. If you know anything about this you know, for this line of work, that a Navy Seal or an Army Ranger is the best job. And that is exactly what I want to do with my life, which makes it a big goal.

Still, those are not my only goals, I have several more. As you may know the military is filled with benefits (that's not why I'm joining) like free housing (on their bases), free food (mostly free), free clothes (if you wear theirs), and much more. Anyway, my point is that money can be easily saved. So I want to spend my money wisely and save. And when I retire I will have enough to open my own small little business, hopefully a paintball field. For you people reading this and don't know what paintball is, well, it is a war game where you shoot little round balls filled with paint at each other with paintball guns at 300 feet per second. It may sound stupid to a reader who has never played, but it is a lot of fun.

My last goal is to stay with and eventually marry my present girlfriend Lauren. I hope she will stay with me too, even though she will have to go through all my military plans. The plan is that I will work, as well as Lauren, and when we retire we will open that business I was telling you about together."

The final assignment for this project was to write an autobiographical sketch.

"If you haven't already looked in the top right and left hand corner of this paper then you now know that my name is Jonathan Dacy. I was born and raised until I was six in

Chicago. Somewhere around the age of six we moved to Florida. We lived there for a year when we decided to move to Georgia. Soon before we were scheduled to move my dad asked for a divorce, and got one. So I was stuck with my mom, brother, and sister for a couple of years in Florida before I decided to move in with my dad and my soon to be step mom (at the time at least). They married, divorced, we moved four times, my sister moved in, then out, my brother in, and soon to be out.

Anyway, I'm rambling here. I guess this paper needs to be about me, well, okay. You will know this if you have read any of the other papers in this scrapbook, I love the military. I guess you could say it's my life. All my money is spent on military equipment, all I read about is the military, and it is practically all I think about. As far as equipment goes I have BDUs (that is fatigues to you), helmets, survival equipment, knives, guns, boots, web gear, ruck sacks, well you name it; I got it, no kidding. By this time you must be asking yourself, "What is wrong with this kid, why does he spend all his money on this junk", so to speak? The answer is simple, because I like it. Everybody likes something and spends a lot of their money on something, and this is my something.

Because I like military so much, I, like a lot of people, play military type games, like paintball. Me and a lot of my friends play and have guns, paintball guns that is. We play as often as we can. In fact, I'm going to a 24 hour paintball game on September 28 and 29.

I guess that's basically everything I can't think of too much more to write so, bye, and thanks for reading."

These five papers were dated in early September, yet there were extra credit papers he completed that were dated in November. The first paper was titled "My Favorite School Memory."

"Well, let's see, that would have to be the 7th grade. I remember being friends with everybody. It is not like that anymore. In the 7th grade nobody was really trying to be better than everybody else so it was easy to get along with everyone and have lots of friends. But now, in high school, it is way different. I liked having lots of friends. It was always easier to do oral reports in front of the class when they were all your friends. It was easier to want to participate in class, and it actually allowed me to think of school as fun.

That is not the only reason 7th grade was fun. I was a real trouble maker, the kind you teachers hate. My good friends and I were always getting detention and referrals. I was written up and given detention 23 times that school year. My teachers probably didn't like me very much but every year during school registration I go and see them and they just love to hear from me. All those friends on the other hand never hear from me. They were just short term friends, I guess. Although, one of them is still my best friend this very day. We stayed in contact and were eventually very good friends and have been ever since.

Sometimes I sit back and think about the way things used to be. I miss it. Sometimes I wish it could still be like that, but, I guess it is all part of life, right?"

The final paper he submitted for extra credit had to be a poem he had written. He explains why before his poem is presented.

This poem is one that I wrote that kind of explained how I was thinking soon after the break-up of my now ex-girlfriend, Lauren, which took place on October 10, 1996. It is not the best poem ever written, but, at the time, I felt it needed to be written whether I used big words or not. There are a lot of things in this writing that you, the person reading, wouldn't understand, it is mostly inside stuff. So now I'm sharing it with you, so just work with me as far as my vocabulary goes in the poem. It just tells my feelings at the time, nothing fancy.

>I woke up that day
>At six in the morn
>It was my birthday
>The day I was born.

I went to school
Everything was fine
There I was after school
With some buddies of mine.

We stayed at my house
We practiced some raids
For a club we wanted
That never became.

We raided her house
How little did I know
That this relationship
Would grow and grow.

My friends scattered home
I sat in that room
I stared at her closely
At her every move.

I soon left the house
With my family to eat
Waiting there was Alicia
To whom we're to meet.

Two days later
To CiCi's we went
My friends and I that is
Our second attempt.

On the way home
I noticed the stars up above
Was waiting for me patiently
My first love.

That was the night
That would change it all
And little did I know
That this love would fall.

Jonathan Behind Blue Eyes

I'll never forget the moment
My lips touched yours
And forever and always
I'd love and adore.

Your beauty, your mind
Your personality too
If someone would have told me
If I only knew.

If I only knew
That this love was true
That you'd die for me
That I'd die for you.

If I only knew
How you felt about me
If it was love or hatred
Or only friends we'd be.

As the months went on
And the days went by
This love grew
But why did I try?

I tried, I tried
And I tried again
To keep this going
So it would never end.

After all this talk
There is one thing I know
My love for you was true
I wanted it to grow.

After all this time
I was honest with you
Were you honest with me?
If I only knew.

> If I only knew
> If this love was true
> It could have been better
> If I only knew.

He received an A for this scrapbook.

To this point, there were two experiences that impacted his life. The first came in 1983 when Kristin was born. This event in itself triggers the "middle child syndrome." Jonathan was 1 ½ years old and up until now, had a mom who was there much of the time. When she wasn't there, I usually was. If both of us were busy, then our best friends, the Johnson's, would watch the boys. There was consistency in his young life. Kristin was born on November 2 with very serious and life threatening congenital birth defects. This rare medical condition resulted in multiple surgeries to correct these problems. In addition, constant monitoring of Kristin's condition was required. Terri stayed at the hospital with her until Kristin was released on Christmas Eve. Terri kept Kristin alive as she scrutinized the doctors and nurses care of Kristin, and she promptly corrected them as mistakes and misunderstandings occurred. I would go to the hospital most evenings while Jonathan and Michael stayed with the Johnsons. These hospital stays for Kristin continued regularly and unpredictably until after her second heart transplant at the age of 14. Jonathan never complained about the attention his sister received or the amount of time needed to care for her. In fact, he always referred to her as an angel, and marveled at how she had gone through life with such a positive outlook and filled with love for everyone.

The second experience occurred in 1988 when Terri and I divorced. Jonathan pointed out in several of his journals and rehab assignments that his life had been OK, but that his parents divorced and that sucked. While Terri and I separated, I would drive from Atlanta to Tampa 2-3 weekends per month to visit with the kids. It wasn't enough for Jonathan and both Terri and I agreed, for his own psychological wellbeing, that he would be better off living with me. Alicia and I were married in the summer of 1989, and shortly after that Jonathan moved in with us to enter the 4th grade.

A year later during Thanksgiving weekend in the fall of 1990, we moved from Smyrna, in the NW suburbs of Atlanta, to Lawrenceville, which is located on the NE side of town. Jonathan and I took our first load of belongings early on Thanksgiving morning, got the truck unloaded, and returned to Smyrna for the next round trip. As we were driving on the interstate, the truck broke down and we ended up on the side of the road. Jonathan was thrilled, this was an adventure, and he talked about maybe having to camp out until the next day when the rental truck companies reopened. A few emergency phone calls later, we got the problem resolved and a replacement truck was brought to us. I'll never forget 9 year old Jonathan's reaction to the incident. There was no nervousness or fear in being stranded, it was "this is what we can do Dad, this is fun!!"

As we were getting settled in Lawrenceville, Jonathan was already making new friends. His first and best friend, Chris, a year or 2 younger than Jonathan, hit it off immediately. They both liked military things, liked to spy, and neither of them was very interested in sports. They started a Spy Club, and the notes and files Jonathan kept represent the first of his writings that I discovered as I unloaded his storage unit. He had a file for many of the neighbors, one for me, and one for Alicia. He would interview people and get their name, age, employer, etc. and make notes about any consistent habits. For instance, he documented when I left and returned from work, when I cut the grass, and my exercise schedule. He charged members $.25 per week to remain in the Club, and he had a little lock box that I assume he used to keep the money to cover their expenses. One of the most serious cases in his files was a situation where 2 sisters claimed they were being verbally and physically abused by their step-father. Jonathan interviewed the girls, and he noted that he and Chris spied on the step-father to get his routine documented. He also mentioned that if they were to witness any abuse, they would call the police immediately.

Shortly after we moved to Lawrenceville, Kristin moved in with Jonathan, Alicia and me. Terri and I decided to move her primary cardio care to a children's hospital in Atlanta. We had no idea yet as to the seriousness of Kristin's defective heart, but her other health problems had stabilized. There continued to be unexpected visits to the emergency room, but not nearly the amount as when she was younger.

As the next couple of years passed, Jonathan began to get angry and said some very hurtful things to Alicia that were quite upsetting. I would confront Jonathan, and he would explain he was angry at the time and that he didn't mean the things he said. In addition, he was getting in trouble in school and was causing some upset in the neighborhood. Alicia and I were concerned and we began to seek counseling for him. As he was capable of doing with many of the psychologists, counselors, and psychiatrists he would see over the years, Jonathan convinced them that he was fine and didn't have anger issues.

Jonathan began experiencing severe migraine headaches when he was 11 or 12. It wasn't uncommon for him to vomit profusely and cry with the agonizing pain in his head. The doctors told us that he was experiencing adolescent migraines and that these would subside as he got older. These subsided, but they never went completely away. Medications would sometimes help, and sometimes not. As he grew older into adulthood, medications would become the answer for whatever "ailed" him.

With Jonathan's interest so heavily entrenched in the military, he was directed to expand his horizons. In 6th grade, he was introduced to his first musical instrument, the violin. He caught on and played fairly well, but after 7th grade he decided that it wasn't for him. I also made him sign up for a sport, and he chose basketball. He turned out to be an excellent defensive forward, and he averaged 4 to 6 points a game to go along with 7 to 10 rebounds. His best game came when he was in the 8th grade and was guarding the leading scorer in the league who played center and was a couple of inches taller than Jonathan. Jonathan held him to 3 points (all free throws), and began to develop quite a reputation as a defensive player. After that season, a couple of the coaches talked with me about starting a basketball clinic for players they thought could play in high school. They invited Jonathan to participate, but he wasn't interested. He had joined scouts and was much more inclined to go camping and be in the outdoors than he was playing a game in a gym.

In May of 1993 I lost my job. The financial burden that this created, along with Jonathan's behavior, Kristin's deteriorating health, and Alicia's efforts to grow professionally, resulted in family counseling. Alicia and I were concerned about Jonathan and his anger, as well as what seemed to be an extreme interest in warfare and fighting. He convinced these counselors that he was fine. In September Alicia asked me for a divorce as it was obvious that the strain on both of us wasn't worth the efforts to keep the family together. I stayed until early 1994 when I found a new job in my profession.

In the meantime, Kristin finished the school year in June, 1993 and then moved back to Florida to be with Terri. It was during her semi-annual heart check-up in December of 1993 that we were informed that she would need a heart transplant.

Jonathan and I found a townhouse nearby so he was able to stay in the same school district. We moved into the place in early March of 1994, and Terri and Kristin moved in a week later. While Terri and I nervously waited for a call stating that a heart donor had been found, Jonathan was in 7th grade and having his favorite year in school. I undoubtedly neglected to give Jonathan the attention he deserved as he was getting in trouble regularly at school. He was reprimanded for talking in class, not completing assignments on time, and displaying a general lack of effort. I can't recall very many of the situations, but my signature was on a lot of slips of paper found in his belongings.

While we waited for a donor, we watched Kristin lose weight and become weaker. It got to the point where she wasn't able to walk more than a few steps at a time before running out of breath. We obtained oxygen tanks to help with her breathing and moved her in a wheel chair. In June we received a call that a donor had been located. The surgery lasted 14-16 hours as not only did they need to do a transplant, but the doctors had to re-route the main vessels around the heart as Kristin's heart was a mirror image of a normal heart. Following the surgery, Kristin had some rejection episodes, but was able to return to Florida with Terri in time for the upcoming school year.

Michael, in the meantime, finished his junior year of high school in Florida and then moved to Georgia to be with the rest of the family. As the summer passed we decided that Michael would stay with me and Jonathan and attend his senior year of high school in Lawrenceville.

After Terri and Kristin returned to Florida, it was time for the three of us males to explore and settle into our bachelor lifestyle. Jonathan was very active in scouts and enjoyed hanging out with his friends. He was also communicating with the local police department. Jonathan had written them for copies of the code and signal list, asked if he could travel with them in a squad car, and wanted to sit in or do any voluntary work for the department. He got his wish in 1995 and was selected to participate in the Law Enforcement Explorer Post. These 14 – 21 year olds were allowed to take part in the Ride-a-long program and experience training in law enforcement.

Michael started school and very quickly found a job delivering pizzas. I was working a part time job along with the full time job so that we could pay our bills. I was resolute about cutting out coupons and looking for sales at each of the local grocery stores. We did many things together, and one of those was grocery shopping. Although I would budget to have the most economical meals possible, the boys came for the ride to make sure we had enough of the "good food" in the house, the sweets and the salties.

One night after work we went out to do our weekly shopping. I was wrapped up in coupons and figuring out what to cook. As usual, Michael and Jonathan were bored so they dismissed themselves to go and look at the magazines. They were gone for about 10 minutes while I focused on our menu for the upcoming week. All of a sudden, the two of them came tearing around the corner of the "meat helper" aisle with a cart. "Dad, we have dinner for the next week!!" they yelled. By now store employees were following them and people within hearing distance were staring at them. Michael was pushing the cart while Jonathan rode on the side. I looked up. They were charging at me with……if a Guinness Book of World Records had ever recognized the most ½ gallon ice cream containers to be stacked in a shopping cart, that record had just been shattered.

I stared at them for a moment as they stampeded toward me down the aisle, and if it is possible for someone to "die laughing," it would have been me that night.

Within the next couple of months I bought a family membership to a health club that was within walking distance of the house. The three of us would work out together regularly, and if one of the boys wanted to go by himself, he could. The football team of the high school Michael was attending was having a good year, so the three of us watched them several times during the year as the team prepared for the state playoffs. We also enjoyed watching movies together, and would often grab a ball (depending on the season) and throw or kick it around. The house was cleaned semi-regularly but not religiously as we enjoyed the pleasure of letting our dishes stay in the sink for a day or two, dusting only when the dust became visible, vacuuming if company was coming over, and cleaning the bathrooms as the individuals who used them saw fit.

Toward the end of Jonathan's freshman year and a few days before his 15th birthday, he submitted an assignment called "Jon's Poems". From what I can gather the purpose of the assignment was to select an author of interest and explain why he had an impact on society, gather poems on a single subject, then use the theme of that subject and write several poems of your own.

The author he chose was Paul Dunbar. He was born in 1872, a child of freed slaves. He was important because he was the first African-American to achieve national renown and acceptance as a writer and the first to become widely known among the people of his race.

Not surprisingly, he chose war as his subject. In his words, "War is a conflict between people and things. I chose war because I find it most interesting. It is important to me because I want to be in the military." He proceeded to write these four poems.

The first poem is called war, and his teacher commented that it had excellent imagery.

War

Soldiers are neat
Because they have lots of
Power.
And then there's the
Uniform
Such neat colors
So crisp and so bright.
Until the blood is spilled on them.

There is a second poem without a title, although it too could be called "War."

War is a good way to solve
Conflicts and problems.
You can die
You will be better off dead.
Dying is good if you are dying for your country
It can be bad
It is bad to die by your own side
By accident.

His third poem was described by his teacher as powerful. It's titled "Anger."

Anger
Anger is cool
You can yell at people
And control them.
If people know you are angry they will listen
And if they don't you can kick their butt.
Then they will know to listen when you speak.
Especially if you are angry
The control should make you happy.

His final poem appears to be based on topic by Paul Dunbar, defining love.

> Love would be nice
> Too bad I don't have
> One.
> Love is great
> Because I said so
> It is a possession
> That should be treasured.
> By all people
> By all people
> Yet not all people view it the same.

At some point in 1995, Jonathan was planning to run away to Florida to be with Terri. He put his list together.

- Put away all military stuff I don't bring so they think I'll be wearing it
- Find out prices on plane tickets and amount for taxi to airport.
- Ask Michael about travel agency and airport.
- Come up with back-up plan and letter to Dad and friends.
- Plan so Dad and Mike are possibly gone, if not, think I'm going to spend night.
- Get maps of Florida, Georgia, and USA
- Find out what curfews are in Georgia and Florida
- Possibly get a backpacking stove.
- Bring jeans, BDU's, socks, boots, blankets, book bag, matches, lighter, money, phone numbers.

He then sketched a map of Florida and identified the three bridges crossing over Tampa Bay. Then, he listed the small towns on the St. Petersburg peninsula with specific directions from our house in Lawrenceville to Terri's house in Madeira Beach. I ask myself why didn't he just ask for a ride, but my guess is he was looking for the adventure of getting there himself.

He kept a journal during the summer of 1995 between his freshman and sophomore years. He described the summer as being OK, but also being bored much of the time. I was dating Laura and would spend most of my weekends on the other side of town. Jonathan would accompany me occasionally, but most of the time he and Michael stayed at our home.

Jonathan would invite some of his buddies over and Michael taught them the art of poker. As they played, Michael, being four years older, was able to good naturedly humiliate them just because he was older and could put the big brother fear into them. It seemed they had a lot of fun together. Whenever I would call to check in on them, they were laughing, playing cards, and having a good time.

One of the highlights of the summer was during the 4th of July weekend. Jonathan and Michael went with Alicia to visit her parents in Tennessee. As Jonathan described it, they had a blast. They swam, played paintball, fished, went water skiing, and knee boarding. The best part was the fireworks display. Not only did Alicia's family have plenty of the legal fireworks obtainable in TN, but Alicia's father, being in the Army Reserves, was able to get his hands on a few loud things.

Jonathan's Journal – 1995

July 10 - I keep thinking about how bad I want to go to the army. I can't wait to go.

August 27 – The closer it comes the more I think about my future. What will I do? Go to the army, college, or do nothing? I think about how much fun high school is supposed to be and as far as I see it, it will be stupid. I hope not. I hope everything goes well and Jimmy and I become closer friends, not that we aren't already.

August 28 – I signed up for the Military Book Club and placed my first order.

August 30 – Today was the first time I sweat on my chest and under my arms, my workouts have been going good.

August 31 – These are my best workout days. Some kid offered to sell me a gun. I want to buy it but I won't.

In October of 1995 Jonathan was in need of money. I called my former employer, a software packaging company, and they were able to hire him as there was a lot of work to do with the Holidays around the corner. Within 6 weeks he had earned a $1 an hour raise and was promoted to lead person, working a few hours during the week and then 8 hours on Saturday. After he received a check for more than $200 over Christmas break, he ordered a Navy Seal Team t-shirt, used authentic army sleeping bag, a GI pup tent, and as I found out later, a knife.

In March of 1996 Jonathan was arrested for the first time. He was charged with "carrying a concealed weapon." He was in a restaurant with some friends and one of the patrons spotted his knife. The restaurant manager was informed and the police were called. A few months later he was given probation and community service. He received glowing remarks for the work he did for the 12 hours of community service.

Jonathan also wrote during the month that he was beginning to recognize his leadership skills. He stated that he was the one who organized their paintball, repelling, and camping outings.

On March 28, the day after his 15th birthday, he met his first love Lauren. Lauren's grandmother lived 2 units down the street from us, and she also had a cousin who was one of Jonathan's best friends. The three of them would hang out together until it became obvious that Jonathan and Lauren wanted some alone time. Lauren's family owned a drum set and it was here that Jonathan was introduced to the drums. He discovered he had quite a knack for playing.

Getting closer to Lauren allowed Jonathan to experience new feelings. He was jealous of her past boyfriends and he wrote angrily about what he would do if he ever saw one of them talking to her. Jonathan let her know that he wouldn't tolerate any of that behavior. His anger would build just by thinking about it, and he expressed this in his journal.

On April 25th he and his friends wore camouflage to school for the first time. They took a little razzing at first, but it wasn't long before their intimidating looks made people stay out of their way. Three days later he wrote "I was in a pissy mood like always. I just want to kill something – I will, sooner or later, I will."

A couple of weeks later, on May 8, he wrote that he was no longer a virgin. I must have sensed something as he wrote – "I got home around 10:00 PM and my dad sat me down. He said he knew Lauren and I spent a lot of time together. He said use good judgment, use protection if I had sex. He said never force myself on a woman. I wouldn't. My first time. From 9 to 9:30 PM on May 8, 1996, a day to remember."

School ended a month later and Jonathan wrote nothing more for 15 months. He and Lauren broke up later in 1996. Her mother and I talked as things were getting serious between them. She thought it best if they stopped spending so much time together. I respected her wishes and consoled Jonathan as they separated. It was the first time in a long time, and it wouldn't be the last, where I held him in my arms as he sobbed on my shoulder.

The Move to Paulding County

Laura and I decided to get married in August of 1997 so Jonathan could start classes at the beginning of the school year. Jonathan had pinpointed this move to the other side of town as another major turning point in his life. Lawrenceville was home to him and he was leaving his best friends. To help alleviate some of that pain, Laura and I bought him an $800 1986 T-Bird so he could visit his Lawrenceville friends on weekends. Jonathan told me later that he blamed the move for the reason he later became addicted to drugs/medicines and alcohol.

In September 1997 he started journalizing again. At school, he met Derek who became one of his best friends for the rest of his life.

> September 10 - I started talking to Derek and sat with him at lunch for a couple of days. We planned on breaking into David's house this weekend since he's been absent, and then duct taping him. I went to Lawrenceville and stayed with Chris mostly. I started smoking. I stayed home one day from school and slept until 3:30, then went out applying for jobs.

During the next 3 months he made many friends, dated several girls, worked on his car often as it broke down several times. Went rappelling 4 times on weekends, dressed in camo with friends and played war games, cut classes a few times, continued looking for a job, almost got into a couple of fights, threatened to get even with a girl who had broken up with him, taken some beer from a friend's house, and stole a $120 knife.

His last entry in 1997 was in December.

> December 8 - On Tuesday me and Dad drove to Tennessee for Grandpa Spurling's (Alicia's father) funeral. He died

while hunting by falling out of a tree stand. He broke his neck and back. The funeral was nice. It was a military burial. We hung around a couple of hours and talked to the family. It was nice seeing them again.

Jonathan was in ROTC in high school and he dressed in his uniform for the funeral. He really looked sharp, and many people commented on how good he looked and how Grandpa was real proud looking down at him.

He continued in his journal "I don't understand how he could die. We are talking about a soldier, Command Sergeant Major, serving his country for 42 years. How can someone like that die from falling out of a tree? I want to say that type of person isn't supposed to die like that. But I've heard it is not tragic to die doing what you love. And God knows he loved to hunt. But did he love that more than anything? I guess we'll never know."

Jonathan at Grandpa Spurling's funeral

He dropped out of school in 1998, started skipping classes, and before he knew it he'd stopped going. He had been in trouble, been suspended for fighting, being absent, and he finally just stopped attending.

In May of 1998 Jon's license was suspended for dropping out of school. Later that summer he and Derek took a vacation and drove to Missouri to visit some of Derek's family. Jonathan was arrested for driving on a suspended license. He had been pulled over because he had a temporary tag.

After Jonathan returned home in mid-July, he wrote a letter to a girl he met while he was in MO.

"I guess I figured since you're the only damn thing I can think about right now I'd write you. I've only been home for 2 hours now and I already miss you. I had a lot of fun while I was there. Just sitting here knowing I can't see you for a while is really bringing me down. I try not to let it get to me but it's hard. All the time we spent together and things we did together is hard to just look past and try to block out of your mind. God this f*@$ing blows. I have half a mind to just buy another ticket and stay up there somewhere for the rest of the summer so I can see you. I'll try to figure out some way to see you before too long. I wonder about us. Is this relationship just natural attraction that will wear off from lack of togetherness? Or is the saying "Absence makes the heart grow fonder" more than the BS it is said to be? What is this I feel? Is it love? Is it the progression stages to love? Or is it merely just the liking a man gets when he is with another woman? I know what it is. Do you? Just think real hard about what I told you that night beside your house and you'll know.

Anyways, I thought I'd write to let you know a little bit about what's on my mind and to let you know I'm thinking about you. Be good, be careful, and write back. Jon"

A few weeks later, on August 6, 1998, he wrote this letter to Lauren, his former girlfriend.

> ""Absence makes the heart grow fonder." Think about that saying. Is our lack of togetherness proving this statement true? Or not? I think of you all the time. Occasionally I cry myself to sleep thinking of all the good times we had together and how much I miss them. I love you so much. I don't understand why I can't bring myself to love a girl as much as I love you, but I can't. I have tried. I think this time apart is doing us good. I believe in the saying I wrote. I hope you do too. I hope you will come to me when you get out of

that home. I think we could have a great future. WE COULD make it work. If there is a will, there is a way. Do you agree? Some nights, when I'm lonely, I drive to Lawrenceville just to sit at the dirt field where we first kissed. That's where it all started, for me anyway. From that point on I would be a new person and would grow to truly love you. What was or is my sole purpose here? Perhaps I will never know. Whatever the case, I would like to spend my life with you. On my outside I am a somewhat intimidating, almost ruthless looking person. But inside I am sensitive and caring and I owe it all to you. You taught me, unknowingly. You taught me how to care for, gently handle, appreciate, and most importantly, love a woman. And you were that woman. Sure, we had our rough times, but doesn't everybody? It was nothing that couldn't be worked through. I know you have Nathan, and that is completely understandable. But, for some reason, I'd be willing to bet money that you two don't have what we had and can have again. I truly believe that the song Champagne Supernova playing those times was more than just coincidence. I know this is more than just natural attraction. Only time will tell.

Love Always and Forever Jonathan Dacy"

Jonathan's Journal – Summer, 1998

Never before and never again do I think I'll have a summer break so full of life lesson experiences. In the last three months or so I've learned more about life than ever before. I've learned that true love isn't always true. That you don't really know what you have until it is gone. That your family should ultimately be your first priority. That true, and I mean true, friends will always be there for you. That the U.S. legal system is nothing more than a crock of shit. That marriage can be one of the most beautiful things ever to happen to a person.

My reasons? Well, this didn't technically happen this summer break, but I say it did since I left school early. After not talking to her for nine months, Lauren called. She had run away and wanted to be with me. After all the talk, after her secretly living with me for a week, after all the positive manipulation she gave me, sex, and thinking "she finally brought me back to love her." And oh did I love her, with all my heart. But I guess all her love was a need to survive, to stay away from home. Because everything is back how it used to be. True love might not be true. It might just be excuses for another cause. A lie.

Your God given, country given, and state given rights should all be cherished just as much, if not more, than anything else. But along with your cherishment should come caution. Because the day you decide to abuse the rights and get caught, that's the day you'll pay. And in some cases, like mine, you'll pay more than necessary. I spent 2 days in jail, completely left in the dark from what was going on around me. That was one of the worst feelings, actually the worst I've ever had. I absolutely hated it and that is an understatement. I had to pay court fees. I had to pay the costs it took to get to court in Neosho, MO. All for simply driving on a suspended license. I was ordered by court to go to school every day this year and make passing grades or I had to go to jail for one year. I had to pay an $86 fine. All for just getting a speeding ticket. That is why this legal system is f*@#d up. People can get away with murder without a terrible amount more of punishment. I think it's f*@ing ridiculous. But through all this, my friends and family were always there. My brother bailed me out of jail. The rest went out of their way to make sure I had money to live on and that I was okay.

I went to one of the most tear-jerking things ever in Chicago, a wedding. Although I didn't cry, it was one of the most difficult things I ever had to sit through. It wasn't so much the fact that I hadn't seen James Johnson and his family in 12 years, or the fact that he was getting married. It was because of the way that through his life, he pulled himself up and is now happy and successful. I just know that can happen to me. He has really made something of himself like I know I will one day.

This writing isn't even close to the feelings and emotions I had when I lived these events. It's merely just a taste. It doesn't sound like much, but it really was. This is just a very few things I learned and experienced this summer. Hopefully I will never make a same mistake twice. I will be successful. Yes, I will be happy.

Jonathan Dacy

Jonathan wrote this poem shortly after his final break-up with Lauren.

"Wasted Money, Wasted Time, Nothing Lasts Forever"

Wasted Money, wasted time
Nothing lasts forever.

They'll give you what you want
And you'll think it's all true
They'll act like they care and really not
Despite the fact they say "I love you."

They use their abhorrent
Just to get you on their side
And you don't know you're being used
You're just along for the ride.

Because it's wasted money and wasted time
And nothing lasts forever.

But they don't all play that game
So don't get me wrong
It's not that bad to take a part
So go out and belong.

But when you're there watch your back
Because "I love you" is what they'll say
And when you decide to turn your back
That's the day you'll pay.

Because it's wasted money and wasted time
And nothing lasts forever.

Trust them a little, but not too much
Because they'll take advantage of you
Right when you think it's going great
They'll leave you without a clue.

When you're sitting back watching TV
They're out having fun
You'll think they're out with a friend
But they could be with anyone.

Because it's wasted money and wasted time

> And nothing lasts forever
> It's wasted money and wasted time
> And you can't be together.
>
> It's wasted money and wasted time
> It's all an evil shame
> It's wasted money and wasted time
> It's nothing but a dream.

Attached with this batch of writings is a list of 24 problems he was having.

1. No license/speeding ticket
2. No car
3. Bad grades in school
4. Darin getting in trouble
5. No job/money
6. Loneliness
7. Pam and I relationship and her father
8. Ear surgery
9. Jail in Missouri
10. Dropping out of school
11. Split up of the team
12. Drugs
13. Not spending time with family
14. No license for David
15. Lack of motivation
16. Boredom
17. Disoriented in my way of life
18. No responsibilities
19. Moving to Paulding
20. Grandpa Spurling dying
21. Missing old friends and girlfriends
22. Michael possibly moving
23. Kristin
24. Family environment

He returned to school again in September to give it another try. The wardrobe was changing from camouflage to black. Black pants, shirt, boots, and coat. He and his friends were nobody to mess with. The primary purpose in going to school was to intimidate, not to learn. He didn't write anything again until the Thanksgiving Holiday.

> November 24, 1998 – December 24, 1998: This sums up what was documented in his journal. During the Holiday Season he dated a couple of girls, spent time with his buddies partying, skipped school several times, got a job, had a court date for speeding, spent time with family, helped Uncle Joe move in with me and Laura and showed Joe the area, almost got into 2 fights (one while at school and the other being chased by 4 cars through Dallas), and took prescription medicines with his friends that were obtained from one of the parents' medicine cabinets. He also made mention of not feeling well, particularly during the week and a half before Christmas.

He began to feel worse after the Holidays. The headaches became more severe and his depression increased. In February 1999 he was admitted to the first of many psychiatric and addiction rehabilitation treatment centers.

In the summer of 1999 he wrote this letter to a friend of his who lived in Lawrenceville.

> Gloria
>
> How is it going? I'm hanging in there. This last week has been the shittiest one of my entire life. I'm not writing solely for the purpose of bitching, but I figure I'd fill you in on what's happening on my side of the neighborhood. My friend is about to go to jail for quite a while for stealing over $30,000 worth of military equipment. Another dear friend of mine abandoned me completely and very suddenly because she felt she needed God in her life more than me, despite the fact I supported her, emotionally anyways. Oh well, f*@$ it, f*@% it all. Those people are dead to me now, utterly absent from my life. I can't remember if I told you on the phone or not but I visited church a few times this week. For the first time in my life I tried to find this God

that everyone talks about. I found Him all right, or shall I say, He found me. I watched a 30 year veteran of Jesus, a man of God if you will; knock 50-60 people unconscious. That doesn't seem so spectacular; it was the way he went about doing it that was truly amazing. By pointing at them with his finger, using the power of the Holy Spirit to knock people on the ground, unconscious. I could not believe my f*@%ing eyes, and that is an understatement. I had to experience it to believe it. And sure enough I did. I walked right up to the alter where the minister stood and when he got to me, after my vision was filled with a bright, white light, the overwhelming power knocked me straight on my back, unconscious. So, for the record, there is a God. And trust me that really means something coming from me. It probably doesn't seem that significant to you, you just had to be there. It happened 2 days in a row. But don't worry, I'm not a hard-headed religious jerk and never will be. You can quote me on that. It's just now I know there is a God, and Heaven and hell. But I'm still the same old Jon, and always will be. I still love to shoot and loot, sneak and peak, and kick ass and take names. With the element of surprise, that is. Okay, I know I sound like a jerk, so I'll just shut up and talk about something relevant to your interests. Sorry

---

Jonathan was seeing a psychiatrist regularly and was on medication for depression. For a couple of weeks he attended this church 4 times a week. Leanne, his girlfriend, was a follower of this church and if he was to get her back, he figured he needed to give it a try. Jonathan talked me into attending service with him, as he was very impressed with the Church. The impact that the veteran of Jesus had on him was tremendous. Jonathan confided in him, telling him of his depression, anxiety, and the dark thoughts he was having. This man came over to the house with a fellow man of God, cleansed his room and performed an exorcism to rid Jonathan of the evil spirits he thought possessed his mind.

Jonathan continued his letter to Gloria.

Okay, I'm a jerk. Why am I a jerk you ask? Because everything you read above the line I wrote 2-3 weeks ago one night real late. I've been so busy it has kept my mind to finish it, but now I am. In fact right now I'm sitting in 4th period in school. Yes, that's right. I signed back up and now I'm going to school. It's so weird, I haven't been here in so long. At least it has allowed me the time to finish this letter. It's not that I don't want to write, it's that I always forget. So I'm sorry. You've probably been thinking "that stupid asshole hasn't written me or anything, I'll never hear from him again." Well, don't think that!! It's just that I'm a forgetful bastard. Anyways, I'm doing a lot better than I was when I wrote the first part of this letter. School is going good and I've been clean of drugs and shit for a while. I think I told you that I went to a family reunion in Wisconsin. It was lots of fun. I stayed in Chicago (my home town) also. I stayed pretty drunk the whole time. You should have been there. Speaking of which, you know, I miss you. I swear we will get together sometime. Once we both have money and stuff I'm sure we can figure something out, right? I don't know what else to write so I'll get going. Before I go, let me reemphasize one thing: I'm not a holy rolling, bible thumper. I don't even go to church now. Just wanted to make it clear for the record so you, in no way, would get the wrong idea about me. Anyways.

Write me back and call me sometime please.

Sincerely, Jonathan Dacy or (as you know it, Jon)

In August of 1999, he was determined to go back and get his diploma. At first, the principal was not going to re-admit him into the school. Having dropped out and getting suspended for fighting, Jonathan had burned some bridges this past year. Jonathan and I both met with the principal and he agreed to let Jonathan come back to school.

One of Jonathan's classes included maintaining a School Journal. Each day the teacher would ask a life related question, and Jonathan was to answer it. Some of the answers to these questions help describe Jonathan's attitude toward life during this time.

"What do I do on weekends?" – Not every, but most

weekends, I do something in the outdoors, or woods, or whatever – wilderness I guess. It consists of rafting, camping, hiking, rock climbing, shooting my guns, repelling, and similar stuff. I don't do all that stuff each weekend I go out, just a couple of them. Like I'll rock climb and repel together. Camp and hike together. You get the idea. I've been involved in these kinds of activities since I was 5 or so.

"What is my favorite sport?" – My favorite sport is probably something you won't consider a sport. I do though, because of my lack of interest in most popular sports. It's paintball. I like it, first of all, because the objective is to shoot everyone who is not on your team. That in itself is fun. Plus, you use tactics, speed, stealth and superior fire power to your advantage. Although they have the same principles, throwing and hitting balls to each other never rang my bell. I'll stick to special warfare oriented related activities, for the most part.

Lawrenceville friends with Jonathan

"I remember when…" – I remember when I left the country for the first time. I went on a week-long cruise with my family. The ship stopped at six different islands including St. Thomas, St. Martin, Dominica and a few others. The ship was the biggest boat I've ever seen. It had 13 stories, 10 elevators, 12 restaurants, dance clubs, a mall, a casino, showrooms, weight rooms, a running track, and a lot more. I lost a few hundred dollars in the casino ultimately, but at one point I was up $300 - $400. Pretty much all anyone did was drink and have fun. It was a big floating party. I guess that is what a vacation is all about.

"What was the worst day I've ever had?" – It was about a month or so ago, the day (night rather) I got back from vacation. I'm not really going to bother trying to make it so you understand, because if I did, this would be 20 pages long. I'll cram it all in a nutshell. My best friend left me (so to speak, we lived together), and my girlfriend left me. Sounds real bad, I know. You just had to be there. You just have to know all the details and know all the strings tied between those two people and everyone else in my life. No real use trying to explain. I'll shut up now. Nevertheless, that day sucked.

"What do I want to be when I grow up, why?" – Military, no doubt. That has been my plan since I was 5. It's the unit integrity, teamwork, and loyalty that really appeals to me. It's like: you make me your first priority and I'll make you mine. I just love that. To be able to jump out of airplanes, fast rope out of helos, scuba dive, shoot guns while getting in shape and to get paid for it, there's nothing better. Oh, it's an Airborne Ranger, Navy Seal, or some kind of Special Operations Group that I want to be. One day I will.

"What song has made an impact on my life?" – A song that has affected me is called "Freeway Time in a LA County Jail" by Sublime. It talks about him (the singer) in jail and how it sucks. It reminds me of the time I was in jail and how much I hated it. In the song he talks about how he misses his life, just like how I missed my life.

"How can I make America better?" – I'm sorry. I sat here and thought about it and thought about it and, being only 18 and in school with no incredible influence over anybody with great authority, I can't think of a way to make America better. Of course, except for joining the Navy, becoming a Seal and eventually becoming the Seal Team Commander, then leading my men into some other country, killing the bad guys and saving the day (or country in this case). But other than that, I can't really think of anything.

"If I could change anything about myself, what would it be?" – It would be my hearing. I was born with crappy ears and I'm 90% deaf in my left ear. It might possibly keep me from getting into the military. My ear canal has grown together and it keeps out most of the sound. Needless to say, it sucks.

"The closest I ever was to someone who died was...." – Probably my Grandma. I used to visit her a few weeks every summer. She used to always make me her famous cinnamon toast. She died a few years back from colon cancer.

"If I could change one event in history, what would it be and why?" – Vietnam, no doubt about it. I would change the timeframe to exactly the timeframe I'll be in the military. I am fascinated by that war; the honor, courage, dignity and camaraderie that went into fighting it. There will never be a war quite like it. Fought in a dense, humid triple canopy jungle. Misery like you've never seen it, what could be better?

"How often do I consider how I want to spend the rest of my life? What do I think about?" – Everyday. I have a pregnant girlfriend, Leanne, and I <u>always</u> wonder what's going to happen. I think about: Are and when are we going to get married? Where will we live? What will I drive? When will I get my diploma so I can join the military to make enough money to support my family? I don't let it bring me down though. I try to keep a positive attitude. I'm much more excited about everything than I'm worried or sad.

"Describe my dream mate." – The most important thing, complete honesty. Also very integral, as in: You make me your first priority and I'll make you mine. Knows how to listen. Very big sense of humor. Likes to think and learn and expand her mind. Looks forward to challenges. Interested in adventurous activities. Plus, pretty and cute and all that stuff.

"What does the word "responsibility" mean to me?" – It is when there are things you just have to do. If you don't do them then you're held accountable for any consequences. Some responsibilities I think most people don't really want, they just get.

The last paper in this folder is dated October 11, 1999.

"At what point do I give up?" – You should never give up. A lot of people, myself included, struggle so bad that they do, and it sucks – when everything gets so bad and you get so overwhelmed that you just want to throw your hands up in the air and quit on life. Take my advice: Don't do it, don't give up.

Adulthood

Jonathan did fairly well the first couple of months of school. By now he was older than the rest of the students and didn't participate in the social games that had been part of the downfall the first two years. He continued to see his psychiatrist regularly and was taking medications to control his depression. He was having problems with his migraines and his ears were bothering him frequently as well. We knew the time had come to see the surgeon and find out what procedure needed to be performed to correct his ear deformity. Jonathan was nervous as we entered the surgeon's waiting room. He sat and prayed silently, as well as talked to me looking for assurances that his dream of a life in the military wouldn't be shattered. But they were. The doctor explained that none of the armed forces would accept Jonathan with either the deformity or the result of the surgery required to correct it. We left the office and Jonathan was tearing up. By the time we got to the parking lot he just broke down and sobbed. I hugged him as he tried to get the disappointment of losing his lifelong dream out of his system.

Jonathan's disappointment and heartbreak never did get out of his system. He dropped out of school again shortly after hearing the news and began working full time at a restaurant.

The depression only worsened. Leanne would write him notes telling him they would work everything out and that their little family would get by. She loved Jonathan and was worried about him. Jonathan returned to the rehab facility that he had been in earlier in the year. He stayed 10 days and this helped Jonathan stabilize for a short period as his depression lessened and his anger was not as easily triggered. In February 2000, Jonathan and Leanne's son, Cullen, was born with trisomy disease. As Terri researched the disease and as Leanne's family kept us informed with medical reports, we realized Cullen would be with us a very short time. He passed a couple of weeks after he was born. For the second time in 4 months, I held Jonathan as he sobbed with grief.

The ear surgery was successfully performed in March and within a few weeks Jonathan was back to himself. He was doing well at the restaurant and would eventually be the manager. He was earning a good salary so he decided it was time to get a place of his own. He and Derek found a nice 2 bedroom trailer in a quaint trailer park. Jonathan and Leanne broke up after Cullen passed, and shortly after, Jonathan met Ashley.

Jonathan and Ashley hit it off immediately. Jonathan became part of Ashley's family as he accompanied Ashley, her parents Hamp and Cindy, and her brother Matt, to the beach for their annual vacation. Jonathan and Ashley seemed to always have fun and they enjoyed each other's company. They fell in love as Ashley and Jonathan were to become parents. By the time May 20, 2001 rolled around, Remy was born. We were all concerned about Remy's health as the research we had done on trisomy disease stated that is was a hereditary condition. Much to our relief and delight, Remy was in perfect health.

Ashley and Jonathan tried to stay together for another year but their lives were headed in different directions. Also, Jonathan's jealousy and anger added stress to the relationship. Although they broke up, they remained best of friends and worked together to provide Remy all the love that they could give.

Jonathan attracted caring and loving companions. Both Leanne and Ashley are wonderful people, and the next two serious relationships he had brought equally wonderful people into our family circle. First, he dated Molly for a couple of years. She was quiet, very patient, and a kind spirit. She supported Jonathan through some of his roughest times in 2003 and 2004, and would always try to be there for him. Molly went away to college, and although Jonathan visited as often as he could, the daily bond needed to maintain a relationship was lost.

In 2004, Jonathan moved to Florida to live with Terri and Kristin. It was there that he met Tiff. Her outgoing personality and creative side attracted Jonathan and endeared her to our family. In 2006, Jonathan and Tiff moved to Georgia and lived with Ashley and her new boyfriend, Ben. The four of them developed a great friendship while providing Remy with love and support. Jonathan and Tiff eventually moved into their own apartment. Problems developed with their relationship and Tiff ended up moving out of their apartment in December 2007.

Both Molly and Tiff were very close to Remy. As Jonathan entered the next stage in his search for a soul mate, he made it very clear to any potential date, as he had to both of them, that he had parental responsibility. He loved this responsibility more than anything as Remy and Ashley were the top priorities in his life. He met people online and dated a few of them, but nothing clicked until he met Tiffany in April 2009.

Ashley, Jonathan, Remy

During the decade Jonathan held quite a few jobs. He had years of experience working in restaurants and was a very good cook. He also had enough experience to know if the restaurant had long term potential employment opportunity. On more than one occasion he would clock in, work a couple of hours, see that the job wasn't for him, and walk out. When he found a job he liked, he would settle in and usually be promoted shortly thereafter. While in Florida, he managed a sports bar and grill where he was highly respected. He also managed a few restaurants in Georgia.

Throughout this time Jonathan maintained his friendships in both Lawrenceville and Paulding County. He also made a new circle of friends while in Florida. The common interest with each group of friends had changed from military games to music. Jonathan bought a drum set and would arrange for some serious jam sessions. He turned himself into a fabulous musician. If the popular video game Rock Band is any indication, he always scored a 98%-100% on the expert drum level.

Over these years Jonathan did burn a few bridges with some of his friends. Borrowed money didn't get paid back or he didn't follow through on promises he made. He also lost one of his best friends, Darin, from Paulding County, in the summer of 2006. Darin was killed in Iraq while serving his country. This had a major impact on his belief system. The potential consequences of war made him think about life at a different level. We spent many hours in my workshop discussing this topic as we addressed the necessity of war against the oneness of love. His journaling continued to change.

Jonathan playing the drums

Jonathan's health was always an issue. He had migraines, back pain, deteriorating teeth, depression, anxiety, and general overall pain. At times it would be worse than others. When it became overbearing was when he would begin to lose control of his life; losing a job, stealing, lying, or manipulating. Getting the narcotics to relieve his pain was paramount in his life. Finally, after a rehab stint in 2007, Jonathan enlisted the help of a methadone clinic to wean off his dependency on prescription narcotics.

He was assigned a counselor who would work with him and monitor his progress as they looked for the optimal level of methadone needed to maintain a pain free existence. Laurie, the counselor assigned to his case, and Jonathan hit it off immediately. They shared common spiritual beliefs. She was the kind of person Jonathan bonded with; intelligent, funny, compassionate, and a great listener. When Jonathan found out that she too was a student of A Course In Miracles, he insisted that I meet her. She told me that Jonathan was her favorite patient and that she equally enjoyed her discussions with him. They maintained this close relationship until The Rollercoaster period started in September 2009.

Jonathan's addiction led him to a rehab clinic twice in 1999, 3 more in 2004, another in 2007, and finally to The Facility in 2010. His battle with pain didn't go away.

Behind Blue Eyes
Introduction

Jonathan lived by two sets of rules and in two different thought systems as he recognized the duality that conflicts within each of us. There's the little devil on one shoulder, screaming and encouraging you to fight tooth and nail to get what is yours. Blame, manipulate, do whatever you need to do to satisfy your ego. On the other shoulder is the angel who whispers loving thoughts and reminds you of the Golden Rule and that love is all that matters.

The first, and the one that seemed to dominate, was the set of rules that needed to be followed in order to satisfy his addiction to medicines. To achieve and "win" the rules of this game, Jonathan would go to any means to meet his needs. These behaviors included lying, stealing, manipulating, etc. He would succeed. His enemy, at times, included anyone but himself; family, friends, girlfriends, employers, doctors, counselors, or anybody else standing in his way to help him obtain his medications. Yet these same people would be his best friends as long as they aided him to get what he needed. Over the years as he realized that these actions and behaviors were selfish and manipulative; deeper depression, anxiety, and guilt set in. As a result, he needed more medicine to make him feel better, thus, he would self-medicate.

Eventually, his actions would become extreme and this led to rehabilitation clinics and to several bouts with the law.

Then there was the second set of rules. This was the set that made up Jonathan's purest essence, which was love. This was the part of him that was connecting with God. He would pray, write, read, meditate, and live these positive words and beliefs as often and as best he could. He focused on love. This is what he wanted to teach, share, and spread to everyone he knew or would meet.

Jonathan knew. He was working towards enlightenment. He could become so focused on his work that he would go days without sleep. He'd doze off now and then, but he was truly committed to becoming a teacher of love, a learner of love, he just wanted to be love.

Somehow though, he wasn't able to maintain this state of mind.

Friendships he developed toward the end of his life were deeply affected by Jonathan's spiritual side. His relationship with Tiffany and the love they shared was founded on this principle.

There was no one he didn't love, yet there was no one he couldn't despise, depending on where his spirit was. In his heart of hearts he knew what was important. His mind knew, his spirit knew, but his body and its control over his mind and spirit didn't.

The duality is illustrated by an assignment Jonathan received during his anger management class in November 2003. He was to write two essays, each describing his life. The first was to eulogize himself as if he had died that day, the second was to eulogize as if he had lived to be 100 years old.

> "Jonathan Dacy, born on March 27, 1981, died November 24, 2003. He lived a full 22 years of unique experiences. Born in Cook County Illinois, he lived with parents Terri and Michael Dacy, and siblings Michael Joseph Dacy, brother, in Schaumburg, IL soon accompanied by sister Kristin Joy Dacy. He lived a happy youth in this area moving two times, until at the age of 6 when his family and him moved to Hillsborough County, FL. Within a year his father had been transferred to Georgia and soon after asked for a divorce. Terri, Kristin, Michael and Jonathan stayed in a nice house in Florida while his father settled around the area of Cobb County, GA. By the fourth grade Jonathan decided to move in with his father where he remained the rest of his life, moving several times in the area and finally permanently settling in Paulding County GA. Jonathan's major interests were always in the military. Ever since he went to his first Army/Navy surplus store at age 5 he had been fascinated with loyalty, camaraderie, and integrity that were associated with the Special Operations Groups of the military. He has always had the goal of becoming a Special Warfare Soldier, but at age 17 these dreams were ruined. Having had reconstructive ear canal surgery he would never be able to be accepted into these organizations due to the fact that he could not be exposed to extreme pressurization changes."

"Jonathan Dacy, born on March 27, 1981, died today, March 27, 2081 from natural causes. He served his country well for 30 years. He went to teach high school until he retired at age 65. Jonathan left behind 7 wonderful children, 17 grandchildren, and his wife who loved him deeply. He will be known for his commitment to his family's integrity and being the great father and husband he was. After putting behind his anger problems in his younger days, he never held a negative attitude and was always there to help others in time of need. Jonathan Dacy will always be remembered by his good name. His family name will proudly be carried on forever."

There may be songs or poetry that better describe Jonathan's life. For the last ten years though, every time I've heard *Behind Blue Eyes*, it reminds me of Jonathan and his life. It describes to me, a person who lives in physical and emotional pain. Yet there is a side to that person who knows within himself, although it may only be a glimmer, what makes up his truest essence.

Behind Blue Eyes: The Dark Side

"No one knows what it's like
To be the bad man
To be the sad man
Behind Blue Eyes."

"Dad, you have no idea what it's like to be me. I can't go into a room filled with people without feeling extreme anxiety, and this makes me very depressed." Jonathan told me this on many occasions. The solitude and depression he would sometimes have to overcome was unbearable to him.

He had seen psychiatrists, psychologists, therapists, and the only thing that would relieve the anxiety and depression was medicine.

On February 4, 1999 I was called by the administration of a local hospital to inform me that Jonathan was in the emergency room and that they needed me to come to the hospital to discuss his situation. As I drove out there, he was writing this letter.

> "Dear Pam
> As I lay here in this hospital bed I think of you. I wish you were here. They tell me they're going to run an x-ray on my hand. They think it's broken. Oh well. I don't know what it is, but for some reason my depression has doubled in the last 2 days. It's doubled again since I'm here in the hospital. I can't stop crying. I can't stop thinking about you. I'm going to try and have a good day tomorrow. Please help me and be in happy moods ALL day, no matter what. Okay!! David's in the room by mine. He registered in the ER at the same time I did for sore throat. I guess Darin is sitting in the waiting room. I raised hell trying to get him in with me. If you would've come, then you would have come back with me or I would have refused treatment and left the hospital. I LOVE YOU SO MUCH!!

> I just got done being examined. The therapists, psychiatrist, and psychologist just loved the artwork carved into my body. Next I get to get my stomach x-rayed because the knife penetrated too deep. Before that two police officers came in and made me give them everything that can cause bodily harm. I had to dispute with them just to be able to write with this pen (it can stab people…….oooooooo). They have already taken x-rays on my hand. They say it's f…….

And that's the end of this letter.

After I arrived I was informed that Jonathan was being committed to the psychiatric wing of the hospital. I was told that his hand was broken and his stomach required stitches. The doctors were also concerned with his mental state. This was to be the first of the 7 admissions into rehabilitation facilities.

He was there for 10 days before he was released. Ten months later I would take him back to the same emergency room for severe depression and his addiction to pain relievers. He was admitted for a second time and stayed for another 10 days.

"No one bites back as hard
On their anger
None of my pain and woe
Can show through"

Although Jonathan would try to control his anger, there were times when he would explode. In August 2002, Jonathan had a run in with an acquaintance of his that infuriated him. The financial impact that this situation had on Jonathan was tremendous, and he lost his temper. After being informed he wasn't getting his money back, Jonathan walked out of work, hopped in his car and followed his "friend" attempting to run him off the road while waving a gun at him. Several people witnessed this, called the police, and a warrant was issued for Jonathan's arrest. He spent a couple of days in jail before being released by the court.

Jonathan's arraignment was held in February 2003 where he was fined nearly $3000, given 80 hours of community service, and ordered to attend and successfully complete a five month Anger Management class. In class, he journaled the causes and effects of his anger for the first time in his life. He answered the questions in class this way:

1. How does your anger build up?
   The primary way for my anger to build up is by dwelling on the sensitive subject that makes me angry. By letting my thoughts lead me to an unreasonable state of mind.

2. What feelings are involved with your anger?
   Jealousy, betrayal, disloyalty, lack of integrity. Hate, violent thoughts, thoughts of revenge.

3. What things or people cause you to think about doing things you may regret later?
   People who steal from me. People who lie to me. Sometimes, thinking about how much punishment I received for my crime gets under my skin. I also don't exactly appreciate people who try to take advantage of me or try to manipulate me. Any negative actions towards my son could make me angry, although it has never really happened.

He addressed why it is important "to bite back", or not act on his anger.

List 5 reasons why it is important to you not to act on your anger.
- Can get arrested
- Can lose friends
- Can lose job
- Can make others upset
- Can cause physical fights

He was asked how to avoid the feeling of his having "pain and woe can show through."

How do you take care of yourself?
- Emotionally – By talking to people (Dad and Molly) about my emotional problems as a release. Playing drums as a release.
- Socially – Really only at work by communicating with everyone there. Not much social interaction in general. I'm mostly around my girlfriend and family.
- Physically – I don't really take care of myself physically. Having to stand all day at work seems to make me pretty tired. That and chasing my son around wears me out.

- Mentally – I read a lot. I'm always trying to expand my mind as much as possible. I believe knowledge is power and can take you far in life.
- Self-will – My decision making process isn't too much based on instinct and intuition. Decisions at work are usually pretty thought out and thorough. Keeping in mind the cheapest or most cost effective way to do things. Or the most presentable….
- Spiritually – I try to keep an open mind and not be unreasonable about people's beliefs. Try to keep a level head and understand people's spirits. By making a conscious effort to better and strengthen myself by analyzing and organizing my religious and spiritual encounters and experiences to develop my faith and set of values.

As the class progressed, he was assigned to identify the effects of his anger on himself and others.

1. How has anger affected my work relationships (include jobs lost or jobs jeopardized)?
   It caused my employer to lose confidence in me from a business or professional aspect. It ultimately caused me to quit another one of my jobs. I've completely lost my temper at every job I've ever had.

2. How has anger affected my marriage or romantic relationships?
   I've lost several girlfriends due to my being unreasonable about ridiculous stuff. My jealousy has played the biggest role in me getting angry with girls.

3. How has anger affected my children?
   My anger hasn't really affected my son at all. The very few times I've become angry in his presence I didn't let him see me out of control, and I treated him the same as always. I've <u>never</u> gotten angry or lost control towards him.

4. How has anger affected my friendships? (including lost friends and strained relationships)
   I'm pretty sure that the only way anger affects my friendships is that it makes my friends kind of scared of me. Not in a way that they are too scared to be around me, but that they might have to watch what they say.

5. How has my anger affected my health? (such as stress and adrenaline levels)
   I've cut and sliced myself from punching things. I've put cigarettes out on myself. It's made me lose my appetite. I've gone days without sleeping.

As the class neared its conclusion, the focus shifted to goal setting. The first assignment was to address his immediate lifestyle. He wrote:

- At home: Be more open minded with my Dad. Try not to get frustrated with my Step-mom.
- At bedtime: Try to get on a better sleeping schedule so I don't stay awake wrapped up in my thoughts.
- In the morning: Try and get up earlier and be more productive with my day before I go to work.
- When I'm driving: Try not to let people going very slow get on my nerves so bad.
- When I'm shopping: Have more patience with people when they're standing in my way.
- With my body: Maybe try to get a little more exercise and it might make me feel better.
- With my mind: Read more and find other activities to keep my mind occupied.

On Graduation Night, December 2, 2003, he completed his final assignment.

1. Do you feel or think that goals are important to have in your life? Explain why.
   Goals are important. They give you something to shoot for. They give you a sense of direction in life. They help you keep in mind what you have to do or need to accomplish.

2. How have you used goals in the past?
   The main goal I had in the past was joining special ops in the military. I prepared for the military for years before I found out I couldn't get in.

3. Define what a goal is to you?
   When there is something you want to accomplish. You don't stop until you have accomplished what it is that you want.

4. How are goals positive and/or negative?
   They are positive because when you reach them they give you a great sense of accomplishment. They are potentially negative if you don't reach your goal by giving up and thinking it's too hard to do.

5. List 10 goals you have for life.
   - Always be a great father and always be there
   - Get my GED or diploma equivalency of some sort
   - Stay out of trouble and don't go to jail
   - Further my education to get a well-paying job
   - Get my medical issues under control
   - Get a nice house
   - Get a nice car
   - Get married and remain faithful

A couple of foods for thought shared on this last day were:
On average, 94% of everything we worry about never happens.
Man can tolerate anything as long as he has a purpose.

"And no one knows what it's like
To be hated
To be fated
To telling only lies."

"Dad, I'm so sorry." I heard this one many times. It's a fact that addicts will go to any extreme to feed their habit. He was a master of juggling money to feed his addiction and try not to go into debt. Buy, cheat, steal….whatever means necessary to satisfy the craving. To lie in order to hide what had been stolen or about money spent on medicine when it was supposed to be for a car payment. To walk around with so much guilt to think you are hated, even by family members who love you unconditionally.

Four weeks before being admitted into his 3rd rehab facility and the day after his graduation from Anger Management, on December 3, 2003, he wrote in his journal.

"The waitress Sarah showed up at 6:00PM to take tables. Beth and James are two lousy restaurant owners. It won't surprise me if this restaurant goes out of business just like their other restaurant did. They have no concept of consistency, cost consciousness, setting a restaurant's atmosphere of vibe and so on and so forth. I have to not take this job too seriously and not put my heart into it in order to avoid being let down. I could run a better restaurant than them handcuffed and blindfolded. They have no recognition of my food business skills or overall potential integrity. If I try and help fix their business up and make things better, I know I'll end up just being let down. They have no appreciation or good business sense for that matter.

I decided to call Daniel (OC/Pill dealer) around 7:45 or so. Finally he got some more Oxycontin 20's in. Twenty of them to be exact.

I called Beth (my boss) and told her Remy got bit by something while being watched by Ashley's parents and was on his way to the hospital due to excessive swelling. She had no problem with me leaving because that other cook was there. It was only supposed to be me cooking tonight anyways. They were going to fire him when they got there (she said when I called her around 7:50PM that they would be there in 2 minutes), but would wait until after he closed tonight since I was leaving. It worked out well.

Right after that I left work and went home. I called Molly, no answer (she was at work). I told Laura to tell my dad that I was going to the store. I told Daniel I would be at his house at 8:45PM. I left at 8:00 or so and took Dad's car. I already had his ATM/bank card from having to have to use it on Tuesday to get out $150 to pay off Anger Management Class on my last day. I had only $37 or so and needed $150 to buy the Oxys (20 Oxys at $7.50 apiece) I stopped at the bank and withdrew $130 then drove to Daniel's in Douglasville, stopping once to get a Gatorade.

I got to Daniels's at 8:37 and he was waiting for me. I only spent 3-5 minutes there, made the deal, then left putting the Oxys in my old "Oxycontin 20mg" medicine bottle. I kind of felt funny when I stepped in his house and for a moment thought it might have been a set-up with the police. But, then again, I always kind of feel like that to a certain extent not matter who I'm dealing with. Except for when I dealt with Thomas, who is dead now. But that's a story for another time.

After I left Daniel's I stopped at the gas station's parking lot right in front of his neighborhood and took 7 Oxys (140mg worth). When I was done I headed home calling Ashley on the way to see if I could come and get Remy so he could stay the night. I swung by Cindy's and Hamp's real quick and picked up 3 diapers for tomorrow. I picked up Remy, stopped at another gas station for an almond Snickers bar and cigarettes then went home. Oh yeah, I also went to Krystal's to pick up some food to bring home (mmmmm…….cheeseburgers).

For the remainder of the night I played with Remy. Molly came over about 10:00 or so. It's 2:24AM now and Remy just closed his eyes a minute ago to go to sleep. Molly brought me $130 to leave on the counter for my dad to get before he went to work. I left the money with a note explaining I took the money out of his account to buy Remy a Christmas present at the store but they were out of stock of the present. I'm supposed to pay Molly back tomorrow with my paycheck (or cash really since I get paid under the table).

I took a couple of polaroids of Remy tonight and got him with the video camera a little bit. I really didn't get to feeling as good as I thought I would off those Oxys. I was surprised. I hadn't had any in 10-14 days or so. I guess that morphine (despite it doesn't make me feel good) keeps my tolerance up. The majority of the day I was just in an okay mood. Not bad, but not great."

In this story he told 3 lies; one to his employer about Remy's accident, one to Laura to pass on to me about where he was going, and finally to me about what he had done with the money.

"And if I swallow anything evil
Put your finger down my throat

And if I shiver
Please give me a blanket
Keep me warm and let me wear your coat."

The amount of medicine he needed to take to feel normal was increasing. He wrote several days later:

> <u>December 8, 2003</u> – Very sunny and slightly cool today. It's about 9:55PM right now. I was too tired and just plain didn't feel like writing last night. I'm pretty tired right now too.
>
> Man, I was so pissed off, or really more disappointed at myself yesterday. I went to bed at like 4:00AM – 4:30AM late, late Saturday night. I had taken 3-4 Somas and 3 over the counter sleep aids. As soon as I opened my eyes, I looked at the clock and it said 6:00, I figured it was early Sunday morning so I'd go to the bathroom and go back to bed. When I walked out of my room I saw Chris' bedroom light was on, hallway light on, kitchen and parents light on and thought "what the f*@k is everyone doing up so damn early?" I took a piss, came in my room and looked at my clock again. It was 6:02PM. I had slept for 14 hours straight without even waking up once, which is unusual. I always briefly wake up at least a couple times a night. That's why I automatically assumed it was 6:00AM.
>
> I was immediately pissed off because I had wasted my whole f*@king day. I started feeling depressed. After basically walking in circles in my room because I was so damn bored and trying to watch some TV, I started thinking back about the good old Lawrenceville days.
>
> After an hour of contemplation, around 9:00PM Sunday night, I decided to throw on some clothes, jump in my Dad's car and head to Lawrenceville without telling them I was coming. Although I tried calling Josh once to see if I could come over, I really wasn't entirely interested to go there and see anyone. I just needed to get the hell out of this house and go for a drive. I was kind of in one of my deep thinking moods. Really thinking about the past and how much fun I had back then.

I didn't realize it at the time, but the ages 14 – 17 were so far some of the best years of my life. It makes me sad when I think about it. I did so much fun and crazy shit back then. Hell, I even did that ages 17 – 20 as well.

As I was leaving here, right before I got in the car (I was standing next to it), I decided to look at the moon. I took a detailed mental picture of what it looked like that night and the angle at which I had to hold my head and eyes to see it from directly in front of my house. I thought to myself that during my "recollection" tour of Lawrenceville that night I would go to a particular spot on a particular road and again take another mental picture. Staring at the moon for those few moments before I left made me feel like Lawrenceville was a million miles away. It seemed weird or significant or something (can't think of the right word) that on that night I would look at the same moon and it would look the very same from two different spots that, to me, felt like were two different worlds.

My old world and my present world. And in each world I feel like a completely different person. Meaning: back in the day, when I used to live right next to the spot where I was going to see the moon that night, during that time period, when I was 15 or 16, I felt like a completely different person. Almost everything about me, not referring to physical traits, is almost opposite now than it was then, 7 years ago.

That night, a funny coincidence happened. It just so happened that the spot which I decided to go to take that mental moon picture is/was located directly on Moon Road. This road runs behind one of our old neighborhoods in Lawrenceville (when we lived on Onyx Court) where me, my Dad, and my brother Michael lived at. That road's name didn't occur to me at all at the time I decided to go or anytime thereafter, until I got there and looked at the road sign.

This is funny; this journal is the only thing I feel like I can be absolutely 100% honest with. Another coincidence: at the very moment, while I write, Chris and Remy are drawing and talking about the moon. They are drawing moons with Remy's new markers. One more thing before

I move on, this Moon Road is the road we would cross to practice our amateur repelling, camp and ride bikes (me, Jimmy, Matt, Clint and sometimes Chris.) This dirt field is where our infamous "plateau" was located.

Anyways, I left for Lawrenceville at 8:58PM and stopped at a few miles down the road to get a Snickers, double cheeseburger combo, and some gas. I continued to Lawrenceville thinking about all kinds of things along the way. I was definitely in one of my thinking moods, as I sort of am right now. I went straight to Alicia's neighborhood. I stopped at her house and the living room light was on. I parked in front of the house, not on the driveway, and walked up to the house. I didn't want my presence to be known unless she was awake. I set off the driveway motion detector light, but she was either asleep or wasn't home.

At this point it was about 10:00PM. I drove down every single side street in the neighborhood remembering all the different things I did and all the different people I did them with as I passed each spot where each event took place. I imagined seeing myself through the car window at the young age of 12 or 13 or whatever it was. I tried to picture everything I did. Geez, I'm getting sleepy right now and I need to pay some attention to Molly and Remy. OK then: I drove through all of my old neighborhoods and down some roads I had kinda forgotten where they went. I also drove the route that I used to ride my bike to get to Lauren's house and I drove through her neighborhood too.

I drove to Holly's street and called Josh. He answered. We spoke for a few minutes and he asked "Where are you at?" I told him I was parked right outside and of course he didn't believe me. He walked out and was very surprised to see me. It had been a few months since we've seen each other. We sat at Holly's for about an hour and talked.

I left there, drove around and tried calling Jimmy – no answer. I left a message. He called back 10-15 minutes later. He met me at the gas station on Lawrenceville Highway and we went to his apartment. We just talked about old times and he let me borrow some movies and video games.

By the way, all I took Sunday was morphine. I left there

about 3:10AM, stopped by the gas station and got some snacks, came home, took 3 somas and 3 sleeping pills and my prescription muscle relaxer, popped in a movie and fell asleep at 6:00AM or so. I was pretty messed up by the time I fell asleep. Those pills pretty much knocked me out. It turned out to be a pretty good day, or night actually, even though I didn't see Molly.

December 9, 2003 – Today I woke up, or got up at 2:10PM. I had my alarm set for 11:00 but just kept snoozing. I woke up, called the doctor's office to let them know I would be late (my appointment was at 2:30PM), and drove to the doctor's. He gave me a prescription for 90 Percocet 10/325mg. After that I drove straight to Wal-Mart to drop off the prescription and went home. Dad was there (he had jury selection duty today). I got home at 4:50 PM. James had called and left a message wanting me to come to work. Rich, the kitchen manager, didn't come in again. After discussing everything about getting Remy and working with Molly (over the phone), my Dad, and Ashley, I decided to leave, pick up my script, go to work from 6:00PM – 8:00PM, pick up Remy, stop and get snacks, and go home. I took 18 Percocets before work. It made me feel pretty good, but I was itchy. When I got home, Dad was asleep. Molly came over. I cleaned up my room and then started writing. Right now it's 11:30 and Remy is playing on the floor and Molly is watching TV. Chris was in here earlier for a while playing a video game and then played with Remy. I must go now, Remy really wants my attention. Write you later – bye.

December 10, 2003 – It's 2:15AM right now. Late Wednesday. Today f*@king sucked. I woke up (I was up at 12:20PM) and almost immediately ate 18 more Percocet 10's. I didn't feel that bad at first but after a couple of hours I felt very nauseous. I kept Remy, made us pizza, dropped him off at Hamp's at 3:00PM, and went to work. I felt sick the whole time at work and threw up around 7:00PM. After throwing up again, Beth called Rich in and I left before he got there. I came home, threw up again, and took an hour nap. I woke up, Molly came over and brought me cigs and lottery tickets (for some reason). She left at 1:00AM or so. I just took 2 morphines, 3 sleeping pills, and 3 Somas and I'm not too tired yet. But don't want to write, talk to you later.

Christmas was coming up and he had no money for presents. He was spending everything on medicine and this added to his guilt and anxiety. Finally, he couldn't take the pain and addiction anymore. The "evil" he'd been swallowing made him ask "for a blanket." Over the next 4 months he would be admitted to three different rehab facilities. The first was 2 days before the New Year.

January 1, 2004 – It's been quite interesting. I went to some groups, I take my meds, I'm a good little boy.

But I have to tell you about two days ago quite possibly being the worst day of my life. I mean talk about the pain!! It was excruciating!! The most annoying and painful lower back pain ever. It was the withdrawal. That back pain might exceed the severe migraines I've had in the past. I felt so shitty!! I hope that I, or almost anyone for that matter, never have to go through that. This has been probably the most extreme experience of my life. On Tuesday December 30, 2003, I finally decided to go to rehab for my opiate addiction. I had gotten 150mg of oxy on Monday. I took it around 12:00 PM on Monday. By Tuesday around 2:00 PM or so I was in so much pain I just said "screw it." I can't take this shit forever. A few days ago I had to take 340mg to feel the effects, and it didn't even work that great. So I called Molly to bring me here.

When we got here I had to fill out a bunch of paperwork. Then they took us to some assessment room where we had to sit for 3 or 3 ½ hours while they processed the paperwork and tried to get through with my insurance. That was when the pain really got bad. At that point it was worse than it was 6 hours earlier. I was in <u>SO MUCH PAIN!!</u> I couldn't sit still, I threw up once, and I was completely restless. At one point, probably around 7:00 PM or so, I said I had to use the bathroom, which I did, and someone unlocked the door for me to go. When I got out, Molly was standing there and I was so frustrated I said "SCREW THIS!!"

I made Molly go and get their attention several times to tell them I need immediate medical attention. They just kept dicking us around, and frankly, I didn't want to be here just because of the damn service. I told Molly "Come on, let's get the hell out of here!!" I intended on having her drive me to the emergency room.

Just as we walked out and got in her car, my Dad pulled up right next to us. I knew I could count on him to quickly get the ball rolling. So I went back in, waited a little longer, and finally got to go to my new temporary home, Cottage C. My Dad and Molly came with, carrying with them my small amount of luggage I'd packed while waiting for Molly to get to my house. It just so happened it was visitation time so they hung around a while. The security performed a safety search making me take all my clothes off except my underwear.

They briefed us a little on how things worked. Almost immediately after my arrival to Cottage C they gave me some pain medication supposedly nearly equivalent to Darvocet for my back. Dad and Molly finally left around 8:30 PM, I think. I hugged them both. I saw tears swell up in Molly's eyes as she walked through those security doors. It made my eyes do the same.

That night I just basically sat around and didn't do much. Smoked some cigs during our once every hour or hour and a half fifteen minute breaks. I really didn't feel good at all. They gave me some detox meds that have anti-anxiety medicine mixed in it. Of course, it had the opposite effect on me and made me nervous. I think I took a little nap, didn't really talk to anyone, and finally decided to try and crash. It was a shitty night's sleep. I tossed and turned most of the night.

I woke up around 10:30 AM New Year's Eve. I just sat around all day and talked some to a guy named John, who is also here for opiate addiction. He's a pretty nice, straight guy, not messed up in the head like most of the people here. John encouraged me to eat, which I tried to do, but I had no appetite. And no energy for that matter. I mean zero, zip energy. Just to walk down the hall made it feel like I'd run a marathon.

Jonathan stayed for 5 days before he couldn't stand being there anymore. My relationship with Jonathan was tense and my patience was wearing thin. After discussing the situation with Terri, the 3 of us decided a change of scenery was in order. He packed his car and moved to Florida to live with Terri and Kristin. Within a month his addiction was taking a strong hold again.

"No one knows what it's like
To feel these feelings
Like I do
And I blame you."

There was a side of him that blamed. Any upset that occurred was someone else's fault. During the severest bouts of depression or anger, he would blame whoever was available. His boss, girlfriend, mother, the guy in the store, another driver, me….it didn't matter.

In February 2004 he entered his 4th rehab center, this one a 12 step program in Florida and he was given an assignment to write a letter to his dear addiction.

"Dear Opiate,
I know I haven't seen you in a few days. I'm writing to you to let you know where I'm at and what's going on with me. But first, I want to thank you. I remember when we first met. You were always there for me. Whenever I started to get a headache you were willing to take away my pain. Do you remember? I'll never forget that. I started having migraines all the time, and so you were there with me all the time. Before I knew it, we were best friends. I wanted to have you around all the time. And you were. Not only would you take away my pain, but you gave me confidence, you made me feel so good. Before I knew it, you were the only reason I wanted to get up in the morning. I appreciate your willingness to make me happy. But just one thing, where the f*^#k are you now? Why did you take all my

money. Oh, it's OK, I only have a son to raise. I only had car payments and rent payments. But you didn't seem to care about that. Oh, it's no big f*^#king deal. I'm only in a hospital now because of you. You wonder where I've been lately? I've been f*^#king miserable....."

In this letter, Jonathan blamed the medicine for his addiction rather than take responsibility for his actions.

However there were periods of time when he would accept responsibility for his life. It was during these times that tremendous guilt would overcome him, resulting in an increase in his depression. During this decade he moved in with Michael for a short period of time, and Michael would hold him as Jonathan cried in his arms for the things he had done.

Years later, he told me he had done some terrible things and he was unable to let these go and forgive himself. We talked about the Earl TV show, and how Earl had made a list of the people he felt he'd betrayed and how he was on a mission to make it right. I suggested to Jonathan that he try to make a similar list. We worked on the list for a couple of days, but he never acted on it. He felt guilt in the way he had treated me and despite my assurances of forgiveness, he wasn't able to let it go. He felt an incredible debt to me. I would pray with him, and we would ask for guidance from the Holy Spirit to bring him peace. It worked for a short period of time, but he would soon lower himself back into a state of depression.

Jonathan stayed with this program less than a week but he did complete a couple of his assignments. There was also a handout included with the information he saved from this visit. This handout listed 148 positive affirmations, and lists of pleasant and unpleasant feelings. He checked off 2 affirmations that hit home to him.

- My life is shaped by my choices.
- I am learning to take life one day at a time.

There was also an assignment called Higher Power Attitude Index. He was to identify 6 characteristics from a list of 24 options that described his attitude toward God. At this point in his life, he defined God as being primarily uninvolved.

Jonathan called Terri and told her he was leaving and asked that she come and get him. This program wasn't for him, and he was leaving whether or not she would pick him up. She did, and the addiction problems escalated for the next 30 days.

Terri had friends who provided holistic therapy. One of those friends introduced her to a married couple who happened to be Reverends in the Spiritual Community, and who specialized in helping people with addiction and emotional problems. The arrangements were made and Jonathan was introduced to the Reverends and their program. Rather than the typical 12 step programs, and waiting to go to, as Jonathan he referred to them, "bull shit meetings," the approach was holistic in nature. Also, Jonathan was the only patient so he received highly individualized treatment. Meditation, yoga, prayer, New Age thinking, were some of the daily routine, as well as accountability for the chores he was assigned. The Reverends also performed numerology tests and a past life regression was carried out. Although this approach didn't solve his future problems, it opened his eyes to a new world of thinking.

After completing the program he went another 3 years before the severity of his addiction overcame him again.

"And no one knows how to say
That they're sorry
And don't worry
I'm not telling lies."

I came home one day in February 2007 to find some of my yard tools and equipment missing. Jonathan told me that someone must have broken in and stolen these things. Deep down I knew he had pawned it, and this was confirmed after his passing. I wanted to trust him, believe him. I think he knew that I knew, and this added to his guilt.

On the evening of April 10, 2007 Jonathan asked me if he could borrow $20. I gave him my bankcard and he assured me he would pay me back at the end of the week. I got home the next day from work and Jonathan was waiting for me at the kitchen table. He looked troubled and he finally burst out in tears. He confessed to taking out over $500 the night before so he could buy some Oxys. We both agreed he needed immediate help. Since he was no longer covered by an insurance policy, we located a state run facility and proceeded to get him admitted.

He kept a journal while going through rehab.

<u>April 12, 2007</u> – It's been another rough night. I've been

fighting hard to keep the tears back. Once again, I'm locked up in another institution hoping to get better. This one is called A Crisis Stabilization unit. The main thing on my mind is my love, Tiff. It's only been one day and I miss her so so much. It feels like it's been a week, She is the love of my life. I'm staying strong for her, only her. I'm going to stay here and fight through this for her. I'm going to get better for her.

During last night's hospital admission to Cobb County E.R., I was at first kind of excited. I was anxious and looked forward to starting my treatment process. But as the night grew on, I got worse. They administered 2 Adovans to me and I didn't like it.

Michael finally left around 2:30 AM and Dad stayed with me all night. Around 9:00 AM Dad left to go shower and sleep and I took turns taking naps and smoking cigs while I waited for the paperwork to process so I could call Dad to come and pick me up to take me to this center. It finally happened between 1 – 2 PM. He dropped me off around 3:30 PM, walked me in, told me "Get better son," and left.

I spent an hour signing admission papers, then smoked, then ate. I was able to speak with Tiff for a few minutes. I've basically been sitting around all night, although I took a 20 minute nap. The meds they have me on are very mild, non-opiate, detox meds. I hope they work good.

I got to call Tiff again at 9:30 PM or so. The nurse was sitting right in front of me so I made it brief. It soothes my soul to hear her sweet voice. It's now about 11:10PM and I'm not tired at all. Almost everyone else is asleep right now.

No one here has really struck me as someone I'll hit it off with. Everyone is between 21-35 years old. They haven't talked to me much. I think I got a roommate who I will be able to relate with more than anyone else here. His name is Daniel with black hair, black goatee, and arms full of tattoos. He seems like he could be my friend.

Right now I'm feeling very depressed and I'm just laying here thinking. I want to feel good. I want to be normal. I want to be a great Dad to Remy and a great family member.

I want to be the man Tiff will always look up to and love. I'm going to attempt some sleep.

April 13, 2007 – It's Friday, at 4:18PM and this day has been soooooo looong. I'm so damn bored. I've been walking in circles all day. I got up at 6:10 AM and got my vitals, then some meds and went back to sleep. Someone woke me up around 7:30 or so because I had a phone call. It was Tiff. I was glad she called. I ate some breakfast and went back to sleep, got up, smoked, walked around, ate lunch, smoked, had some gay bingo meeting, then met with the doctor's assistant. I had earlier met with the doctor. He seemed pretty nice and thorough and said I would leave on Thursday. It's going to be an eternity so I took another little nap, read a little bit, and here I am now. I've tried breaking the ice with a few people so we could relate and help each other pass the time. It hasn't really worked. I'm hoping over the next few days I will come up with some kind of creative idea to help. Otherwise I'm going to go nuts. Physically, I haven't been that bad. The lack of energy and mild back pain being the worst things. I've had some little headaches and diarrhea too. But all and all, not nearly as bad as the first place I went to in 2004.

The next several days passed and he wrote about the daily routine. Meetings were held throughout the day and regular smoke breaks were provided, but his boredom escalated. Tiff and I took him a care package that contained several books and a carton of cigarettes. Reading helped the time pass, and daily conversations with Tiff and periodic calls from me, Terri and Remy helped, but he was going stir crazy as his anxiety would build at the thought of being locked up. Finally, the day before his release arrived.

April 18, 2007 – Well it's 10:15 PM and I'm getting ready to go to sleep here for the last time. It was another routine day here schedule wise. I taught Clark and Daniel (crazy boy) how to march and we marched the hallways. Everyone was laughing at us. I watched six people have a farting contest and stink up the entire hallway. The cool tech, Tony, let me, Clark, and Jeff sweep the smoking deck which was a treat. Everyone was jealous because he let us smoke while doing it (extra smoke break for us). I know Tony picked us because he liked us best. Particularly me. I believe because I was exceptionally kind and polite to him. Most of the employees here have made it clear to me, in one way or another, that I was one of their best patients and they were glad to have me. It made me feel good, I guess. They let me get by with things, little things, here and there that they wouldn't have done for anyone else. Physically, it wasn't too great of a day. I had a moderate (as opposed to mild) headache most of the day. I had some bad anxiety but it came and went and I dealt with it in the same usual fashion – did nothing. I guess I will read some now to get sleepy and pass out. Tomorrow morning I will be up by 6:00 AM and ready to go by 9:00 AM, when Tiff is going to pick me up. It's been an adventure here. It's been difficult. I've been clean for about seven days now. I don't know what will happen from tomorrow on. It is only my hope that all my future endeavors utilize my full potential so I can stay the course. What that course is exactly, I don't know….I guess I'll just have to wait and see….

Tiff arrived at 9:00 AM to pick up Jonathan. As they were driving home, Jonathan insisted that they go directly to his Oxycontin source. Tiff tried to persuade him not to go and reminded Jonathan that he had been clean for a week. Jonathan began to get angry and demanded that they go immediately. Tiff tried to convince him otherwise, but despite her best efforts, Jonathan was determined to take his medications.

And like clockwork, nearly 3 years later he was admitted into The Facility. That would be his final trip to a rehabilitation center. In May of 2007 he took the first steps to kick the Oxycontin addiction and began methadone treatment for his withdrawal This helped him to stabilize for a while, but the deep rooted feelings of sadness, depression, guilt, and anxiety eventually manifested itself in blame, anger and manipulation.

"I have hours, only lonely
My love is vengeance
That's never free."

Lesson 22 of A Course In Miracles states:

> I see only the perishable.
> I see nothing that will last.
> What I see is not real.
> What I see is a form of vengeance.

At the end of each practice period, ask yourself:

> Is this the world I really want to see?

The answer is surely obvious.

Although Jonathan later understood this lesson, he spent many years with feelings of vengeance filling his mind. Nobody could have one ups-manship on him. Not only could he get mad, he got even, and then some. Until he graduated from the Spiritual Healers Program in April 2004, getting even was in the back of his mind. The teachings of this program however, provided a new way of looking at life's problems. This stimulated a seed in Jonathan's mind that had always been there and he began applying some of the ideas presented to him and dug deeper into alternative ways of thinking and perceiving.

<u>April 9, 2004</u> – This letter was written to Jonathan upon his completion of his rehabilitation with the Reverends.

> "Dear Jonathan
> Today you begin a new life with independence and freedom from addiction. In addition you have seen your headaches disappear or become non-existent based on the excellent diet and water intake of approximately 170 ounces a day. This intake of water has helped to remove the toxicity and as toxicity leaves your physical body so too does the desire for the addictions that caused the toxicity. The almost total elimination of red meat and sugar from your diet will help you to continue to release toxicity and greatly improve your overall mental, emotional and physical well-being.
> So now with re-entry into your new life you have achieved all the important aspects of the elimination of the causes of your initial distress. For example: your first

session with us in doing a past life regression gave light to your desires of being a soldier, a hero and a suicide, because of the memory so strong within you of that past life. Once you were able to recognize the fantasy that existed and once you were able to put truth to the lie of you becoming a soldier of fortune, a security agent and joining other spy type organizations, as well as paramilitary organizations you realized that you were making a clown of yourself and you were a parody of your own truth.

Today you have grown up and left behind the make-believe something that you are not. The reality, Jonathan is that you are a gentle soul, not a killer, a special agent, a spy or any other absurd and ridiculous and self-created image. Your real image is, as we said, gentle, kind, eager to learn, wanting an education, seeking improvement mentally, spiritually, and physically. And learning that there is more to life than the Culture of Death for which you have so long espoused.

It could be a long time before all the toxicity is out of your system enabling you to function at optimal levels as a young man. Commitment with this will be the necessity for you to realize that everything you do from this point on will be matter of even greater choice than before, because the spiritual and mental demons that have infested and infected you are now dispersed. There is no one to blame but yourself from this point on. You must be especially vigilant and mindful of the excessive use of manipulation that you employ in particular upon those close to you. It is sometimes difficult to break these old habits. You can overcome this excessive manipulation by remembering there is no longer room for this destructive component in your life.

While the above is all well and good in all that you have accomplished you need to understand that the reason you accomplished it was because of your spiritual work, your meditation, your prayer, your yoga and journaling and without God you would have been able to accomplish little. You are here at a most significant juncture of the year, the sacred Holy Week and the energies expended over you by nine priests in doing the Liturgy of Baptism with exorcism has eliminated the initial cause of your hardships, which may at times have become an excuse to hide your own choices. No longer can you say, "the devil made me do it." You can now truthfully say, "God made me do it."

We wish you only the best and look forward to seeing you put in to practice in your life the spiritual, physical and emotional teachings that we have passed on to you. We stand ready to help you and continue to be of service. We anticipate in the immediate future to having you return at a schedule that will be coordinated with your father, your job, etc.

We have made an electronic document from your handwriting and in your words and in agreement with all that we have taught you. Attached is a list of items that will help you in your strength and quest for a continued Culture of Life rather than a Culture of Death.

Love, Life and Blessings,
The Reverends Francis and Ariadne Romano

He kept a journal while he was with the Reverends and they encouraged him to be honest with his writings.

March 25, 2004 – I got to the Reverends I think around 5:30PM. We talked a while. We ate dinner and talked a little more. I fell asleep around 9:30 or so then woke up at 1:20AM. I felt very shitty, my back was hurting some and I couldn't go back to sleep. I came downstairs and watched TV, smoked some cigs, had to take some more medicine and finally went back to sleep at 4:20AM. Today I learned that red meat is not good for you.

March 26, 2004 – I'm almost 23. I woke up at 9:30. I did not feel well. Not a very big appetite and very low on energy. I took some meds (Darvocet), smoked, and we ate breakfast, oh yes, right after taking Sasha (the dog) for a short walk and taking a shower. I helped clean up a little and smoked some more. I threw up outside while smoking and came in to take a 1 ½ hour nap. I feel shitty. Ariadne and I went on a walk which just about killed me. Francis and I talked awhile before Ariadne came into the bedroom and showed me how to meditate her way, which is what I learned for the day. I went to sleep about midnight or so and woke up from 4:20 – 6:00 AM on 3/27.

March 27, 2004 – I'm 23!!! I woke up at 9:00 AM. Laid in bed for a bit before getting up. I felt like shit. Ariadne and I took Sasha for a walk then we came in and made a little breakfast. I went upstairs and talked with Francis awhile and Ariadne left around 1:00 PM. Francis and I went outside for a little while. At first I walked a few hundred yards down the beach and back to see all the people. I took a little swim in the Gulf. We then sat on the downstairs back porch and talked for a bit. We came in and I took a shower, then went outside and called mom while I smoked. I called dad, Chris answered, and dad was gone. It doesn't even feel like my birthday. I believe this is the most weird birthday ever. I'm lonely. Francis and I got in our dispute. I talked with Ariadne about it and then Francis. Between that I called dad. I was very upset. Eventually, at about 8:30 or so we went to a restaurant to eat dinner. We all came home. Ariadne, the nice woman (I forgot her name), and I meditated a bit. Before which they gave me some birthday presents. They all sang Happy Birthday at the restaurant. It's 11:35 PM now and I'm tired.

March 28, 2004 – Well shit. I woke up this morning about 8:00. I went outside, smoked, took the dog for a walk with Ariadne, then went out on the beach and she showed me some yoga; the 5 rights I think. I felt kind of stupid because there were other people around. We finished, I cleaned up, shaved, showered, cleaned the room, then we got to go out and wash her car. It's 3:00 PM now and I've just been chilling since then. My mind keeps jolting around with positive and negative emotions. I feel kind of torn, kind of confused in a way. It's hard to know what to make of all this. I just hope the answers are coming. I decided to go with Ariadne and Lena to a wedding Ariadne had to do. It was pretty nice. The couple was Daniel and Vanessa. Of course I knew no one and just sat in back. We drove home and ate a nice dinner with Francis, and Tom. Lena and Tom left, Francis and Ariadne went to bed, all by 10:30 or so. I stayed up and watched some of "Apollo 13" and went to try to sleep around midnight. I could not fall asleep, despite how tired I was. After getting in and out of bed to smoke cigs and stuff, I finally fell asleep around 2:30. Except for trying to fall asleep, it was a pretty all right day, I guess.

March 29, 2004 –I'm a little more nervous and frustrated than yesterday, but I'm trying to deal with it. I feel like leaving right now. Shit…this is hard to deal with. I went and sat outside and on the beach a while to write in thinking pad. Ariadne and I discussed some things for me to do when I leave here and I did the "Wheel of Life." I just chilled around until 6:30 PM or so when everyone started coming for class. I talked to a guy named Dave before class and Bill after class. I liked Bill. He was kind of inspirational to me. Among other things, he was taking 400mg of Oxy's at a time. Class was pretty good. By the time class was over and I got done talking to Bill, it was about 10:30.

March 31, 2004 – Francis and I got into it again. I found out that I'm staying until next Friday now…that SUCKS!! Francis gave me a choice: "Either pack your shit and get out and go to jail in the next 24 hours, or stay here until your parents finally come to escort you home." We had cleaned my car out and Ariadne went through all my stuff. She took away a bunch of my shit and found some Imitrex pills and such that I wasn't trying to hide. They said they had asked me if I had any more pills and I said no. I don't remember that, but if I did I was saying I had no more narcotics. You can't abuse Imitrex type medicine!! After getting defensive and knowing that I wasn't going to win the argument unless I wanted to go to jail, I gave in, said "screw it" to myself, and bit the bullet. I gave hugs and got over it, mainly because I'm scared shitless about going to jail. Basically, I've been blackmailed to stay here.

April 1, 2004 – Tom and Lena showed up and eventually another woman (I can't remember her name), and we headed towards Orlando to see the author Elaine Pagels give a speech. The lecture was OK, I guess. Hard to follow on written Jesus documents and such. The college campus was kind of inspirational to me. It made me feel, when looking at all those students, like going to that college, or a college at least.

April 2, 2004 – I really haven't elaborated on my feelings too much since I've been here, so here it goes……..
It's been very, very difficult. I get very bored and feel confined a lot. I'm forced to be here. All I want to do is go home, but I can't do that right now, I have no choice. So instead of thinking about how miserable I am and how much I want to go home, I've been trying to stay positive and deal with this. My patience has worn thin. I'm very lonely. I cannot wait until next Friday when my family shows up to get me. I will be ecstatic. I don't even give a crap about drugs anymore, I just want to go home and see my beautiful little boy. Usually, the day starts out with me feeling shitty. I mean, I'm better than I was when I used to wake up – no withdrawal symptoms, but it still sucks. As the day goes on, usually I start feeling better and better, but then it starts back over the next morning. I can't tell if it's the yoga and little bit of physical work that I do that makes the day get somewhat better, or the fact that the day is coming to an end, which brings me closer to going home. Today is my 6th day clean. I haven't talked to Molly or anyone, except my mom and dad briefly on my shitty birthday. Even if I could just talk to them it would help. But the rules here are very strict. I'm scared to be myself most of the time because I'm scared of Francis' or Ariadne's reaction. I am myself, just much quieter, less whiny, and I do exactly what they tell me to. I don't want them to think I'm trying to be manipulative. But I really am trying, with all my might, to get through this so I can be with my family and friends. This is a very rough road, but I suppose I brought it on myself. I must get better and I will, or my life will be destroyed. And I have a son to raise so that can't happen.

April 3, 2004 – Francis, Ariadne, and I meditated for a while. Immediately after, Francis insisted that Ariadne and I take an hour to an hour and a half walk on the beach, after they did a little work. It was as if Francis had some sort of breakthrough about me right after the meditation. He said "It's gone Jon, you're going to be fine." Does this mean that I'm stable now? I won't push it and ask. Francis wanted us to leave so he could clear the house of all negativity. And that's what we all did. It's 4:04 PM now and Ariadne and I just got back from a long beach walk. Francis "cleared" the house while we were gone. I can still smell the deep incense aroma from his works. I have no idea what we are doing the rest of the day. I never do. They don't tell me anything that's going to take place on any day. I wonder if that has anything to do with my morning anxiety?

April 4, 2004 –It's 8:40PM now. Ariadne, Francis, Tom and I are all sitting in the living room. They are watching a CNN special on Jesus. At about 3:30PM, after Francis and Ariadne were done working on their publishing company, Ariadne and I went and sat on the beach for an hour and a half. We came in at 5:15 after first walking Sasha. Tom came over and by 6:15 we left and went and ate at an Oriental Buffet Restaurant. They had some normal food there. It was pretty good, but then, I was starving too…..It's 9:34PM now and I've been thinking. I've been thinking about it a lot lately: my old Lawrenceville life. Looking back, that was so great. All the very many laughs we all had. I was happy, healthy, clean, had many friends, made decent grades, life couldn't have been better. It was so great. I remember when I was weight lifting. I was so strong and healthy. I was getting thick. I remember riding my bike everywhere. It never even fazed me. I never thought twice about involving myself in a strenuous or difficult situation. It just wasn't my nature. I never thought of it and therefore it never existed. I was fearless. I remember how great high school was and all the gambling we did. I remember Lauren. I remember all of our camping and paintball trips and our ops. Everything was so great, it was perfect. And I didn't even notice any of that at the time. Those great friends, those great times. I have to change my thinking; I have to change my lifestyle so I can live like that again. I remember my brother and I being so close. I remember the 5th grade, the 7th grade, the RSIA, I remember everything!! Everything was so great, so fun, so perfect, and I was sober the whole time. Was it just my ignorance? I think not. I want to be like that again, it'll be perfect. I feel these intense emotions from those experiences, and I'm only 23 years old. What more fun can I have? Thank you my Lawrenceville brothers, with all my heart……..After we got back from dinner I had to sit there and watch about 3 hours' worth of religious TV programs. After that, Tom went home and Francis and I talked for a little while. Then he went to bed. I stayed up until 1:00AM watching some more of "The Gladiator," then I went to bed.

April 5, 2004 – I just want to write that all I can think about is Friday. I want to leave so bad. I wish I could keep it off my mind so the time would go by faster. But I'm so bored. Francis is upstairs resting (he doesn't feel well again), and Ariadne is working. I wish we could, or I could, do something entertaining to help not think about the time. But instead, I do exactly what they tell me to. So the day went on with me writing and smoking some. Ariadne and I went through my CDs. I have to get rid of a lot of them. Ariadne then did some channeling from Blessed Mother Mary. That was interesting. Eventually 6:30 PM rolled around and people started showing up for class. After everyone left I came upstairs and talked to Tom, Francis and Ariadne some. I read them "My Relationships" paper. They said it was good. Tom left about 10:00 and Ariadne and Francis went upstairs. Oh yeah, they also "tested" my healing stones while we were talking. After all that I watched the rest of "Gladiator" and a little TV. Then went to bed at about 11:30 – 12:00. I felt much better at night than during the day – go figure.

April 6, 2004 – Mom's Birthday. I woke up at 9:25 and did the rituals. Today was the first day I did the yoga by myself with Ariadne watching from the balcony. I felt pretty stupid. I'd rather do it in private. Ariadne let me call my mom after that. I was very happy to talk to her. To give me a little reassurance, she said that Friday is definitely the day. Outstanding. I talked to her for 10 minutes and 7 seconds (Ariadne said 10 minutes, there was a timer on the phone). Mom said Dad is going to leave at about 4:00AM Friday morning to come get me. That's great!! I can't wait!! I'll write later....it's 6:12PM now. I listened to the beginning of a new Wayne Dyer series today. I have to finish that, among other things, before I leave. I just went upstairs to see what's up (I'm bored) with Ariadne and Francis and she said they are resting. She's watching her show and will be done in an hour. So I guess I'll sit here, write, and watch the clock tick by.......

This was the last entry during this period. He had to spend the next couple of days completing his assignments in order to graduate on Friday.

MY 3 TOP PRIORITIES
- Staying healthy, happy, clean
- Making sure Remy is happy, healthy, and forever taken care of.
- Recognizing everyone who loves me and who has helped down this path.

THE 10 STEPS FOR ACHIEVING MY 3 PRIORITIES:
- Forever continue to be spiritually active
- Stay at Mom's house until I feel ready for Georgia
- Go back to Georgia and make amends wherever possible
- Establish a secure place to live
- Start keeping Remy as often as possible
- Surround myself with positive things and positive people
- Strengthen my relationship with Molly
- Help Dad with as many outdoor chores as possible
- Spend as much time with loved ones as possible
- Love myself, everything, and everyone in my life

Answer the following questions in writing, use as much paper as you require – think about it carefully. Be honest and realistic about your answers. When you answer, list the most important point first.

What are the ten best features, qualities, you see or perceive about yourself?

Being spiritual, intuitive, intelligent, loyal, loving, family oriented, a great teacher

What are the ten worst qualities, features, you see or perceive about yourself?

Addictive personality, manipulative, forgetful, temperamental, being dishonest, impatient, slightly overweight, bad diet, claustrophobic

What are the ten things you hate in your life (could be self, others, things or situations)?

Having been an addict, having misused my loved ones, having lost my loved ones trust, not having diploma/degree, my probation and criminal record, some of my family being so far away, my bills/debts to businesses, not having money

What are the ten things you love in your life (could be you, others, things or situations)?

So many people helping me and being by my side, my growing spirituality, the fact that I am clean, myself, Remy, Mom and Dad, brother and sister, Molly, Ashley, the rest of my family, my family life and family situations, having a nice home and nice possessions.

How do you think others see or perceive you? List ten points

Addicted, friendly, polite, manipulative, intelligent, intimidating, a leader, one with lots of potential, spiritual

If you could change yourself immediately, what ten changes would you make?

I would not and never again be an addict, a completely trusted friend and loved one, a highly highly developed spirituality, more intelligent, wiser in the ways of the world, always see only the positive in every single situation, lesser personality flaws (not manipulative), skinnier and stronger, sharper memory

What are the ten goals you can set for your future growth and development?

Strengthen relationship with God and Self, to stay clean and sober, continually practice spirituality, yoga and meditation, always be a great father and never have to leave again, stay very close with family, get diploma or GED, continue job training with college or technical degree, eat a healthy balanced diet, exercise very regularly, stay clean, orderly and organized with everything I do, surround myself with positivity and avoid the Culture of Death

Can you define how you think, what steps you take for making a determination?

I'll perceive something, think of it as either a more positive or negative perception, analyze how it affects me, how I can benefit, try and interpret from certain points of view, convince myself that I perceive it correctly, make a determination

What do you want to really do with your life?

I want to stay clean and sober. To live life close with God and expand my spirituality every day. To be a great father so my son will be the very best at anything he does. I want to continue my education so I can get a fun, well-paying job and eventually be put in a position to teach. I want all of my family and me to stay very close together forever and have large family reunions regularly. I want to get married and one day have more children. I want to stay happy forever and be able to impact other people's lives in a very positive way.

MAKING AMENDS

With Father: I have much to make up to my dad. For lying and stealing from him. For putting him through so much unnecessary stress. I will show him my appreciation for all he has done for me. I'm going to be with him and my family a lot more now and I will help him around the house more and pay him back as quickly as possible. I'm going to show him that I am better and can do this by being more responsible than he's ever seen me. I'm going to show him just how much I really love him.

With Mother: I'm going to discuss with her our need for good 2-way communication. I'm going to be in much closer contact with her than in the past. I'm going to make every effort to see her more often than the usual once or twice a year. I'm going to make sure she knows just how much she really means to me. I'll make sure that she knows that all her good wholeheartedness and loving and caring is very much appreciated.

With Sister: Me being caught up in my drug lifestyle surely hasn't helped this relationship very much. In the past we haven't talked much. Kristin is a very special person and I will make sure we get together and talk much more often. She is too wonderful of a sister to not be close to and be in close contact with.

With Brother: I've definitely neglected this relationship. My brother loves me and cares about me so much and most of the time when he tried to find out how I was doing I just blew him off. I will not allow this anymore. My clean lifestyle will allow us to do a lot more fun things together. I plan on paying him back the money I owe him and being very close, like best friends. Just how we used to be.

With Laura: I need to make things up to Laura by being responsible. My stupidity that caused my dad so much stress put a strain on their marriage. For that I am very sorry. I'm going to show Laura that we all can live together happily, that there is no need for her to stress about me anymore. That with my new lifestyle the family life will be great.

DEALING WITH THE CULTURE OF DEATH

I'll start by cleaning my room as soon as I get home. I'll get rid of my equipment, negative stickers, books, photographs and music. That will all be separated into "throw away," "sell," and "pack it away" piles and moved away accordingly. I will completely dust, clean and vacuum everything. Then, as efficiently as possible, I will rearrange my furniture and items in my room. When driving, I will avoid songs on the radio that potentially bring across a negative message. I will keep my head clear of negative thoughts by commanding that Satan and the dark forces be gone from my presence in the good name of Jesus. I will refuse to have the culture of death anywhere near me. By listening to positive music, reading uplifting and inspiring material, yoga, meditation and prayer, attending AA meetings, and surrounding myself with the wonderful people who love me most. The culture of death will cease to exist in my life. The darkness will move on when it understands that in the light where I dwell, it's just too bright for shadows. In the name of God, so shall it be!!!

DAILY ROUTINE
- Wake up and immediately think of God/ thank God
- Say all prayers and call on angels

- Go to inner temple and meditate for as long as necessary
- Make bed and change clothes
- Begin drinking water (170 ounces daily for a month, 120 after that)
- Take a walk/exercise
- Practice yoga/breathing exercises daily
- Eat a hearty, nutritious breakfast
- Take a shower and clean up
- Begin journaling/food log
- Listen to/read positive material wherever possible
- Eat a healthy snack sometime in afternoon if hungry
- Continue throughout the day keeping positive thoughts and attitude
- Eat a nutritious dinner/supper/lunch
- Make sure you're finished with water, food log, and journal
- Thank God for the day and say prayers
- Call upon angels and return to inner temple/meditate before falling asleep
- Last thoughts at night of God
- Maximum 12 cigarettes per day
- Go to AA meetings at least once a day and as often as needed

MY RELATIONSHIPS

With God: It is everlasting and continuously increasing relationship. Over the years this relationship has gotten stronger and stronger. It is a relationship of unconditional love for He will love me no matter what I do. I'm in the progressive stages of learning my will for Him. My relationship with God is an indestructible and inseparable one, as long as I choose to have it. He knows only light and love; therefore as long as I exercise my free will to do so, We will forever remain closer and closer. God and I will stay united for all of my many years to come. I thank you God for my wonderful life.

With Family: This is a great relationship. I believe this also is one of unconditional love. This relationship for the past few years has been distorted due to my wrong doings/bad choices. My parents and siblings have loved me dearly my whole life and for that I'm deeply grateful. The time has come for this relationship to strengthen. I don't think you could really ask for a more loving and supportive family. I know from this point forward this relationship will only bring great things. Thank God for such a wonderful family.

With Remy: This relationship is very special to me. Seeing the little one that you created, your own blood, walk around is an overwhelming feeling that only a parent can experience. Our relationship is great. Remy loves me and looks up to me very much. I love him with all my heart. It is time for me to concentrate on making better this relationship with my new, clean, healthy way of life. Remy and I will remain life partners and forever remain a loving father and son unconditionally. My positive influence on Remy plays a crucial role in his wellbeing and I will succeed in his being raised properly, with great love. Thank God for such a beautiful son.

With Molly: This relationship is also very great. Molly loves me and believes in me very much. She is a terrific girlfriend. Any damage caused in this relationship is my fault. My lies, deception, and manipulations have caused somewhat of a strain. With my new life I believe things between us will be great. She has stuck through me with these rough times and now it's time for me to stick by her. Our relationship will always continue to grow and strengthen. It's a very special love between to integral partners. One I intend on forever participating. Thank God for such a great woman.

30 DAY PLAN

When I go home I'm going to spend all my time with my family and Molly. For the first few days it will be Easter weekend. I will help my dad in the yard and help cook. Remy will come over as soon as I get home, clear my room of all negative possessions, and get organized. On that following Monday I will contact Uncle Vito's Pizza and let them know I am ready to come back to work. During this week I will do all necessary research to find out the best way for me to obtain my high school diploma or GED. If classes start during this month, I will attend them and work approximately 25 – 30 hours a week. If classes take a while to start, I will work full time. Whatever the case, I will keep Remy as often as possible. During my off time I will spend my time with my family and Molly so I can begin to mend the relationships in which I've damaged. I will practice my yoga, praying, and meditations on at least a daily basis. During this month I will continue brainstorming on a career path to take and will take necessary steps to initiate this career. With the money I make at work I will start paying back as much as I possibly can to my dad and Molly. Any debts that I owe will be dealt with as soon as financially possible. If I have any moments of weakness I will contact Francis or Ariadne immediately. If they are not available I will turn to family, meditation, and prayer. Calling upon my angels and praying will be the first thing I do if I begin feeling down or weak but I will make calls if I need to. I will eat more healthy and exercise whenever time allows. I will maintain my water consumption to at least 10 glasses a day and will continue to reduce sugar and soda intake. I will live a happy and healthy life and I will raise my boy the very best I can!

SO BE IT!!!

WHAT I'VE LEARNED

I've learned so much since I've been here. Here are some of the main points and underlying principles I've learned during my stay.

I've learned that God loves everyone. He is everywhere and in everything. He is in everyone. To know God is to know yourself. We all have free will and God embraces us no matter what we do. He knows only love and light. I know now that there are no sins, just stupid choices. I've also had a glimpse of some of the original teachings of Jesus, and that he did not die on the cross. He did not heal others; he showed others how to heal themselves.

I've learned about spirituality and the power of the mind. I've learned techniques to help control pain. I've learned some yoga and the 5 rights, and how to use alternative nostril breathing for clarity and natural euphoria. I know yoga helps open your body's energy and helps open a person's chakras. The mind is the most powerful tool a person can have. Anything you want in life is yours, all you have to do is go out and get it. The ability to use your mind can bring great things. Everything you encounter in life is all about how you perceive it. With the right state of mind, you can find positive in anything.

I've also learned about vibrations. Everything puts off a vibration. It's important that you surround yourself with good vibrations and not bad vibrations, or the culture of death. Surrounding yourself with the culture of death is surrounding yourself with negative vibrations and can greatly influence your conscious and subconscious mind. These things must be avoided.

I've learned about the importance of meditation and how one can call on the angels. The stilling of your mind can bring great insight about yourself. Daily meditation is a crucial part of clear consciousness and self-awareness.

I've learned about the importance of nutrition and that there are chemicals in some foods that can clog up one's thinking. I know it's important to have balance in your diet and to stay away from sugars, junk food, and MSG. I know to stay away from red meat and that it can cause aggression. And to eat lots of greens. Water consumption is very important. It helps flush the body of toxins and give a clear mind. I know that exercising is very important. It helps bring oxygen to the brain and can help with my headaches, not to mention, it's good to be in shape.

I've learned about personal habits. It's good to be neat and orderly in everything you do. It helps set a good, positive atmosphere for where you're living or working. Personal hygiene is also important. "Cleanliness is next to Godliness."

In "Tuesdays with Morrie" I learned that one can find happiness no matter how bad it gets. That staying positive is one of the best things you can do. In "Bruce Almighty" I learned that perhaps God works in mysterious ways. Because of free will, He will let everything take its course. You only get yourself into what you set yourself up for. God answers everyone's prayers, just maybe in a way you're not expecting.

Above all I've learned the importance of life. It does no good to go around pissed off all the time. There is a good purpose for everything; all you have to do is look for the light. A clean, healthy sober life is the only way to truly live. Drugs ultimately only bring you three things: institutions, prison, and death. That is no way to live. Life is too precious and short to screw it all up with drugs, negativity, and petty bullshit. Everyone needs to seize the day. Every day, with its sunshine, is a gift from God and should not be taken for granted.

Behind Blue Eyes: His Truest Essence

*"But my dreams, they aren't as empty
As my conscience seems to be."*

It is these two lines of the song that describe Jonathan and his innermost beliefs. His dreams were not as thoughtless and selfish as some of his actions may have led one to believe.

There was a period of time, prior to The Rollercoaster and after Jonathan met Tiffany (June – August 2009) where he was documenting profound ideas, not necessarily all new, but he affirmed to himself in his own words what was true to him. Also during this time he believed and practiced these affirmations. This may have been the time of his greatest spiritual growth. Even though his attachment to the world remained very much intact, there was a part of him that was expanding and growing, probably more than we realized. When he was in Spirit, he was truly in Spirit. And being in Spirit, he knew only Love.

There were people who loved him dearly and unconditionally. His aunts and uncles loved him as a nephew, his siblings as a brother, and his parents as a son. There were 3 people who came into his life later with whom he developed a special relationship, where despite anything; unconditional love was the underlying feeling between them. Chris, his step-brother, came into his life when Laura and I began dating in 1994. His son, Remy, was born in 2001. His wife, Tiffany, entered his life in April of 2009.

Chris

I had known Laura for over 6 years before I asked her out on our first date. We had worked together for the first 5 years, so we knew a little about each other's families and lifestyles. I asked her for a date that would include our kids, so we agreed to meet at Chuck E. Cheese. Matt and Chris were

7 and 6, while Jonathan was a month away from turning 13. 10 year old Kristin was with us too, as she awaited her heart transplant. We had a good time as we played games and ate pizza. Chris was intrigued with the older kid, Jonathan, and followed him around playing games together, jumping in the plastic ball pit, and just having fun. "What a cool kid," Chris thought to himself as we said our goodbyes.

Laura and I continued to date over the next several years. Kristin moved back to Florida to live with Terri after her transplant, and Michael moved in with Jonathan and me. I would usually drive out to Laura's house and spend the weekend with her and her kids. Occasionally, I would bring Jonathan and Michael with me, and at times Laura would bring her kids out to my house.

When the six of us were together, the boys would pass the time playing games with each other. A lot of times the games would pit the oldest and youngest, Michael and Chris, against Matt and Jonathan. One of their favorite games was Nerf War. Chris always wanted to team with Jonathan as Jonathan always had a strategy and seemed to know what needed to be done to win the game.

When Laura and I married, Jonathan was 16 by now and Chris was 10. The war games continued as by now Jonathan had started collecting an impressive array of camping, military, and paintball gear. Chris was fascinated with it.

The house we moved into had a large backyard, about 70% uncut and natural. Trees, weeds, and brush were 6-12 feet high; and it was very dense bush. The favorite game was flashlight tag. After dark, Jonathan and his friends would dress in full camouflage gear. They would then go to the rear of the backyard and hide, while Laura and I stood on the deck sipping a cocktail with flashlights in hand. Matt and Chris usually joined us too. The goal of the game was for Jonathan and his friends to sneak up to the clearance area, about 20 feet from the deck, and touch the deck before we could tag them with the flashlight beam. This game proved to be a lot of fun for everyone. As the weekend routine continued, Chris began asking Laura permission to let him be a "sneaker-upper." We had no idea what kind of critters were out in the woods, so Laura's initial responses were always "No." Chris continued begging and was finally granted permission to be a "sneaker-upper." Jonathan took him under his wing. He pulled out some of his older, smaller camo gear; got the camo face make-up on Chris' face; and led him to the starting point. Times like these continued to solidify their older-younger brother relationship.

A demonstrative form of affection that seems to be almost exclusively male is the flip of the bird. As Chris and his best friend Zach stood at the bus stop each morning awaiting the school bus, Jonathan would get in his car and leave for school. As he drove past them, he would flip them off. True male bonding.

After Michael moved out of the house in the spring of 1998, we decided to finish the storage area attached to the back of the garage and turn it into a studio apartment for Jonathan. Chris would go downstairs to visit, and began to idolize Jonathan and his lifestyle. Jonathan would play his drums while listening to his tapes. Posters of Rambo and Sublime, and other military and music groups hung on the wall. Jonathan smoked, was never at a loss for friends, and was just cool. He was a tough guy. He could be intimidating and scare people, or he could be the life of the party. Chris would watch this in awe and amazement.

The years passed and Jonathan began having his troubles. Despite his addictions and anger problems, he and Chris never fought nor did they ever get angry with one another. Chris would listen to Jonathan during these trying times, as this allowed Jonathan a vent to release. Chris, in turn, would seek Jonathan's counsel and advice with the growing up issues of turning from boy to young man.

At a point in Chris' mid-teens, he picked up a guitar. The glue in their relationship that had been curing came to its lifelong bond. The interest that Jonathan had in his little brother changed, from the big-little brother to friendship. They began to jam together as Chris learned how to play the instrument. These jam sessions continued until Jonathan left for Florida in 2004. The addiction problems had become severe again, and Jonathan needed a change of scenery to help him with recovery. Chris was heartbroken that Jonathan was leaving, but at the same time wanted his brother to get well.

While living in Florida in 2004 and 2005, Jonathan found work and began to make new friends. One of his friends happened to be a very good guitar player, and they would jam together. Jonathan would often call Chris during these jam sessions, play the music, and encourage Chris to learn how to play a particular song, many times music by Sublime or The Beatles.

Chris, a naturally talented musician, continued practicing the guitar and learned how to play the piano. He would play with Zach for hours on end. By the time Jonathan returned in early 2006, Chris and Zach were seasoned so that they could keep up with Jonathan and play some serious music together. Chris had an idea that would allow them to play more effectively together.

He had been eying a guitar that plugged into the computer, produced better audio, which in turn made better recordings.

When Jonathan returned to Georgia, he brought the new love of his life, Tiff. The first time Chris met her was on an evening that Jonathan had to work. Jonathan dropped Tiff off at the house, introduced her to Chris, and left. Tiff and Chris hit it off immediately. They hopped into Chris' car to drive an hour and a half to the other side of town to buy this guitar. They talked the entire way there and back. It was if they were brother and sister catching up with each other's lives.

Jonathan and Tiff were living with some friends a couple of miles from the house. As his schedule was free most of the day, he would sometimes pick up the booze for his underage brother and friend, and they would play their music together. They learned how to play 40 songs fairly well. They played a variety of music, The Beatles, Sublime, and Simon and Garfunkel to name a few.

They began writing music. Most of the lyrics were about partying and as Chris said, "These songs just didn't work." They decided to take a different approach to their lyrics and came up with a song called "Hey Girl." This was a three part harmony played on acoustic guitars that was about dancing. This turned out to be their masterpiece and as Chris describes it, "We sounded good and our voices blended well…..we almost sounded like the Bee Gees."

The three of them continued to play on and off over the next couple of years. Their relationship grew closer. After Jonathan moved back into the house in 2008, they would play in Jonathan's room with the windows open and the volume turned to maximum. I could hear them as I approached the house and they did sound good. So good that one of our neighbors overheard them and offered them a job to play at his daughter's 16th birthday party.

The house next door was up for sale during this time, and I let Jonathan and Chris know to keep the volume down if they saw anyone looking at the house. The house did sell and I went over to introduce myself to the new neighbors. The couple who bought the house was about my age, and I let them know that if the music got too loud, just to let us know and we'd keep it down. He laughed and replied, "I'm a part time musician and I get gigs during the weekend every now and then. When we pulled into the driveway to do our final walk through, I could hear them playing. I thought to myself, "Good, I can play my instruments and there won't be any complaints from next door."

When The Rollercoaster time period hit, Chris was affected as much as anyone. Like the rest of us, he didn't understand what was going on. There were days he would carry Jonathan back into his room and lay him down because Jonathan was so intoxicated. There were days he'd be totally fed up with his behavior, like we all felt, and became disgusted. But Chris never stopped loving his brother, he just felt hopeless at times.

Monday April 19, 2010 was the last time Chris saw Jonathan. After Chris read his tearful eulogy during the funeral service, he was hoping that he might feel a little comfort and be a little more at peace. He was hoping to feel some closure, and even expected it, but it didn't happen.

As people began getting in their cars to leave the cemetery, the grave digger approached the burial site with his shovel. Chris walked up to him and asked if he could use the shovel to bury his brother. The grave digger handed it to him. As Chris began scooping the dirt onto the casket, he thought to himself, "A brother needs to bury a brother. I have to bury him." He continued to shovel as Zach and Dustin walked over to assist. A second shovel was given to them and the 3 of them alternated shoveling the dirt for the next 20 minutes. While Chris was shoveling, he felt as though he was burying a body, not Jonathan. Then a moment of clarity hit him, something he'd never felt before. He felt or heard Jonathan's voice. "I appreciate what you have done for me, but this was meant to happen."

Chris stood there, and for a brief moment, the world seemed different.

Jonathan and Chris

Remy

On October 3, 2003, Jonathan sat in his room and resumed writing in his journal. He wrote:

> "Let's see....today I woke up around 12:00PM or so. Remy spent the night last night. He is my perfect little boy. I just paused and thought....it almost seems crazy. I wouldn't trade him for the whole world and everything in it. I mean literally the world and everything in it. We got up and sat and played around in my room for a little while.
>
> October 4, 2003 – Remy spent the night again. I gave Remy a big coloring set that folded together and snapped. Kristin gave this to me to give to Remy a few weeks ago when I went to Florida to help Kristin and Mom move. I tried to put the coloring set away a few times and get Remy ready for bed and Remy threw a fit (that is quite unusual). The set consists of markers, crayons, colored pencils, charcoal pencils, and so forth. Remy loves it. His rainbow scribble filled pieces of notebook paper are funny. He is also trying to figure out how to cut the paper as the kit also came with a pair of scissors.
>
> October 6, 2003 – Remy and I got up about 12:15 and we ate and played for a little while. Then I took Remy to the gas station to get some chocolate (he wanted peanut butter cups) and I got an almond Snickers. We sat outside the gas station for a moment to eat Remy's chocolate. I dropped him off at 4:00PM so I could go to work.

One evening during The Rollercoaster period, Jonathan came into the workshop and explained to me how much he loved Remy. He repeated what he said on October 3, 2004 and he went on to tell me that no one could know exactly how he felt about him.

Jonathan loved no one as he did Remy. He would proudly dress Remy in Jonathan's favorite attire, camouflage; and parade him around town and introduce him to people he knew, as well as perfect strangers. The annual ritual for Halloween was for Remy to go trick or treating early with Ashley, and then Jonathan would pick him up and take him around our neighborhood, ensuring he was dressed in camo, to collect his goodies.

Jonathan demonstrated remarkable patience toward Remy while teaching him how to do things. It's not uncommon for a father to calmly endure time spent teaching his child to do something, but Jonathan showed such peace as he taught, and it was completely unlike his reactions to some of life's other events. Oft times I would sit, watch, and marvel at the commitment of love he had for his son.

Jonathan taught him how to ride a bike. He would balance Remy on the bike, then push him off and yell "peddle, peddle!!" Jonathan stood in the street as he encouraged Remy until he was riding in circles around the cul-de-sac.

He helped him with school work and taught how to shoot a bb gun. Remy would accompany Jonathan to work on many occasions and help with some of the chores; sweeping, washing pots and pans, and preparing the food. Despite not having a lot of interest in sports, Jonathan assisted Remy with hitting and throwing a baseball, catching a football, shooting a basketball, and kicking a soccer ball."

Jonathan and Remy, Halloween Ready!!!

Jonathan and Remy

Jonathan shows Remy how to play games

When Remy was 6, he had the duty of being the ring bearer for Kristin and Matthew's wedding. On rehearsal night, we all went through our steps and Remy suffered from a severe case of stage fright. He started crying and said he didn't want to do this. We all tried our best to console him, yet he was scared to death and didn't want to participate. On the wedding day Jonathan assured him that he would be with him as they walked down the aisle. And he was. He walked about 6 steps behind Remy and would quietly whisper encouragement as Remy needed it. He was there for him then as he is there in spirit with him now and forever.

After Remy turned 8, Jonathan began teaching him the power of the mind. When Remy visited with his Dad and Tiffany, he was fascinated by Jonathan's meditation shrine. They would sit together, and Jonathan would teach Remy to close his eyes and try to empty his mind. Remy grasped this concept, and enjoyed the unusual practice his Dad was teaching him.

Jonathan, Remy and I were at a local family entertainment center one afternoon watching football while Jonathan met some of his friends. It was in November of 2009 during the time when Jonathan seemed to be stable. Jonathan decided he was going to give a lesson on the power of the mind. Remy had been playing some games trying to collect tickets so he could use the tickets and "purchase" a toy. He wasn't having a lot of luck, so Jonathan took him and sat him down. He told Remy to close his eyes and focus on abundance and spinning the wheel on the Wheel of Fortune game to hit the jackpot. They sat and meditated for about 10 minutes and then Jonathan took him to the game. He told Remy to close his eyes and focus on where he wanted the spinner to stop. A minute later Remy came running to where I was sitting with 1000 tickets in his hand. "Grandpa, I hit the jackpot!!!" he yelled. "Dad taught me how to use the power of my mind!!!"

There was another time that Remy had a bad headache. Jonathan wanted to teach him to focus on healing himself. Remy went with Jonathan to his meditation shrine. They closed their eyes and Jonathan led him in some prayers and meditations. Within a few minutes Remy's headache was gone and he felt fine.

While Jonathan was teaching Remy to use his mind, Remy's perception of his Dad didn't go unnoticed. Remy asked me several times while he was visiting and Jonathan was resting in bed, "Why is Dad always sick?"

As Remy gets older, he will miss the words of wisdom his Dad would have shared with him. There are also the positive affirmations and brief essays that Jonathan had written, and Jonathan would have shared these with Remy to help him learn his life's lessons.

Jonathan would say, "Remy, when you are worried and feel guilty about something, or are upset about something from the past,

- Be still and know - Don't believe everything you think.
- <u>Today is Perfect!! -</u> Most people spend 80% of their mental energy and capacity on trying to change, or being upset about, the past.
- The first place we lose our battles is in our minds - Think about your thinking."

When moments of discouragement surface in Remy's life, Jonathan would tell him,

- "Never, never, never give up - If you contemplate with thoughts that match originating spirit, you have the same power as originating spirit – which is an endless, limitless source of energy that creates nothing of which is not derived from pure non-judgmental love."

During those teenage years we experienced when we all knew everything and our focus was completely on ourselves, Jonathan would mention to Remy,

- "Contemplate like God does, with thoughts like "How may I serve?" rather than "What's in it for me?......Come only from love!"

As Jonathan and Remy would take a walk through the woods while camping out, they would come across 2 boulders where each could take a seat and rest. They would sit silently for a moment and observe the beauty around them. Then Jonathan would say,

- "Learn to think like nature. You have a nature – a faultless, perfect nature. Allow yourself to live from that perspective. Practice non-interference. Hang onto nothing. Think small. Stay kind. Stay humble."

Perhaps on Remy's 18th birthday, Jonathan would have called him into his workshop to present Remy with a copy of the Tao Te Ching by Lau Tzu. Jonathan would explain:

- "Some people call the Tao the wisest book ever written.
- In the book "Lau Tzu and Jesus", observations comparing Jesus and Lau Tzu are made. Everything on the pages was almost identical.
- The Tao Te Ching was written 500 years before the birth of Christ.
- 31 verses of the Tao teach us the importance of water. Our brain is 85% water. Be soft, be flexible."

Jonathan would then point to The 4 Virtues by Lao Tzu presented in the 51st Verse.

1. <u>Reverence for all of Life:</u> Don't kill. Allow everything to live its dharma. Don't judge. Always know, and let everyone know, we are not alone.
2. <u>Sincerity/ Honesty:</u> True nobility isn't about being better than anyone else – It's about being better than you used to be. Always be honest. Be honest to yourself. Start staying in a state of gratitude. This is when God really starts to show up.
3. <u>Gentleness:</u> Practice kindness wherever you go. Send love to everyone, even the seemingly mundane – the waiter, a cashier at a store, people who are rude, and especially the ones that piss you off to no end. Be gentle, be kind, and send love. Work on making this your way of life.
4. <u>Service:</u> Living your life in a place of not "what's in it for me?" How may

I serve? Think of this question in every circumstance of everyday. Get the focus off of yourself.

After Jonathan and Remy finished their discussion, Jonathan would conclude,

- "The Tao that can be named is not the Tao. Because the moment that something is labeled, you have the label and the thing being labeled – that's two-ness. The Tao is only Oneness. The Tao cannot be separated, it cannot be divided, it cannot be sliced in half. You have to learn to trust in THAT!!"

Above all else, as Remy goes through the ups and downs of life, Jonathan would remind Remy often,

- "In everything, give thanks. Live your life with your heart and love, and remember that being happy is most important."

Nobody is going to replace Jonathan as a father. Hamp, Remy's maternal grandfather, spends time with him working on motorcycles and mechanical things. Harry, his maternal great-grandfather has been there for Remy since he was born, and playfully teases him while they watch TV together. They both love him and spoil him rotten. They are wonderful elders for him.

He has his uncles who adore him; his 3 Uncle Matts, Chris, and Michael all enjoy his company and are great uncles to him. They all play video games, compare phone applications, play ball, and have fun together. Michael involves himself with the hobbies that Jonathan would have been very active in. Michael takes him camping, has taught him how to ride a dirt bike, goes bicycling, spends long weekends in the mountains hiking, goes zip lining, and does anything having to do with the outdoors that both he and Jonathan loved to do.

Ben is his step-dad. He reminds me a lot of the relationship I have with my stepsons. He's close to him, has fun with him, and is supportive in anything Remy does. They play games together and he is a constant male figure in Remy's life. Remote control cars are a common interest. He also recognizes that he's not his father and he's not going to force himself or his will onto him.

I'm his grandpa. I help him with school work and provide general support in his outside activities; Cub Scouting, BMX bike racing, and learning how to play football. I love being a kid at heart with him, and I think he enjoys that. He's told me on several occasions that I'm the funniest guy he knows. We'll keep it that way.

There would have come a time when Remy would have asked Jonathan, "Hey Dad, can we go to your workshop and talk?" And Jonathan would have led him and they would sit down. Remy would go into some of the problems he was having and Jonathan would reply. Instead, the workshop doors of Ben, his Uncles, Hamp, Paw Paw Harry, and mine will always remain open.

Tiffany and Remy

Jonathan and Tiffany: A Love Story

"He was the best thing that ever happened to me." Tiffany told me this as we sat down 6 months after Jonathan's passing to talk about their relationship and the positive impact he had on her life. "He was my teacher. He taught me what love really is, along with patience, forgiveness, and compassion. He taught me the most important things I've learned in my life." She went on to tell me that he was the most giving person she had ever met. He was selfless, and if he had a dollar and someone needed it more than he, he'd give it to him. He tried to help other people. He could identify people who needed to be talked to, needed compassion, and he would introduce himself and listen to what they had to say about their lives or themselves. After Tiff had left Jonathan, he eventually got evicted from his apartment as he couldn't afford the rent on his own. He moved back in with Laura and me, found some work, and started to explore online dating as a means for finding his soul mate. He had met several women on line and had dated them, but nothing serious developed. Then on April 24, 2009 he came across this profile.

> *"I am single, never been married, have no children or scary exes. I am fun when the time is right and serious as well. I am an RN and I love my job. I want to get back to working in Pediatrics at some point. That is really where my heart lies. I love to read. My first major was art at UGA. I am using that for pleasure instead of paying the bills. I like painting and photography best and am doing more of both lately. I have a wonderful family and we are very close. I have 2 cats. They think they rule the house. Actually, they may. I live in a 1930's bungalow that has cracks in the plaster and lathe walls from settling. It also has a claw foot tub (awesome for bubble baths) and a front porch that I spend a lot of time on in warm weather. I love that house. I don't attend church, but I talk with God every day. I feel like we're old friends. When I lived in Atlanta I really enjoyed going to hear local bands play. I miss that, living in Rome. I like all kinds of music...take that back, most kinds. I don't care for rap, except old Beastie Boys. Oh, not a big fan of the Grateful Dead either. My favorite ice cream is Ben and Jerry's New York Super Fudge Chunk. I spent 2 summers in New Hampshire as an arts and crafts teacher at a summer camp. That has been my favorite job so far, even though it paid the least. I'm looking for someone who likes to laugh, enjoy life, learn new things, teach me new things, actually enjoys conversation, can be silly and also serious. I am looking for something real. It's that simple, really :)"*

He liked what she had to say so he marked it as a "fave."

She noticed that he had marked her as a fave, so she decided to check out his profile before responding and it read:

> *"My name is Jon. I'm now living solo in Dallas with my new doggie, Sam. My life just took off on a new course-things happened, people left, and I'm what remains. I'm smart but lost. I'm loyal but alone. I'm alone but not lonely. I'm here, and I'm open to it all.*

I'm too serious but I have a great sense of humor. I'm stubborn but extremely open-minded. I'm shy but I love to meet new people. My son, Remy, is six years old and is my role model. He is the only one I know with a truly pure mind. He is my first and foremost, and that must be accepted before anything can start with me. I'm a kitchen manager in a local restaurant and have been in the industry for a long time. I'm very well mannered. I refuse to waste anymore of my life beating around the bush and insinuating, so I'm here for experience and truth. I'm brutally honest so if that frightens you then I'm sorry (you'd be surprised how many people this has scared off). I'm intelligent and love to learn new things. I'm very observant but often blinded by passion. I'm sometimes overly spontaneous but probably one of the best strategist, tacticians, or planners you will ever meet. I'm aggressively protective of things close to my heart. Profanity is one of my favorite ways to emphasize and merit attention. I'm an artist. I'm a musician. I'm remarkably sophisticated in an utterly simple way. I think too much. I consider myself old fashioned and it shows. I have a unique ability to calculate numbers in my head. Sometimes I have clairvoyant moments. I experience deja vu more than the average person. Despite the fact I'm currently deeply engrossed in it, I'm not a big fan of technology. I'm very spiritual yet very impious. I feel most at home in the deep wilderness. I'm filled with random, almost useless, but fascinating talents. I frequently drive for hours with no destination in mind. I love romance and savor passionate moments. I want to share. I have a heart full of love...So now what do I do?"

She liked what she read and decided it was worth sending a note. So at 3:15PM on April 24, 2009, their first communication took place.

"I saw that I was on your faves and took a little look. I love the way you express yourself in words! I'm an avid reader and lover of the written word, and you hooked me right in. I laughed out loud when I read that smoking cigarettes was an interest...I'm more than an occasional smoker- actually, I think I'll have one now. Your son looks just like you. I love the Mohawk/fauxhawk. I have a picture of me with my niece with her hair like that. She was only 6 months old, so she really couldn't say "NO!" She's now 2 and a half and says it a lot! She is my heart and soul. She sang Happy Birthday to me on the phone this week and I almost cried it was so sweet. I get to see her Saturday and am so excited. Sorry to ramble- I am very good at that. I'm adding you to my faves because you seem like an interesting juxtaposition of many qualities- Sadie Cate"

Over the past year or so I had seen Jonathan on the computer looking for a potential mate. He'd type away furiously using his 2 finger hunt and peck method (at which he was pretty fast) and reply to posts on the dating board.

4/24 5:51 PM: "Well hello there, Sadie Cate. I am so glad you wrote. I was excited to see an email from you when I signed in, which ironically was my specific reason for doing so. After many weeks of seldom use, I got on POF last night to search through profiles to see if I could find anyone who, to quote a corny movie line I heard recently, "dazzled" me, lol. After several hours of searching and having virtually no luck at all, I came across your profile. I was blown away;-) It was so refreshing to find someone who had substance and obvious intelligence. You would be surprised to see what some women put on here, lol. I love everything you had to say about yourself...from your occupation (I don't think there are many professions as honorable for a woman to have as being a nurse, or as hot, lol) to the fact that you don't really like rap, haha:-) Trust me, I know exactly what you mean. You reminded me a lot of me- which is a good thing in my eyes. The fact that you live a reasonable distance from me and that, to me, you are an ideal age was all definitely a bonus too (I am 28 by the way). I was a little taken back by your pictures too. I understand you may think this sounds like a generic one-liner, but you are very beautiful. As I reviewed your pictures I had a smile stretch across my face, which does not happen too often. I was all around very impressed and intrigued by your profile. I knew it would be crazy not to try to write you and at least tell you how awesome you seemed. Since at that point I was in a hurry to get off the computer, I just added you to my faves so I could jump on this afternoon to shoot you an email...and look who wrote;-)

So, I would be very interested in learning more about you and talking to you somehow. I realize your email wasn't necessarily suggesting that we do so, but if you are up for it then it'd be great. I suppose just let me know what you think. :-)

Well, I have to run off to work now. I hope what I said wasn't too blunt for you, lol. I know of no other way to be more honest or sincere. I'll be looking forward to hearing back from you. Have a wonderful day!

Jonathan"

Tiffany replied back about an hour later, with a new subject line;

Subject: I'm smiling...

4/24 6:48PM: "Thank you for being honest and not afraid to say nice things! It is strange that you say I remind you OF you, when, as I was reading about you, I had that same feeling. Really, no kidding. I feel like I'm a very odd/quirky mixture of so many things, and always have been. Like I wrote in my profile, I love art, but am an RN. Two very different fields, and yet I love them both. In high school (long time ago) I was a cheerleader who didn't care for football, and a skater chick. I could go on and on :) What restaurant do you work at? I worked in that biz for quite a while myself. Hope you are having a great night at work. I am staying in and reading Dickens' David Copperfield. I have all the windows open and there's a nice breeze blowing. I've got sweet tea and cigarettes and I'm ready for the night! No, you were not too blunt. I AM interested, and I love the dimples:) Hope to hear from you-SC"

Jonathan had worked that night and as would happen so often, he didn't get home until 4:00 AM. He checked messages as soon as he got home and replied.

For the next three days they continued learning more about each other as they regularly texted, emailed, or conversed on the phone. On April 29th, they began another text conversation.

> Jonathan– "I want to meet you."
> Tiffany – "You are going to meet me."
> Jonathan– "No, I wanna meet you now and see if you like me."
> Tiffany – "I already know that I like you."
> Jonathan– "No, I want to see if you like me physically."

Jonathan was still self-conscious about his weight. The methadone treatment he was on to help him get off the Oxycontin addiction created a huge sweet tooth. His diet consisted mainly of doughnuts, candy bars and ice cream. He had gained 100 pounds over a 15 month period and weighed in at about 270. By the time he met Tiffany, he had dropped 30 pounds but was still concerned with his body image.

> Jonathan– "When can we meet?"
> Tiffany – "Tonight."

Jonathan drove over in his 1994 Cadillac. It had seen better days but he kept it in running order and neat when he was meeting someone for the first time. It had power everything and in its day was considered a luxurious car. Tiffany fell in love with the car the first time she stepped into it.

That night they were both nervous. They hopped in the car and drove down to a pizza place and bought a $5 pizza to eat and a couple of soft drinks. After eating, they took a walk down to the river and then strolled around Rome. They small talked and Jonathan was being a bit of a smart-ass. Tiffany was thinking that he doesn't like her and that he will end up thinking of her as a friend.

They eventually worked their way back to the car and drove back to her place. They continued to talk and realized just how much they had much in common. The subject eventually got to spirituality and Jonathan asked her "Do you believe in hell?" To which Tiffany replied, "No, I don't believe a loving God, our Father, would put us in a place like that." She reminded him of her profile; that she and God are good friends and they talk on a daily basis. Jonathan liked that. And they continued to talk about deep subjects, the kinds of things you don't talk about until you get to know each other for more than a week. Tiffany cried three times that night as they talked about her Dad, who had passed away years ago. They discussed philosophy and religion, family and friends, and the meaning of life. Finally, at 4:00AM, Jonathan hopped in his car and drove home.

As he drove off, Tiffany knew that she was going to marry that man. Without a doubt, this was what she had always wished for; a man who was intellectually, emotionally, and spiritually on the same level as she. And to top it off, he was nice to look at as well.

This was the guy.

The next day Jonathan got off work and drove 60 miles in a torrential downpour to see Tiffany and participate in The Relay for Life. The sponsors of the event had postponed it due to the weather conditions, and Tiffany told Jonathan this. He insisted on coming anyway because he had flowers for her and he wanted to give them to her.

This night they went to a coffee shop and again conversed for hours. Finally, Jonathan stopped in mid-conversation and said "Do you love me?" This caught Tiffany a bit off guard and she responded "You can't ask me that, it's just our second date." Jonathan, never one to let up, replied "Why not, do you?" Tiffany stammered "Well….yes, I do…but you can't ask me that."

But she already knew, and when I spoke with Jonathan about his date later that day, he knew too.

Tiffany would be going on a family vacation in two weeks, a traditional week together where they would go to Florida and kick back and relax. So for the next two weeks they spent all their free time together and continued to develop their relationship. The day she left, Jonathan and I talked about the dread he was feeling. For the first time in his life he had met someone who he felt at one with on a spiritual level. Even though he had known her for only a few weeks, he felt this was the person he would marry and spend the rest of his life with. His thinking was that while she was away, she would forget about him, find someone else, or something negative was going to happen. I could only assure him that everything would turn out as it was meant to be.

As it turned out, they spent quite a bit of time on the phone together wishing that they were with each other. They also decided that they would give each other a gift to remind them of their time apart.

Tiffany decided she wanted to bring a gift that each of them could have; here's something for you and I got one for me type of thing. She explored the stores and finally came across a gift shop that had hundreds of rings. She spent over an hour looking through the selections until she came across two that hit home for her. One ring said "Unity" and the other had "Integrity" inscribed on it. She bought two pair, a matching set for each of them.

When she returned home late on May 23rd, Jonathan went to visit after he finished at work. They exchanged gifts. He had made her a set of dog tags while she was gone, as well as one for himself. His stated "With separation we have nothing....integrity....true love conquers all...many many bunch (pet way of saying I love you) 4/30/09."

The one he gave to Tiffany had "With unity we have everything. True love conquers all...to the moon (another pet way for I love you) 4/30/09" written on it.

They sat there in somewhat disbelief, yet marveled at the thought of all the gifts they could have selected for each other, they both decided on Unity and Integrity as the theme. They agreed that this was more than coincidence, that they were soul mates, and they were just going to have to get used to these types of things happening to them.

This was the first time they talked about marriage. They had known each other only a month but felt as though it had been years.

The next evening Jonathan showed up with a little box. As he presented the box to her, he told her 'This is not an engagement ring. This is a ring telling you that I'm going to ask you to marry me very soon."

Tiffany opened the box and in it was a huge cubic zirconia, bordering on gaudy. Tiffany loved it and put it on. She proclaimed that she was so excited and proud of it that she would wear it to work the next day. Jonathan told her that she didn't have to wear it; it was only a symbol, and a rather large one at that. Tiffany though couldn't contain her excitement. "I'm engaged!!" "I love this!!" "I'll wear this tomorrow and show everyone!!" "I'm so proud of this!!"

Jonathan asked her, "So when I officially ask you, and it will be soon, you will say yes?"

To which Tiffany shouted, "Yes, yes, of course I'll say yes!!"

Since Jonathan worked 40 miles from her apartment, he would spend some evenings with me and Laura, depending on his work schedule, and the others with Tiffany. When they did see each other they would spend time getting to know one another on a deeper level, and would pray together and focus much time on their spiritual development. They were each other's medicine. They would hug and press their hearts together, and their anxiety would be relieved. They talked about things that serious couples talk about; finding a new home, future family plans, places they'd like to travel to, getting a pet to be their "baby", among other things. It was during this time that Jonathan began writing his lessons and affirmations that were mentioned earlier in the book.

It was also during this time that on an evening in early June, he got down on his knees and proclaimed "Do you know that I love you more than anything in the world?"

"Yes", she answered.

"Do you know that I want to spend the rest of my life with you?" he asked.

Again she replied "Yes."

"Will you marry me?" was his last question.

"Yes, Jonathan Dalmond Dacy I will marry you!!"

This, Tiffany later described to me, was their best moment as they were so happy together.

The date was set for September 12, 2009.

Family Reaction

As you might imagine, there was skepticism from most members of their families. This conversation could apply to both sides of the family when they announced their engagement.

"You just met this guy/girl!!"
"I'm going to marry that man/woman."

"You don't even know him/her!!"
"Yeah, I do."

"There's no reason to rush into anything!!"
"There's no reason to wait when we both know that we're supposed to be together."

July 2009 – Jonathan entered this quote from a revised edition of a book by Thoreau. He certainly would have shared this with anyone who had any doubts about their relationship.

> "If two soul mates do not keep the same pace as other couples, perhaps it is because together they hear a different drummer.....let them step to the music which they hear, however measured or far away."

It was clear to both of them: they were each other's soul mates.

From: Michael
Sent: Wednesday, May 27, 2009 11:17 AM
To: Mike

Hey there old man,

So how do you feel about Jon's engagement? A bit premature, I'd say. I pray he's making the right decision. A failed marriage could be devastating for him.

Did he talk about it with you beforehand? When I spoke to him on Monday it sounded like he was trying to speak confidently, and with surety, but it seemed forced.

I'm really worried about this decision. Despite his insistence, he cannot truly know, trust, and understand Tiffany after only a month! And there's no way she really knows him!!!

From: Mike
Sent: Wednesday, May 27, 2009 11:55 AM
To: Michael

I do know several things that point as to why they came to this decision so quickly. That being said, it does appear, from a linear time standpoint, to be premature.

1) Not that this makes a lot of difference, but they've been talking to each other and getting to know each other for closer to 2 months than 1.....I know, big deal.
2) Jonathan has been looking for the "right" person to come along ever since Tiff left him. He has had ample opportunity to get to know people and spend more time with them had he chosen to do so. In almost all cases, after a date or conversation or two, he would "know" the person wasn't right for him and would end the relationship.
3) They have had spiritual and deep intimate conversations about things that generally don't come up in a relationship for 6 months to 1 year, sometimes even longer. He's also brought up his insecurities, and she's brought hers up as well, and have reached compromise/

agreement on those issues. It seems they have pushed their relationship to see where it would take them.
4) He's moving in with her over the next several weeks and the living together should help them get to understand each other even more. I trust that if something comes up that puts the relationship in jeopardy, they will work it out or end it at that point.
5) Jonathan originally bought the ring to act as a pre-engagement ring. After talking, they decided to make it engagement.
6) He's been in the process of manifesting this for himself for the last year. I thought that once he found the right person, it would move quickly. I think the same can be said of Tiffany.

They obviously have uncovered territory to explore. I think they will have the good sense not to rush into a marriage if they sense something isn't right. Plus they have to have the money to pay for it, and that will take some time to save for. On the other hand, he might run off and invite only 2 people to his wedding……no wait, one of my kids already did that. *(Mike and Cherie had done this, but I was one of the lucky ones invited!)*

I would only say not to worry; things always have a way of working out. Even if something were to happen, he'll only learn and grow from it.

From: Michael
Sent: Wednesday, May 27, 2009 12:57 PM
To: Mike

I agree that living together should allow them to sort out any overlooked differences, and hopefully they'll be able to work through them. They're bound to happen.

You're right about #6…he's been determined to find a mate…similar to how he was determined to have a child.

I advised Jonathan to allow the engagement to last as long as possible, no less than 6 months, so they could really get to know each other. But he all but disagreed with me. It's EASY to fall in love, but difficult to STAY in love.

Hopefully he'll have the wisdom to understand that, and be able to provide for all of Tiffany's needs (and vice-versa) so it stays that way.

He'll be in my prayers.

In early June, Jonathan began moving in some of his things to Tiffany's home. He was still commuting to Dallas on days he worked, and on some occasions would spend the night with Laura and me. He was happy with his relationship, yet feeling the need to get his education completed so he could begin a career in helping other addicts. He had consultations with his counselor at the methadone clinic, and she offered advice to him on what needed to be done to get a certification in counseling. He checked out what needed to be done to get his GED, and corresponded with several schools about certification.

Because they worked such different schedules, Tiffany from early morning until evening, and Jonathan from mid-afternoon until close, they had very little time to talk face to face on 3 or 4 days a week. To communicate, they would leave each other notes and letters. They created a notebook called **Jonathan's and Tiffany's notes <u>ONLY</u> Love Diary.**

When they were together, he would tuck her in every night. He would lie next to her, holding hands placed over her heart, and they would pray for guidance and give thanks for whatever the day had brought to them. He would tuck her in, give her a kiss, and leave her to sleep.

As Tiffany slept, Jonathan continued his spiritual studies and writings. As he would be reading 4 or 5 books at a time, the sources of the quotes he documented varied greatly. These quotes and his personal work focused on love. Tiffany would get up in the morning as Jonathan slept and read his night's previous work. Reading this work is what made Tiffany realize that Jonathan was her greatest teacher, and that he had so much to give and share with the world.

July 1, 2009 Jonathan wrote:

> To My Angel,
> As I read through the word I felt passionately called upon to relay to you these most truthful and healing passages. I pray to God that their eternal nature ring as deeply with you as they did me and that you may keep them close to your heart on this day, and all the days of your life. At the remembrance of these divine words of wisdom, our

true love as soul mates, beautiful life and marriage, and Holy Destiny together shall never cease to exist.

> "Love is patient, love is kind....it is not rude, it is not self-seeking, it is not easily angered, it keeps no record of wrongs. Love does not delight in evil but rejoices with truth. It always protects, always trusts, always hopes, always perseveres. Love never fails...And now these three remain: faith, hope, and love. But the greatest of these is love."
>
> 1 Corinthians 13:4-13

I love you with all of my heart and soul, Tiffany. I thank our God every single day for leading me to cross paths with his most perfect angel, and for having created us to be soul mates. You have indeed been an angel to me. You have saved me in ways I never thought possible. You have shown me beauty in places I before saw nothing. You have given me love, the most precious thing of all. For all of this I thank you...so very much. I <u>LOVE</u> you. Forever.

Jonathan

The Miracle Day: July 5, 2009

Tiffany had been down in the dumps during the last couple of weeks, feeling a little depressed and out of sorts. She was staying in bed and lacking motivation except to get up and go to work. When finished at work, she'd come back home and go to bed.

On the 5th in the afternoon, she told herself "I gotta get up and do something to get out of this rut." She asked Jonathan if he would go for a walk with her explaining that if she got outside, perhaps she would feel better. He agreed and out the door they went. They stopped at the convenience store and picked up a couple of drinks and cigarettes. Tiffany then suggested that they go back to where they had their first date.

They jumped into the car and headed to the park. First, they walked around the levy and then decided to follow a path that runs parallel to the river. They strolled down the path, not saying much, but just walking in a comfortable silence. While wandering down the path, they both noticed what appeared to be a drawing on the sidewalk next to the path. They couldn't tell what it was until they were almost on top of it. It was a woman with long hair, and she immediately thought of Mother Mary. She had been looking at some of the pictures on Jonathan's meditation and prayer shrine, and the resemblance was uncanny. They both stood and stared at the picture for 5 minutes before they began to walk away. Tiffany looked at Jonathan and asked, "What's the first thing you thought of when you saw that?"

Jonathan simply replied, "Mother Mary."

She agreed and for the first time in weeks, the depression and sadness Tiffany had been feeling vanished. In that miracle instant, she was overcome with an inner peace and a happiness that seemed to have grown foreign to her. She grabbed his hand and they continued down the path.

Approaching a small neighborhood, they began to notice some of the houses along the river. These homes were built about 50 yards from the river with the back of the houses facing them. They became aware of a big green house with a deck, and Jonathan suggested, "Hey, let's go look at it."

They proceeded to go up the hill to look at it, and when they got there they could see that it was vacant. They peered into the windows before detecting that the next door neighbors were sitting on the deck.

Jonathan walked over to them and asked if they knew who owned the green house.

"Why yes, we do. Would you like to go inside and take a look around?" The kind elderly couple led Jonathan and Tiffany to the house, opened the door, and let them in. The home was a large home, 5 bedrooms and 4 baths, but was in need of major repair. In addition to being in need of a good handyman, the asking price was more than Tiffany could possibly afford. The couple mentioned to them, that although there wasn't a For Sale sign, the smaller house across the street was on the market. Just then a car pulled up into the driveway of the home that was being pointed out. Jonathan and Tiffany thanked the couple and went across the street to introduce themselves to the people getting out of the car. The couple confirmed that they owned the house and were in the process of making repairs in order to sell it. They asked if Jonathan and Tiffany would like to come in and look around.

They entered the front door, looked around, grabbed each other's hands, looked at each other, and smiled with a huge beam on each of their faces. "OK" Tiffany smiled and quietly told herself, "I'm not going to beam too much. Need to be serious so I can effectively negotiate."

The couple led them around the home showing the beautiful built in mahogany book shelves, a gorgeous dining room chandelier, the fenced in back yard with tool shed, sunroom, 2 bedrooms, 2 fireplaces, and several other small traits that made this house somewhat unique. After all, it had been built in the late 1800's and still had the original mahogany hardwood floors with matching bookshelves.

The four of them sat down and began to talk about not only the house, but chatted just to get to know each other a little better. Finally, Tiffany stated "I don't know if you've ever considered this, but have you thought of doing a lease/purchase? My credit is not that great."

The owners admitted that they hadn't thought about it, but hadn't ruled it out either. The four of them continued talking about the house and some of the repairs that needed to be done, about themselves, and before too long the tone of the conversation changed from the repairs needed before they would sell it, to "Before you move in, we'll do this and that. If you're sure you would like to move in, we'll get the papers ready and meet tomorrow to get them signed."

Jonathan and Tiffany were blown away. Two perfect strangers, who didn't know them from Adam, had offered them a chance to move into this little dream home not one hour after meeting them. The owners told Tiffany later that they had seen a true and honest love in each of them, and that they wanted to help them get on their feet.

Jonathan and Tiffany had their dream home!! They walked back to the car pinching themselves!! "How did that just happen?!? We have our home!!"

As they reached the park and walked up to the car, a little puppy ran up behind Tiffany. They both sat down and the pup approached them and proceeded to receive their petting. The puppy was a little shy and would periodically run around the car. They sat and played this little cat and mouse game for 15 minutes when Jonathan noticed something by the garbage can. He whistled and out jumped another puppy, this one not shy of anything, and hopped right into his lap.

They sat awhile longer playing with the pups before they got up and started asking some of the people in the area if they knew anything about the puppies. The responses they received were close to unanimous. Someone had dropped them off earlier in the day and left. The puppies had been running around all day, begging for food, and just wanting to get some love. None of the business owners or other people in the area wanted either of the puppies, so Jonathan and Tiffany talked about their options. They decided to bring both of them back to their apartment, as the two of them were obviously sisters and they didn't want to break them up.

What a day it had been!! It started with depression and ended finding a dream home and acquiring two sweet little dogs!!

Time passed as they prepared to move into their new home. The synchronicities that had been in their lives since they had met continued to occur. Each day something would happen that would reinforce their knowledge that they were meant to be together. Tiffany told me later "The feeling was odd, but every time something happened, it was so right."

While sitting on the porch together, both of them would feel God within each of them. They would talk about it and feel it; in joy and spirit at its purest essence. They could look into each other's eyes and see God.

They spoke of abundance and gave thanks to God each day for what they had. They prayed the Prayer of Jabez regularly, asking for God's blessings, asking God for abundance, asking God to stay close to them, and asking God to keep them from harm and evil so they wouldn't cause anyone any pain.

Shortly after they had found their new home, he quit his job in Dallas and moved in permanently with Tiffany. As there are many restaurants in Rome, he was confident he could find a position immediately. It took a little longer than he thought, but he eventually found a position at a chain restaurant as a cook.

His depression and anxiety started to increase. Although he spent nights working on his spiritual development, there were times that he got lost in his past mistakes and his current physical pain. Toothaches, headaches, chest pain, backaches, and numbness and tingling in his limbs were becoming more common. The guilt he was feeling only deepened his depression.

In August Tiffany wrote this to Jonathan to try and lessen his depression.

> My Love
>
> I so hope you have a good night at work. I felt lonely on my drive home today, knowing you wouldn't be here. I put our picture up on my locker today. It made me very happy. Now I know that all I have to do for a quick happy boost is walk in the break room and look at you. I love you so much. I DO know that God brought us together. I DO know we can get through anything. Love does conquer ALL and I love you infinitely. I'm sitting on the back deck watching the puppies run around. They are so sweet. They love love too. Imagine that! I'm leaving you some cigs so you don't nic-out tonight. I pray you have a happy night

and sleep well, knowing that I will always be by your side – and whether I'm here, at work, or asleep, the heart that beats inside of me is yours forever. It's a curious thing that when a person is critically ill, the whole body shuts down to protect the heart – the core of our being. I love you to the core of my being. You are my life, my love, my everything. NEVER forget that, and everything else will fall into place. Goodnight my angel.

Tiffany

It was somewhere in mid-August that The Rollercoaster started. What occurred during this period didn't make Tiffany love Jonathan any less. In fact, her heart opened even more than ever in hopes of doing whatever she could to help him. There were periods of frustration, desperation, and helplessness that occurred over the next 8 months. They did come to a realization that they needed to postpone their September 12 wedding date until they could get their financial situation under control, and until Jonathan was able to handle the life situations that were being dealt to him. They decided to wait 3 months and reset their official wedding date to December 12.

September 7, 2009

Jonathan wrote: True love is when there are two souls working as <u>ONE</u>, which never stop growing. True love conquers all. Thank you for your <u>true</u> love, Tiffany. Thank you for being my soul mate. Thank you for being you. Together, forever, we can conquer all things, using love as our weapon, we will serve. There is no higher purpose, my Love.

I love you. Jonathan

September 12, 2009

Tiffany got home from work in the late afternoon and entered their home. She found Jonathan in a white dress shirt and a pair of his dress polyester pants. He had 6 bouquets of flowers and candles lit throughout the house. She thought it was just beautiful when she walked in that night. Despite some of the problems they had been having, they both knew it was the day they were to get married. They talked and agreed that marriage is defined by "two people in the eyes of God." And since God is with us all the time, she said "Stay here," and she ran into the bedroom. A tear came to her eye as she noticed that Jonathan had placed several more flowers in there.

She changed into a dress, grabbed the flowers, came out of the bedroom, and walked to the fireplace. (The original plan called for them getting married at their house in front of the fireplace) As she stood by the fireplace, she said "Come up here. We can still get married today. Two people and God."

They said their vows. It didn't matter that they lacked a piece of paper, or that she couldn't legally use his last name yet, he was still her husband and she his wife.

The Teachings of Jonathan

The reading and studying Jonathan had been doing periodically over the last 5 years was beginning to make sense to him. As he wrote his works, he began to realize that what we see in the world of 5 senses is not what is true. He realized that we are here, in these bodies, for a short period of time and that our True Self, our Higher Self, is with God.

Unless italicized, all of the following words are taken from his journals. *As I read through his work, I realized everything he was writing was what he was trying to become. It was as if he was telling himself what he needed to be reminded of and what he had to do to overcome his illness. He was telling himself what he needed to do to become closer to God.*

These are also the words he would have shared with fellow addicts, or anyone who felt lost and needed another direction to their life.

On September 10, 2009, as he was writing his notes, Jonathan wrote this to himself.

"I wrote this one evening during a moment of clarity (April 2009) long before I fully understood, at least as much as I do now, the power of love. It may be difficult to understand exactly what I am getting at here. But until I finish this, upon many essays, just ask me upon reading and I assure you a clear explanation will follow:

Upon reaching the end he said, "Follow not in my footsteps for I have ample riches, extensive wisdom, and beautiful scars. But turn back to your brethren and learn to love, because in the end, it's all that will ever matter."

He wanted so much to help his fellow addicts and share with them what he had been through. He wanted his brethren to forgive themselves, and to love themselves and each other as God loves us.

I imagine him getting ready to speak to a group of people who are trying to kick their addiction..........

He walks into the classroom and looks at his fellow addicts. This is the first class he will lead since he's accepted the position of Spiritual Counselor at the new Rehab Clinic. He has been clean and addiction free for over two years. He has spent that time educating himself; first receiving his GED, then a counseling certification, and finally a spiritual ministry diploma. He moves from the back of his desk to the front. He sees there are 12 people in therapy today. He is dressed in his favorite business attire, a pair of green double knit slacks, a white shirt, and a green and beige tie. His confidence is high as he is dressed for the occasion.

"You've read about my dark side?" he asks, referring to the Behind Blue Eyes: The Dark Side handout each person was given upon their entrance to the clinic.

"Not too pretty. Can some of you relate?" He smiles, looks at each one of them with love and understanding flowing from his eyes.

"It doesn't have to be this way." He takes a sip of water, clears his throat and begins.

> "It is only by becoming Godlike that we can know God – and to become Godlike is to identify ourselves with the divine element which in fact constitutes our essential nature, but of which, in our mainly voluntary ignorance, we choose to remain unaware." Aldous Huxley, paraphrased from Plato.

"So who is it that doesn't identify with the divine element deep inside each one of us?"

> "The False Self: The nature of human unconsciousness and dysfunction as well as its most common behavioral manifestations, from conflict in relationships to warfare between tribes or nations, is part of the ego and not the real you. Such knowledge is vital, for unless you learn to recognize the false as false, as not you, there can be no lasting transformation, or even recognition, and you would

always end up being drawn back into illusion and in to some form of pain.

On this level, it's important how not to make that which is false in you into a personal problem, for that is how the false perpetuates itself. The false self is E.G.O., Edging God Out. We cannot fix a problem with the same mind that started it, as Einstein once observed.

The false self is concerned with how they look (we are all very beautiful in the eyes of God), what people think of them, with what material things they own, and with the need to always want to be right. Ego exists only in your mind, and exists only in the world of 5 senses.

It has been proven that we have far more than 5 senses, most of them spiritual. No spiritual sense can truly and fully exist in the world of 5 senses (also known as the world of 10,000 things). The false self is all an illusion of your mind, it is fake, and serves no purpose other than to keep you on the surface, so you can remain a highly trained robot – one that many, all actually, have been given to us to live with for years. We must change the way we look at things, so the things we look at change." JDD

He takes another sip of water and asks "Did everyone follow that?"

Blank stares looking back at him is the response.

"OK, how did we fall into this trap of the False Self? Here are a few quotes from some of the world's great thinkers that I'd like you to digest along with what I just said."

> "The hell to be endured hereafter, of which theology tells, is no worse than the hell we make for ourselves in this world by habitually fashioning our characters in the wrong way....we are spinning our own fates, good or evil....." - *The Principles of Psychology* by William James.
>
> "From childhood upward, everything is done to make the minds of men and women conventional and sterile." Bertrand Russell

> "Every human being's essential nature is perfect and faultless, but after years of immersion in the world we easily forget our roots and take on a counterfeit nature." Lao-Tzu

A woman in her mid-20's, Jane, in the back row asks, "So if I'm understanding this correctly, there is a part of me that is capable at looking at things differently than what I see? Where did you say we're stuck? The world of 5 senses?"

> "Set your minds and keep them set on what is above (the higher things), not on the things that are on the earth." Colossians 3:2

"So how is it we can begin to recognize the desire to change?" Jonathan asks the class.

> What is more mortifying than to feel that you have missed the plum for want of courage to shake the tree?" Logan Pearsall

"Here are some words to think about and I encourage you to begin to start looking at things from another point of view."

> "Though no one can go back and make a brand new start, anyone can start from now and make a brand new beginning." Carl Bard

> "So many fail because they don't get started – they don't go. They don't overcome inertia. They don't begin." W. Clement Stone

> "There are two mistakes one can make along the road to truth....not going all the way, and not getting started." Buddha

Jane stands up again and says "I don't know what I'm doing. I'm too unsure of myself."

> Maturity of the mind is the capacity to endure uncertainty." John Finley

Jonathan looks at the class and asks "Are there anymore questions or comments before we move on?"

A young man in his early 20's, Robert, wearing ragged clothes stands up and says "I don't know how to think like this, this is way over my head." Jonathan smiles and walks over to Robert, puts his hand on his shoulder, and says,

> "Contemplation is the highest form of activity." Aristotle

> "To rid yourself of excuses, you must learn to practice contemplating what you INTEND to manifest, and simultaneously DETACH from the outcome." JDD

"So how do we do that? How do we put ourselves in a position to recognize that we have been held prisoners in our own minds?" Jonathan walks over to the easel and flips the cover page.

The time has come. It is always the right time. When you read this has no relevance to when it was written. The time for it is now, and now is never too late.

Let it go.
All of it.

SURRENDER.....
Then just let it be.

You came here with nothing.....no – thing
And you shall leave with nothing.....no – thing

With this truth, no things matter.

So surrender, and praise the sun that rises for you daily. Then go live from moment to moment, and love it, for love is the only thing that can truly overcome anything. Now, go find love, and with it, just surrender. JDD

Jonathan looks at his class to see its reaction. Nobody comments, so he continues,

"God is dead." Nietzsche's famous statement. What did he mean?

Not being able to stop thinking is a dreadful affliction, but we don't realize it because almost every single person on earth suffers from it, so it is considered normal. This constant mental chatter and noise prevents you from finding that realm of inner stillness that is inseparable from being. JDD

"I think, therefore I am." Descartes

"He had in fact given expression to the most basic error; to equate thinking with being, and identify with thinking.
    The mind is using you. You are unconsciously identified with it, so you don't even know that you are its slave. It's almost as if you were possessed without knowing it, and so you take the possessing entity to be yourself. Knowing this enables you to observe the entity. The beginning of freedom is the realization that you are NOT the possessing entity – the thinker. The moment you are able to start watching "The Thinker," a higher level of consciousness becomes activated. You then begin to realize that there is a vast realm of intelligence beyond thought, that thought is only a tiny aspect of that intelligence. You also realize that all things that truly matter; beauty, love, creativity, joy, inner peace – arise from beyond the mind. You begin to awaken.
    It is not uncommon for the voice to be a person's own worst enemy.
    The good news is that you CAN free yourself from your mind. This is the only true liberation, you can take your first step right now – listen to the voice in your head, be there as the witnessing presence." JDD

A woman in her late 50's, Maria, has been addicted to pain killers for nearly 20 years. She stands up and says to Jonathan, "This stop thinking and getting wrapped up in our thoughts is all well and good, and so is surrendering, but how do you do it? What proof is there?"

Jonathan smiles again and reflects on the questions. He replies:

> "Wake up each day and say "I have the favor of God" or any one of many affirmations to stay focused on your divinity. Scientists have proven that these thoughts and words do impact all of the matter that surrounds us. "As you think, so shall you be!!" JDD

He pauses again for a moment, and then continues. "A good habit to get into is to begin each day with meditation."

"Meditation can be defined this way:
- Interesting
- Familiar
- Sensual
- Extremely productive
- Natural
- Powerful"

"Also", he continues, "there is power in affirming to yourself each day, single words which hold meaning to you. For example, these words are placed around my meditation area."

- Blessed
- Faith
- Cherish
- Believe
- Beauty
- Enthusiasm
- Love
- Inspiration
- Purpose
- Harmony
- Wisdom
- Joy
- Integrity

"In response to the proof you are looking for,"

"Every thought that we have has an energy component to it. Nothing happens until something moves. <u>Everything</u> in the universe is energy – there are NO exceptions. Energy isn't right or wrong, good or bad, moral or immoral; energy is high/low and fast/slow. And higher and faster energies are the energies that nullify and dissolve lower and slower energy. One of the goals of our lives should be to calibrate our lives at a higher and faster, or a more spiritual energy.

When you concentrate any form of energy, including mental energy, you gain power. This power is that which can overcome and defeat any ailment, physical and mental, emotional and spiritual, and the same power with much practice allows you to move objects with your mind. This premise is a common misconception. The world, in fact, is made up of nothing more than energy, most commonly, vibrating energy. Everything exists at a vibratory level or frequency. Under a powerful enough microscope you can take any object and see that it is nothing more than atom or molecules and such moving radically, rapidly, and randomly. Take a wooden table for instance – it is nothing more than a bunch of particles moving so quickly that it appears solid. It is a scientifically proven fact, that with much practice and training of the mind, you could stick your finger without force yet physically, right through it with no effort, injury, or "special effects." That is the nature of our universe. With spirit, or source, or whatever you want to call it in our illusionary perceptions, that anything is possible. Impossibility is impossible, but that's about it." JDD

He pauses again and adds:

There is a law in psychology, that if you form a picture in your mind of what you would like to be, and if you keep and hold that picture there long enough, you will soon become exactly what you have been thinking. William James, 1842

"When you are inspired (inspiration), this is the level of mind where we can create anything for ourselves. You lose any touch of fatigue, and you transcend everything. Silence is the voice of God – listen to Him. Allow yourself the precious gift each day of stilling the mind and listening to the ultimate wisdom which He always has available to you. You have no need to listen to any worries of the mind. When you are inspired you are in spirit, and when you are in spirit you are connected to your Source. And what you are doing is moving out of the mindset of in-form, or information, which is where all problems occur in the world of the physical, and you are shifting into the world of spirit.

If your gaze is upon the ground and not focused on any of all possibilities, then you are looking blindly in the wrong direction and risk missing out on all of God's will. Think in terms of the Prayer of Jabez, ALWAYS!! It's a spiritual, psychological, and scientific fact that we move toward what we focus on and what we see in our minds. Your life will always follow your deep-seated and true expectations, not what you want to expect or wish you could expect. What we think about is ever expansive, and the universe and God have unlimited resources to give you just that. Your subconscious mind will always provide you with what your thoughts are aligned with – good or bad – positive or negative. Always enlarge your vision, pray from Jabez, and maintain your ultimate expectancy. ALL religions practice this logic; they just vary slightly in terminology and form." JDD

Maria raises her hand again and says to Jonathan, "You said all religions practice this logic. I'm familiar with the Bible, but I don't recall anything like that."

Jonathan replies, "Very good. Let's talk about the Bible for a moment."

"We are God's workmanship." Eph. 2:10

This implies that we are all a work in progress. God is always here to help shape us if we desire his will. JDD

"The things which are impossible with men are possible with God." Luke 18:27

This is great news from scripture. Since God lives within each of us, so does His power. This makes all things possible by man through God in his heart. JDD

"And God will give to you, upon your belief, as you call all things that are not as though they were." Romans 4:17

This confirms the law of attraction principles (and the Power of Intention) on the scientific level, as we have seen, but also God operates in this way. So either way you look at things, what you conceive and believe you will receive. JDD

"Neither do men pour new wine into old wineskins. If they do, the skins will burst, the wine will run out and the wineskins will be ruined. No, they pour new wine into new wineskins, and both are preserved." Matthew 9:17

So what is he saying? We must release old, restricted thinking habits of the past and recognize, without judgment, where they have limited us in the past. We must open our hearts so God's will can take root in our hearts. We CAN stretch our faith and vision to be open to new, life enhancing thought processes ridding ourselves of old negative mindsets which have held us back our entire lives. Be thankful for our blindness to this point for it has brought us to this moment – the most precious gift in the world, AND all that we will ever have. Our close-minded ways is the best thing that could have ever happened to us as it has given us the insight to what God has in store for us – a boundless, limitless life in which ALL things are possible. ANYTHING that can be conceived CAN be achieved. We must conceive it in our open hearts AND our open minds before it will be received. The process can be as quick or as slow as we allow it, knowing that it is our true faith that transforms and IS NOT EVER limited by the laws of time and space. To God we are all equally worthy of love, blessings and miracles. It lies all in faith. JDD

"Faith without actions backing it up is dead." James 2:20

Remember: With love, all things are possible. With God, all things are possible. God IS love. JDD

"Well done, good and faithful servant; you were faithful over a few things, I will make you ruler over many things. Enter into the joy of your Lord." Matthew 25:21

Always keep your faith. Just trying and having faith over a few things is enough for God to bless you with far more abundance than you would think not having faith over many, many things would bring. God loves to see us always trying and will bless us greatly for our efforts. Faith, and pure belief in it, is what ties everything to God. Without it we cannot excel and reap God's supernatural blessings. JDD

"We are more than conquerors through Him who loved us." Romans 8:37

This isn't saying that we will one day become conquerors. It's saying we are conquerors right now – we possess all the power and wisdom we will ever need. We must look and search and reach for the truth that lays dormant deep within us. It is this that gives us the Power of God. Our collective society has not taught about the truth within so it can be difficult to find – but it has always been there, and will remain so. We can never escape this truth, although we can ignore it. In this truth lies our salvation. And it's in this salvation that the conqueror within us resides. When a person is ready, and has found certain understandings, their bodies, their minds, and God are all there to assist and perform miracles. When you allow this to be you will have mastered your life and conquered all adversity. When the time is right, and your eyes remain open, the universe and God will show you the path – the path to the ultimate freedom – the ability for love without exception. JDD

"I know the Lord is always with me. I will not be shaken for He is right beside me." Psalm 16:8

Ken has been sitting in the back of the class looking bored. He finally blurts out, "I don't believe in the Bible. I'm an atheist. This stuff isn't doing anything for me." Jonathan smiles to himself and remembers when he felt exactly the same way.

> "I would have lost heart, unless I had believed that I would see the goodness of the Lord in the land of the living. Wait on the Lord; be of good courage, and he shall strengthen your heart, wait, I say, on the Lord." – Psalm 27:13-14

> "Summing it all up, friends, I'd say you'll do best by filling your minds and meditating on things true. Noble, reputable, authentic, compelling, gracious – the best, not the worst; the beautiful, not the ugly; things to praise, not things to curse. Put into practice what you learned from me, what you heard and saw and realized. Do that, and God, who makes everything work together, will work you into his most excellent harmonies." Philippians 4:8-9

> "Let this mind be in you which was also in Jesus Christ." Philippians 2:5

> "Let us hold unswervingly to the hope we profess, for He who promised is faithful. And let us consider how we may spur one another on toward love and good deeds." Hebrews 10:23

> Here "He" is the Lord. When you sew the love seeds, you will reap all that you hold on to with great faith. In due season, you will eat the fruit of your works. Patience + Affirmations = Limitless Miracles. JDD

Ken says, "I still don't buy it. And what's up with Limitless Miracles?" Jonathan looks lovingly into his eyes and says "I am your counselor for the next 3 weeks and perhaps we'll be friends long after that."

> "When we partner together, miracles happen." JDD

> "What is a friend? A single soul dwelling in two bodies."
> – Aristotle

He stops for a moment to clear his throat and says, "Ken, here's something not from the Bible but from my favorite contemporary spiritual leader."

> Be strong and courageous. Stop making excuses, as the Wayne Dyer book "Excuses Begone" suggests to step out in faith. "God has already approved and accepted you, so acting outside your comfort zone is perfectly safe. Our High God is always with us no matter where we are or what we are doing, so your comfort is merely a worldly illusion – God's divinity inside you goes anywhere with you."
>
> The fact that you are alive should be your comfort zone. Thanks to God, any feelings of disconnect are social and ego driven illusions that do not exist in spiritual realm. Deep down, when we truly look within, lies honor and valor seen as the only truths by God. If we practice silencing the mind the whole Holy truth will reveal itself to us. Silence is the most profound and most important sound in the universe, both on the physical and spiritual planes. JDD

"If God is for us, who can be against us?" - Romans 8:31

Robert blurts out "Man, I can't step out of my comfort zone!! Whenever I do, I screw up!!"

> "There are so many lessons we have to learn and then relearn all over again. It doesn't matter. God is not keeping score. Perhaps we are, but we shouldn't expect perfection. Progress is all we are asked to make, and willingness opens the door. – Karen Casey from <u>Fearless Relationships</u>

Jane jumps in and agrees. "Meditation, looking within, trying to understand all of this, I can't do this!!"

> The presence of excuses in your life is evidence that you focus on what you can't do or have, rather than the infinite possibilities that ARE inherent in your <u>DIVINE CREATIVE SELF!!</u>" Think about the other 89% of the brain that scientists say we don't use!!!! JDD

> When you rely on excuses, you allow your false self (ego) to concentrate on what you DON'T want, what's MISSING and things that aren't "working out", or why you can't create it yourself. JDD

Jane comes back and says "I'm not trying to make excuses. Whenever I try to meditate, I don't get anywhere. I feel like I'm butting heads within my own mind."

> "In the confrontation between the stream and the rock, the stream always wins – not through strength, but through persistence." – Buddha

> "Enlightenment, and living a life that is inspired, is not so much about learning anything new, it's about remembering." Recognized by many spiritual leaders.

"Here's a poem I wrote back in April 2010," Jonathan says. He walks back to the flip chart and turns to the next page. Jonathan's Dad stands in the back of the class watching Jonathan teach. His Dad remembers the first time Jonathan showed it to him. He still thinks it is absolutely beautiful and profound.

> I have long feared that the empty canvas that sits
> In the back of my mind for God to draw on
> Would remain blank.
> My life's colors have no meaning.
> The universe has sketched none.
> What is it to say that God will lead the way?
> As I look inside to find
> Just like the blind leading the blind
> I find nothing but to see
> That my life's true artist is God
> And God <u>IS ME!!</u>

Maria raises her hand and states "Isn't it rather arrogant to think that you are God?"

> "Greater is He who is in you than he who is in the world."
> – I John 4:4

Treasuring our divinity means being in a constant state of appreciation, looking for occasions to be joyful and happy, to be in a state of gratitude. Treasuring your own divinity doesn't mean not having respect for God, it means respecting the God that is always with you. JDD

Everyone has a certain time to understand God, but He and all His peace, joy, love, abundance, and contentment are but only one thought, and one belief, away. JDD

Ken asks, "OK, suppose there is this God you talk about. How do we know when we understand?"

Jonathan pauses for a moment and reflects how to answer Ken's question. He replies, "Ken, since you're not much into the Bible, let me answer your question this way."

In the movie The Shift with Wayne Dyer at 56 minutes, it's described as: A shift, a movement from ambition to meaning, from the morning to the afternoon of your life – generally it's preceded by a "Quantum Moment" – this refers to what it's like to have a peak experience. They have certain distinct qualities.

- It's very vivid
- It's a surprise
- They are benevolent/they always feel good
- It's enduring – it doesn't just come and go, it lasts with you forever.

Beyond the ego though, there is an extremely profound transformation of human consciousness – not a distant possibility, but available <u>NOW</u>– no matter whom you are or where you are. You are shown how to free yourself from enslavement to the mind, enter in to the state of enlightenment of consciousness, and sustain it in everyday life. When in this mind set you are directly connected to your source, making all things possible and knocking down all walls of restriction and boundaries and opening the door to everlasting happiness, joy, contentment, and gratitude – among many other things. This mode is also referred to as being inspired, or in spirit. We are only one thought away from being Christ-Like.

Since every person carries the seed of enlightenment, you should address yourself to the knower in **you** who dwells behind the thinker, the deeper self that immediately recognizes spiritual truth, resonates with it, and gains strength from it.

All the great teachers throughout the history of our species have merely taught one thing over and over and over, in whatever language and whatever time, all have said very simply "Give up weak attractions for the strong attractions, period." Individuals of great power throughout human history have been those who totally aligned themselves with powerful attractors. Again and again they have stated that the power they manifested was not of them. Each has attributed the force of the power to something greater than himself. ALL OF THE GREATEST TEACHERS!! JDD

"When you are inspired by some great purpose, some extraordinary project, all of your thoughts break their bonds, your mind transcends limitations, your consciousness expands in every direction, and you find yourself in a new, and a great, and a wonderful world." – Patangali

"We have only 10 minutes left before we move on to the next class. Let me open it up for questions or comments," Jonathan says.

Ken immediately stands up and says,"I still have a hard time believing any of this."

"As a man thinks in his heart, so he is." - Proverbs 23:7

"Whatever the mind of man can conceive and believe, it can achieve." – Napoleon Hill

"And you talk about this inner knowing", Jane blurts out. "I don't know anything."

> "Real knowledge is to know the extent of one's ignorance."
> – Confucius

> "Whatever you can do, or dream you can do, begin it. Boldness has genius, power, and magic in it. Begin it now." - Goethe

Robert is looking lost and confused. "I can't EVER imagine becoming enlightened."

> "Imagination rules the world." – Napoleon Bonaparte

Robert continues, "OK, I look at some of the people here, and they seem to get it. I'll never be like them."

> "True nobility is not defined by how much better you are than someone else; it's defined by each day being better than you used to be." – Unknown

> "When a man's willing and eager, God joins in." Aeschylus

"All right", Ken says, "After 3 weeks, I get outta here and go back to the same shitty routine I've always lived in."

> "Things do not change; we change." – Thoreau

"I have a card, I can't remember where I got it, that I keep on my meditation shrine," Jonathan continues.

> "Change is hard but it is inevitable. You can become part of a change or you can resist it. Change is essential…..change can be a great experience."

Ken replies, "I don't think I can go back to that and stay off the booze and drugs."

Robert and Jane chime in together, "Yeah, me neither."

> Your thoughts are actually like things that act to begin the process of materialization.
> When contemplation is a vibrational match to

originating spirit, you gain the cooperation of the divine mind, attracting and fulfilling your any desire.

If you contemplate with thoughts that match originating spirit, you have the same power as originating spirit – which is an endless, limitless source of energy that creates nothing of which is not derived from pure non-judgmental love. JDD

"Dormant forces (that is forces that you thought were dead) that you thought weren't accessible by you, facilities and talents come alive and you discover yourself by far to be a greater person than you ever dreamed yourself to be."
– Patangali

"How do I know that by changing my thinking that my life will change?" Ken asks.

"Faith is being sure of what we hope for and certain of what we do not see." Hebrews 11:1

"It shall be done to you according to your faith." Matthew 9:29

Since we all come from God, His spirit is alive inside each and every one of us. JDD

Jane adds, "I'm still worried I'm going to go home and get stuck with the same crap I've always had."

Most people spend 80% of their mental energy and capacity on trying to change, or being upset about, the past.

The biggest fact of life that you can do <u>absolutely nothing about</u> is the past. JDD

"True peace exists in not separating ourselves from the will of God." Thomas Aquinas

"But all I've done with my life is screw it up," Robert says with tears welling up in his eyes. "I'm a loser!"

"When you see only black and white, you miss the infinite array of colors that exist in the spectrum of life." JDD

"That is, don't see yourself as capable of being only a "winner" or "loser." You are not a loser," states Jonathan. "I keep a copy of <u>A Winner's Creed</u> on my shrine to help keep me focused. It goes:

> If you think you are beaten, you are;
> If you think you dare not, you don't;
> If you'd like to win, but think you can't
> It's almost a cinch you won't.
> If you think you'll lose, you're lost;
> For out in the world we find
> Success begins with a person's will,
> It's all in the state of mind.
> Life's battles don't always go
> To the stronger or faster hand;
> But sooner or later the person who wins
> Is the one who thinks "I can."

"I keep a bumper sticker at my shrine and in my office. It is from the Bible, Colossians 2:6-7, and reminds me that I have a long way to go in this seemingly never-ending process of life. It simply states:"

LIFE UNDER CONSTRUCTION

We must learn to be happy with who God made you to be. We should easily be able to find great value in ourselves as God has made us, absolutely unique, nobody is, ever has been, or ever will be just as you are. This is an affirming and awesome truth. JDD

Jonathan picks up his Bible, Tao Te Ching, and class notes and turns around to leave the room.

And nobody ever has, or will be, like Jonathan. His purest dreams and his deepest conscience were not what they seemed to be.

The Rollercoaster
Introduction

As the students are picking up their things and preparing to leave, Jonathan stops and turns around to offer one final lesson. He clears his throat, smiles, and begins.

"This is how my family communicated and did their best to help me. Your OBJECTIVE is to simply observe, and use, or don't use, any of the methods they saw fit to help me. The six of them, Mom, Dad, Michael, Cherie, Kristin, and Tiffany shared both completely different AND common viewpoints, with their common goal being to help me. Mom knew the medical repercussions of addiction, and the consequences that existed if the scientifically proven steps weren't followed. Tough Love steps needed to be taken. Dad's approach was more spiritual in nature. Let it BE, and follow the flow of destiny. Michael's approach was that of a big brother; kick me in the ass if I'm screwing up. Yet he complimented this hard-hitting approach with the love and guidance of a devout Christian. Cherie had experiences within her family that she shared in order to help. Kristin was beginning her life with her new husband, and wanted her big brother to heal any way and by any means possible. Tiffany only wanted her soul mate back."

He turns his back and heads toward the light.

The rollercoaster began in early August 2009 and continued for the next 9 months. In late July, there was an incident that triggered Jonathan's reaction to outside events. Despite his spiritual development and commitments to wean himself off of all his medications, he found it necessary to explore other medicinal avenues to relieve his pain.

As this period of time progressed he would agree with his doctors to change his anxiety and depression medicines in an attempt to relieve his symptoms. He added over the counter meds that he thought might help. He got off the methadone and switched to Suboxone. Heart medications for his high blood pressure were prescribed. The result of the experimenting and self-medicating led to, at times, an increase in his anxiety and depression. This resulted in some extreme and unusual behavior.

In mid-August 2009 I received a call from Jonathan. He was sobbing, telling me that Tiffany didn't love him anymore, that he needed to move out, and asked if I would come and get him. I explained to my boss David that Jonathan was having some problems and I needed to pick him up and take him back to my house. I left to get Jonathan with an underlying thought. I would try to offer counsel, guidance, advice....anything to help the two of them work through the problem. When I arrived, they were sitting on the front porch. Jonathan continued to sob as he wondered why she wanted him to leave and why she didn't love him anymore.

This wasn't the case. I spoke with Tiffany briefly and she was exhausted. She didn't know what was happening as she'd never seen him like this before. She described him as being over-emotional and taking every non-positive comment as a stab to his emotional heart. She was confused, concerned, lost, angry.....any emotion you can describe when dealing with someone as emotionally unpredictable as Jonathan was behaving. She didn't want him to leave, but she couldn't live with the over exaggerated drama either. She loved him....they were soul mates. What was happening?

Jonathan came home with me. We spoke often and he cooled off, regained his self-esteem and composure, and moved back in with Tiffany after three days.

A week later I received another desperate call from Jonathan. I went to pick him up and the same emotional scene from 10 days earlier repeated itself.

The Rollercoaster period was filled with some of the most intense emotional mind rides imaginable. Every negative emotion we have was experienced by all of us. His sometimes outlandish behavior resulted in a wide spectrum of reaction. There were feelings of fear, anger, despair, judgment, and disgust to name a few. Not only did we get angry with Jonathan, but we would also become angry with each other and worse yet, turn some of these feelings inward and feel guilt within ourselves or blame others.

On the other hand, the compassion, love, understanding, faith, forgiveness, and trust we ultimately expressed in each other outweighed any of the negative attributes.

There WAS much frustration and confusion.

These were some of Jonathan's indirect lessons to us. Our reactions to his actions tested our willingness to practice those positive attributes described above, as well as learn to release the negative feelings harbored within each of us.

The core of Jonathan's immediate family, that is, Michael, Terri, Kristin, and me communicated almost daily via email or over the phone to keep us all posted regarding Jonathan's current status. Each one of us has our own religion, belief system, and experiences to call upon and these would often clash. Although we disagreed regularly on how to provide Jonathan with the help he needed and how he should get that help, we all agreed on Jonathan's favorite passage from the Bible. "And now abide faith, hope, love, these three; but the greatest of these is love." – I Corinthians 13:13.

All of us entered this next period of time not knowing what was to happen, but with this thought in our hearts.

Up until now I'd like to point out that I was the only family member who had developed a relationship with Tiffany. I knew what a loving, caring and wonderful human being she is, but the rest of the family hadn't been introduced to that side of her. They saw the weary, frustrated side that, in fact, all of us experienced. As a result, they hadn't seen the positive effects she had on Jonathan, and there existed doubts about she and Jonathan's compatibility. This, of course, has changed as they got to know Tiffany and see the strength she displayed and the love she has for Jonathan. Tiffany is part of our family and always will be.

During the last week of August, Jonathan received a Leave of Absence from his employer due to his unstable mental and emotional condition. They were concerned for him as they had noticed that his usual impeccable work ethic was missing. They understood his problem, encouraged him to get well, and told him to come back when he was able to continue working.

Monday, August 31

I'd been receiving calls from Jonathan about his depression and self-medicating, and I let him know how it was affecting his personality and behavior. He disagreed, but it started to become obvious to people outside the family. It was end of month and the busiest day of the month for me. Jonathan called me about 11:30AM and told me the Methadone Clinic would not let him drive due to his intoxication. He asked me to come get him, as he had Tiffany's car, and there was no one else available. At this point I recognized (and not the first time) just how fortunate I was to be employed by a company that supports family and will do whatever it takes to help and understand.

When I arrived at the clinic, I discovered Jonathan had not had his methadone administered to him. He was furious as we stood outside the front door and he described what had happened. He worked himself up to such a frustration level that he yelled "F*@#!!!" and proceeded to march down the street boiling mad at the situation. "Patience," I said to myself as I knew he would eventually get his anger under control.

He continued storming down the street totally pissed off about not getting his meds. I sat there and watched as his counselor came outside and chatted with me. After 20 minutes, he returned to the car, still furious, but knowing there was nowhere else to go.

Jonathan had recently started using a new anti-anxiety medicine. This, combined with his anti-depressants and the methadone, and his self-medicating, resulted in some extreme behavior. From outrage to sobbing uncontrollably to fear, reactions to any possible negative event in his life, these feelings surfaced often yet inconsistently.

As we drove back to his house, he started crying at the thought of Tiffany wanting him to leave. That's not what she wanted but he had convinced himself that it would happen. We returned and an argument between Jonathan and Tiffany ensued. I stayed in the background initially hoping they would work things out. The arguing became more heated and he came out to the porch, sobbing uncontrollably and screaming in a very loud voice, "You've let me down!" He repeated this continuously. By now, some of the neighbors were coming outside to see what was going on.

He continued crying and said to me "Dad, she doesn't love me anymore! She wants me to leave!" I tried to assure him that this wasn't the case, but to no avail. The three of us agreed that he should come home with me so things could simmer down for a couple of days.

He went to the bedroom to gather a few belongings, and I spoke with Tiffany. For the third time in less than 3 weeks the same scene was unfolding. She told me again that she didn't want him to leave, but she wasn't able to deal with the mood swings. She was weary and wasn't getting the rest she needed to effectively work. She was a nurse at a hospital working with patients in the surgical recovery area. She needed to be alert in order to treat her patients and she had 3 days of 12 hour shifts coming up. I assured her things would work out and I would spend some time with him working on some of the misperceptions he was having.

Jonathan came out of the bedroom with 6 duffle bags for a couple of nights at our house. I asked about this, and he explained that he NEEDED all of them. I wasn't going to push the issue so I helped him load the car. As we prepared to leave, the uncontrollable sobbing and pleading started up again. The pleadings turned into accusations and the yelling began as well. The neighbors again came to see what was going on. After what seemed an eternity, I finally got Jonathan into the car and we drove away as the sobbing continued.

A few minutes after we left, he composed himself and explained to me that he would be in pure hell if he didn't get his methadone dosage. He'd missed doses before and while there was some discomfort, he was able to function. This was not his mindset today. My patience was working so I stopped into an emergency room on the way home to see if he could get dosed. ER's usually don't prescribe methadone, but 4 hours later, after explaining the situation to them, much to Jonathan's amazement, the doctor prescribed his medicine.

September

What follows is the first of many emails that Jonathan's family exchanged during the next 8 months. The email address, date, and time have been eliminated.

Wednesday September 16

Michael to Mike

Hi old man,

How did Jonathan do last night? Is your car bad? Cherie had a lot to say about Jon's struggles…her wisdom with this stuff is amazing. Long story short, she believes he may be exhibiting the exact symptoms of a speed junkie…lack of sleep, appetite, chewing on tongue, mood swings, etc. This might make sense, given his addiction struggles. Has it come up with him? With his recent blood work, were you given the permission to see his files and/or speak without barriers to the doctor? Jonathan could be hiding this… hopefully Cherie is wrong in her suspicion…but she wasn't last time.

Mike to Michael

As for Jonathan and the car, the headlight is shattered; the air bags popped; the right tire, when making a sharp left turn at a slow speed, sounds like a train (or tornado) as part of the encasement scrapes the tire; and the bumper is dented badly. Don't know how I'm going to handle that. What I'm thinking is that the mixture of the anti-anxiety and methodone, with lack of sleep, really messes his head up. It's like he's drunken slob. Now that you mention it, he did have something like that a few weeks ago, but the doctors took him off that. I truly believe he's got some deep deep rooted issues that he must let surface to his conscious so that he can address them and let them go……but I don't know what these are. I talked to him about going to a hypnotist, but he has no desire and you've got to want to be hypnotized in order for it to be effective.

The blood results are due to be discussed on Monday. I'm not sure about patient confidentiality or how that works.

Do you have Mom's email address at work? If so, can you forward this to her and copy me so I can add her to my address book here.

Michael to Terri and Mike

Thanks for responding quickly, Dad. And hello Mom.

As I see it, despite any deep rooted issues he may have that need to be surfaced (which obviously there are many); I think he's simply a junkie. His actions are the same as any other junkie…the struggle between right and wrong, the incredible anxiety associated with not receiving his fix, the Mr. Nice Guy attitude to disguise his self-loathing, the violent mood swings, the lack of sleep and appetite, the incredible weight loss, the lack of judgment, the lack of initiative for his responsibilities, and the lack of care for those he would otherwise do anything for. Whether it's methadone, anti-anxiety medicine, anti-depressants, or possibly a street drug…he's an addict and is quickly regressing.

I don't say this lightly…but I believe wholeheartedly that Jon's soul is being tormented by a darkness, a demon, the depth of which we do not, and cannot, understand. I believe Francis and Ariadne helped rid his body of certain evils, but they have come back stronger than ever, which is supposedly what evil spirits do. At this point I am 95% in favor of having Jonathan locked up. The fact he threatened himself (again) is one thing. But having crashed 3 times in 2 weeks and having threatened both Tiffany and you is enough to put him away. I called Ashley last night after we hung up and told her not to allow Remy in a car with Jonathan under ANY circumstances. I also warned her to be careful allowing Remy with Jonathan at all, at which point she admitted a sincere discomfort with it herself. Did you know Jonathan bought (probably stole) a very sharp knife as a gift for Remy? He is far too immature for a blade. Fortunately I could tell Remy was very uncomfortable with it, and he seemed content to just leave it in his pocket. Ashley also said Jonathan came over the other night with "10 dozen roses" to wrap up and give to Tiffany…it seems Jonathan may be groveling again. Just where did he get money for that?

Jonathan MUST be stealing or conning to get money for these things. Ashley said he was on the kitchen floor talking on the phone the whole time he was there. Unfortunately I think it is now an appropriate time to invade Jon's privacy and take his phone to see who he's always talking/texting with. Though he won't return many of our calls, I KNOW that he is constantly using the phone. Just who is he speaking with? Perhaps a dealer?...a conspirator? Who knows? Forgive the imagery and the suspicion, but how do we know Jonathan isn't hanging in bars or on the streets and being a male prostitute? Seriously! He is quite obviously very sick, and an addict will eventually do ANYTHING to get a fix. How low can he go? He'll go lower.

Based on what you're telling me, Jonathan is not taking adequate steps to help himself, especially if he refuses alternative treatment methods.

What the hell...does he expect all the things he's been doing to eventually work?!?!? He has good days, then he has terrible days. That is the life of an addict...until their life is over. I think it's imperative that you sit in with Jonathan when the blood test results are revealed. Insist upon it. If Jonathan won't allow you in, tell him to walk home and leave. Tell him when he gets home, his things will be on the driveway. He'll let you in.

I don't believe a word Jonathan says anymore. I have about a 10% trust level, and that 10% is only because I know his intentions are pure. But his soul is corrupted. If he won't voluntarily lock himself away, it's absolutely time... hell it's well past time...for the toughest love he could possibly imagine. And that means he gets to live on the street! But everyone must be on the same page and committed. I am.

Sorry to babble, but I'm just typing my thoughts as they come...I am sincerely worried. And angry! I will not let my family be destroyed...not even by my own brother.

Terri to Michael and Mike

OK, I am sitting here stunned....from the sounds of these emails, I am getting the impression that, in the time that has transpired since I hung up from talking to you last night, Mike (Dad), a lot more things have happened. Am I interpreting correctly that Jonathan had ANOTHER wreck, now in YOUR car? I assume this was last night or this morning? And what is this about him threatening people?

As far as Remy is concerned, I absolutely do NOT think he should be around Jonathan when he is under the influence of the Klonopin...he is not himself, not clear thinking or responsible enough, and, DEFINITELY he should never drive with him (nor should anyone) as Jonathan would be at risk of possibly killing himself or someone else. He has no business driving at all when he is taking any medication that affects his mental faculties and impairs his judgment. Also, I noticed how upset the whole situation was making Remy when Jonathan was carrying on the weekend I was there. Remy was so worried about him, and kept asking him if he was ok, poor little thing…he should not have to be subjected to this….he is too young to understand. He had tears in his eyes several times, and I could tell he was very scared.

I have to say, and I've said this before, I definitely believe Jonathan is in need of some serious medical/mental health treatment, and, the sooner the better. There will always be time for his spiritual growth to continue, and I do agree he has come a long way with it over the last few years. But, his situation is, in my opinion, almost as severe as it gets regarding the bottom of the barrel disparity of chronic depression and addiction. It's good that he has seen a doctor, finally, but I do not personally agree with the doctor's belief that Jonathan needs to be on the anti-anxiety medication (at a high dosage already), and then didn't think twice about giving him an even higher dosage when Jonathan ran to him the other day with the severe anxiety that had worsened. I believe that Jonathan needs to be admitted, especially now while he still has insurance to pay for it, to a competent mental health facility, preferably one that deals with patients who have addiction issues, as well, so that he will get the evaluations, testing, and medical help that he needs to get on the right track. We have all waited a very long time now for his spiritual growth to save him, but, when one's mind is not in a coherent enough place to even practice the spiritual lessons, it is time for whatever other intervention is necessary, even if it is forced by the rest of the family members who love him. He is not going to do this on his own, I'm convinced of that.

If anything, he seems to be getting much worse lately, even now casually conversing about going out to sell some drugs to get money, as though it's like going to the convenient store to buy a loaf of bread. There is something VERY wrong here.

Michael, I must agree with you that Jonathan needs major intervention, tough love, etc….on the other hand, I believe Jonathan is about at his lowest point and I fear that he might just give up completely, as he has already been having increased suicidal thoughts, which I take very seriously, so all of us, as a family, need to be united, strong, and with extreme love, and gently hand Jonathan over to those who are well trained and know how to best handle patients with these situations. This is far too big for any of us to take on, and time is wasting in getting Jonathan the help he needs before it's too late. Mike, I do not want to offend you or anyone in any way, as I know how much you believe that his spirituality is all he needs….maybe if he wasn't so severely ill, I might agree, as I, too believe that spirituality and the belief in self-healing is very powerful. However, as much as it breaks my heart to say so, I have a very powerful and real fear, almost an intuition that just won't go away, a feeling that something really terrible is about to happen....and, I think this has gone too far.

Jonathan does not seem willing to do anything any of us has suggested so far....and, maybe it's because he is "waiting" for his healing to happen based on knowing that you (Mike) are so certain that it will, if he just continues to do what he's been doing and stay on his spiritual path....I hate to say this, but I truly am starting to think that Jonathan is using this as his excuse to keep screwing up....that he is a work in progress, he can't be expected to be well overnight, etc., etc. Now, he continues on with one problem after the next, getting more severe each situation, KNOWING he is hurting himself, others, acting irresponsibly, ignoring his entire family, including his own son, and just not caring! He has taken advantage of you, Mike, as he knows you are going to always bail him out. Since he knows you won't "judge" him, he has no issues with doing whatever he chooses, even telling you he's going out for a while to sell some drugs, and he knows you won't do anything to stop him. I'm sorry, but I do believe you need to stop him!! Certainly, you can't control what he is doing when he's not in your home or getting help from you....but he should not be allowed to put you into his nightmare on a daily basis, not to this extent.

Please, will someone call me and tell me what has happened last night and today?

Jonathan had taken my car out the night before and had his third accident in a 2 week period. He ran into a light post at a nearby grocery store hard enough to do the damage described above.

I spent some time looking for rehab clinics in the area and sent information to Michael and Terri. The task of researching clinics would become a routine for all of us. We exchanged dozens of emails assessing the clinics we came across as we looked for one that would fit Jonathan's needs. The two we turned to in the future are referred to as "The Facility" and "211."

Thursday September 17

Mike to Michael and Terri

Just to let you know I checked on him at 4:00 AM and he was sleeping in his meditation position. I rechecked before I left at 5:30 and he was asleep in his bed and is catching up on his sleep. I have to take his medicine to him about 9:00 today, so I'll let you know how that goes after I get back to the office.

Also, I just spoke with Tiffany and she talked with him last night and said he sounded much better.

Mike to Michael and Terri

Just got back from giving him his meds. He's still somewhat wobbly but talking a bit more coherently.

Jonathan spent the weekend with us although he did spend much time on the phone with Tiffany. They had made amends and he was going to move back in with her to continue to work on their relationship.

Monday September 21

Mike to Terri and Michael

Jonathan appears today much better than he has in a week. As opposed to yesterday when he fell asleep just sitting in a chair. He slept about 10 hours last night and this is probably much of the problem.

Doctor update:
1) Nothing out of the ordinary detected in the blood work. He said it was nearly perfect.
2) Jonathan had to sign a release stating he was refusing treatment with Klonopin.
3) He is going to try a different anti-depressant. I think it begins with an "a".
4) No explanation for the stumbling. Didn't consider the effect of the air bags smacking him as he shows no sign of head trauma.
5) There's a 3 month wait to see the shrink that the doctor recommends, so we'll pass and pursue another avenue.

He's in the process of moving his stuff back in with Tiffany. As Michael knows we're having flooding issues around here, so I'm not sure when he's going to get here to pick me up. That being said, my phone is about to die and I won't be picking up to answer. I may need it tonight and don't want to use the last of the juices.

Email me back if you have any questions and I'll try to speak with you later tonight.

Michael to Mike and Terri

Has there been any talk about eliminating anti-depressants entirely? Does Jonathan truly believe he needs drugs to be happy? Could it be psychological at this point?

Terri to Michael and Mike, Mike's responses in bold, Terri's response in italics

Terri: Did you mean another anti-anxiety medicine (this is what Klonopin is)....or did you really mean another antidepressant? Is this doctor still insisting Jonathan needs to be on medication? I would like to see him just try it for a while on nothing at all besides his methadone, since he was doing just fine this way up to a couple of months ago.
Mike: We all want him off the stuff. And he wants to be off too. His logic is that it's there if he needs it.
Terri: Ok...but just trying to differentiate what he is going to take...an antidepressant or an anti-anxiety medication?

Terri: Very glad to hear his blood work was all normal....that's almost surprising and I am very relieved about those results. Well, did he say anything about ordering any brain CT scans or an EEG to help diagnose his neurological/psychological disorder?
Mike: No.

Terri: If the psychologist is booked up for 3 months, maybe this doctor needs to call him and tell him this is an emergency situation and then he can fit Jonathan into his schedule.
Mike: He did and that's what he was told. Not sure who can pay for it anyway.
Terri: Does Jon's insurance not pay for any of this? And, what did the doctor recommend as an alternative to the doc who can't see him for 3 months? Drs do this all the time! He should not have to wait any longer for the help he needs.

Terri: I am surprised to hear he is moving back to Tiffany's so soon. I was under the impression he was feeling like he was healing better and was more comfortable at your house.
Mike: He is more comfortable at our house but they miss each other and that's where his home is. I hope they can work it out.

Terri: I thought Jonathan wasn't driving at all? He's out with your car?
Mike: Yes, he's out with my car. He didn't have time to come and get me for the appointment, and quite frankly, I've taken way too much time off as it is. He got plenty of sleep and was just fine this morning and sounds fine each time I speak with him on the phone.
Terri: *That's good to know. Glad he is ok now regarding that aspect of things.*

Tuesday September 22

Mike to Terri and Michael, Terri's responses in bold
Mike: Got in early to get this to you. My cell died at work yesterday, so I didn't get any calls if you tried calling me. Seems more than a couple of hours on the phone and the juice is drained.
Terri: **No, I didn't even try to call you last night, since you had said your cell juice was running out. By the way, I think I know why your cell phone battery keeps dying…remind me to tell you about it later…I learned this from the spiritual ministers I met with on Saturday…very interesting.**

Mike: That being said, I'm not going to be able to discuss this today. I need to get a lot of things done as I have 3 meetings that require prep. I won't be answering my phone, so if it's an emergency, please leave a message and I'll call back as soon as I can.
Terri: **You have done more than enough over the last several weeks/months…take care of YOU for a change….you are absolutely right in telling Jonathan he needs to start taking responsibility for himself. He can't continue to drain the life out of everyone around him. That being said, I'm not entirely sure he does that intentionally, as I believe that has to do with his emotional/psychological issues….all the more reason he needs to go get some help somewhere. When you have time, there is an organization called 211 which operates all over the country. I looked briefly at their website last night and they have resources in the Atlanta area. Anyhow, maybe there is something for Jonathan they can recommend.**

Mike: Jonathan called me this morning at 4:45, and I didn't call him back until I was on my way to work. He slept about 5 hours, and sounded sluggish until I pissed him off with a comment about accepting responsibility for everything in his life, and voila, he sounded fine. He hung up on me, and I'm hoping he's getting a hold of the clinic so he can make arrangements to pick up his methadone today as he doesn't have a ride tomorrow (his beginning of the day stress activity), and I can't help him. At this point, I would rather see him pissed at me than at Tiffany, which was where he was going when our conversation started.

Terri: He has a lot of nerve hanging up on you, after all you've done for him. He really needs to step up and show a little appreciation and stop assuming you will take care of his every need. He seems to be far too dependent on you...I know he is feeling down, but maybe he will be more inspired by some tough love from you at this point...as you have seen, he seems to have instantaneous ability to be "fine" (as with your conversation this morning) as soon as he realizes he can't wallow around you. Believe me, he doesn't want to lose your support and respect, so pretty much anything you say to him (when you put your foot down, as you do once in a great while) seems to hit home. He is a master manipulator in many ways, but he also is intelligent enough to know when he's pushed you too far and then he immediately backs off....the tough love seems to work when you apply it. He doesn't want to be "left out in the cold" where you are concerned, so I don't think he really wants to make you mad. This puts you (and maybe only you) in the position of influencing him to some degree the rest of us don't seem to be able to do.

Mike: Anyway, I don't know what today will bring. He may call you for support. I sincerely doubt he will call me, but I will be there to talk to him if he does, as always.

Terri: Have a good day....please let me know if anything major transpires. Thanks for everything. You're a good man, Charlie Brown.

Mike to Terri and Michael
I had a moment to check out the 211. That could be a real possibility. There's a location in Hiram very close to the hotel you stay at sometimes.

Michael to Terri and Mike
I spoke with Jonathan during my lunch break. He is with Tiffany for the day, and they are shopping for home decor. He seems mildly content to just be along for the ride and be with her in a relatively happy setting...but I also sensed frustration which he could not elaborate upon because of her presence.

I asked him why he was mad at you this morning, Dad, and he said he feels like you "take sides" against him and that your insistence upon his feelings being "an illusion" frustrate him because he doesn't see it the same way. He was very unspecific, so I'm unsure exactly what he's talking about.

I asked how things were last night with Tiffany and he said they were ok, but after she went to bed he experienced bouts of depression. I asked him for specifics, most (if not all) of which we already know about...no money, poor dental health, lack of education, etc. He mentioned his job also, which surprised me a bit. I had the impression he actually liked the job, but he says he hates it. I asked why, and he said it's because of the people, at which point he said he had to go help Tiffany, so I was unable to encourage him to hang in there and deal with it...that EVERYBODY hates their job sometimes. It probably just boils down to not wanting to cook any longer. I think he feels emotionally ready for a new career, but hates that the reality is he's stuck unless he gets a GED, which is probably quite true. To get past the feeling of incompetence, he needs to get that GED, and he knows it...but I think maybe he's not ready (or willing) to work hard enough to get it...I don't know. I can't imagine it's really THAT difficult to get one, especially in the information era we're in.

I asked him to call me again tonight, but we all know how that usually goes...he seemed in generally good spirits as we hung up, but by no means would I say he's happy...he's just hanging in there the best way he knows how, which is one-minute-at-a-time, not one-day-at-a-time as we'd all like to see him achieve soon.

The medicine he's taking, by the way, is Lexapro.

Thursday September 24

Mike to Michael and Terri

The last I talked with Jonathan was at 3:45 PM before he walked into work. His car was broken down in the parking lot. FYI - He's at his and Tiff's house. He moved back on Monday.

Michael to Mike and Terri

Tiffany just called me because she wants to visit our store today. I asked how she and Jonathan are doing. She says fine. She loves Jonathan and looks forward to him getting better. She has a positive outlook.

Terri to Michael and Mike

That's good to know. Hopefully, Jonathan spoke with his boss (or maybe even worked the shift) yesterday. I'm worried about him losing his job.

Whoever does talk to him, please encourage him to call those phone numbers I gave him for 211 as they may have resources readily available to help him.

The weekend rolled around and Jonathan was staying at home with Tiffany. Tiffany had to work 12 hours each day from Friday through Sunday, so Jonathan had a lot of time to himself. I went to visit him on Sunday as we were going to get some things and do some work around the house. We went to a home improvement store and he tried telling me he could steal the things because he never gets caught. I forbid it, and told him to get everything out of his pockets and put them back; I would buy what was needed. We separated at the store and after a few minutes he started yelling for me from the other side of the store. Although we had seen this "man-child" behavior at home, it was the first time I'd seen it displayed in public. It unnerved the employees as well as some of the customers. I took Jonathan and led him to the cashier and we promptly left. We got back to the house, attempted to repair a couple of things, and he fell asleep. I woke him, let him know I was leaving so he could get some sleep, informed him I was going home to spend the rest of the day with Laura, and left. Based on his behavior at the store and the symptoms described to us later, he had been taking Klonopin again.

He went to a restaurant for dinner, ordered his meal and proceeded to pass out while eating. The restaurant managers called 9-1-1 and the paramedics examined him and took him to the emergency room. I received a call from him in the emergency room, and he was extremely upset but didn't want me to come to the hospital. I called Terri, Michael, and Kristin to let them know what was happening. Terri immediately called the hospital to see if she could help and to give them information regarding Jonathan's recent history. An hour later, I received another call from Jonathan. He again insisted that no one pick him up AND that no one call the hospital. I got off the phone and immediately called Terri to let her know of his wishes, but it was too late as she had already made the call. He was discharged later that evening. None of us heard anything else that evening. The next morning we exchanged emails trying to find out about Jonathan's whereabouts. Messages were left on both Jonathan's and Tiffany's phones.

Monday September 28

Michael to Mike and Terri

Tiffany just called me. Jonathan is at home sleeping.

She said she picked him up from the ER around 12:30 this morning. She also said she asked the nurse about Jon's urine and blood tests, but they would not give her the results...she seemed to get the impression that Jonathan specifically asked that she does not know them. It may be he's hiding further drug use, which she fears as well. Or it could be simply they were following the law, but her impressions were that he may be wanting the results hidden.

Dad, your dream about the cat was not a dream. Tiffany's cat is suffering heart failure and she had to cancel a job interview to be with the cat and Jonathan today. Apparently she is seeking further employment so they don't lose the house.

I asked Tiffany to take and hide Jon's keys and to blame me if she's uncomfortable with the responsibility or feeling Jon's wrath. She didn't say no, but she didn't say yes. She did say she knows a manager at another restaurant who might allow Jon's car to stay there for another day or two so it doesn't get towed. I offered to help move the car if necessary, but I was very adamant about her not allowing Jonathan to drive, if possible.

She agrees with me that Jonathan is suffering some sort of delirium, and she believes it is fully because of his lack of sleep. She said he'll stay up all night every night, studying and forcing himself awake, taking copious notes and trying to better himself spiritually. She says he is insistent about his ability to stay awake for days at a time and being perfectly fine...he tells her he's always done it and that it's just mind over body. Yet she believes fully that he experiences delusions because of it.

Though Tiffany "knows" Jonathan is taking the correct dosage of depression medicine, she has no idea if he is taking the correct amount of methadone, nor does she know if he might be taking anything else. I suspect he is taking something else, and I fully intend to find out the truth. If/when I speak with Jon, I will be insistent that he allow me to know the results of his urine/blood tests. Hopefully he'll be accepting of it, but if not I will threaten police interference (because of his recent illegal drug sales).

I'll let you know if I hear anything else. Dad, please let Uncle Joe know the news when you speak with him again.

Terri to Michael and Mike

They did not give me any results either...they didn't even want to tell me when he was discharged or where he went. Finally, I convinced them to tell me since we were concerned for his wellbeing and mental health status. They wouldn't tell me anything, and they aren't supposed to....some do tell more than others but they can get in big trouble for it if they get caught.

Jonathan may not even know the results of his tests. They don't always tell you unless there is something worth mentioning. Again, I don't believe they'd let him leave if they saw anything seriously out of whack.

Do you know why it took her so long to call you? Does she not care anymore?

Michael to Terri and Mike

I didn't get the impression she doesn't care. She's been dealing with her sick cat all day, and apparently she slept late into the morning because of Jon.

Terri to Michael and Mike

I am sad about her cat.

I wonder what will happen when Jonathan wakes up....if she is annoyed about having to go pick him up, having to miss her appointment today, etc.; she may be aggravated when he wakes up...therefore, maybe another long night ahead.

I'm hoping Jonathan will talk to me again at some point, and I hope someone will point out to him that I was trying to help him by giving the medical staff more information to treat him appropriately and to the best of their ability. Hopefully, when he is in a better state of mind he will realize this was done out of love and concern for him. I feel very inadequate as a mom when he won't even talk to me.

Should I come to Georgia? I've already informed my boss I may need to, so they are aware. If we are going to do something as a family to intervene, I would like to be there, too, so we are all together. Let me know what you think.

Michael to Terri and Mike

It's too early to decide to come here, Mom. Hold off. Jonathan wouldn't be accepting of it anyway. It would probably spark unnecessary rage.

Jonathan just called. We spoke for about 20 minutes before we both had to hang up…he promised to speak with me again later. He explained all that happened the other day. He went through a lot of medical trauma, and says he was quite anxious and confused about the whole scenario. Apparently he's mad at you, Mom, because he specifically asked that you NOT intervene because he "just knew" you would blow it out of proportion. His feelings were escalated when he had to be guarded by 4 armed police officers so he couldn't leave. And then further when they stuck a tube down his urethra because he couldn't urinate. (He says they refused to give him water after asking for it over and over again.) He was pretty frustrated with the experience, humiliated, and angered because of the inevitable expense (which he deems entirely unnecessary).

He was hurt by you, Dad, because he thought you were going to spend the day with him Sunday. He says he was excited to see you, but he took it personally when you spent the day with Laura instead. I tried to explain you have more things in your life than just him…and he understood…but he's admittedly quick to anger and unfair to judge. He'll get over it.

I couldn't talk about much else…but will inform you of the rest when I can. I will be working tonight until midnightish…so it might be morning before you hear back from me.

Terri to Michael and Mike

As both Dad and I tried to explain to him last night, the decision for me to call was made before Jonathan told Dad he didn't want anyone from the family to call there. It was too late. And, I didn't blow anything out of proportion. I stated the facts, nothing more, nothing less. I knew he had been catheterized last night, and I don't understand the reason for that, quite frankly. There is no reason I can think of that they would refuse a patient water unless they were not supposed to have anything in their stomach. Jonathan should have questioned that.

And, if there were armed guards to prevent him from leaving, then how did he leave? They should have kept him. I don't understand what was going on there.

Tuesday September 29

Mike to Terri and Michael

I spoke with him last night, mostly about the way he was treated at the hospital. He's pissed and he said he's going to get a hold of a lawyer today to see if he can file suit against the doctor.

He also said he's taking sleeping pills now so he can try to regulate his sleep. He slept 13 hours yesterday.

I also mentioned he owes you Terri a huge apology. He didn't get defensive, just kind of sheepishly agreed, so he realizes he overreacted. When he'll apologize, I don't know.

All in all, he sounded normal. No mumbling or sluggishness in his voice.

Michael to Terri and Mike

I spoke with Jonathan for about a total of 40 minutes. He seems fine. He has his wits about him, but as Dad says, is VERY angry about the hospital care.

He promised me he'll regulate his sleeping, though he didn't mention sleeping pills. I don't know how to feel about that.

I also made him promise NEVER to drive his car if he's the least bit sleepy or if he's even mildly impaired. Initially he was angry with me because I asked Tiffany to keep his keys from him. Mr. Temper got pretty pissy. I had to yell to shut him up...so I know EXACTLY why you've had to do the same a few times, Dad. Eventually after speaking awhile I told Tiffany to let him drive because of his promises to me. I told him the consequences will be dire if he screws up again. He knows I'll take his keys from him permanently.

I believe he'll keep both promises to the best of his ability and stay on the straight and narrow (for the most part).

I asked about the drug sales. He is defensive about it...insists there's no risk of being caught and that he's not hurting anyone. I still need to talk with him more about that. But at this point, like Dad, I don't believe Jonathan is on any other drugs. (I forgot all about insisting to see his lab results...at this point I'm not going to bother...he's just trying to pull his life together and doing too many things at once.)

I wasn't able to address his anger with both of you, but I did insist that any negativity he is sensing is because of his own actions, and he reluctantly agreed that he brought it all upon himself.

I think slight progress was made yesterday, but he is bound to revert quickly if he doesn't stay on the ball...as we all know. He promised to call me every other day or so to keep me informed.

To an extent I think maybe we have overreacted. His intentions don't seem to have been amiss, but his judgment has obviously been horrible. We talked about that, and he will try to make better judgment calls. Time will tell.

Mike to Michael and Terri

Spoke with him this morning and he was crying because of an argument with Tiffany. We are giving the impression to Tiffany that Jonathan has never been able to be trusted, so she is hesitant to trust him……I think. We only talked for a few minutes as he was about to sign in at the social service appointment he is having today. I encouraged him to get his wits about him so that they don't end up seeing something wrong and get someone (police) involved. He seemed to snap out of his funk.

He did sound well rested and coherent other than the crying.

Michael to Mike and Terri

Jonathan did comment to me that he thought she might be upset with him because I got further involved. He also mentioned she was upset about him being hauled off in an ambulance and that she had to get him…… perfectly understandable. Though he didn't seem mad at me, there was definite frustration and anxiety in his voice.

Probably all because I asked her to keep his keys.

That being said, trust has to be earned. And if he hasn't done enough to earn it, then he must be more consistent with her.

Terri to Michael and Mike

Honestly, even if I'd known before I called the hospital that he didn't want anyone to do so, I probably would have called as a caring family member. I don't think anyone should have to be afraid and feeling the way he did, sitting alone in an ER, and simply because of everything he's been going through, I thought it important that those taking care of him should be as informed as possible about his current situation. It never even crossed my mind that Jonathan would not want a family member to be able to talk to the hospital staff about him, considering he was there all alone. I actually thought he might appreciate my stepping in and assisting him to get help. I was a mom on a mission to help my son, and I'd do it again. I am not just going to sit still from a distance and watch him kill himself slowly over time. Maybe that sounds a bit overdramatic, but I have said it before, I have a very bad feeling every day of my life that something bad is going to happen to Jonathan and I want to do everything I can to stop that from happening. Since he won't talk to me, I wish you two would PLEASE try to convince him to go to a good mental health facility in the area and get thoroughly evaluated, or, at the very least, make an appointment with a good shrink so he can get counseling to work through some of his deep seated problems.

As far as the ER scene the other night, I am really furious if he was treated poorly, and, no wonder he is angry with me, as the circumstances of that day being that he was simply severely sleep deprived and suffering side effects of his medicine turned into them strong arming him, apparently, and I'm sure he blames me directly for that. That is why he made the comment that I called and blew everything out of proportion. I truly did not blow anything out of proportion, I only stated the facts of Jon's recent history, and our family's concerns for his wellbeing....I am glad they took my request to further evaluate him seriously, but there was NO reason for him to have been treated with anything other than professional and caring demeanor.

I truly did NOT know Jonathan was against me talking to them in his behalf...I was trying to do the right thing and be his advocate. I think he has a very wrong idea of how all of that took place and the reasons behind it. But, please do tell him that I want to discuss with him the details of what happened regarding his treatment and I will personally help him with getting something done about it (assuming he will talk to me). Just let him know I am offering to help him. If he doesn't want to talk to me, that's fine... just let me know what he says.

Michael to Mike and Terri

I will let him know next time I speak with him.

I called him during lunch and he answered. He was on the way home from his government appointments, and he's just waiting "up to 14 days" for response now.

Wednesday September 30

Mike to Michael and Terri

I need to be brief as I just got here. Been with him this AM to get his meds. He slept no more than 3 hours so I didn't let him drive me to work today. He didn't put up too much a hassle.

He goes back October 14 for another meeting to qualify for $256 per month cash, then another meeting for food stamps.

He may be around the corner as far as being too weepy is concerned. He and Tiffany calmly discussed their situation without arguing. They agreed to give it 3 more weeks and will decide then.

Busiest day of the month for me, so I need to go. My phone is almost dead too, so you won't be able to reach me until it's recharged.

Terri to Michael and Mike

Thanks for the information. Glad he didn't drive today. Very glad he is getting some of his feelings of self-worth back again. Did he seem ok or was he depressed? Will be interesting to see what the next 3 wks bring.

Maybe he will want me in his life sometime soon. I hope so. I am on his side and I wish he realized that.

Michael to Terri

Sorry I can't answer the phone now because my minutes are gone and I'm not paying 40 cents per minute...plus I'm at work.

I spoke to Jonathan briefly last night. At first he asked me to come get him away from there. He wanted me to help him take everything out of her house, and he didn't have anywhere to go. But he thought about it for about an hour, then called back and said he and Tiffany are going to give it another try. I didn't know about the 3 weeks. So he's doing the right thing right now.

At this point I don't believe he needs psychotherapy because he's not ready for it. If he begins to realize a need for it, then it would be worthwhile... otherwise it's like trying to bandage a severed artery with a Band-Aid...not gonna' work. He seems to have his head on relatively straight, but he's a very angry man right now. He feels like he's been mistreated by everyone around him, including me. Obviously he is only seeing the negative side of all this right now, but in time he'll be humbled by it, I'm sure.

I'm going to try and see if he'll spend some quality time with me this weekend...an all day kinda' day. I intend to talk with him about lots of things that our phone conversations never allow. Hopefully he'll go for it.

Terri to Michael

I very much hope he will spend quality time with you, and I sincerely hope you can succeed in getting through to him just how much we all love him, despite his negative feelings that we don't. There is no one in this family he should be angry with, as all any of us have tried to do but help him and love him unconditionally (when it could have been easier to walk the other way...I'm sure he does not realize the extent of pain, heartache, and anguish all of us have endured trying to find a way to save him over the years).

Dad and I have both suggested having a hypnotherapy session, as he might be surprised at how much of his subconscious issues might surface. My friend Kelli says they can work wonders at getting to the bottom of deep rooted issues such as Jon's.

Please tell him I love him very much and that I hope he will try to understand and forgive where I am concerned. I truly want nothing but the best for him, and, above all, for him to be healthy and happy.

I want a good relationship with Jon, just as he stated at Dad's house when I was there that he wants one with me.

Please try to get through to Jonathan in my behalf. It means the world to me. I am really hurting over this whole situation. When I saw he had sent me a text message the morning after he screamed at me and disowned me on the phone at the hospital, I was so happy as I was expecting it to be an apology for being so hateful to me...instead, the text message said to please not ever call he or Tiffany again and that if they ever decide they want to talk to me, they'll call me. You can imagine how hurtful that was.

At least you are getting somewhere with Jonathan and he's talking to you. I am so very thankful for that.

Michael to Terri

I'll do my best to get through to him. I'll talk to him about hypnotherapy, but I'm skeptical he'll even briefly consider it. I get the impression he wants to fix his life by himself. He's tired of the burden and I think he may not want outside help because he has seen no real progress over the years with it. Maybe he thinks if it's going to be done right, he's gotta' do it alone...I don't know. I'll keep you in the loop.

October

Monday October 05

Michael to Mike and Terri

I spent a few hours with Jonathan on Saturday night. He is an angry man, and upset with Tiffany. He told me he intends to keep trying every day for the remainder of their 3 week commitment, but he feels 90% certain he will leave thereafter. I admire Jon's persistence. He is trying really hard to maintain positivity in his life. His home is filled with notes, signs, and artwork reflecting this. There are flowers everywhere. He strives to keep the atmosphere positive. Though I don't agree he is truly "disabled" he is trying his best to get every dollar he can from the government. He says he goes out every day in his suit and seeks "under the table" employment. He all but begged me to provide him with some work so he can earn some money. (Unfortunately I don't have any…work or money.)

I spoke with him about his disability, and I expressed the importance of taking advantage of the government benefits only temporarily. I told him it is both unethical and unwise to depend upon the government for extended time periods unless it is truly needed. He agreed in principal, but I didn't get the impression he really cared.

We spoke about his counseling at the methadone clinic. He is actually excited about the prospect of working with a new counselor because his other one has proven worthless. Apparently the lead counselor offered to help Jonathan personally. Jonathan sounds like he really likes the guy and looks forward to sharing and growing with his help. But Jonathan is torn. This counselor is in Cartersville, 23 miles away. He has the opportunity to move to the Rome office *(only minutes from their house)*, but he feels like he'd be starting over if he does it. And he has no reliable method of transportation for the Cartersville location. A true quandary for him.

As for Mom, Jonathan feels like you do nothing but remind him how much of a loser he is. He says every time you speak, you keep telling him over and over the same thing…things he feels like he's already addressed. Next time you speak with him, whenever that may be, I suggest listening to him more…even if he has nothing to say…then cut the conversation short. He doesn't want to be scolded, and he has obviously rejected you because of it. I think subconsciously he feels like you don't have a right to tell him how to live. I think the relationship he seeks with you is truly that of a mother and son, but he can't just jump in feet first…he needs to wade into the relationship slowly and gently. He doesn't trust that you have his best interests in mind. He believes that you TRY to have his interests in mind, but doesn't agree AT ALL with your feelings about certain things. I believe he feels like you don't listen to him, and if you do your feelings outweigh his own.

Jonathan is worn from the bombardment of everyone telling him how he should live, behave, work, handle things, etc. He expressed disappointment that he doesn't receive any positive reinforcement from anybody, only negative reinforcement. Nobody ever tells him good job. Everyone tells him he should've done this or that another way. I reminded him that if you do something right, it doesn't usually necessitate a pat on the back…it's expected. He understands that…but I think he feels like nobody notices his efforts when he does the right thing.

Jonathan is STARVING for appreciation. He needs it probably more than anything…especially from Tiffany. But if/when that relationship ends, it will be extremely important to come from you, Dad. He seeks your approval more than anybody…just like he always has. Jon's rope has become quite short. He is angry, sad, lost, hurt…broken. It will not be an easy road back to health unless he has some sort of emotional/psychological growth spurt. To some degree, it is back to square one with Jon. It was a very sad ride home for me, but I believe in Jonathan if he has the staying power necessary to make it through all of this.

Terri to Michael and Mike

I completely agree that Jonathan has reached the bottom of the barrel emotionally, which is why everyone in this family has bent over backwards trying to help and encourage him.

Terri then explains the steps needed to help an addict and the tough love steps necessary to get that person sober.

And, though my heart is broken that he feels so much hatred towards me, I have come to the realization that if he needs to hate me in order to get well, then I can deal with that if I have to....but I'm not in a position to do this alone. I need the rest of the family to be more forceful, too (if you are willing)....I believe, with every inch of my being, that he needs to have inpatient therapy, initially, so that they can start detoxing his body, a little at a time, combined with therapy and proper evaluations of his condition.

He always talks about how broke he is, how much he hates his job, etc. but he never does anything about it. We even talked about it when I was there Labor day weekend and he told me he is really bad about procrastination and he really WANTS to do it, but when he feels so depressed he has no motivation to do anything. This is very typical of someone in his situation and he needs someone to **motivate** him constantly, lovingly but **firmly**. I believe (again, we also have to be very careful not to do one of the worst things which is to become **enablers** or co-dependents ourselves – as it is, Dad is taking care of him financially and in many other ways (maybe too many), and Jonathan may be just too dependent on Dad's help. He definitely wants his meds until he is able to get the help he needs to wean off everything ...and the way things are now, it sure doesn't seem that the meds are making him well.

I can't imagine that anyone in our entire family has ever been negative to Jon...his PERCEPTION is that everyone is negative towards him and his situation but that is simply NOT TRUE. I know Dad doesn't agree with me on this, but I have believed for a very long time, and now more than ever that Jonathan desperately needs psychological help. I remain extremely frustrated and heartbroken because **he is my child** and I cannot control my intense feelings of knowing how badly he needs help and watching him suffer...and wanting to do whatever it takes to get him well again. I am very sad that he sees my constant encouragement (and yes, I'm sure I do sound like a broken record, but I have always hoped that, in just one conversation, one time, it might sink in and make some sense to him) as a negative perception.

Unfortunately, all the experiences he had in the past with rehab centers, etc. have given him negative feelings about them. Though I absolutely believe that there is a huge amount of importance in one having spiritual peace and growth, I do not believe that Jonathan is strong enough to be able to apply the wealth of knowledge he has gained from all his reading and meditating. I know how hard he is trying and how much he wants to believe he can heal himself (and he is, in a spiritual way!) But, he needs more than his books and meditation to get well...don't forget that his brain chemistry is severely altered. He cannot be expected to heal himself with "mind over body."

Can we all please just accept that we need professional help on this situation? I don't feel that it is fair to him to keep insisting to him that he can make himself get well by himself if he just BELIEVES he can....of course he doesn't want to feel this horrible, thus he keeps pouring everything he has into this one area, waiting for the day it will all come together for him. Though his spiritual being is getting much healthier, the physical/psychological issues need to be addressed by a qualified doctor who can treat the chemical dependency and brain imbalances he has.

Terri then addressed the financial situation and pointed out a couple of state run facilities that might offer a sliding scale.

Sorry to go on and on, but I am very upset and concerned that this is just a constant vicious circle that is in need of serious intervention, and I am very frustrated at spinning wheels.

Michael to Terri and Mike

I've said this before, and I maintain 100% confidence in this statement. Jonathan does NOT need psychiatric help if he is unwilling to accept it. Forcing him into a facility because "research" says it's best or because others have experienced success with it or because a doctor/counselor we know says it's a good idea is the absolute OPPOSITE of what needs to happen. Jonathan will only further destruct. The only thing that may need to be forced in Jon's life is chemical detox...but that would also likely prove detrimental because he'll reject it. He is too stubborn and I suspect he would only regress. The fact he is encouraged by his new counselor at the clinic is a MAJOR step forward, in my opinion. We must all nurture that possibility... AND we must remember that Jonathan needs to take BABY steps. Dad, do you know the phone number to his clinic? I'd like to speak with the counselor personally.

Jonathan is, indeed, making positive strides with his life. The primary contributor to his depression/anxiety at this time is Tiffany, and to a lesser extent, his misperception of Dad's feelings about everything. With Tiffany eliminated from his life, assuming (and hoping) it doesn't further depress him, Jonathan can be relatively free to focus on the other factors in his life that need addressing...largely improving his relationship with you, Dad. He had GED information available that he shared with me, and I believe he'll pursue it just as soon as he gets past this government money stuff. However above all Jonathan seeks love and companionship in his life. It may prove very difficult to keep him focused on the big picture, rather than that of temporary satisfaction with a girlfriend. I know this will be a struggle, and we'll all have to stay on top of him about it. I intend to speak with him about it if/when he and Tiffany break-up.

So Mom, despite your strong feelings about introducing a shrink into Jon's life, I don't believe it's the right thing right now. It is good to keep talking with Jon, and perhaps reminding/encouraging him about the option, but he needs to pursue that avenue on his terms only, lest we all push him over the edge. Seriously. As long as his mind is occupied with things to do, he will maintain a sense of purpose. That purpose will be the driving force behind his emotional, psychological, and physical growth/maturity. We must never take away his purpose…but we must constantly remind him of it (in a gentle, non-offensive way, if possible)

My $.02.

Terri to Mike and Michael

I agree that he must want the help….no argument there. I believe all of us have to gently and lovingly express to Jonathan how much we want to see him well and that we are trying to ask him to just seriously consider the benefits of seeing a counselor on a regular basis, or even join a support group or a church.

Also, Jonathan might meet some friends who have experienced the same things he is going through and there is a lot of help in that alone, just knowing you are not all alone. I think it might help him a lot not to feel like a "loser" when he realizes what a huge problem it is and that there are many, many other people who suffer from the same problems.

I'm not saying we should put him in a straitjacket…I'm just asking if everyone could stop telling him to heal himself, and try to encourage him about the good we believe it might do for him to find someone he likes and trusts to confide in and get to the bottom of his deep rooted issues. Obviously, if he refuses, then this plan won't work.

I think he is looking for approval and for love and support to get help and he is not sure how to do it.

The remainder of the week focused on Jonathan changing from the methadone clinic in Cartersville to the clinic in Rome. Laurie, his counselor at the methadone clinic, and Jonathan had remained close the entire time. However, when she questioned Jonathan about some of his recent actions, he became defensive and argumentative. He wanted to either switch clinics, or change counselors. The Rome clinic was only a mile from he and Tiffany's house, so a transfer made sense. He began calling and checking the Rome clinic protocol.

Tiffany was working the upcoming weekend so I picked Jonathan up on Friday after work. We spent a lot of time discussing the need for counseling. We also had conversations about how true happiness comes from within ourselves, our own minds, and is not dependent on what we perceive the outer world to be. We discussed the need to stop blaming, and to accept responsibility for <u>everything</u> in our life. Practice on how to perceive with love, and forgive.

This conversation was not only to help Jonathan, but it was to help me in the months to come.

Monday October 12

Mike to Terri and Michael

Jonathan is seeing a psychologist this morning. I haven't heard back yet even though his appointment was at 8:00. I'll let you know when I hear something. Incidentally, the appointment was made through the 211 hotline.

Mike to Terri and Michael

I just got off the phone with him. This group therapy stuff is not for him. He said it makes him more depressed. So, the psychologist was actually a group counselor. He sounds good, he's heading home to clean up some of his mess.

Michael to Mike and Terri

What inspired him to try it?

Terri to Michael and Mike

He has never felt comfortable in the group therapy sessions, which is one of the reasons he hated the rehab programs he went to, as they are so regimented about everyone going to the groups and standing up talking about themselves to everyone. Jonathan would do much better with a psychologist he can meet with one on one, someone he trusts and respects...perhaps the counselor he likes so much at the clinic can refer him to someone good. I am very glad he has considered going to see a psychologist, and hope he will continue to find the right person who he can feel comfortable to go and see on a regular basis.

And, yes, my question, too…what did inspire him to try it?

Mike to Terri and Michael

This was someone his doctor wanted him to call. He finally called on Saturday and they wanted to see him first thing this morning.

Terri to Mike and Michael

Why don't you try suggesting to him to TRY the group session counseling again? Maybe it won't be as bad as it was the last time. After all, he was in a completely different place spiritually and was still not really ready to accept the help back then.

Mike to Terri and Michael

I did, and he didn't rule it out completely. It's just not something he wants to participate in today.

Michael to Mike and Terri

Surprise, surprise. Jonathan doesn't want to leave his comfort zone. I'll try calling him for encouragement also. Maybe he'll answer.

Terri to Michael and Mike

Well, I'm sure you are correct…he is not going to be comfortable, necessarily….but, with the right group of people, he may find that his spiritual growth will help him to help OTHERS in the group…funny how that works. He may realize that when he looks around the group of people who are all in the same boat, he may see how much he truly has to be thankful for, after all. I'm sure there are many people there who are just starting out in the journey and don't have the spiritual growth to help them. Jonathan could be possibly very helpful and comforting to others, which, in turn would do wonders for him, and also give him a sense of purpose and something to feel good about.

Mike to Michael and Terri

An excellent point!!

Michael to Terri and Mike

Helping others is, ironically, something Jonathan insists he strives for. If he realizes that possibility and he's being honest with himself about that ambition, then maybe he'll have a change of heart/attitude about it.

That evening Jonathan and I were in the workshop and I encouraged him to look at the group therapies as Terri had suggested. He agreed to give it some thought.

Tuesday October 13

Mike to Terri and Michael

He was depressed last night because he hadn't heard from Tiffany. Thinking only the worse, he thought he was getting thrown out. She texted him several times later in the evening stating she loves him and wants him to come home. Nothing like working yourself up over nothing.

He is making much more sense in the morning and has been getting up with no problem the last two days. He went to the clinic after dropping me off and then went to his house. He called to let me know and I haven't heard from him since…..that was at about 10:30, so I'm assuming all is fine at the moment.

Wednesday October 14

Mike to Terri and Michael

I spent about 3 hours with Jonathan last night, primarily filling out paperwork for the disability claim. He spent a wonderful day with Tiffany. He told her he was going to have to move back in with me until his car got fixed, which will more than likely be a couple months from now. After he left to pick me up from work, she arranged for insurance on the car for the both of them. She even had him listed as the primary driver. He'll be going over there tomorrow for a couple of days. My guess is that I'll be picking him up on Sunday…..don't know for sure yet.

He's got an appointment today with the Dept. of Labor. I'll let you know how that goes after he updates me.

We emailed a few more times and I let them know that Jonathan had qualified for food stamps, but had been turned down for any financial assistance. I also suggested to Jonathan that he should consider going back to his employer to see if they could give him a few hours. He was still feeling reluctant about returning back to work.

Tuesday October 20

Terri to Mike and Michael

This was in our company newsletter today...thought you might find it informative. Any more news today?

The company newsletter described depression and some of the signs and symptoms of the disease.

Mike to Terri and Michael

I spoke with Kristin last night, and she said that you send her all the emails we have going on to keep her informed. Can you add her email address to this? I don't know her email address off hand.

Regarding the newsletter, except for post-partum depression, these symptoms describe all of his behaviors, including the bi-polar.

I've been on the phone with him today. He is sounding completely sober although a bit angry. I didn't point out to him yet that he seemed to be doing fine on his way to the clinic, despite the drama of last night about going through withdrawals. After he got to the clinic, they informed him he was being dropped back to an A-1 status *(going to pick up his methadone 6 times per week)*. He demanded the transfer to the Rome clinic, so that is supposed to be in process now. He's going to go to the Disability office today (missed yesterday's appointment) to see what he needs to do.....but like I say, he's fine today and could be working without issue.

He also mentioned that there is a Pest Control Company across from the Rome clinic, and he's going to apply there today or tomorrow.

I'll keep you posted as I hear more today.

Terri to Mike, Michael and Kristin

Here's Kristin's newest email address in the cc: field. Yes, I have forwarded her the emails so she is up to date.

I can't imagine why Jonathan was surprised at the clinic this morning. After all, he, once again, put himself in the position of acting that way there yesterday and having his status changed as a result. Just as I was saying yesterday, he (as all addicts) does not consider repercussions or consequences in anything he does...once again, why he needs professional help. Obviously, he thinks he is invincible. So, now he wants to go to the Rome clinic again? Guess that means he'll move back over to Tiffany's? And, I thought he wanted to be close to the new counselor he wanted to work with....what happened to that? Was he able to talk to him at all today?

Hmmm...pest control? Wonder if he'll like doing that? Maybe he would, though, who knows? Sounds like a possibility.

Michael to Terri, Mike and Kristin

Obviously being away for business I didn't get the update on Jonathan yesterday. What happened at the clinic yesterday that was so bad?

Dad, please tell Jonathan to call me about the auction on Saturday. I want to personally express the importance of being clean and looking nice. If he doesn't call me, please don't bother bringing him...I don't want any drama or distractions...no time or energy for them when trying to conduct a very busy auction. Is Matt planning to come?

That Saturday marked the fourth annual auction at Michael and Cherie's furniture accessory store. Family and friends would volunteer their time to assist with this gala event. There was wine and appetizers, cake and Sangria. Michael and Cherie would select about 150 items to auction off. Matt, Jonathan, and I were going to be there to assist. As expenses were tight, I was asked to be the auctioneer. Having no experience, I said "What the heck. Sure." Matt was going to assist Michael with moving the furniture to the stage and Jonathan was to record each piece sold with the buyer's number.

Terri to Mike, Michael and Kristin

Apparently, Jonathan was having a bad day and he decided to take some Klonopin, which made him get slurry and stumbly, as before when he took it. When he went to the clinic yesterday morning, they thought he was "intoxicated" and refused him his meds. I'll let Dad tell you the rest...that's the jest of it.

I didn't know Jonathan was working at the auction with you. I'm sure he'll be fine, Michael. Dad said he's been doing much better until he took that extra medication. Dad talked to Tiffany yesterday and she saw for the first time how it affected him shortly after taking it. She'll make sure he doesn't take it around her again, and she'll do what she can do to keep it from being prescribed to him.

Mike to Terri, Kristin and Michael
Just so you know I won't even bring him if he's out of sorts.

Wednesday October 21

Terri to Mike, Michael and Kristin
Wow…for once, the update is coming from me! Yes, Jonathan actually called me this morning; first while I was still at home getting ready for work, then he called me back again after I arrived at work. He was in Tiffany's car, had gotten up early and dropped her off at work, has lots of errands today and was stopping at the Rome clinic to take care of whatever he needed to do to complete the transition over to their clinic.

We hung up as he was pulling up to the Rome clinic. Then, when he called me back a while later, he had experience a bad situation there; apparently there was, according to Jon, a very rude girl working at the desk who told him they cannot accept him as a patient at the Rome clinic because he does not meet their criteria (he mentioned something about his dosage being so high, as well as his being on "benzos", which he explained that he has a prescription for from his doctor and the other clinic is completely aware of the situation and is fine with it)…I think they were mostly referring to the Klonopin, which Jonathan said he told them he was no longer taking and that he had gone off that medication but he wanted to tell them about it in case there was anything still left in his system so they would not be surprised if it showed up in his urine analysis)… I'm sure that was why he decided to list that medication on the paperwork or whatever, as he knew it would show up.

He said he was very nice, very polite, remained calm and respectful, but this girl would not even continue the conversation with him. So he asked her to please give him the name and number for the clinic director, or her supervisor, so that he could call and try to rectify the situation with someone who is a decision maker. But, she wouldn't give him the name, even as he stood there with a pen in his hand to write down the number. She told him he needed to leave, kept ignoring his request for the director's name, and the next thing he knew, apparently at her summons, two big burly guys came up to Jonathan and physically removed him from the building. He was not happy, to say the least. He again, stated to me that if I was there to help him with those kinds of situations, it would have been a lot different. He said he is sick and tired of being treated by everyone like he is a lowlife, and he is tired of being disrespected when he went out of his way to be polite and respectful to them. Jonathan said he gets treated this way a lot, whether it be emergency rooms, or whatever the case, as soon as he truthfully tells someone that he is in addiction therapy. Then, they immediately start talking down to him, and insulting his intelligence.

If he was treated rudely and disrespectfully, and they refused to give him the clinic director or supervisor's contact information, he has every right to follow through and speak to whoever is in charge of the clinic and explain the situation. Again, Jonathan said that kind of thing goes over so much better when he has a parent with him. Maybe you (Dad) can help him with that…if he truly was treated this way, he deserves the right to be heard.

Jonathan just called me again and he had left the other clinic, got his dose, and was headed to his doctor's appointment. He did not have time to stay there at the clinic to talk to anyone about the situation over in Rome, as he was pressed for time. So, he, for now, I guess he will continue to go there until he can get it straightened out.

He seemed completely normal and rational in our conversations, and I didn't speak much at all, purposely…I just listened, for the most part. I was glad to finally hear from him….he didn't mention anything about the last conversation we had…nor did he apologize….but, he did end the conversation by telling me that he loves me very much, and he thinks of me every day. I told him the same. Hopefully, he will call again someday soon. He did say that things with him and Tiffany are going well. So, he was glad about that.

So…..that's all I know.

Kristin to Terri, Michael and Mike

I spoke with Jonathan last night for the first time in about 4 months. He told me that dad told him what was going on with me, with my mild anxiety problem, and he was calling to see how I was feeling. We had a nice conversation I think. He asked me exactly what symptoms I've been having, and he asked me what all my medications and dosages were. He was trying to talk me into going to the psychologist and asking him to put me on something for my anxiety. I told Jonathan that I will call the psychologist when I am ready. I also told him that I would rather not be on any medications for this problem, unless it gets really bad. That was about all we talked about. He said that he loves me and that he is not avoiding me, he just has been sick lately. I told him that I understood and that I loved him too. I am supposed to talk to him again tonight, so we'll see. I love you all!!

We all shared our stories about our personal experiences with anxiety and some of the tricks we had used in the past to relieve that pressure.

I received a call later in the day from the Methadone clinic, and because of Jonathan's recent behavior, they asked me to come in and meet with them the next day.

Thursday October 22

Mike to Terri, Kristin and Michael

Just got back from the clinic after meeting with Jon's treatment team. I met Karey, the head counselor, and I can see why Jonathan likes him. A very nice, sincere guy.

They wanted me there to primarily get my side of the story regarding Jon's behaviors. I gave it to them. Jonathan was in there as well, and although he got a wee bit defensive on a couple of issues, he was forthright, honest and polite during the entire meeting. He did interrupt on occasion and they asked him a couple of times to stay silent so I could speak. He apologized and would try to keep his mouth shut.

He did get moved to a B-1, which is 4 times a week instead of 6, so that will help. Also, he talked about what happened at the Rome clinic and JM, the Director, is going to call and find out what the protocol at that location is. It could be that they are so strict that Jonathan won't be able to go there until he meets certain conditions. Oh, they also lowered his methadone dosage to 200 mg (from 220). Jonathan is concerned about this, but it sounds like the Team is ready to start dosing him down and working to get his mindset out of the "if I'm broke, I need a pill." I think that Karey will be a big help with this.

Terri to Mike, Kristin and Michael

Terri expressed her relief that Jonathan would be weaned down and her gratitude for Karey and the help he would provide.

I know, just as recently as yesterday when he talked to me, and he stated that he has told you, Mike (Dad), this, as well....he said that he absolutely will not go through the agony and pain associated with being without his medication (he was referring to cold turkey situations and how horrible they are for people who get themselves in trouble and end up going to jail, etc. and their meds are just jerked away all at once with no weaning process) that he would commit suicide without question if he ever had to go through that. That kind of statement from him scares me to death, and this is not the first time he has said that to me. I believe he is serious, and I know he is scared to death of the unknowns in trying to go through the difficult and trying parts of weaning off the meds permanently. I also do know that what he says is true regarding the danger of being taken off the methadone suddenly like that.

When you were being completely honest and open with answering their questions about how you feel about Jon's behavior, etc., I'm very curious exactly what you did say to them...and which parts Jonathan tried to interrupt....I bet that was a very interesting meeting. I'm very glad Jonathan remained calm and respectful, which says a lot to everyone involved.

Mike to Terri, Kristin and Michael

Well, they didn't really ask me how I felt about it, except once and I told them I was learning patience and practicing unconditional love. Mostly they wanted to know what Jon's behaviors are during time of duress. I told them it can be from deep depression to the point of incessantly crying to extreme anger where he says he wants to kill something or someone, including himself. They asked about specific examples, probably to get a feel for how to treat him based on what I said, rather than what he said. He tried interrupting at points when what I said, in his eyes, made him look bad. (killing someone, crying uncontrollably, etc.). He felt the need to defend himself, I guess, as he probably feared what they would think of him and what the consequences might be.

By the way, Jonathan has an appointment with a psychiatrist on 11/20.

Terri to Mike, Kristin and Michael

That's good news....was this at the new counselor's recommendation or someone who personally referred him?

Terri expressed her hope that Jonathan would develop a good rapport with the psychiatrist.

He told me yesterday he is so sick and tired of being treated like a lesser person and being categorized and treated disrespectfully, and I agree with him that it is a terrible stigma that is all too often attached to people with addiction problems, in spite of the fact that it is a widespread epidemic with millions of people affected with the same situation. Unfortunately, for many, they do not have the support or the means to get the help they need, so, for that, Jonathan should feel blessed that we have all hung in there for him. I wonder if he ever really realizes or appreciates that fact. Somewhere deep inside, I'm sure he does, but until he gets well he will never fully see it, I'm sure.

How was he towards you after you left the clinic? Was he aggravated over the things you talked about?

Mike to Terri, Michael and Kristin

Not a bit, we went out and had something to eat. I just got off the phone with him....he may be eligible for some other benefits he didn't know about. Not sure what they are.

I had told Michael earlier in the week that if Jonathan was out of sorts, I wouldn't bring him to the auction. Jonathan was fine as we got into the car to leave, although he did admit to feeling a bit nervous. I assured him he would be OK, and that I would be directly in front of him and would assist with his task as need be.

About 25 people showed up to bid on the furniture. Matt and Michael were hustling around showing each piece of furniture as it came up for bid. Cherie would introduce many of the pieces, give a brief history, and explained the great value of many of the pieces. I jumped into my auctioneering assignment and as I gained my on the job experience, I began talking a little faster and with more confidence. Jonathan was staying busy tracking the purchases, and although his hands were shaking, he seemed to be holding up and doing his job well.

The auction lasted a little more than 3 hours, after which we collected payment and helped customers get their cars loaded with their new purchases. Jonathan assisted as well, but would disappear out back on occasion to take a smoke break. Tiffany arrived toward the end of the auction as she was picking up Jonathan to go back home with her.

After the last of the customers left, the six of us sat around, caught our breath, and talked about the day's events. Cherie then noticed that a bracelet that was not up for auction was missing from its display. I thought to myself "Oh no, maybe it's been misplaced." We began searching the store and Cherie noticed that there were other things missing as well. Jonathan had disappeared again and was outside moving his bags from my car to Tiffany's. I went out there to check to see if my worst nightmares were true. Had Jonathan stolen from his brother's store? I approached Jonathan and told him what was going on. He had taken some Klonopin and was slurring his words and began crying. I looked in his bags and there was the bracelet as well as a dozen other knick-knacks.

I went back into the store to let everyone know what I had found. Michael went storming out the door ready to beat Jonathan to a pulp. Cherie asked me to follow Michael and make sure things didn't get out of hand. Michael was furious, and rightfully so. Who would steal from his own brother? But with each step Michael took toward Jonathan, his anger would slightly diminish. He knew deep down that Jonathan, in his right mind, would never do this to him.

Plenty of angry things were said. While Michael and I searched Jonathan's bags, Cherie stayed in the store and explained to Tiffany and Matt what Jonathan was going through. She had seen the same behaviors from a couple of members of her own family. Cherie knew it wasn't Jonathan taking her things, it was his addiction.

For the next two hours, tempers flared while immediate plans were being made. Tiffany was, as we all were, completely in a state of bewilderment. How could something this bizarre be happening? But it was.

While all of us were in the parking lot, the volume of yelling amplified and the intensity of emotions increased. Tiffany wanted to leave. Michael's frustration swelled as he uncovered additional items that Jonathan had taken from the store. Jonathan sobbed and threatened to kill himself. This scene was causing people dining at an adjacent restaurant to stop and stare at what was transpiring.

Before the police were called, we decided to take the cars and drive a mile from the store. We parked in a grocery store parking lot to sort out what was to be done. After Jonathan told us he didn't have any more of his medications, a bottle of his anti-depressants fell out of his pocket. Being caught in the lie caused Jonathan to cry again and to profusely apologize. We examined his bags, found additional medicine, and took it from him.

Ultimately, whether it was exhaustion or utter frustration, everyone's attitudes calmed down. Tiffany reluctantly agreed to take Jonathan home with her. Michael and Cherie returned to the store with the items Jonathan had taken. I had called Laura several times during the evening to keep her posted. She told me after Matt and I returned home that she would have asked me to take Jonathan to a hotel if he had come home with us.

Who could blame her? The craziness of the last 8 weeks was catching up to all of us. What was next?

Wednesday October 28

Terri to Mike and Michael
Has anyone talked to Jonathan today and, if so, how is he feeling?

Mike to Michael and Terri
I spoke with Jonathan about an hour ago. He was feeling generally ok, down from great this morning. He started delving into his depression a bit, and says he doesn't know why.

He has a busy day of errands to run, so his mind should be occupied for the majority of today.

Terri to Mike and Michael
Thanks for the update. It will probably take him some time to get into another routine again. He has had so much changing at once in his life. Glad to hear he is at least generally ok, as opposed to being very depressed like he was. Did he mention where his errands are today? I'm wondering if he still had follow up appointments with the unemployment office and work force to help him find a job.

Mike to Terri and Michael
I'm working from home today in order to spend time observing and to let him get out and do a few things.

I've noticed that immediately after taking some of his meds he slows down. It seems to affect his mental capacity....making meticulous to-do lists over and over. He is very defensive and I have to remind him that I'm pointing out behaviors I'm observing, not being critical. He is looking forward to hearing back from the 211 folks; he even called today, so he can begin therapy.

We also went next door to see if our neighbor was home. She has the brother in charge of the Celebrate Sobriety group out in this area. We're going to set up a meeting with him.

I'll let you know how the afternoon goes.

Thursday October 29

Michael to Terri
I was already sleeping by the time you called last night. With Jonathan on top of the store and planning Chicago, I've had an exhausting week!

I didn't talk to Jonathan any more yesterday...just the one time around lunch when he was preparing to run errands. He left me a message asking not to answer or return any calls/texts from Tiffany. I think he wants her to suffer not knowing what's happened to him. Another example of how he is not the peaceful, all-loving man he wants to be, or thinks he is. The other night I was awakened to an arrogance he has about his spirituality that frankly scares me. Despite Dad's best efforts, my opinion is Jonathan is spiritually lost...completely. He boasts peace and love, but that night he was moments from killing...literally! THAT is spiritual warfare if ever there was any. That night when I tried to sit down and talk with him about my feelings... how I truly felt God orchestrated the series of events leading to that night (including his stealing from the store), and how God's mercy is selective, that He blesses certain people (like me) and uses others as examples (like him), and that Jesus encourages us to be as God-like as possible by offering mercy to those who may not necessarily deserve it (Jon), just like God did for us through his son...well, Jonathan became defensive of his "beliefs" and started boasting how we can all be EQUAL to God, which of course is sinful thinking and sacrilege. Then the anger came. And the rage. And the yelling. And the knife.

The previous Monday night Jonathan gathered some of his belongings and moved out of his and Tiffany's home. Michael and Jonathan's friend, Zach, were there with their trucks to assist. Since the auction, the arguing intensified between Jonathan and Tiffany. Tiffany's uncle was there to make sure Jonathan moved out and to protect Tiffany if need be. Words ensued between the uncle and Jonathan, and Jonathan became furious. Tiffany's uncle stepped outside to cool off, and Jonathan pulled out his knife and was ready to attack him. Tiffany and Michael were terrified! Jonathan was filled with rage at everyone, and Michael feared for each of their lives. Fortunately, Michael and Zach calmed Jonathan, and the three of them left before any harm was done.

Michael continued his email:

The enemy is inside Jon, and fears my presence in Jon's life. I've seen it multiple times now. My presence creates spiritual tension. Next week, and every subsequent week, I will ask Jonathan to visit church with me. Hopefully his presence with other like minds and the leadership of the pastor will be awakening for him. I cannot communicate the truth well enough to break through Jon, but he does want spiritual growth...he just doesn't respect my place. That's fine for now, but I will be making strides to get through...hopefully without any further violence.

In the meantime, Dad's peace-loving nature is good for Jon, despite being misleading for him. This will be a difficult struggle.

I'm leaving for Chicago tomorrow morning. I still don't have everything ironed out, but I'm working on it.

Terri to Mike

Michael's thoughts are so disturbing to think about...

I tried a couple of times last night to call Jon, he didn't answer and I left messages both times that I was just calling to say hi and that I hope he is feeling a little better and to please call me back when he can. Never heard from him, though. I think the last time I tried was around 10 or so last night.

What transpired last night? And, how is he doing today?

Mike to Terri

He was unloading the car past 12:30 last night and then straightened his room. He called me about 9:30 this morning to let me know he'll be with Chris today and that I'll need to pick him up at Chris' school. (it's located about 2 miles from where I work) I'm focusing on his body right now, which means food and rest. He received a C- for yesterday. I didn't wake him up with me today as that would have left him with 2 hours sleep. Michael has a good point about not practicing what he preaches. I continue to work with him about this and he'll eventually get it. My job is to try and bring the light to him by practicing what I have learned……I still have a long way to go.

I'm going to try and get him to come home tonight and study during what had been my "class time"…..4:30 – 6:30. With what has been going on the last few months, I've gotten away from that. I'm hoping Jonathan wants to work with me and start learning A Course in Miracles.

Terri to Mike, Michael and Kristin

Maybe he is just very anxious to have some "order" in his life and it is probably very important for him to get all of his things together and organized in his new world where he is looking to "start over". My guess is that he is on a mission to get everything in order first so he can not have any more chaos in his life than he already has….maybe we should not grade him too harshly for the rest of this week while he is trying to put his ducks in a row to hopefully begin getting help starting next week and then he can focus and know he can come home to a peaceful place.

Where is he going in the truck today?

I'm sure it will be an adjustment for him to start getting the rest he needs, as his body clock is so screwed up, and don't forget the insomnia that is a side effect of his antidepressant medication. Never mind the fact that he has a million things overwhelming his head and his heart right now, so it's no surprise he finds it difficult to sleep. He is keeping busy instead and trying to accomplish things as long as he can't sleep anyway.

I'm sure he will get his schedule turned around, but it's just going to take some time for him to get things in order. He seems to be trying hard to change things.

Mike to Michael, Terri and Kristin

Good news!!! I just got off the phone with Jonathan and he sounds better than he has in months. Ironically, he hasn't taken his methadone or anti-d's today (or last night). He went to school with Chris this morning and checked out 18 books about self-help, Thoreau, and some other topics. Chris also has a credit of several hundred dollars from books he returned so Chris bought Jonathan some more books. He actually sounds like he has his IQ back. One of the books Chris bought him was GED prep. Jonathan said the book is thicker than the Bible.

Anyway, again it all points to mind over body. His inspiration level is soaring right now, and he sounds just fine.

Michael to Mike, Kristin and Terri

That's fantastic!!!

(You might sneak the Thoreau book away from him or he'll probably drown himself in pity.)

Is he going to be ok tomorrow when the meth withdrawal symptoms slam him? Why didn't he medicate? Intentionally?

Terri to Michael, Mike and Kristin

That is great news! Especially the GED part! Just caution him about weaning from his meds the correct way…cold turkey will send him into some severe withdrawal symptoms if he's not careful to regulate everything. But, if he is not needing the antidepressant, he might want to wean off that medication as directed, then he will only have the methadone to contend with, and he can continue the wean down process each week a few milligrams at a time.

Mike to Michael, Terri and Kristin
He would rather do it when he starts to feel like crap. That will probably be tonight. If he reads Thoreau, maybe he won't complain if he goes to jail.

Terri to Michael, Mike and Kristin
Guess I can't relate as I'm not familiar with the writings of Thoreau.

Michael to Mike, Terri and Kristin
He's a wallower, a sissy boy, somebody Hemingway probably would've enjoyed beating up.

Mike to Terri, Kristin and Michael
He went to jail because he refused to pay taxes to a government that passed laws to slaughter the Native Americans. Perhaps he was the original hippie.

Halloween, Saturday the 31st rolled around and Jonathan continued to sound good. He was at a level A-1 at the clinic, so he needed to get his methadone for the weekend. I trusted him to go by himself, but to pick me up immediately following as we had some errands to run. He left the house about 7:00 AM, so I expected him to be back no later than 9:30. At 10:00 I hadn't heard from him so I tried calling. No answer. At 10:30 he called me, sounding somewhat slurry, and told me he had rear ended someone in Hiram, past our house. I asked him why he didn't pick me up and he told me he had to meet a friend.

The accident wasn't serious, but the police could have arrested him. They didn't as Jonathan explained to the officer that he was suffering from severe anxiety and depression, and asked the officer if he could call his dad to come and pick him up. The officer had a heart and felt sorry for Jonathan; he let Jonathan call me so I could drive him home.

Although the accident wasn't serious, the damage to my car that day coupled with the light post incident a month earlier, affected the battery and the cooling system in the car. We stopped at a gas station on the way home, and the engine started smoking. Laura and I spent the rest of the day and into the early evening looking for a car, settling on one, and getting the financing approved.

One of the Halloween traditions between Remy and Jonathan was that Jonathan would always take Remy trick or treating. By the time I drove Jonathan to Ben and Ashley's that night, it was after 9:00PM and Remy was done. We visited for a while, ate a couple pieces of candy, but we could see that Jonathan was still under the medication mixture that affected his being.

November to Early December

I picked him up after work on Monday November 2 and took him to see one of his psychiatrists. Jonathan explained the effect that the combination of the Klonopin and the Methadone seemed to have on him. The doctor switched him to a different anti-anxiety medicine, and from an outward appearance that looked to be the answer. During the next several weeks many changes occurred and he seemed to be getting back to his normal self. His over sensitivity stopped. He began cleaning his room and helping with other household chores. Although he spent a lot of time in his room, he would come out each evening and socialize. We all complimented him as to how much normal and coherent he seemed. I told him I felt like I had my son back for the first time in a long time.

But this medication had its side effects. I found out later that this medicine was used in the 1960's to control and calm patients who were being held in mental institutions. Jonathan, although he didn't talk about it until later, was actually more depressed. He also suffered from severe constipation. But the most obvious side effect was the bug eyes the medication caused him to have. He could stare a hole through you while talking with him. Nobody said anything to him about this, but he began to feel self-conscious about his appearance. Yet it was good to see him seemingly have his wits about him.

With all that had happened at the Methadone Clinic, Jonathan had been dropped to an A-1. This meant that he needed to go and get his dose each day (except Sunday). We would leave the house about 5:00AM, pick up his buddy Derek, and proceed to the clinic. We had it timed where he would be one of the first 12 patients to get his meds, I'd drop him off at home, and I'd get to work about 7:00AM, a half an hour later than my scheduled starting time. Again, I thanked God for the patience and understanding of my employer.

Friday November 6

Terri to Mike
How was Jonathan last night and this morning?

Mike to Terri
Still a little depressed. He sees the psychiatrist today and he's hoping to switch to Zoloft. His therapist also left a message for him yesterday so he's calling her back. Hopefully he'll get something scheduled today. He's feeling guilty about putting me through such inconvenience and I tell him I'm not feeling inconvenienced so neither should he. It still bothers him though. I'll be with him most of the afternoon, so I'll have a chance to try and get him out of the doldrums.

Terri to Mike
I am sorry he is still feeling depressed, and hope he will have a good meeting with the therapist and the psychiatrist. I just sent you a page I looked up on Zoloft. I was about to look up the drug interaction between Zoloft and Methadone but I didn't find it yet. I will send it to you when I do. The Zoloft info clearly states a lot of the same exact side effects he is having now, and also that others should keep a very close watch on someone who is taking the drug, especially in the first few weeks.

Is Jonathan going to go camping and dirt biking with Michael and Remy this weekend? Maybe it would help him feel happier to spend time with them.

Please let me know how his appointments go.

Jonathan decided not to go camping with Michael and Remy. He wanted to stay at the house and rest. He didn't feel very good, and spent most of the time in his room.

In the meantime Terri talked with two of her friends who were acupuncture practitioners. They recommended to Terri that this treatment could help Jonathan with the overall pain and body aches he was experiencing, and gave her some guidelines as to where to find a good practitioner in the Atlanta area.

Tuesday November 10

Terri to Mike and Michael

This is the information (acupuncture benefits and practitioners in the Atlanta area) Kelli sent me this morning. Read this information when you have time.

Mike to Terri

I just scheduled an appointment with an acupuncturist on Saturday. She looks good but it'll be $85 for the first session and $65 per after that. I didn't see this email before I scheduled so I'll take a look and see what I can find from a cheaper standpoint.

Terri to Mike

Darn! That sounds pricey! Well, I'll see what I can find out today, and you could always cancel that appointment you made for Saturday, if we find someone else who won't cost so much and is a participant of one of the "Community Acupuncture Clinics" mentioned in the article. Will let you know what I find out. You didn't say…how is Jonathan feeling today?

Mike to Terri

I just checked a few places and that price looks competitive. I haven't talked to Jonathan today as I think he'll spend most of the day in bed as he's taken all his methadone and won't have any more until tomorrow.

I just got an email from Laura and her company is laying off people again. Someone who she's worked with for the last 28 years was let go.

Terri to Mike

Oh no! I'll keep my fingers crossed that Laura does not get laid off, too. That would be terrible. Sorry about her friend's situation.

Why is Jonathan out of methadone already? Was he taking more than he was supposed to? Did you check on him this morning before you left? Will he call you when he wakes up? I'm worried about him being there alone without knowing he is ok.

I'm sure those acupuncturist prices are competitive. Hopefully I will be able to get some info today.

Mike to Terri

I check on him every morning. He asked me not to wake him today because he's taken all the methadone and he knew it would be a tough day. He may sleep the entire day, don't know. His anxiety is worse when he awakens.

Terri to Mike

Why is he out of methadone? Was he taking too much?

Are you going to call the place I talked to last night? If Jonathan could go there for the week inpatient detoxing, the acupuncture would probably be very helpful after he gets all the chemicals out of his body, and it could help him with his anxiety/depression issues, along with going to regular therapy and counseling, etc. I know he is scared of not having his medication, but if he already feels like crap, what are another few days of it if it will make him well.

Mike to Terri

I'll talk to him tonight but he isn't going to go if he doesn't get his methadone. And yes, he took it all, didn't sell it.

Terri to Mike

There are no drug rehabilitation/detox programs that are going to give him methadone (or any other narcotics)...after all, that would be defeating the purpose when the goal is to help someone become drug free, not give them more.

Terri explained why Jonathan needed to admit himself and that he could overcome his addiction.

Continuing what he has been doing (though helping him in a spiritual way) has not and will not alleviate the drugs from his body. Doing the same thing over and over will only result in the exact same results over and over. Please try to convince him to get the detox that he needs to get well. A few days and all the hard part will be over for him.

I know I'm making it sound like it's easy, and I don't mean to at all....I know this could be one of the hardest things Jon's ever accomplished, but it would be a major accomplishment and give him the chance to start over and take his life in a new direction, free of drug dependency.

She then expressed her fears about losing him, and that I was the one person who could talk him into voluntarily admitting himself.

Please, Mike, I'm begging you to be tougher with him about this, lovingly, of course, just be CONVINCING, even though I know it is tough for you to do...just do it **for him**, as you are the only person he will listen to... if you are steadfast in your conviction that this is what he needs to get well, and you keep convincing him that he has exhausted all his other resources and attempts at trying to fix this himself, maybe he will finally see the light. We MUST be tough on this, Mike, PLEASE!!! I am so worried about him.... as you are.

Sorry for the novel....I am just so certain I am right on this....I have done a lot of research and had conversations with many people who know a lot more about this than we do....and I have consistently been told and have read the exact same thing over and over again...the ONLY way for someone to become drug free is to go through the very difficult task of detoxing, safely, with the help of medical professionals who know how to help the addict get through it.

Are you getting any closer to agreeing with me that things are far too out of hand at this point to take a chance of leaving things as they are?

We can't just keep watching him go further down until there is just nothing left of him to even want to try anymore...and I see him getting this way, Michael said the same....Jonathan sounds like there is nothing left but a shell of where our Jonathan used to be. I can't sit still and watch this any longer. Even at the risk of him getting angry, I still think we need to do this, for his own good, to save his life, out of love for him. He cannot do this alone...truly, he can't....we have to take charge of it in his behalf. He is not even able to think like a rational person....his thinking is too jaded on the subject because his thoughts are more concerned with the aspect of not getting narcotics.

Terri continued to reiterate the urgency of Jonathan's situation. She also reminded me of the variety of treatment centers available.

Let me know what you think about everything, please....and not just one sentence, I want details so I can really understand where you are on this....

I spoke with Terri later that evening about the acupuncture option and then talked with Jonathan about it. He wasn't very keen on the idea, and he had pointed out to me that he didn't want me spending any more money. I cancelled the appointment the next day. We also spoke of going to a hospital, but Jonathan was not ready to give up his methadone. Another option was to fill out the form 1013 that allow 2 family members to have him committed for 4-10 days. This was not something I wanted to do at this point.

Wednesday November 11

Terri to Mike

I am concerned that Jonathan is not going to therapy sessions...he had said he was willing to go at 5 days a week, remember? What happened to him getting help?

You never responded to my lengthy email about the inpatient detox programs, or about the other one I sent you the link for the rapid detox program. I sincerely do want to know where you stand on all of this, in detail. I want us to find help for Jonathan....another week has gone by now, and he hasn't really accomplished anything towards getting himself drug free except listening to the tapes and reading. I don't mean to be cynical or negative in any way...I think you can tell by my email I sent that I can't get this off my mind....I never heard back from you re: what I wrote. Just wondering....

Thursday November 12

Mike to Terri

He's a 28 year old man who will get the help when he wants it. Allow him to BE. He will be as he is supposed to be without your judgments, my judgments, or anyone's judgments.

He is making tremendous progress albeit not to what you want it to be. He is less anxious and depressed. I used to hear from him 2-4 times a day and he'd be sobbing. That's not happening anymore. His job when he moved into our house was to relax, gain composure, get professional help, and contribute with housework. He's done all this.

You mentioned yesterday that while on methadone, acupuncture treatment would be minimal. At $85 a shot, and Jonathan's MIND not set for it (remember, our minds control EVERYTHING), and him being declined his unemployment compensation, I decided to cancel the appointment.

I will not force him into a place he doesn't want to be nor will I attempt to coerce him into it.

Terri to Mike

We have allowed him to BE for many years now, and I don't think there is anything wrong with all of us doing our best (especially you, who he actually talks to) to keep trying to lovingly **convince** him (coerce seems harsher than it needs to be) and **encourage** him to be strong enough to get detoxed, in order to have his clear mind back again and have the chance to start over on a healthy track towards being a genuinely happy and productive person.

You say he is making tremendous progress, but, unless you haven't told me everything, I don't see why you are saying this. It was less than one week ago when you (and he) told me he was the most depressed and had the most anxiety he has EVER had. I'm very glad he is feeling less anxious and depressed at the moment, but he seems to go through these extreme ups and downs in cycles (in fact, I'm not convinced he may possibly have severe clinical depression/bipolar disorder himself, as there is a very fine line separating the two diagnoses). Again, I am not being negative, but just realistic.

You know this better than anyone...one day he SEEMS fine, the next he is at the bottom of the pit, and him remaining emotionally unstable like this is not making him get well. He has some good days, and, if he is lucky, maybe a couple or three in a row. But, you and I both know this is not at all true happiness, not for Jonathan and not for anyone, just barely scraping by emotionally, going through the motions, having no real joy or true happiness in his life. It is not fair, and I hope you will forgive my pursuing this constantly, but I love him with all my heart and I see this differently than you, have researched it greatly, taken the time to speak to others who know and understand these things far better than we do, and yes, Jonathan, by age definition, is a 28 year old "man", but he is not living his life as a man at all, but more like a helpless, vulnerable little boy, and it breaks my heart to see him remain this way any longer.

At what point would you ever agree that it might be time to try something different that may yield different results? (I'm not being sarcastic here; I am genuinely asking what it would take for you to change your mind on this?) I do not mean this as an insult or to be rude or unfeeling, and I hope you know this....I know better than anyone that you have tried your very best, nearly singlehandedly, especially lately, to help Jonathan. But, he is my son, too, and I do not have the advantage of influence over him that you do....as I said to you before, I know that it is not necessarily comfortable for you to go outside of your comfort zone, or even to encourage him in a way that goes against your belief that everyone can heal themselves by just willing it to happen. I am asking you to please look outside the box on this....if there was any way on God's green earth I could fix things for my son, there is nothing I wouldn't do. But, unfortunately, my hands are tied...you, on the other hand, have the power of his having a lot of respect for your opinions.

Terri explained how I was the only one to whom Jonathan would listen and she offered to take all of her vacation to come up to Atlanta and help. She pointed out how tough this would be for Jonathan, but it was his only hope for true happiness.

    I apologize if anything I say here upsets you in any way, and I reiterate, I am not insulting your thinking on things...but I am begging you to at least give this a try...yes, it has to be his decision, but MAYBE if he sees the benefits outweigh the fears, and can maybe talk to people there who do this every day, I'm sure they would be more than happy to speak to him. They were very nice when I called and bent over backwards to be helpful and compassionate. Would you agree that this would be worth the effort to at least try?
    That's all for now...I've said too much already, I'm sure, and I know you are probably angry now....I hope not, but I have to say how I feel. I am sorry, I can't help it....my motherly instinct to protect my child is just too strong for me to be idle on this. I hope you understand my feelings, too, as I always try to understand yours.
    Thanks for everything you have done and are doing, and don't ever think it is not recognized, appreciated, and respected by me. I just think it is time to do more, much harder stuff, yes, but necessary if we ever want our son back. I just can't sit back and keep watching the situation just repeat itself, and I believe Jonathan needs us to do the hard stuff for him. He may fight back but eventually I think he will give in to it, if he can just understand finally that his life without drugs will be the best thing he's done in years. It is not too late for him to take hold and get his life back without being a slave to drugs to get from one day to the next. PLEASE, Mike, will you at least try to do this?
    Thanks for listening....as for the acupuncture, you misunderstood what I meant. Dani did not say the treatments would not be very beneficial to Jon...she said they would be....but they will be MORE beneficial after the

drugs are not there anymore. For now, anything is better than nothing, as long as the price is reasonable, which is why she said to call and ask about the sliding scale participants that may or may not be listed on the website yet.

Saturday November 14

Mike to Terri

I don't expect you to change your belief, nor do I think 99%+ of the world population would believe any of this. It doesn't make me right and you wrong, or vice versa.

The most important thing or feeling for me is that of inner peace. This is not something that is attained through the world of 5 senses (wo5s), or as the Tao refers to it as the world of 10,000 things, or as The Course in Miracle refers to it as the dream or illusion. This feeling comes from within me when I feel and allow the love of God to flow through me. Unfortunately, I'm not always in this state. The trials and tribulations over the last several months have been great learning lessons to show me that this feeling needs to apply to everything, not just those things that make me happy in the wo5s.

There are certain behaviors that can bring this inner peace, and other behaviors that can bring it down.

1) Judgment – To judge in any way is to attack and when I attack, I am not demonstrating out of love. If I judge anybody because of a certain behavior, I am attacking by accusing him of making him responsible for my lack of inner peace. And I point out again that the wo5s is not where I find inner peace, I find it in myself. For example, the car that I just bought has a few things wrong with it. I spent days scheming what I would do if they didn't fix the problem; from writing nasty letters to holding demonstrations outside their car lot holding nasty and accusatory signs. It wasn't until I forgave myself for feeling this way and forgave them for taking advantage of me that I finally got my peace back. As for Jon, if I insist he get help, I am holding him responsible for disrupting my inner peace. In addition, I am attacking him by saying he's got to do this my way so that I am happy (the tough love approach), and I have judged against him as such.

2) Love – The Course teaches there are 2 basic actions that we perform. We either act out of love, or when we are not in spirit, we call out

for love. In either case, the proper response is love. To love is not to judge and when I don't judge I don't accuse Jonathan of behaving in such a way that disrupts my inner peace. I look at this as a call for love, and again the proper response is love. So how do I define that? First, I point out that I don't always respond this way. In fact, over the last few months I have responded quite the opposite many times. However I am starting to get it thanks to Jonathan and the lessons he is bringing to me. Love is patience, kindness, a willingness to let anyone follow his/her own path (non-judgment). I point out how he has come along. Two years ago he was an opiate addict. He is now by his own accord seeking methadone treatment. Several years ago he didn't know God existed and would damn Him without thinking a thing about it. He now is cutting back on his foul language, prays daily, and seeks guidance from a higher source than the wo5s. He's had his ups and downs. He suffers from depression and anxiety yet last week he saw a counselor twice and a psychiatrist. He's lost his fiancé and his transportation in the last couple of weeks. In this same period he has eliminated Klonopin, has cut his anti-depression meds in half, and cut back on the anti-anxiety meds the psychiatrist prescribed for him. He is trying to become drug free on his own.

3) Respect of all others and acceptance of whatever behaviors or actions we perceive. Again, by not judging anything we can accept all that we perceive with the love that is in us. It is arrogant, as The Course points out, to think that we know best. We have no idea, the Holy Spirit does. Jonathan is going through what he is going through to teach us all about love and forgiveness. Look at when he stole from Michael. This was a lesson for Michael to learn how to forgive and get rid of his anger. Most people won't look at it that way, but Michael forgave him and has learned a lesson in true love. Jon's done some things over the years that would cause him to be disowned in many families. Some of you have even suggested I let him go to the streets (tough love). I've come to respect how he has affected this lifetime and the lessons he has brought me. I will respect his wishes forever and stand in his corner as long as he needs me to. He brings the same lessons to all of us and it's how we decide to use our minds in response that will help determine our spiritual growth.

Like I stated early on, most people don't get this line of thinking and would judge against it saying it's nuts. Four or five years ago I would have agreed. And even over the last 3 months enough has happened to make me question this. Jonathan through his repeat actions has taught me how to love unconditionally and it is now my turn to help him down his path. When he says he wants to quit cold turkey, I'll drive him. Until that day comes, I'll hold his hand.

Tuesday November 17

Mike to Terri

Jonathan saw his counselor last night and he said they still don't click. However, they came outside together and were talking and joking. I chatted briefly and they seemed to get along fine. He told me she seems to talk down to him. She wants him to get started on a daily outpatient sequence, but he doesn't want to right now. We talked about it and I'll work with him to perhaps reconsider his thinking.

She also suggested family counseling and he agreed if it were to be only him and me with no step family. He'll talk to the psychologist tonight about it.

He went to Tiffany's last night and I haven't talked with him to see how that went. Will find out more tonight.

Wednesday November 18

Terri to Mike

I'm so disappointed that Jonathan doesn't want to participate in the daily counseling sessions, and that he is not really clicking with the counselor he is seeing. I'm sure these types of situations happen sometimes, and, after all, part of the counseling is to be completely honest. Maybe Jonathan should just come right out and ask if he could try a different counselor, and if they want to know why, he could just be honest and say that he doesn't feel like he can relate to her, plus the closeness in age, lack of similar experiences, whatever....if he is nice about it, I doubt anyone would be offended, since different personality types just relate better with certain individuals with similar commonalities and personalities.

How did things go with Tiffany's visit? I was very surprised, as I thought you had told me part of your "contract" was that Jonathan could not go over there or see her for at least a month. I hope this didn't set him back emotionally, when it seemed he was getting a little better with the depression episodes. Did Jonathan talk to you last night about how it went?

Mike to Terri

Things went fine with Tiffany. They had a very nice visit and he left her house about 10:00 PM.

His meeting with the psychologist was cancelled yesterday as she informed that he needs to see the nurse before he can see the psychologist. So he was/is trying to make an appointment with the nurse.

I also got a message from Laurie, the methadone counselor, and she informed me that Karey is supposed to call me to discuss moving Jonathan to once a week visits.

Terri to Mike

It seems Karey is his favorite, hands down. I wonder if Karey would be willing to be Jon's counselor. Does he have any assigned patients or is he just the supervisor of everyone? Is Jonathan going to ask them to continue weaning him down every week or two on the methadone?

I wonder why no one informed Jonathan that he needed to see the nurse first....hadn't he already had one appointment that was canceled with the psychologist and have a couple of conversations with her? She should have known this....that kind of thing is just so frustrating. Hope it won't delay his meeting with the psychologist for too long, as he already had to wait as it was.

What did Tiffany and Jonathan talk about? Did he say? Just curious if they had a "state of the relationship" conversation. Are they still considering themselves engaged or just friends now or what?

How's Jon's depression/anxiety now? Is he still continuing with the weaning off on those two meds?

Mike to Terri

Tiffany still wants them to get back together. Jon's not sure but didn't tell her that. They both agree he needs to continue to improve.

He's about stabilized for now with his meds. Half the dose for each. He hasn't cut back anymore at this point as he feels the anxiety and depression increase. He told me he still feels anxiety, it's just not as severe. He doesn't feel he can work yet.

Don't know what to say about the appointments other than the psychologist said she received an email that morning stating all patients must be seen by the nurse first. Perhaps a new policy.

Thursday November 19

Mike to Terri

Just spoke with Karey. He's checking with Laurie to see what they (we) have to do to get Jonathan going less than 4 times a week.

Jonathan's trying to get a hold of the nurse today. He's also trying to get a hold of Laurie. They spoke very briefly this morning but I think she wants to meet with him. I just don't know when that can happen based on car circumstances.

For the next several days Terri and I exchanged emails and talked most evenings. We discussed treatment options, costs, locations of each facility, and Jonathan's overall wellbeing. Jonathan was working hard to cut back on his medicines, make peace with his counselors, reestablish his relationship with Tiffany, and continue his spiritual growth.

Tuesday November 24

Mike to Terri, Michael and Kristin

The doctor had wanted to cut back on Jonathan's methadone dosage. When I spoke with Laurie, she said she wasn't sure. Right now Jonathan looks better than he has in months, and she wants to be sure he maintains. He has a meeting with Laurie on Wednesday, so we'll find out more then. The doctor had wanted to lower the dose by 20mg, which in Laurie's opinion is too much. So perhaps by 10mg.

The counselor cancelled his appointment yesterday, as she too said he has to see the nurse before she can see him again. He sees the nurse at 4:00 this afternoon.

Terri to Mike

Jonathan actually called me last night and I was so happy to hear from him. He said that the self-hypnosis cds had not helped him at all, though he did have one (not from the same guy) that did seem to help, or at least helped him to fall asleep easier. He said that his sleeping schedule is all messed up because he is so tired all the time that he sleeps a lot during the daytime. He told me he was feeling a little better yesterday, and that he is trying to feel better each day, but things haven't really changed too much. He said the anti-anxiety weren't really helping too much. I told him you said he was really trying hard and that we are very proud of him and his efforts, and also told him that you said he was really helping a lot around the house and that it was very appreciated. Overall, his voice sounded better than it has in a long time, and he was calm and communicative, not overly so, but definitely more than he has been in the last few months. He sounds better and that made me feel good that he is feeling better one day at a time.

I am looking forward to seeing him on the 9th. I still have no idea how I'm getting there, and really don't want to drive if I can help it. But, I'll just have to see how it goes.

Let me know how things transpire.....

On Wednesday the 25th, Jonathan had the meeting with Laurie and Karey. They both came out to the parking lot and hugged him, telling him how good he looked and sounded. Both were delighted to see he was back to the Jonathan they had grown to know and love. It was determined that his dosage would be reduced by 10mg, and he would be required to pick up his medicine 4 times a week.

Thanksgiving was on the 26th and we had a good uneventful day. Some grossly undercooked smoked turkey (courtesy of my smoking skills; I gave it to Laura so she could finish the last couple hours cooking it in the oven), a little football, and relaxation.

I had wanted to go to the weekly ACIM study group that was held on Sunday mornings at a Unity Church about 20 miles from the house. I'd been holding off because of Jonathan's condition, but this weekend I felt I could go and not concern myself about the home front. I attended and shared Jonathan's story with the group. To describe my thoughts and actions to people with common beliefs was therapeutic for me. I let the group know that I had thoroughly enjoyed myself and would return the next Sunday.

Tuesday December 1

Terri to Mike, Mike's responses in bold
Terri: Did Jonathan tell you I talked to him this past weekend?
Mike: Yes he told me about it.

Terri: He sounded good....mellow, as you said. Not happy, not sad...just complacent. I can't wait to get there! Only a week to go!
Mike: He told me that yesterday is the best day he has had. No anxiety

or depression. He went to Tiffany's last night and they got a 10' tree. He was excited when I spoke with him this morning although he hadn't slept yet so I encouraged him to go right to bed after I left for work.

Terri provided me with her travel arrangements; gift ideas for the kids; and baking arrangement requests so she could make her famous nuts and bolts.

Terri: How is everyone? Any updates?
Mike: He is scheduled to see the counselor next Monday, the psychologist next Tuesday, and the nurse any day this week to get his TB test. He is probably going to drive me to work tomorrow as he's talking about going out and finding a job.

Terri: I asked Jonathan if he'd go shopping with me after I get there and help me look for stuff for him and Remy and he said he would. That way at least I can get him something he'll actually like!
Mike: Not sure how we'll work driving arrangements. My guess is that Jonathan will take me to work and then pick me up.

The rest of the week was quiet. No emails and minimal conversations just to keep everyone up to date. Although Jonathan had his bug eyes, his speech and coherence were excellent. That is until Saturday as we were driving home from the clinic. His speech slurred a little bit at first, and got progressively worse as we continued driving. I asked him about it. At first, he said he was tired and hadn't slept much the night before. I pressed on as his speech became harder to comprehend. I accused him of going back to the Klonopin or some other medicine. He got defensive, and then finally admitted that he had taken Klonopin before we left for the clinic. One of the doctors he had seen in the past wrote a prescription for him that past Friday. We got home and he went to bed. I sat there and wondered what would happen next, knowing I wasn't going to the ACIM study group the next day.

December to The Facility

The next 10 days provided witness to some of the most bizarre and extreme behavior any of us had seen to date. Jonathan began self-medicating again, and the results were Jonathan stumbling around the house and passing out while eating, among other things. As the following week progressed, the strain on Laura, Matt, and Chris was incredible. The tension around the house could be cut with a knife. We looked forward to Matthew, Kristin, and Terri arriving later in the week to see if they might be able to help provide a solution as to what was taking place.

Sunday December 6

Jonathan slept much of the day, and when he wasn't, he stumbled to the living room to visit. His speech was slurred, and he asked me to use the car to drive to Tiffany's. I explained there was no way he was driving while he was in this condition. He argued, stating that he was fine, dozed off a few moments in mid-conversation, and angrily walked away after I insisted he wasn't driving.

He called Tiffany later that evening and made an arrangement for her to come pick him up the next day. Their plan was to spend a few days together until the family arrived from out of town and Jonathan would return to our house on Thursday.

Tuesday December 8

Jonathan called me from Tiffany's and asked that I come and get him. His speech was sluggish and he was crying. I told him I wasn't picking him up and that he couldn't come back to the house while he was in the condition he was in. We got off the phone and he was angry with me, not sure what to do.

He called his friend Zach, who picked Jonathan up to let him spend the next few nights with him. Zach's parents, who had been our next door neighbors for 10 years until they moved in 2007, saw Jonathan after he arrived at their house. They informed Zach that Jonathan could spend the night, but that he had to leave the next day. Who could blame them? Jonathan was not in his right mind.

Wednesday December 9

Zach dropped him off at our house in the early afternoon on a dismal, rainy day. Jonathan got out of the truck sobbing. "I'm officially homeless" he cried. He looked pitiful in his outfit: slippers, sweat pants, coat, and stocking cap with tears pouring out of his eyes. I knew deep within me I wouldn't let him go homeless; the tough love approach didn't work for me. I went up to him, hugged him and told him he was staying here at the house. And if not here, I would go stay with him elsewhere.

I left the house later that afternoon to pick up Terri, Kristin, and Matthew from the airport. Jonathan wanted to accompany me, but my small car allows for only 4 people to travel comfortably. Although I didn't tell him this, I also needed to explain and prepare the three of them for what they might observe during their visit.

As the four of us drove home, I described what had transpired over the last couple of days. We stopped at my house so they could visit with Jonathan, before leaving to stay with Ben and Ashley for the weekend.

We talked for a while, and Jonathan continued to stumble and speak incoherently. We finally convinced him into going to bed so he could get some rest and go shopping the next day.

Thursday December 10

Terri drove me to work so she could use my car to run some errands and visit with Jonathan. However, when she returned to my house to spend time with Jonathan, he was stumbling and needed to sleep. She told him to go to bed and she would return later in the day to take him shopping.

Terri returned to Ben and Ashley's home and spent the day visiting with them, Remy, Kristin, and Matthew. Later that day, Terri and Kristin picked me up from work and we returned to my home so that they could get Jonathan and do some shopping. Terri was going to give money to Jonathan so that he would be able to buy a few small gifts. When we arrived, Jonathan was groggy. After a couple of hours "waking up", Jonathan was dressed in his suit and ready to shop.

As soon as the three of them entered the store, Jonathan disappeared. Kristin and Terri thought nothing about it at first, as Jonathan needed to look for Christmas gifts. After 20 minutes, they searched the store and were not able to locate him. They were at the store for an hour when I called Terri to alert her that dinner would be ready in 15 minutes and that they should finish their shopping and return home. Kristin located Jonathan in the store, but he wasn't ready to leave. For the next ½ hour Terri and Kristin attempted to persuade Jonathan that it was time to leave. Finally, after threatening to leave him at the store, Jonathan got into the car. He had a plastic bag filled with gifts that he said that he purchased. Yet he had no money that we were aware of, nor was there a receipt in the bag. When I asked him if he had stolen the merchandise, he became angry and defensive. I yelled at him for getting angry, and proceeded to yell at him for not doing the chores he was to have completed earlier in the day. As he retreated to his room because I had hurt his feelings, I didn't know this would be the first of many times he would "push my buttons" this weekend.

Friday December 11

Matthew and Kristin left early in the morning to go to the hospital so that Kristin's annual heart testing could be administered. I took the day off and spent most of the day with Terri as we tried to figure out what to do about our son. We called several rehabilitation facilities during the day and researched online for any option that might be available. As the day progressed, we were unable to find anything tangible to use that might help Jonathan.

Laura got home from work in the early evening and the three of us continued to try to come up with a solution. I had received my bonus check from work, so I had a little extra money. Having spent the past few days watching Jonathan's depression, crying, and obviously being affected by his medications, I suggested that the two of us could move out into a weekly inn until we determined what the next steps would be. We agreed that was a strong possibility.

It wasn't much later when we tried a new approach, one that hadn't been discussed. Jonathan got up from his nap and went downstairs into the workshop to call Tiffany. It wasn't long before we heard Jonathan yelling and arguing. I went downstairs to see what was going on and told him to keep it down as we could hear what he was saying in the kitchen upstairs. I left him and after few moments the arguing started again. He began throwing things. I called 911 and explained the situation; what had transpired during the week and what was currently going on. The police and a medical team were on the way.

Since we didn't want Remy, who was present at the time, to be in the house when the police arrived, Matt took him to the family entertainment center. Kristin and Matthew were on their way home from Kristin's all day appointment and we redirected them to meet Matt and Remy.

As there is only one entrance into the workshop, my job was to go and settle Jonathan down and make sure he stayed down there so he couldn't escape. The police arrived after a few minutes and entered the workshop. The officer asked Jonathan how he was doing, and like a flip of a switch, Jonathan sobered up. The medical team examined him, looking for a reason to hospitalize him. They found nothing. The officer explained to Jonathan that if he didn't want to voluntarily have himself admitted, he would handcuff him and take him to jail if he had to come out there again. Jonathan told him he was fine and assured him there would be no more disturbances. The rest of the evening was quiet.

Saturday December 12

Terri, Jonathan, and I left the house at 11:00AM with a full afternoon planned. We had a trunk load of Remy's old toys to drop off at a donation center. There were also several stores we wanted to visit as some of Terri's gifts to Jonathan were to be clothes that Jonathan insisted he badly needed. Jonathan also requested that we stop at a Christian Book Store as he wanted to browse and look for presents for the family.

The first stop though was the drive through bank teller. While waiting in the line of cars, Jonathan began insisting that he be let out of the car so he could unload the toys. We explained to him that we were at the bank and the donation center was the next stop. He continued to argue that he needed to unload the car until I finally turned around and yelled, "Jonathan! Sit down and shut up! We're at the bank!"

That quieted things down for a moment and we soon proceeded to the donation center. Jonathan jumped out of the car and began to happily unload the trunk and talk with the center's employees. His mood had changed from quietly crying in the back seat of the car only moments ago to being the happiest man in the world.

Terri and I wondered silently what the rest of the afternoon would bring.

In the clothing store, Jonathan took a couple of outfits into the dressing room. He was in there for an extended period and Terri suggested that I go into the dressing room to check on him. I found him on the floor sobbing. The alarm on his phone had sounded earlier and when he looked at the message, it read "Jonathan's and Tiffany's Wedding Day." It was exactly 3 months after their original planned wedding. Today was the day they had rescheduled their wedding.

I hugged Jonathan, helped him to his feet and led him out of the dressing room. I quickly explained what had happened to Terri and she immediately consoled him. Store employees were concerned and offered to help. Terri and I explained the situation, the employees offered condolences, and Jonathan eventually regained his composure.

In less than 2 hours he had gone from gently crying due to hurt feelings, to being happy and grateful for being alive, and finally to severe depression over an event that didn't happen.

As the day wore on and we visited more stores, the unusual behavior continued. He began walking around the counters to talk with store clerks. At one point he ran out of a store with a package of socks in his hand asking me in a loud voice to get these for Remy. Our final stop was a Christian Book Store that Jonathan frequented, and we caught him stealing merchandise. Terri described what she saw in an email the following week.

> "Actually, he seems mentally ill even beyond the drug addiction, in my opinion....even when he is "normal" he has such strange behavior, the shoplifting issues, inability to think straight or concentrate, even short term memory of something that was just said or that he said to someone else. His behavior seems very bizarre and so sad, like a little old lonely man just walking aimlessly around, talking to anyone and everyone about nothing...it is alarming and shocking, uncomfortable to others the way he invades their personal space, etc. as when he walked behind the cash register and was bothering that young cashier at the department store who was clearly unnerved by his behavior...she was trying to be polite and I kept trying to get Jonathan to come back around to the customer side of the counter but he then decided to confront the poor girl and asking her if she was uncomfortable with him being there by her, putting her on the spot, embarrassing her and making himself look like a complete fool. That type of behavior is just not socially acceptable, he scares people, he is embarrassing and he doesn't even realize it because he is so out of it all the time."

After the incident at the Christian Book Store, we went back to my house. Laura was preparing dinner as we were celebrating our Christmas together that evening since Terri, Kristin, and Matthew were in town. Michael, Cherie, Joe, Ashley and Remy were on their way to the house to join in the celebration.

We ate dinner after which, at Remy's insistence, we proceeded downstairs to the Christmas Tree to exchange gifts. Throughout the gift giving, Jonathan was quiet and appeared to be depressed. Each of us in one way or another tried to cheer him up, without much luck.

After we opened our gifts, Michael and Cherie packed their car to return home. Ashley and Remy left shortly after that. Matthew and Kristin were going to stay at a hotel for the night and they began packing their gifts to take with them. Kristin noticed that a gift card she had received was missing. Someone had noticed that Jonathan was rummaging through the gifts while the others were outside saying their good-byes to those who had left. Laura and I looked through the bags of trash in hopes that the card was accidentally thrown away. We couldn't find it.

I asked Jonathan if he had taken the card. He exploded, "How could you accuse me of that!!!" He blamed Kristin for implying such a thing and I yelled at Jonathan that she hadn't, it was me asking the question. The arguments heated up and Kristin began crying. Laura was ready to call the police, and I let her know that I would take Jonathan to the hotel. Matthew tried comforting Kristin as they packed the car to leave. Kristin continued to cry as Jonathan remained furious with her. I yelled at Jonathan, letting him know that we were packing his bags and that I was taking him to a motel as his behavior wasn't to be tolerated in the house any longer.

Matthew and Kristin left, and no sooner got half way up the street before Kristin insisted that Matthew turn the car around. She couldn't leave Jonathan this way.

Matthew parked the car and Kristin opened the door and ran to Jonathan with tears flowing down her face. "We all want you to get better," she cried. "I'm not blaming you for the card. I just want you to get better! If not for me, do it for your son!"

She hugged Jonathan, crying, and Jonathan hugged her back and began crying too. They held each other for a few moments and told each other that they loved each other.

"See you tomorrow," Kristin said as she released Jonathan and headed back to the car.

In the meantime I had lost my temper and my ability to think rationally.

I yelled for Jonathan to get his things packed as we continued to argue. As he became angry, I became angrier. I scared him. He began crying as we drove to the hotel as I insisted that it was time for him to get some help!

Fortunately, Terri and Joe were with us to help calm me down.

We checked into the motel. I threw Jonathan's bags into his hotel room while Terri tried to console Jonathan. I went out to the car to wait for Terri and talk with Joe. After a few minutes, Terri came out to the car and told me that I couldn't leave Jonathan this way. He was scared and he didn't want me being angry with him. I knew Terri was right, and I had some time to simmer down. I went back into the room, apologized to Jonathan for my behavior, told him I love him, and that I would see him in the morning.

Sunday December 13

Before Jonathan went to sleep early this morning, he called Kristin and left a voicemail on her cell phone. He wanted to know if Kristin would go to church with him in the morning.

By the time Kristin listened to the message in the morning, it was too late. She called Jonathan to let him know that she and Matthew were packing to leave for the airport, but that she would stop by the motel with Terri to say good-bye.

Terri, Kristin, Matthew, and I arrived at the hotel at 11:00 AM. The knock on the door didn't arouse Jonathan, so Terri let herself in with the extra key I had. Jonathan was passed out on the bed. While she gently tried to awaken Jonathan, the three of us remained outside the room. A short time later, Terri and Jonathan came out of the room.

Jonathan hugged Kristin, exchanged an "I love you," and said good-bye. He walked over to Terri and did the same thing. We got into the car and drove off, none of us knowing that Terri and Kristin would never see Jonathan again.

During the next few days I visited Jonathan every morning and night. I had begun administering his medications a week earlier, and each morning I would drop off his daily dosage.

While in the motel he continued to force himself to stay awake and read or study, or get lost in his own world. He made out countless to-do lists. He would fall asleep where he was sitting; while eating, reading, or writing. He decorated his room with many positive affirmations in an attempt to heal himself. We went to the grocery store so that he had plenty of food to eat, and we went back to the house so he could gather some of the things he needed to live in the room.

Monday December 14

Mike to Michael, Kristin and Terri
Good Morning Everyone

I hope you who traveled got in OK last night without too much delay. It was wonderful seeing everyone this weekend, as hard as it was for all of us.

I spent some time with Jonathan last night, and his mood was depressed. He was complaining of staying in the room alone and he wanted some friends. Unfortunately, it looks like his friends are avoiding him while he is in this state. His stomach was really bothering him due to the constipation as well. I stopped by this morning to drop off his methadone and he was sleeping comfortably. I went to use his restroom and what I saw assures me he's not constipated anymore........if you know what I mean.

I have calls to make today and will keep you posted as I get information about the form 1013, and any advice I might receive.

Michael to Mike, Kristin, Terri and Cherie
Thank you.

I had further conversation with Cherie yesterday. Though we both agree it is imperative he rid his body of the drugs, we must remember that simply getting Jonathan committed (especially involuntarily) into a state run drug rehab facility won't be enough to cure him. His addiction, though very physical, is primarily spiritual and emotional/mental. Being uncooperative and unwilling to accept that particular fact leaves Jonathan extremely vulnerable to relapse (yet again) when he is released. I know the state will have programs/classes/counseling for him, but if he is of the mindset that is won't or can't help him, then it won't work (as we've seen happen for years already).

If we can all agree Jon's addiction is spiritual/emotional/mental, then we must attempt to "prove" it to Jonathan when he is released. Cherie had the idea of videotaping him while he is in his "high" state of mind, then showing it to him later once his body has been freed of the drugs. As we all know, a big part of Jon's problem is that he thinks we're all overreacting. He seems to really believe he's fine. That, of course, is the drug and the Great Deceiver within him. By later showing him how he's behaved, perhaps a breakthrough can be made. God willing. Dad, do you have a way to do this?

As for continued "education" when Jonathan is released, somehow we must convince him it's the right thing for him. If that means participating with him or forcing him to attend, then that's what we need to do. If that means placing him into a program we all believe in, then Cherie and I are prepared to help financially. Whatever the case it will most certainly mean STRICT supervision, especially if it isn't a live-in type program. I know you and Laura have reached your limits, Dad, and if that means Jonathan has to find his own place to live, that's entirely understandable and nobody would think less of you for it. But it also means Jonathan will be free to plummet back into this personal hell again, and that is likely EXACTLY what will happen.

Dad, when you speak with Jon's counselor again, please express these feelings. Let him know we've all gone through this before with Jon. He has been physically cleaned more than once, but his spiritual/mental addiction to the drugs always persists, and ultimately wins out again. If he hasn't done so already please ask him to encourage Jonathan to voluntarily commit himself. It is the best way, I believe, but it would require a certain level of humility and admission of failure on Jonathan's part.

As for the specifically spiritual side of things, Jonathan NEEDS a personal savior in his life. He NEEDS to recognize the mercy and the love and the strength he will find in Jesus Christ. Whether one agrees with Christianity entirely or not, at the very least it is a simple concept for Jonathan to grasp, that this man died to save his soul. When I speak with Jonathan about "religion" I grow frustrated because he is arrogant and haughty about who he feels God is. He ties multiple religions and concepts together to make God his own little pet. He takes the parts he likes about God and dismisses the parts he doesn't like. This is DANGEROUS!!! And I believe it is the primary factor in Jon's recent fall from grace, so to speak. We cannot, and must not, attempt to control God. Jonathan needs Christianity right now more than ever, if for no other reason than to realize that he cannot do it all on his own. Jesus Christ teaches us this many times, and it cannot be ignored. It is not simply a mind over matter principle for Jonathan, as simple or as easy as it might seem. He needs to be SAVED! I say all this to encourage all of us to expose/introduce Jonathan to Christ. Though you believe in many other concepts, Dad, you are by far the one most capable of helping Jonathan with this. If you're willing and able, please try to focus on Jesus and the Christian Bible with Jonathan. Disregard the other methods, at least for now. Sit with him and listen to the various messages I've referenced with you before. Read the entire New Testament together. Purchase a Bible study book, perhaps something focused on Jon's struggles with addiction. Your personal involvement may be the only way...I can think of no other. And at the very least I promise you a spiritual enlightenment of your own.

Michael then described a Christian based 10 month program he was familiar with through his church, and he would begin researching that option.

"Everyone, please let's strive for a plan of action before we involuntarily commit Jonathan. Without it we may be spinning our wheels (again)."

We spent the next few hours pulling up government forms to look at options to have him committed and making calls to his counselors, doctors, and psychiatrist. I arranged a meeting with Karey and suggested to Michael that he attend if possible.

Terri to Michael, Kristin and Mike
Terri replied in agreement with Michael that Jonathan needed more than a state run facility. The anger he might feel toward all of us would outweigh whatever good might be accomplished in 4 – 10 days. She located a facility about 20 miles from my house that would help with the methadone withdrawal. She explained in detail the personal hell Jonathan would be going through for the first several days. After completing the withdrawal, there would be intensive work with the staff to get to the root of the underlying mental issues. Terri also brought up a place in CA that offered a rapid detoxification program. She concluded her email....

"All the above being said, I do believe we would get the best results in doing everything possible to get Jonathan convinced and psyched up for the process of being admitted, so he will be dedicated and devoted to receiving the help. Otherwise, I don't know how it will turn out...there are no guarantees either way, I suppose...It seems he may be getting a bit closer to just finally giving in with just a little more of us being lovingly forceful, as he seems to be very much at the bottom of the pit and they say when someone finally hits rock bottom in their life is when they finally give in to getting the help they need...when all their friends, family, landlords, employers, and everyone else gives up on them and they are left with NOTHING...I think Jonathan got a very big awakening to the reality when he was forced to leave Dad's house, live alone in a motel room with no friends, no car, no job, no money, and no future unless HE makes the efforts needed to save himself (with our help)..

Voluntarily admitted or not, I talked with Dad this morning about the fact that Jon's biggest fear and his reason for being so adamant about not going into an inpatient detox program is because of his belief that the detoxing cold turkey without weaning off gradually is not just uncomfortable but more like falling into the category of downright inhumane, which is why we need to convince him HE CAN GET THROUGH IT and he won't die from it, with all the empathy and love/support to let him know he is not alone and it will be ok throughout and after the process. I think he is so vulnerable and frightened and doesn't know what to think about anything right now. Maybe if HE could finally feel like it is the right thing to do, he would go willingly so he can get himself well. He says he wants to just continue working with Karey's one year plan of weaning him off the methadone that way...if he does that, then all of those doctors/counselors need to take a serious look at the meds, dosages, and combinations of all of them that are making Jonathan unable to function like a normal person...there is no way he can get a job, ever think about driving again, or anything until this is addressed."

Mike to Terri, Michael, Kristin and Cherie
Just got off the phone with him. He's tried calling 7 places to see what they can do about his car. Only one guy seemed very helpful. He's also depressed, sounds like he may be on something, maybe not, but he definitely sounds miserable. He'll call his psychiatrist right now to see if he can get an emergency appointment. If that happens, I'll be leaving to take him.

Agreed, the 1013 is not the way to go, especially initiated by family.

Michael, please make sure Karey knows you're his brother. Mention my meeting with them tomorrow and it would be great if he invited you too.

Mike to Terri, Michael, Kristin and Cherie
I just got off the phone with Jonathan and he meets his psychiatrist at 12:30 tomorrow. I'm not sure how the timing of all this is going to work.

Michael to Mike, Terri, Kristin and Cherie
I just finished a lengthy conversation with Karey. Karey was unaware of many of the specific issues...stealing, car accidents, Klonopin abuse, etc. He has invited me to attend an already scheduled meeting with the clinic director at 8:30 tomorrow morning. He said the goal of this meeting is to discuss the need of in-patient care for Jonathan. He figures my presence and candor will better equip the staff to help Jonathan receive the help he needs. I'm getting the impression they are going to strongly encourage in-patient care, and I urged Karey to be the primary voice in this. He understands and

agrees that he may be the only one able to convince Jonathan of the benefits. (He said he also distrusted his family's recommendations when he struggled with heroin.) He mentioned in passing that they were already planning to make Jonathan come in every day for his methadone again, as they obviously were aware of some recent regression.

Dad, he would like you there if possible. And he said Jonathan is invited, but he sounded like maybe Jonathan would present barriers. I am going to see about getting the time off, and I'll touch base later.

For what it's worth, Karey admitted the state run in-patient facilities are more appropriate for someone who acknowledges the need for that type of help. He said privatized in-patient facilities usually offer better care because they maintain a strict focus and can afford more personalized attention.

Michael to Terri, Mike, Cherie and Kristin

Karey called back and said Wednesday at 8:30 works better for his staff. If you're able to come either day, that is preferred. However he said Tuesday is still possible if it's the only way you can make it. He'd really like you to be present if possible.

Please let me know and I'll get back to him.

Terri to Michael, Cherie, Kristin and Mike

Michael, thank you for calling Karey...it sounds like you were brutally honest, and I believe that type of honesty is what we all must present to each other and to the professionals working with Jon. I know Dad has tried to not disclose certain things in the past, as to avoid Jonathan's help from there being jeopardized in any way, i.e. if they found out he was selling his methadone, etc. it might make them drop him from the program completely. But, after what I saw this weekend, I believe wholeheartedly that the only hope for Jonathan now is some serious intervention with total honesty with all involved, as he seems to be going downhill faster and faster and he needs help badly, the sooner the better. Obviously, the fact that they were about to start making him come in on a daily basis again indicates that the clinic, too, is recognizing negative changes occurring, and probably until you spoke to them today, they didn't realize just how severe things were/are.

Can you find out from Karey at your meeting where the best places might be so our chances of making a difference in his life would be best served? Maybe we can figure out some type of payment arrangement with one of those places, or maybe they might be willing to do a sliding scale consideration. We won't know unless we ask.

I wish I was there to attend the meeting with you. Maybe I should have stayed longer.

Jonathan called an old friend, Jerry, that evening and asked him to pick him up and take him to church. The two of them walked into the church and suspicions arose within the clergy. I got a call a few minutes later from Tom, the Social Director of the church, asking me if Jonathan was OK, and did he need to worry about anything. I assured him Jonathan was harmless and I offered to come and get him if I needed to. He told me not to worry, they would talk with him for a while, and he'd call me back if something came up. Nothing did, and I saw Jonathan the next morning when I took his methadone to him.

Wednesday December 16

Mike to Kristin, Terri, Michael and Cherie

Let me quickly fill you in on today's meeting at the Methadone Clinic. They are all very concerned regarding the mixture of meds Jonathan is taking. They are particularly interested in talking to the psychiatrist to see what he is thinking in relation to mixing what he is prescribing with Klonopin.

We are meeting tomorrow again at 8:00. At this time Jonathan will be told:

1) He is getting Friday's dose at a reduced amount of 180 mg.
2) We will discuss his voluntary admission into a rehab clinic, located in Rome. They help methadone patients by administering the meds while the patient comes down. As you know, this is Jon's biggest fear about going into one of these places. I understand the minimum stay is 3-6 months. This gives the staff the time they need to thoroughly evaluate.

If he doesn't opt for this, he will be told that in order to continue to receive meth at the clinic, he will need to see a psychiatrist that will be referred by Karey. If the psychiatrist thinks Jonathan is suicidal or can harm someone else, he will issue the papers to have Jonathan committed.

Way behind with work so I won't go into any more detail. Let me know if you have any questions.

Terri to Michael, Mike, Terri and Kristin

This may sound "sneaky" but since you told me earlier that you are planning to tell Jonathan tonight that he doesn't have to stay where he is anymore, I would like to suggest that you don't tell him this yet, since he hates being there alone so much, if he doesn't know you are taking him out of there he might be more likely to consider the Northwest Regional idea where he can get the methadone, possibly meet some new friends and it sounds more like a place where he won't feel "locked up"...he told me again this morning that he WILL NOT go to one of those places again and that it is like being in jail. He said again that he would kill himself first before he'd go into a mental hospital (institution as he calls it). So, maybe this new one might appeal to him better since it is more of a long term place where he can settle in and perhaps it would be more thorough in his treatment program. However, I still have my doubts about him agreeing to it UNLESS he has nothing better in view than where he is at now, alone and depressed with no friends and no way to get anywhere. This is why I would suggest holding off on making him think things are going to get easier for him tonight, as I think he will feel differently once he realizes he can go back to your house where things will only go back to exactly as they are/were, most likely.

Michael to Mike, Terri, Kristin and Cherie

Dad, I didn't know you were considering bringing Jonathan home again. He shouldn't be allowed to return unless you lay down VERY STRICT ground rules, and make it known they will be enforced 100%. Any break means he's on the street that day, no exceptions, and no hotel or help of any kind this time around. THIS MUST BE HIS LAST CHANCE (if you're offering it). Otherwise it will be a never-ending cycle and he'll never stop trying to take advantage. Let me be clear on my opinion also...he should not be allowed back in with you UNLESS and UNTIL he completes the Northwest Regional program. NO EXCEPTIONS. He's your son, and you want to be the most loving father possible, so it's hard to see him "on the street," but he won't improve until he hits rock bottom. He hasn't, and he won't as long as he can come home. Please allow me to be involved with setting the ground rules if you're going to bring him home. And allow me to enforce them. I will not be flexible, even if it means he doesn't like me anymore. It is for his own good. Remember Jonathan CANNOT be trusted... not even a little bit.

And I agree with Mom, by the way. Don't let him know he has the option of coming home, especially not prior to tomorrow morning.

Cherie to Kristin, Michael, Mike and Terri

Michael...I didn't know you were sending this out. But you are so right. Letting him come home at this point is a form of enabling. Don't do it, please????

We had the meeting with Jonathan on Thursday and he agreed to go to the facility in Rome. He initially argued about having his daily dosage reduced, but quickly gave in when he saw there would be no option.

Friday December 18

Mike to Cherie, Michael, Kristin and Terri

I received a call from Jonathan at 3:45AM this morning and he informed me he was in jail for shop lifting. Bail is set at $132. I told him he is sitting in there for a while as I need to go to work as I've taken enough time off. Not to mention I was asked when all this stuff would end so I could get back to focusing on my job. I was debating what to do and how long to let him sit. After a few minutes of trying to personally judge this situation, I told myself I'll let the Holy Spirit decide. I then went off to get my Course in Miracles book to do my daily meditations and prayers. I opened to my daily lesson not knowing what it would be. It stated:

"Let all things be exactly as they are."

Talk about receiving an answer. All things will work out as they are supposed to. Could be that Jonathan couldn't consciously admit himself for treatment, so he has continued to steal as a cry to get help....I don't know.

I'll call Karey today and see what he suggests. Obviously, what are all of your thoughts? Should he be bailed out or should he stay to receive the treatment he needs.

My inclination is to let him stay in there and see what can be done to get him the psychiatric care he needs and to make him as comfortable as possible during the next month. "Let all things be exactly as they are."

Keep in mind he will probably attempt suicide if he has to stay in there. Ask yourself if you can live with that if he is successful.

I'll let you know Karey's thoughts after I speak with him. Perhaps he can pull some strings to get Jonathan to a place where he can be observed and comforted as much as possible.

Thoughts, ideas?

Michael to Mike, Terri, Kristin and Cherie

A cry for help it may be, or it may be simple mindlessness. I think a call to the jail, letting them know Jon's continued assurances that he'd kill himself if ever imprisoned, would immediately get him admitted into a psych ward of some type where he can receive at least minimal protection from himself. Or maybe it's not that simple. Surely a phone call to the jail from Karey would speak volumes, not to mention the fact he sees both a psychiatrist and psychologist and is prescribed multiple "head" medications. That should be step #1, in my opinion.

If that doesn't get him out of jail and get him the help he needs, I don't know what to do. I somewhat doubt that he'll have the guts to kill himself because he's talked about it for so long (years), yet he's never even attempted it softly (for attention). That's not to suggest we take it lightly, just something to consider.

Realistically how long would he be in jail before they released him anyway? I'm guessing they'll put him out after 4 or 5 days because it was a misdemeanor shoplifting crime, and it's not worth spending the money on it. Though I suppose it depends how Jonathan plays it...if he pleads not guilty, then it'll probably drag out.

Let's try to get him into the right facility, then go from there. My initial feelings are leaving him in jail if that doesn't work. I'll pray about it, and everyone else please do the same.

Terri to Michael, Mike, Cherie and Kristin

As soon as I am able, I am going to make a call to the jail number Dad gave me and see what kind of information I can get. If anyone makes the call first, please let me know.

She expressed her concerns about withdrawal symptoms, but was thankful he was on suicide watch.

Mike to Terri, Michael, Cherie and Kristin

When I spoke with Jonathan this morning, the jailers sounded very nice to him. Keep in mind this is Paulding County, not Atlanta or St Pete, so I think we can find some relief in that.

After I hear back from Karey and Anne (psychologist), I'll let you know what they have to say.

Mike to Michael, Cherie, Kristin and Terri

I spoke with Anne and it doesn't appear she'll be much help. She's only met with Jonathan 3 times, and she is thinking he needs to get off the drugs. She asked for a list of his meds, but I let her know that Karey is taking care of that. She then said "Just keep me posted." Haven't heard from Karey yet.

Terri to Michael, Mike, Kristin and Cherie

I spoke to the nurse who is caring for Jonathan who was VERY helpful and comforting. She told me that with all inmates who have addiction illness are given Vistaril, which eliminates all withdrawal symptoms during their detox period.

She said he is very polite, and "a very sweet and pleasant young man" and has not been crying, acting depressed, or acting out in any way at all. She said he is remaining very calm, seems to be comfortable, is sleeping a lot, but is very cooperative and is eating.

She said he is in good hands, is being well taken care of, and treated with kindness and respect, and we should not worry about it.

So, now the question is, should we let him continue his detox right where he is or try to get him transferred to a facility for continued mental health? Either way, he will be detoxed.

She said the Vistaril works absolute wonders on ALL addicts, no matter how severe or what drugs they are addicted to…amazing that no one ever mentioned this to us before. What do you all think about all of this?

Michael to Cherie, Terri, Kristin and Mike

If he is receiving adequate care in jail…not to sound harsh, insensitive, or sarcastic…but you do the crime, you do the time. This could be an awakening for many aspects of his life. If he hates jail as he has always stated, and continues to hate it just as much, this may be a valuable lesson about the idiocy and ignorance of being a criminal, however petty he may have been. Unless the medical care becomes inadequate, I think he should remain there and grow up (hopefully). But I encourage you or Dad to caution the nurse against the use (and Jon's abuse) of Klonopin.

This may be worth talking about now. If Jonathan stays in jail, or wherever he ends up, I think it might not be a good idea to visit him. It's certainly not the "nice" thing to do, but he might realize nobody is interested in him or his behavior if nobody visits. Maybe he'll realize he needs to fix himself before anybody cares to speak to him again. That, too, could prove beneficial to his maturation.

Remember jail is a form of rehabilitation also. Time for Jonathan to grow up, and this just might do it.

Terri continued to look for places for Jonathan over the weekend. She located a place 25 miles from my house that looked to offer everything we were looking for. Dual diagnosis, trained staff and a doctor to assist with withdrawal, holistic treatment, financial flexibility, and a nice apartment setting to live in.

Sunday December 20

Terri to Mike, Michael and Kristin

I spent a great deal of time talking to one of the intake counselors this morning and I have a very strong instinct that this is the program that Jonathan needs.

At this very moment, he is gathering information to get grant funding to help us to have all of this in place by Monday so that Jonathan can go directly from his jail release and immediately into their hands. He is trying to get information from their IT person to try to do a conference phone meeting with all of us today. In the meantime, he may have to speak to all of us individually. I have given him all of the history and information about Jon's situation, as well as an idea of the entire family dynamics and how this has affected all of us, where we are all located, the financial concerns, etc.

His name is Ed and his phone number is 770-555-3371. He is located in Norcross, GA. He would like to hear from all of you today. Please, Mike and Michael, call him at your earliest convenience. Kristin, you are welcome to call, as well, or I can pass on the information to you if you are uncomfortable making the call. However, if we are able to get a conference call set up, I will attempt to include you in the conference call, if you are available.

Time is of the essence. We are trying to get this in place BEFORE Jonathan gets released so he can go directly into their care.

Call me as soon as you can.

Terri and I spoke about the program and I agreed with her that it looked like the type of protocol that Jonathan would benefit from; Holistic in nature, with a unique weaning off process. I called Ed and we spoke at length about Jonathan's condition and a potential plan of action.

Monday December 21

Kristin to Terri, Michael, Cherie and Mike

Any new news about Jonathan? I checked out the website. It looks like a nice place that Mom and Dad are trying to get Jonathan into straight after he leaves the jail. I understand that mom and dad want to help him. We all want him to be better. But I also feel that Jonathan should be able to want to do this. If Mom or Dad make him go and Jonathan doesn't agree to it, it could get uglier later. Jonathan is a smart guy. He will find a way to get away if he doesn't like it. Let me know of any news you hear. I love you all!!!

Michael to Cherie, Kristin and Terri

I just spoke to Dad. He is on the way to pick Jonathan up from jail.

The intent is to take Jonathan to the live-in rehab facility immediately. The cost after receiving qualifying financial aid is $16000. And yes, Jonathan can conceivably walk away. However Dad has assured Jonathan he will not have a place to stay if he leaves. You're right...Jonathan must be clear this is what he wants and needs, not what he's doing to temporarily satisfy our desires to see him get better. It's a very tough decision.

Jonathan was released and sentenced to 1 year probation. Prior to going in front of the judge, I spoke with the Public Defender about Jonathan's recent history. I asked the PD to recommend probation so that his case would remain in the court system. The PD looked at me and explained his job was to defend Jonathan and obtain the most minimum sentence possible. Jonathan's first time misdemeanor would result in a small fine and jail time already served. I again emphasized Jonathan's recent condition. The PD looked at Jonathan and asked him if he was OK with that sentence. Jonathan replied that if that's what his Dad says, it's OK with him.

Tuesday December 22

Terri to Mike, Michael and Kristin

I did speak to Jonathan last night, too, prior to the time you spoke to him. I also talked to him this morning and he was very upset over the conversation with Tiffany last night so you must have caught him right after that happened. I told Jonathan he does not need to concern himself with that right now, and that he just needs to focus on getting himself well. He called several times last night and had good conversations with Ed, asked a list of questions he had, was explaining that the only reason he didn't have Dad drive him directly there was that he just needed a little time to organize his things, pack up what he wanted to take with him, say goodbye to Remy, and "psych" himself up for this journey ahead. He was/is nervous and anxious, scared of the unknown, and has never even so much as seen a picture of this place, so Dad agreed that he had some valid points. Though we would have liked him to go directly there, even Ed, after speaking with Jonathan, knew that Jonathan just needed this little amount of personal time before he headed over there. This is why Dad dropped him off at his motel room.

I spoke to Ed late last night and he said that he and Jonathan had talked many times throughout the evening; in fact, it was Ed who Jonathan called when he needed to vent about his argument with Tiffany, and subsequently with Dad, I believe. I think he called Dad and was upset with him, too, as Jonathan didn't realize Dad had told Tiffany he was in jail and Jonathan tried to lie to her and tell her the reason he had not called her was because he'd lost his phone. He got caught red-handed in his lies and that apparently was what led to the horrible argument that just escalated from there.

Ed said last night that he and Jonathan have already developed a great rapport and he thought Jonathan was a wonderful and kind person, who seems truly grateful for this opportunity. He just needed some time to get on board with all of it, some time to ask questions and let it all absorb. Ed said he has absolutely no doubt whatsoever that Jonathan would be there today, as promised.

Now, for the update...I talked to Dad on the way to work this morning and he and Jonathan were in the car almost at The Facility. Jonathan was having some horrible withdrawal effects last night, besides the anxiety he told you about. It apparently got so severe that he had to go to the emergency room because he had severe heart palpitations and was feeling like something horrible was about to happen to him. I think he did the correct thing in obtaining medical care, as it turned out that he did have a crisis in progress with his blood pressure being 180/140 (or something like that) and his heart rate racing. They had to give him nitro and were able to get his heart stabilized again. He had a horrible migraine headache as well, and they offered him narcotics for the pain which he refused, as difficult as that was for him to do. He was very proud that he was able to say no, and when I talked to him while he and Dad were in the car this morning, he felt pretty horrible and is having horrible anxiety right now, but he sounds relieved that he is going to get the help he needs and seems to welcome it. This is huge, and quite a breakthrough so I am feeling blessed right now.

Dad and Jonathan were not supposed to be there until 11:00 this morning, but Jonathan was ready to go. They were driving around the grounds just looking and checking things out and were going to go get some breakfast while they wait for Ed to get there.

Jonathan was up all night, not feeling well, etc. but was still very appreciative, and ready to do this. Ed said last night he had the same impression in his several conversations with Jon.

Ed arrived at The Facility at 8:30 and gave us a tour. Their building had many offices, classrooms, and a large recreation area that consisted of a big screen TV, several sofas, recliners, and a massage table.

After the tour the three of us went to a conference room and listened to Ed describe what would happen during the next few days. Jonathan was to see the doctor later that day and check into his apartment after the appointment. He would accompany the other patients to the office each day and continue with his detox while he watched TV, read or received light massage therapy. After he completed the necessary detox period, he would then begin therapy.

While we listened to Ed, Jonathan was experiencing chest pains and severe headaches. We agreed that a trip to the ER was to be the first step to his rehabilitation. Jonathan and Ed got into my car and the three of us drove to the nearest hospital. As we walked to the ER entrance, Ed assured me that Jonathan was in good hands and that Ed would take care of Jonathan from that point on. I shook Ed's hand and thanked him, hugged Jonathan and told him I was proud of him, and drove off to work.

Michael to Terri, Mike and Kristin

I spoke with Jonathan momentarily a few minutes ago, and he unfortunately will be unable to see the doctor until 7:30 tonight. So he is contemplating staying in the ER until his appointment. They will figure it out together, I'm sure.

I told him I was proud of him for being open-minded enough to try this and that I look forward to him getting healthy. I told him I'd try to see him on Christmas day also. I truly am proud of him...may God bless his fragile soul.

Terri to Michael, Mike and Kristin

Thank you, Michael, and thank you for still caring for Jonathan, after all that has transpired. You are absolutely right, he is in a very fragile state right now, and I am disappointed to hear he won't be able to see the doctor this morning.

We don't want him to have any medical crises while detoxing, especially his heart. Someone does need to be monitoring his blood pressure, for sure.

Thank you for letting him know you care and that you love him and are proud of him. He needs all of our love and support now, more than ever. This is very scary for him, more than any of us can possibly imagine, I'm sure.

Kristin to Mike, Terri and Michael

I spoke with Jonathan this morning. He sounded like he was scared and anxious, but he sounded ready to face this. I told him that I loved him and that I am happy that he is finally getting the help that he needs. He told me that he appreciates me calling him and that he loves me too. Dad told me that he is going to drop Jonathan off at the ER at a hospital about 20 minutes from the place. Jonathan told me that he would be in his new apartment tonight and he will make sure to call dad and let him know the phone numbers so we can all reach him.

Terri to Michael, Mike and Kristin

Ed just called me and said Jonathan is doing fine, and they are back from the emergency room. Jon's BP was high again and they hospital gave him BP medicine to get it back down to a more normal reading, and they also gave him Ativan to help with the severe anxiety he is experiencing. Ed was with him the entire time.

Ed said he just loves Jonathan and they get along great! Jonathan seems very genuinely humble and grateful for being there, and has really opened up to Ed and feels completely comfortable with him. Ed said they had originally set Jonathan up for an immediate stay in a detox hospital they use for incoming people who are still in the beginning difficult stages of detox, in order to have nursing care by medical professionals for just such things as BP issues, etc. However, Jonathan really did not want to stay alone or in a hospital, I'm sure partially due to the bad experiences he has had with hospitals in the recent past. Jonathan has an appointment with their doctor at 7:30 tonight so he will take over his medical protocol from there. For now, Jonathan just needs to rest.

Ed was more than happy to stick by Jon's wishes and so now Jonathan is sleeping, not in his apartment, but in a special detox area that is near where Ed is located so he can be constantly checked on. Jonathan is exhausted after being up all night, as well, so Ed said he just needs to sleep right now. However, he said Jonathan is fitting right in, has been going around introducing himself to people, despite not feeling well. Ed said he knows, and he believes Jonathan knows, that this is the best thing that has ever happened to him. Jonathan is embracing the whole program sincerely and wholeheartedly and is glad to be there.

I feel like a ton of weight has been lifted from our shoulders and we can all rest easy knowing Jonathan is in great hands. I could not be any more grateful from this divine gift our family is receiving. Thank you to all of you for hanging in there, supporting and loving, even when it may have been almost more than you could bear. Everything will be good for the future; I am confident with all my heart and soul. Especially, thanks to Dad who has endured this pain on a daily basis for several months now and I want him to take care of himself now and put aside his worries, exhaustion, heartache and stress this has caused to him personally. Michael and Kristin, thank you, so much, for all you have endured and for still believing in your brother. Somewhere in there is your wonderful brother, and mine and Dad's son, and I know all of this will result in a complete transformation for Jonathan's life, actually the beginning of his life in many ways, as he probably has no concept after all these drugged years of what normal even is....I love you all. Thanks for hanging in there! I know there are good things ahead for the New Year!

The Facility

Wednesday December 23

Mike to Michael, Kristin and Terri

I just got off the phone with Jonathan and he sounded good. The van load of people with him just arrived at the main office and he had to get off the phone. Here's the update:

1) He spent the night with Larry, another counselor last night. Jonathan says he's a good guy and he made them omelets for breakfast. He said that these apartments are not that great. (He will be staying in another complex and hasn't seen them yet.)
2) He saw the doctor this morning and was given Suboxone to wean him off his addiction. He says they work pretty good and he'll continue to receive these for 10 more days. After this, the treatments will start.
3) He says this place is unusual. There doesn't appear to be a lot of regiment to their methods. They cater to their patients' needs as best they can, and are in general a bunch of very nice people who treat their patients like real people. I guess Jonathan isn't used to that, so it looks like he's being treated, as he so often preaches, how patients should be treated.
4) It doesn't look like he's going to do a whole lot as he is being weaned. He has a headache right now so I suggested he go get a neck and head massage. He's going to check into that.
5) He will need to make his own breakfasts and dinners. The van takes them out for lunch every day.

He told me he'd call later, so I'll let you know as soon as I hear from him again.

About 2 weeks had passed. The family went to visit Jonathan for Christmas. The focus during these two weeks was to get Jonathan off the Suboxone, have his teeth examined, and get prepared for the treatment. He would see the doctor every few days, and the weaning off process was taking longer than anticipated. This meant treatment would be delayed. I sent an email introducing the family to Tom, the Social Director of the church Jonathan had been frequenting, as Tom had asked me to keep him abreast. We had a few email exchanges during this period, most commenting on how well Jonathan seemed to be doing. However as the time passed, it appeared that The Facility may have been the wrong place to send him. We had been misled into believing this was a dual diagnosis facility. In fact, there was only a nurse on staff full time and an independent psychiatrist that Jonathan saw a couple of times a week. There was much turmoil going on between the staff and patients, and it seemed as though the staff lacked control of the patients. Drugs and alcohol could be found, many of the patients were using, and Jonathan was afraid to mention this to the counselors as he didn't want to be black balled by the other patients. We again began a search to locate another rehab facility. Terri emailed me a list of places she came across during her research.

Wednesday January 6

Mike to Terri

The first one looks like it might be in FL as it's licensed there. Price is $21000 if you want to check into it. Jonathan is frustrated today. There are protestors outside their facility against their beliefs and treatment methods. Also, Jonathan has heard rumors that Larry thinks Jonathan is going thru Larry's bags looking for Jon's meds.

Terri to Mike

Yeah, he just called me about 45 minutes ago and he was very upset. This situation, if accurate, is highly unprofessional for the director of the detox program to say something like that to Jonathan in the first place, especially if she asked him not to say anything to Larry. For anyone to add additional stress or heartache to him is truly upsetting to me. Now this will make Jonathan feel that Larry is not looking out for Jon's best interest, nor will Jonathan feel he can talk to him or trust him again. Also, Jonathan deserves the right to have open and honest communication and should not have to feel that he cannot talk to Larry about this. If Larry truly does think something like that, why wouldn't he come to Jonathan on his own and have a private conversation with him? I have to say I am very upset about all of this.

When Jonathan hung up, he hung up abruptly and very upset, and told me that now there were a bunch of cop cars out there pulling into his own building. He said he had to go and he'd call me back and I have not heard from him again yet.

I asked Jonathan if he wanted me to get to the bottom of things, as I will call the director of the whole place, if necessary. Jonathan is worried that they will make his life a living hell if anyone calls. This is NOT sitting well with me at all. Jonathan said when he talked to you, you told him to just forgive everybody and forget about it. Though I do think forgiveness is necessary, he should at least have the right to be spoken to honestly and not have to feel that the very place/people who are supposed to be helping him are not "on his side". The more I am hearing, the more concerned I am.

I am sincerely thinking about going ahead and calling them to find out what's going on, even without Jon's blessing. Certainly, at the very least, he is in a very critical part of his healing process and he deserves to be able to have calm, serenity, and medical professionals, as well as counselors, available to him at all times. It appears this is not happening. His very best chance of recovery is to help him stay hopeful and peaceful throughout the process, and it appears this is getting worse by the day.

We need to get to the bottom of this or get him to a different place, in my opinion. What do you think?

Mike to Terri

Perhaps give Larry a call, not mentioning the drug incident, and ask about the cops/protestors and how upsetting this is to Jonathan. Mention your motherly concern about the way he is feeling. BUT, if Jonathan asked you not to call, then I wouldn't if I were you. Remember the hospital incident and how he blamed you for his misfortune. Also remember a couple of things. Is Jonathan telling the truth? I'm not sure he's reached the point where he can be trusted completely. These people are overworked without a doubt. I'm not sure that anyplace he might go would not have the same issues. He's also going through detox, so he's going to feel crappy and irritable. He is trapped. If he leaves, he's on probation and I can't support him anymore other than a roof over his head as long as he doesn't get back into drugs.

Are you going to research that place that appears to be in Florida?

Terri to Mike

Yeah, actually I read their info to Jonathan over the phone. He called me back a little while ago. He definitely wants me to keep checking into other places, which I will do. I tried to encourage him to talk to Larry tonight himself, and I think he is going to do so.

I'm leaving work now. Talk to you later.

Thursday January 7

Terri to Mike

Hi…I was on the phone with several places last night.

Terri explained that she had found three potential places, one which was located very close to where she lived. She also talked to places in TN and in CA. Each place was dual diagnostic.

I'm still looking every chance I get. I have not heard from Jonathan anymore last night or today. Did you? Do you know if he ever talked to Larry?

Mike to Terri

I just left him a message. I talked with him last night to let him know you are checking on other places. I also pointed out that if getting his medicine promptly is the most important thing, we can go to a state funded facility. I pointed out that the patient-counselor ratio anywhere is not 1 to 1, and that he has been given an opportunity to practice patience as well as forgiveness. Also, I'm not sure what kind of picture is being painted regarding Jonathan sitting in a room with a TV. It's a huge open area where he can receive massages, read, listen to CD's, visit with other people, and actually do about whatever he wants. Many people refer to this atmosphere as vacation and look forward to it twice a year.

This place looks nice, I'm concerned about funding. The one thing about The Facility is that we've been approved.

He hadn't talked with Larry last night when I spoke with him. I think he was leaning away from confronting him.

Terri to Mike

From my understanding, Jonathan is not receiving massages, but rather something called "nerve assist" which is not massage therapy; it is a VERY light touch (designed to calm the nerves) where someone just rests their hands on your back for a few minutes, and in many cases the patient can't even feel them doing it at all. I don't think Jonathan has access to actual massage therapy or acupuncture unless it is specifically ordered by his doctor, at least according to what I was told by Ed.

I really believe that in order for Jonathan to stay where he is, all the issues of concern need to be addressed and some questions need to be answered as to why all the "secrecy" and not allowing Jonathan to participate in rehab skills and learning when he is already there anyway and is anxious to learn and move in a forward direction.

As far as Jonathan having his meds being distributed to him as ordered, he has every right to expect that. No patient should have to hunt down someone for any reasons related to their care and wellbeing.

The issue of what happened yesterday needs to be addressed, or Jonathan will never feel comfortable there again and the program will not serve him well. He can't stay in the mindset of not trusting the very people who are supposed to be helping him. He needs some answers to a few items of concern and he deserves the right to sit down with those concerned and get those things ironed out once and for all. Either his comfort level will increase or it won't, but I don't see him changing his feelings unless this happens.

Michael is also helping me to look for other places. I didn't realize that he knew nothing about any of this. I thought you and/or Jonathan had been keeping him up to date.

Oh, I understand your concern about finances, but if you were able to get approval once, you shouldn't have a problem doing it again, I wouldn't think.

Mike to Terri

I just spoke with him as he's on his way to the doctor. Keep in mind Jonathan has found fault with everyone and everything in his life for the last 6 months. He's now talking about going to a state facility....SO HE CAN GET HIS MEDICATIONS ON TIME......does this seem to be his biggest problem? When I talk to him it is. Got to go to meetings. Talk to you soon.

Terri to Mike

I'm sure that is one concern, no doubt. In fact, my guess is that his appt with the doc today will end up that he is going to start weaning off the Suboxone and maybe the BP meds. Therefore, I don't see this as Jon's primary concern. I don't hear him focusing on the drugs when I talk to him, but rather his being upset at all the unprofessionalism and disorganization, and especially the constant drama and ridiculous situations that surround him with what he believes are incompetent people who he can no longer trust.

However, I do try to take everything with a grain of salt as I do agree that Jonathan is easily able to find fault with everyone. On the other hand, if he could sit down and have a meeting with you and the director, maybe he would feel better about things once it was all addressed. I would be curious as to the answers and explanations to all the situations of concern. According to Jon, the Director won't even make herself accessible to anyone or any family members, regardless of their concerns or needs to talk to someone with authority there. I am only going by what Jonathan tells me and quite a bit on my perception of the way his voice sounds (whether sincere or manipulative) and I am fairly good at my intuitions. I hear sincerity and true disappointment and frustration coming from Jon, and I would also like to know why they are keeping him apart from the rest of the group when he is over there all day.

Mike to Terri

Perhaps you are correct. My perception, and this is no exaggeration, is that he called me multiple times daily over the last 6 months, crying, ranting, raving, etc. about the ineptitude, cruelty, or stupidity in everyone or everything. Now he is doing the same thing with coherency. I honestly don't know that sending him elsewhere will result in him feeling better. His issues are within himself and the way he looks at the world.

Terri to Mike

Would you be willing to go over there and request a meeting to discuss things and ask for more clarification of the program and address Jon's concerns so that the environment is the best it can possibly be to ensure his successful graduation into a new life? It is too important to just let this go.... maybe if Jonathan had some answers to what is bothering him, he might once again embrace the program .

What do you think?

Friday January 8

Mike to Terri, Michael and Kristin

He calls whoever will listen to him gripe in order to manipulate a situation to what he thinks will be an improvement. He's done it to me many, many times over the years. Although there may be cons, and you are only hearing Jon's side of the story, there are positives which if taken away would make him unhappy at a new place.

1) He gets to keep his phone. This is important to him and if he were to go anyplace else, it would be taken away.
2) Financing is approved. Trying to arrange for different financing may or may not be approved. If not, he's going to a state run facility.
3) The program is open ended. He can stay as long as he needs to. Other places charge additional after 30 days. No one has offered to help me pay for this and I'm not going to work until I'm 70 paying this off.
4) The people there are caring, albeit overworked. Jonathan doesn't get the answers he wants when he wants and he goes into fit. He has to deal with it. I promise you he would complain regardless of where he was.
5) We selected this place because of the success rate of the treatments. No other place offers this, and within 40 days all the crap will be out of his system.
6) Sales people from any institution are going to tell you what you want to hear. (see The Facility) What happens when he goes someplace else and he's not happy? Do you call and find him another place? He's not going to be happy anywhere. He's recovering from a drug addiction.
7) He's not going to be brain washed. People in these situations usually come from broken homes and are looking for love in one way or another. He has a supportive and loving family helping him through this. Plus, his intelligence is much too high and the spiritual effect I have on him would cause him to get my opinion on any different path he may choose to travel. And if he decides on their belief system, who are we to tell him he can't.
8) This is not a 12 step program. He has specifically stated he wanted something different than this and that is what he has. A couple of the links you sent me look like they use the 12 step as their foundation for healing.

I appreciate you being loving and concerned about what is going on. If you were to come across an open ended program that was "affordable" and offered a holistic approach to healing, I'd be more apt to exploring further.

As far as meeting with people, this sounds like something you want to do to satisfy yourself. Please arrange a conference call and I'll gladly sit in. I told Jonathan last night to check the protocol in regards to me meeting with his doctor tomorrow. He didn't sound too enthused. Does this mean he's not telling the truth about what is being told? Maybe, maybe not. Perhaps his blood pressure is 140/90, not 170/100. Maybe the doctor suggested that Jonathan go into the hospital. Perhaps Jonathan refused. Going to the hospital means losing his phone. Remember, this place lets patients make their own decisions. I talk with Ed and Larry several times a week and what they are telling me about Jon's behavior is nothing different than what I've seen over the last 6 months. He's de-toxing, miserable, and will blame anyone but himself for what he is going through. I've told him on several occasions that if I could take his pain, I would. But I can't, he's got to get through this himself.

Michael to Mike and Terri

Mom, I agree with Dad. Of course Jonathan deserves the medical attention necessary, and the fact Ed and Larry are overworked doesn't excuse any neglect that may be present, but like Dad said...we're hearing this from Jonathan, the great manipulator. I don't say that as much sarcastically as I do to remind you (and perhaps better inform you) that Jonathan does indeed modify truths to suit his wants/needs. He's done it with all of us, but perhaps mostly Dad and me more so than you. He may be telling the truth...he may be stretching the truth...he may be outright lying. I think leaving Jonathan where he is, given all the reasons Dad listed below, is what's best.

That said I do plan to call Larry today. Nothing confrontational...just calling as a concerned brother...following up, so to speak. I'll feel him out and let you both know my impressions.

Terri to Michael and Mike

I hear you both...and I agree on everything you said regarding Jon's not always being truthful and having very manipulative ways.

Terri had spoken with Jonathan the previous night and encouraged him to confront Larry. She also wanted to know more about his care, and was thankful that Michael and I would be meeting with the doctor the next day. According to Jonathan, his BP was very high and he was having problems getting his medications promptly. Terri expressed her concern over the rules and protocol of The Facility, and suggested setting up a meeting with management.

We have to make this simple for Jon...if he sees we have done all we can to fix the problems that he is having, he might rest easier...I don't know what to think. As far as the cell phone, most of the other places I talked to DO allow cell phones, laptops, and encourage communication with family members and support people. One more suggestion...Jonathan is being GREATLY influenced by Tiffany (who he texts with all day long)... and she has pointed out to Jonathan that their activities are illegal (especially the part about how they are storing/administering the meds irresponsibly, etc.)...she wants him OUT OF THERE...even to the extent that she talked to several of the doctors at her work last night and they all agreed that Jon's BP was something they would have admitted someone into the hospital for immediately.

Michael to Terri and Mike

All fine points, but I actually think Jonathan could, and possibly would, abuse blood pressure medicine, too. Not because he seeks a high, but because his answer has always been to overmedicate himself to "fix" his problem, whatever it may have been. Jonathan doesn't need those in his hands. Not yet. But yes, he should be supervised. Perhaps his blood pressure isn't as bad as he indicates, perhaps it is. If Dad is visiting with the doctor today, we'll find out for sure.

Terri to Michael and Mike

Michael, perhaps you are correct there...however, I want to know he has access to his middle of the night dosage. He would have no reason to take it if it weren't being taken to control BP, as this is the only quality it possesses.

I thought you and Dad were going to the doctor with him Saturday. Michael, if you are able to go, I would be grateful, as you are more inclined to ask specific questions and get solid answers, where Dad tends to be more passive. I so wish I were there so I could do it...but unfortunately I am not. So I have to depend on you guys.

He is desperately needing love and support and he is trying to get it from anyone he can. We should all try to stay in closer contact with him. I told Kristin to try to send him a text and say hi and let him know she is thinking of him. I have a routine of texting him every evening after I get home from work to say "can you talk?" He then calls me and we talk and he gets the chance to vent and be heard. I know Dad talks to him at least once a day, and Michael, he told me he rarely hears from you, and he misses you. If you are able, could you send him a text occasionally during the day as he really loves to hear from all of us?

We have to find a way to convince Jonathan that he is doing the right thing and somehow find the answers to his concerns so he can rest easy and move forward again. He has a huge fear of the unknown parts of the program now, where before he was fully trusting in their guidance and protocols. He just deserves to be clear on what to expect.

Michael to Terri and Mike

I just spoke with Larry for about 15 minutes. I could tell he was initially being very careful about what he said to me, but after a few minutes he opened up. Basically he believes, but cannot necessarily prove, that Jonathan is manipulating the doctor into keeping him medicated. The medication is the only thing prohibiting Jonathan from moving onto the treatment, but Jonathan has the mental addiction to it. Larry said he sat with Jonathan at the doctor once, and Jonathan began to "perform" as we have all seen him do before. He said Jonathan started feeling sick, dizzy, etc. when up to that point in the day he exhibited nothing of it. He was careful to say it COULD have been happening, but he didn't believe so. He then reminded me that the doctor is independent, and he will prescribe Jonathan medication based upon Jonathan's answers to questions, etc. Larry said the Suboxone is intended for addicts who display much greater symptoms than those Jonathan shows, and he also said Jonathan's blood pressure is checked three times daily by a nurse, and that she has never given Larry an indication that it was irregular or dangerous. He mentioned the particular blood pressure medicine Jonathan takes also has an ingredient for relieving agitation, and that it is quite conceivable Jonathan is wanting it primarily for that property alone. He also said the Suboxone will give Jonathan a mild "high", for lack of a better term, and that Jonathan may be staying on the meds simply because he's addicted to having "some kind" of medicine. Larry believes 100% that Jonathan is ready to move forward without medication, but he states Jonathan calls him regularly about getting his doses ON TIME, though Larry knows a few minutes here or there isn't going to make a difference. Larry says Jonathan is not ready because he won't stop his addiction to medication, and the doctor is the only person who can stop that. Larry also admitted that he doesn't pussyfoot around with Jonathan, and that maybe Jonathan has a negative impression of him because of it, but I did not allude to this…he admitted it freely, which to me says there is no real dishonesty existing. His example is that Jonathan often wants things his own way, but gets mad when he can't have it that way. Dad has gone through this more than anyone, so this is nothing new.

Larry is checking to see if I can visit with the doctor tomorrow also, though he didn't know anything about Dad...nor did I indicate Dad was planning to come. He did say the guy in charge of taking Jonathan to the doctor is currently in the hospital himself after having hurt himself on the ice this morning...so there is some question as to whether he'll be able to take Jonathan tomorrow or not. I volunteered to do so, if necessary, and he is checking on that also.

Long story short...it sounds like Jonathan is manipulating the doctor so he can maintain a dependence on medicine. That's probably why Jonathan wasn't thrilled with the idea of having you come, Dad. We need to encourage the doctor to push Jonathan forward unless he feels Jonathan will be doing harm to himself without the 2 medications.

Terri to Michael and Mike

How do we know for sure that this information is accurate? If there is not a nurse onsite, how can Jon's BP be checked 3 times a day? It is my understanding that there is not any medical professional there, except the nurse who monitors the patients during the treatments I, too, believe that meeting with the doctor and also with Larry and Jonathan together and get Larry to admit in front of Jonathan what he stated to you. Then, Jonathan will know that they are "on to him" and he will have the ability to try and defend himself or bring up his own issues to be open to rebuttal, if necessary. Once and for all, everything out on the table from all parties involved... complete honesty in a caring but firm way, while letting Jonathan know his best interest is at heart.

Mike, are you going to go? And, is the appointment tomorrow or today? Time for a showdown here....I would love to be a part of the meeting, too, if I can be conferenced in somehow. Is there a way you can call Larry and Ed and set up a specific meeting time for everyone while you are there, so it is scheduled in advance?

Michael to Terri and Mike

Yes it's hard to know the truth, but right now we only know of 1 person with a history of lying. The others deserve the benefit of the doubt until proven otherwise. The doctor appt. is tomorrow.

And by the way, you commented how much you think we should all be trying to talk to Jonathan and show him love daily. I disagree wholeheartedly. By consistently "showing him love" by listening to him complain and actually entertaining his stories (true or not), it is a form of pandering to his needs (however unintentional) and, in my opinion, a way for him to maintain status quo in a comfort zone of "support" instead of progressing while struggling to face his demons and tackle his actual problems...certainly the more difficult task. Without us "behind him," he might dip further into depression in the short term, but ultimately he will learn to cope and improve himself if he has any will to live/survive whatsoever. Karey made this very clear to me, and it makes perfect sense. It may have something to do with the reason The Facility doesn't want patients to keep cell phones...maybe not.

Terri to Michael and Mike

Just because he complains to us does not mean we are agreeing with him...even if it means just listening to what he says and saying as our only response "just hang in there, Jonathan... I know it is very difficult, but you can do this...this is the toughest thing you'll ever do but it will be worth it", etc. and make the conversation short...just say we are calling to say we love you and hope you are feeling better....and leave it at that.

Remember, he was (and could be still) suicidal in his thoughts/tendencies...every place I have called said it is VERY important for the person in treatment to know their family's love and support is behind them.

Jonathan admitted to me on the phone the other night that he actually attempted suicide not all that long ago...he took nearly 50 Klonopin at once in hopes he would not wake up in the morning, and was disappointed and depressed that it did not work....so, I believe Jonathan is too fragile to make him suffer more than the lovingly forceful amount that is necessary...he still needs to know we haven't given up on him...

Michael to Terri and Mike

I understand. That's the most logical answer.

But let me ask you this...how in the heck did you know about Jonathan attempting suicide and not say anything?!?!? I'm very disappointed in you (or somebody) not telling me. If that's not a clear reason to have him locked up, I don't know what is. Knowing that, I think the state facility is the best option...and against his will. When did this happen? I'm PISSED!!!

I'm leaving work shortly. Please forward any additional emails to my home email.

Terri to Michael and Mike

He just told me two days ago. I don't know when it happened, as he didn't say. But, he was telling me in the context of when he was talking to his psychiatrist about how excessively high his tolerance level is to huge amounts of drugs. He told me the doctor even agrees that he is one of the most difficult patients to detox because of this. He said he told the doctor about taking that many Klonopin at once.

I'm not 100% sure that this was not just another one of Jonathan's attempts to sensationalize his ability to ingest such huge dosages, or for him to make a point of how severe his withdrawal and detox is. "High dosages that would kill anyone else don't seem to have any effect on me whatsoever" he told me.

Jonathan was mad last night because he thought he should have been admitted to the hospital due to the BP problem and he was scared something would happen to him without nursing/medical supervision and the inability to get his BP medicine without having to wake up and anger Larry. He was very clearly upset and frustrated, as well as genuinely afraid. We have to get to the bottom of this situation tomorrow while with the doctor.

Will you please give me a call tonight so we can talk about a plan of action? I'm leaving work in a half hour and will be available after that, anytime.

Michael and I met with the doctor, Larry, and Jonathan on Saturday. The doctor spoke with Jonathan briefly to find out how he was doing. The doctor then explained to us that Jonathan's withdrawal was uncommonly lengthy due to the amount of methadone he was taking. The doctor couldn't give a definitive time frame for completing the weaning off process. We also found out that the only nurse on staff worked at the building where treatment was held several miles away. Jonathan's BP was not being monitored regularly, and when it was, it was by an available member of the staff. I bought Jonathan a BP monitor so he could watch it himself.

Monday January 11

Terri and Michael exchanged emails expressing their concerns and sharing ideas as to what the next steps might be.

In the meantime, I sent an email to The Facility.

From: Mike Dacy
Sent: Monday, January 11, 2010 9:35 AM
To: The Facility
Cc: Terri Dacy; 'Mike Dacy'
Subject: Jonathan Dacy's Blood Pressure

Good Morning,

My name is Mike Dacy and I am the father of one of your patients, Jonathan Dacy. He is withdrawing right now and taking Suboxone to help with the pain. Jonathan's brother and I met with Dr. Smith on Saturday to express our concern about Jon's BP and to discuss the treatment. Dr. Smith didn't seem to be too concerned about the blood pressure, although it was 185/98 while we were in the office.

Below is a link posted by the American Heart Association that describes a systolic pressure of over 180 as Hypertensive Crisis, Emergency Care needed.

What is being done to monitor his BP, and at what point do you consider this an emergency? He's supposed to have it taken 3 times per day and we found out on Saturday it is checked once per day. I'm concerned for his health as are the 2 people copied on this email, his mother and brother. I want to know that his welfare is of equal concern to the people watching over him during the day.

Please describe to us what is being done.

Thank you
Mike Dacy

Terri to Mike and Michael

Thanks, Mike...hopefully someone will respond back shortly. FYI, properly spelling of the drug he is taking is Suboxone.

Michael to Terri and Mike

FYI, Mom, following is the correct grammar of the sentence, "FYI, properly spelling of the drug he is taking is Suboxone."

"FYI, <u>proper</u> spelling of the drug he is taking is Suboxone."

Terri to Mike and Michael
HA! I know this...just seeing if you would notice! LOL

They answered.

> **From:** The Facility
> **Sent:** Monday, January 11, 2010 5:44 PM
> **To:** Mike Dacy
> **Subject: Re: Jonathan Dacy's Blood Pressure**
>
> Dear Mike,
> These are the blood pressures today 126/89, 114/75, 122/77. He is doing fine.
> We will keep you posted.

Tuesday January 12

Michael to Mike and Terri
The numbers look great...let's be sure to compare her numbers with the ones Jonathan gives us. And let's ask Jonathan if they actually took his BP 3 times yesterday. I guess she missed the part that says, "Please describe to us what is being done."

I spoke with Jonathan yesterday. I tried to give him encouragement about the way he was being treated...that Larry told me personally he felt Jonathan may have been manufacturing symptoms to stay medicated, but that it was based on experience, and was in no way a direct reflection on Jonathan personally. Jonathan didn't think that was excusable...he doesn't seem to understand that everybody cannot have a custom tailored plan to suit his/her needs. I had to get a bit testy with him about his negative reaction. He still refuses to acknowledge being just another addict...he has this superiority complex...you'd think 4 days in jail would've humbled him some.

He says nobody has approached him about our conversation regarding leaves of absence, but that Larry has been very responsible recently with his medication. I told him to remind Larry about the LOA's so we can plan a day together soon. I expected him to react positively to that idea, but frankly I don't think he cares anymore. He's just angry at the world despite his best efforts not to be. He won't acknowledge the simplest of compliments and he doesn't even try to be pleasant. It sure is hard not to take it personally, because it's easy to tell myself I would act differently, but none of us really knows how we'd act, I suppose...so I try to give him the benefit of the doubt about his rude/unpleasant demeanor.

He mentioned another thing that is particularly concerning, and I'm unsure if either of you have been made aware; but he says drug/alcohol abuse is rampant (he says 95%) at The Facility and that many (he says half) of the patients intentionally skip classes/treatments throughout the week because the program is not taken seriously. He says these abusers will leave at night, unsupervised and go buy drugs/alcohol to get loaded, then return and act like nothing's changed. He says he is ostracized by the others because they view him as antisocial, but he says he stays away because of their interests. He asked me not to say anything because he doesn't want to be labeled a rat, but I think it's something of which at least all of us need to be aware, if not the actual program facilitators. I encouraged him to tell Larry or Ed, if not face to face, then anonymously so they can be better prepared and can help those who obviously need it, but Jonathan says it will just make things more difficult for him. I understand...he's just trying to do his time and get healthy as quickly as possible...but so much for all his altruistic talk about helping others...it always comes back to him first, to heck with the greater good. I'm disappointed about that, but again I'll give him the benefit of the doubt. I don't know if we should say anything or not. Thoughts?

Mike to Michael and Terri

When I spoke with Jonathan last night the BP's were comparable. He said he took his 10 times and the average was 122/77.

I wouldn't say anything about what others are doing. He's mentioned this before and I've suggested that he learn from it, and focus on getting himself well. What others do should not affect Jon, although if it does, then Jonathan has another problem to deal with. If he's going to be Mr. Crabbypants, we'll all eventually stop talking with him. I only talked with him for 5-10 minutes last night and he didn't have much positive to say. And like you say, we have no idea how we'd act in his situation.

Terri to Mike and Michael

He had mentioned to me on several occasions that there were people there accessing drugs, etc. but I just figured there is bound to be some of that at all rehab facilities, as they are, after all, treating drug addicts who are very sly when it comes to finding ways to get drugs.

Terri expressed her concerns about the management and how she felt bad for

Jonathan in that he didn't feel accepted. Even Ed would hardly speak with him anymore.

Any ideas on what we can do to make things better? I know Jonathan fears repercussions about us talking to people there, but honestly we do need to know exactly what is going on and Jonathan and our family can expect to be accomplished by the time he comes out....just how to do this I don't know. This information is discouraging to me, but I know it is not up to me to decide. What do you guys think should be done, if anything?

Michael to Terri, Mike and Kristin

I don't think anything can be done. I believe they're doing everything they can with the limited resources they have available. Larry is first to admit they are stretched thin. The students/patients are adults, and are treated as such...they have free will, and if they're not going to make strides towards improvement, the administrators cannot force them. I'm guessing a forced approach would only serve to push the students away anyway...at least being passive leaves the door open for these students.

Let us not forget the spiritual side of all this. There are dark forces present amongst the masses there, and those forces will not go away. The enemy will manipulate as much as he can to maintain that darkness, and that includes affecting minds and actions. Jonathan is most certainly not excluded from this...indeed the enemy will likely work harder against Jon, and may eventually attempt to use Jon's leadership abilities to negatively influence others. Jonathan is still fighting a spiritual war...let that not be forgotten or taken lightly.

That being said, at this point it's up to Jonathan to make the best of the situation. Resources are available if he chooses to access them. If he wants to talk with someone, he can. If he wants to be alone, he can. If he wants to exercise, he can. If he wants to make a phone call, he can. If he wants to read, he can. If he wants to write, he can. Eventually when he's allowed to attend classes, he will be able. The possibilities for extending his mental health are nearly limitless if he will simply apply himself. It's ironic he compares this to jail when a more positive minded individual could see this as the most freedom Jonathan could possibly have...no responsibility whatsoever...no bills, no job, no parenting, no chores, no broken car, etc. Just Jonathan. This is probably the most freedom Jonathan will have for the remainder of his lifetime, so he'd do best to embrace that as soon as possible...of course that means he'll have to "get it," which he doesn't yet. All the more reason that this is a good program for him, because he's allowed to be there as long as he chooses, as Dad continues to reiterate. Jonathan will need the time.

I think we should do and say nothing. Wait and see. Even after treatments, he should not be allowed to retreat simply because he's physically clean and the pending classes are controversial. This must remain his only option... or the street. When he makes the best of the situation, the situation will make the best of him. I'm certain of it. I have faith in it. This opportunity is tremendous for Jonathan, not only for him, but eventually for the minds and souls of others who may be served by Jonathan's wisdom and charity...true greatness can be achieved here, if only Jonathan acknowledges/embraces the will of God.

Dad, do you have any CD's about not feeling sorry for oneself or taking responsibility for one's own actions? He could use this reminder/encouragement right about now. If he'll listen. Also I encourage both of you to read the book of Daniel and ask yourselves how the faith and thanksgiving exhibited in the story can be related and applied to the life of Jonathan. Dad if you'll ask Jonathan to read it after you're finished...talk to him about the ideals before he reads it...I'd appreciate it. He respects your perspective on religion, but I believe a strong, sometimes physically violent, spiritual barrier exists between Jonathan and me...one I have not yet been able to breach.

Then read Luke 15:11-32 for yourselves.

Terri to Mike, Kristin and Michael

Given few alternatives, if any, I'd say you are probably correct. Actually, that is an excellent positive I can see as a possibility to be presented to Jon...your words, Michael. Helping Jonathan to turn this around into a positive experience, i.e. the fact that he is able to find himself conquering the situation on his own, building pride and personal strength and character, with the help of God, even if Jonathan feels he has no one else on his side, and no matter how difficult it is, or whether he relates to any of the people are who surround him over there. He doesn't really have to agree with, or condone anyone or anything, as long as he stays focused on his own personal journey and avoid the negatives in order to do so, even if it means remaining somewhat isolated from the others there who have negative influences/energy directed in Jon's direction.

It is such a shame Jonathan has no one with whom to walk this path....he is not alone, though, and he is forgetting this, since God lifts him up all the time and Jonathan just isn't feeling/recognizing it right now (otherwise, I have no doubt he would not even be with us today after all that has transpired in his past). I truly believe with all my heart that God has a special purpose for keeping Jonathan here, and that Jonathan will, in fact, make a profound difference in the lives of others (as he does, even now) . He could sure use a mentor right now, another reason why I wish they had the ability to spend at least a little quality time with the patients on an individual basis. Larry and Ed have been through this themselves and would be the perfect people to sit with Jonathan and reinforce the positives.

Anything to get Jon's hope and faith back up where it belongs would be great. I remember when he called on Christmas day and sounded the best I have heard him in I don't know how many years....he was excited about going through the classes, even staying on and becoming a counselor there....what happened????

Michael, thanks for your wise words....In spite of what you may feel, though, I know Jonathan loves you very much and respects you, as well. You are his big brother. Your words of encouragement can do nothing but help him, so don't stop....I would suggest writing him a letter and mailing it to him, as I intend to do in the next few days. Maybe it will cheer him up to actually receive mail, and it will also be something encouraging he can read over and over again when he is feeling down.

Mike to Terri, Kristin and Michael

Well stated. He has a tremendous library of easy reading, easy listening, comprehensive reading and listening, thought provoking materials, a variety of books on different spiritual paths, Dr. Wayne Dyer's works (the person he admires most), and much more than I can possibly imagine at his disposal. I've suggested he read Dyer's book "Excuses Begone" but he doesn't want to at this time. As you state he can do anything he wants, and if he wants to be miserable, that's his choice. I point out to him often, and I know I sound like a broken record to him, when he decides to change the way he looks at things, the things he looks at will change; another way to point out the positive you describe below.

There are some websites on the book of Daniel. I'll take a look during my lunch break today.

Terri to Michael, Mike and Kristin

I just heard from Jonathan (via texting). He told me things are much worse than before. I told him we as a family all love him very much and are trying our best to do the best we can to help him, but we are all as frustrated and stressed as he is about the situation, and that he needs to know we feel the pain, too. I told him I am looking into alternative treatment programs, and I also told him I have very profound information to share with him when we are able to talk regarding what my astrologer last night revealed to me at MY appointment about my "middle child". After I gave her Jon's birth date and time for her to look further into the signs about Jonathan that she was seeing from my own chart, the planetary alignment in Jon's birth chart is at a place in 2010 that only comes along once every 30 years in one's lifetime, and whatever he chooses in his life path during this year will profoundly affect the next 30 years of his life. Of course there was a lot more detailed explanation (with her knowing nothing about Jon) regarding his perfectionist tendencies towards others, etc. Very interesting.

Wednesday January 13

Terri to Mike, Michael and Kristin

Ed called me back a little while ago and I have been on the phone with him for quite a while discussing all the issues of concern.

Ed admitted that he rarely sits down and talks with Jonathan one on one anymore, but that he had always told Jonathan he is always welcome to come and sit with him anytime. However, he did acknowledge that he has been extremely busy and that perhaps Jonathan didn't feel he could interrupt him.

I told him about all of the concerns of Jon's. He was aware that Jonathan had been "attitudinal" at times regarding receiving his medications ON TIME and having to "hunt down" Larry. For this reason, he said he, too, had felt Jonathan was still exhibiting "drug seeking" behavior, indicating that he was not far enough along in his detox yet.

I let him know that I feel Jonathan is in crisis mode and is ready to walk, is very depressed, anxious, uncomfortable, and feels he has no one to talk to, no one he can trust, and that he feels ostracized by the other students when he refuses to participate in their parties. I also told him what happened last night when Jonathan (at our encouragement) finally did go and try to talk to Larry, and what transpired afterwards, and that Larry had tried to make Jonathan give him names, etc. of the people using drugs and that Jonathan did not feel comfortable with it at all, also that Larry would not promise Jonathan to keep their conversation confidential and might even call him down to the administrators today to force him to give names.

Ed was very upset by this information and said that he was going to hang up immediately and get to the bottom of this. He found it very shocking to hear that Jonathan believes this much rampant drug usage to be happening (in fact, he, at first said there was no way that it is true)…but, as the conversation went on and he found out that Larry had gone downstairs last night and had to kick everyone out of their party and make them all go home and how Larry came upstairs and was extremely angry, slammed his door, and never even finished talking to Jonathan after he left him hanging there like that..Ed's attitude was becoming more and more concerned.

We also discussed the BP crisis issue, and again, at first he came out immediately with "oh, that's not a problem, as Jon's BP is being taken 3 times a day" (he was referring to the email that you wrote, Mike, which ended up in the Director's office) and Ed was made aware of it. But, I reminded him that the concern was not after the email, but before the email when the doctor specifically told Jonathan to make sure he received his medication every 6 hours until the BP was under control and that Larry had even told Michael that Jon's BP had been taken 3 times a day when, in fact, it had not. I told Ed that Larry had even apologized to Jon, stating that he was not aware that his BP was not being taken, and that now things have improved, but that Jonathan now also has his own BP machine, thanks to his Dad.

I also mentioned that Larry had gotten testy with Jonathan a few times that seemed perhaps underserved. Just hearing the way Larry acted last night, Ed stated that his behavior was completely unprofessional and it should not have happened. Also, he said that Jonathan should never have had to feel intimidated to go wake up Larry if necessary, even in the middle of the night if need be.

As we were hanging up, Ed thanked me for everything, said he does not want Jonathan to feel he needs to leave, and he was very disturbed about the alleged drug use…he is immediately ordering a UA (urine analysis) on every student in the place to determine who is or is not on drugs, and for those that are, there will be big problems for them…… and he is going to have a meeting with Larry and the Director today. He said he is going to have the Director call me directly this afternoon, and Ed will also call me again tonight. He was NOT happy, and I feel that being completely honest about everything was the right thing to do, as this situation has gone too far. I hope Jonathan won't be upset/angry that I had to tell Ed what I did, but I had to do what I had to do. I hope you all support me in my efforts there.

So………..it will be very interesting to see what happens now. If Jonathan is exaggerating or being untruthful about the drug use, they will know it once and for all…for everyone concerned.

Michael to Mike, Terri and Kristin

From all outward appearances, given the alleged neglect at The Facility, I believe you did the right thing. If Ed needs to hear it from me also, please let him know I'll make myself available to talk about it.

You mentioned Jon's "need" for counseling. Did Ed make any promises or offer any insight about this? Did you talk about Jon's fear of a violent confrontation with some of the patients? His reaction?

Terri to Michael, Kristin and Mike

Michael, maybe it would not hurt for you and/or Dad to call Ed, as well, and I bet he will shed some light as some time has gone by now and I bet some sh** is hitting the fan over there. I just hope Jonathan is not caught up in more drama…I don't have a good feeling now, after the text he sent last night that things have worsened. I fear that this might have caused a major shakedown over there and this was exactly Jon's biggest fear, which is why he didn't want us to talk to The Facility about any of it.

Mike to Terri, Kristin and Michael

I just got off the phone with Jonathan and left a message for Ed to see if Jonathan can come back to my house on Friday and return to The Facility on Saturday. He didn't seem too upset to me, but did describe that people are running around.

Terri to Mike, Michael and Kristin

Running around, meaning what? Did he indicate anything specific or whether Ed had talked to him yet? I wonder why he is saying things are worse than before now.

Mike to Terri, Michael and Kristin

Running around – a slang term used to describe people behaving in a disorderly fashion; to react rather than pro-act.

He left me a message last night about getting a hold of Ed again as he still hasn't called back. Jon's meds were reduced to 1.5 for the next 3 days and then 1.0 for 2 days.

Thursday January 14

Terri to Michael

Hi there, birthday boy!!

It was Michael's 33rd birthday. Michael had asked for information about the astrologer, and Terri provided it. Terri also briefly described a Christian based facility in FL that she had communicated with the night before, and was trying to arrange a conference call.

Mike to Terri and Michael

I don't really have time during the day to talk. I trust your judgment completely, and as I told you earlier, if you and Jonathan want to work to change facilities, that's fine with me. He hasn't made me aware of all the negatives like he has you.

I'm picking him up after work tomorrow so he'll get to spend some time with Tiffany and Remy. I'll need to get him back Saturday afternoon or evening. His phone may be turned off at some point today but should be restored tomorrow.

Terri to Michael and Mike

Well, if Jonathan has not been telling you the negatives, does this mean he now wants to stay where he is? I don't know what's going on. He never called me last night, so I know nothing further than yesterday when you said there were people running around and Jonathan texted me that things are much worse now than before. I told Jonathan I needed to know what was going on if he wants me to help him so I have my information accurate and up to date. I texted him last night around 10 and I haven't heard back.

I am NOT happy that Ed never called me last night as he said he would, nor did the director call me, as he said would be happening yesterday afternoon. He knew that everything I discussed with him was of urgent concern and that I was concerned about Jonathan having one bit too much and walking out the door. Apparently he is not so professional, either. Did he ever call you back? If so, did he or Jonathan or someone tell you what has transpired? Do you have anything at all to report?

Mike to Terri and Michael

Only that Jonathan didn't sound bad today. Not happy, but not depressed. I'll talk to him in detail tomorrow about the future.

I picked Jonathan up for the weekend on Friday afternoon. He was anxious to leave as we loaded the car and he was looking forward to seeing Tiffany and Remy. He was able to spend quality time with both of them.

After I dropped him off at The Facility on Sunday evening, Terri and I started a discussion that ended up in a heated argument. With all that had transpired and the tension building up, we both said some things we didn't mean.

Sunday, January 17, 2010

Terri to Mike

I have spent a great deal of time since then taking a close look at myself and just want you to know that, in spite of my feelings about all that transpired previously, it is simply not in my nature or in my heart to hold grudges or feelings that are anything but happy and healthy ones.

Please know, once you read the previous email, that it is all in the past and that all I ask is that you will please keep me updated regularly on Jonathan and his ups/downs/progress, as he will always call on you first, and, as much as I would love him to truly understand how very much I love and support him throughout this very trying ordeal, I don't feel that he will ever come to me for motherly advice. This has all been a very horrible and stressful situation for all of us; after all, addiction is truly a family disease. I know that you, more than the rest of us, have endured the heartache and vast other emotions on a daily basis for a very long time, and I give you the utmost respect and support for everything you have done.

I hope you will understand the heartache that I am enduring, as it is especially tough on me being so far away and not being on Jonathan's priority list for people to call. Therefore, I rely very much on hearing from you on a daily basis, with good news or bad news, just to stay informed of the details.

Please forgive whatever I have done or said to offend you, as this was and never will be (for future reference) intentional. It is important to me that the strength and love of our long history continues to endure the trials and tribulations that seem to be the norm in this family. We have to stick together, if only for the sake of our beautiful children, as they deserve this.

I wanted to send this to you since I am not working tomorrow and I know you will see the first email I sent when you get to your office. If you respond, please send the email to this, my home email. Again, I hope we can move on from here, as there are so many much more important issues to pray for than my feelings or soft hearted sensitivities. I only want our children to be happy and healthy, and I am counting the days and praying for no setbacks during the road to Jonathan's complete recovery. It will be one of the happiest days of my life to see him happy and whole again for the first time since so many years ago, even happier to see the transformation that will allow him to truly realize the beauty and pure joy of being the best Dad ever to that precious little Grandson of ours, who loves him so dearly and unconditionally.

I hope to hear from you as soon as you hear from Jonathan again.

Thanks for everything,

Terri

Monday January 18

Mike to Terri

Please understand I didn't mean to upset you....I didn't even want to tell you what Jonathan had told me. In no way did I mean to hurt you and I'm sorry I pushed my own buttons and got angry for a moment.

I said I love you as we were hanging up, and of course I mean it. We have a long history together, 99% of it very positive and I know it will always be that way.

Just know that I encourage Jonathan to be open and frank with you, and as he sobers up, I'm sure that whatever needs mending will eventually be mended.

This has been hard on everyone and I'm not always good at being compassionate towards others, and I appreciate your forgiveness. I'm sorry that I hurt your feelings.

Jon's relationship with Tiffany seems to be improving and his feelings for her are becoming deeper. He is struggling with the reduction in Suboxone but is seeing the doctor today to determine next steps.

I'll let you know should I hear anything today.

Mike

Tuesday January 19

Terri to Michael and Mike

Have you heard anything from Jonathan at all since you dropped him off on Sunday evening? Any news on his doctor's appointment yesterday?

Mike to Terri and Michael

I spoke with him for a few minutes last night. He's staying on 1 Suboxone for four more days and then sees the doctor again. I'll pick him up Friday again and take him to Tiffany's. He feels like crap, says he feels like he did 3 weeks ago. More withdrawal I guess.

Terri to Michael and Mike

I just texted Jonathan and asked him how things are going, and what the doc had to say. He responded "Not doing very well. The doctor was the same as always. I don't really have a plan. I still want to find another place to go. I am interested in that 28 day program by your house."

I responded to him that it appears the money has already been paid, unbeknownst to any of us, and that I don't know if refunds are an option.

Michael to Terri and Mike

Not to sound completely pessimistic, but I am curious. How do withdrawal symptoms disappear then reappear? Is it possible Jonathan is manifesting symptoms because he's feeling alone again? What happened to all the positivity? He should be starting treatment soon...things are supposed to be looking up...?

Terri to Michael and Mike

He is in withdrawal from being weaned off the Suboxone, as it, too is a narcotic and is addictive when someone is on it as long as he has had to be, which is why they try to take people off of it a lot sooner. He is down to only 1 pill twice a day now, from what I understand.

As my credit was not approved for the funding, Terri's brother Scott offered to use his good name as the applicant. Scott had given the pertinent information several weeks prior and we hadn't heard a word. We found out that 2 loans had been approved, and the money paid to The Facility. This was completed without any paperwork or notification as to how the money was being obtained.

Terri to Michael and Mike

Did Jonathan call you? He said "great!" after I told him it looked like the money has already been paid to The Facility. I think he was going to call you to find out if any portion of it can be pro-rated (refundable) because he still wants to find another place to go for the rehab.

In that case, Jonathan could finish his detox there and then go to this other place, maybe, depending on the amount of money that might be deducted if he left The Facility early. Just a thought....either way, I hope you are going to call Ed. I am thinking of calling him myself, as I was the person he initially talked to about all of this and he was downright deceitful in the way this was handled. Plus, I'm still curious to see what he has to say about never returning my phone call (or yours)...I still don't feel too great about this place.

Mike to Terri

Ed's out on vacation for the day. Jonathan called and he sounded fine to me. I let him know about the money and he seemed fine with it. He's filling out paperwork to get his LOA this weekend. The money thing doesn't look favorable.

I still contend that he won't be absolutely happy anywhere and that The Facility is open ended as opposed to limited to 28 days. But, I'm flexible.... but not rich.

The rest of the week was quiet. Each of us spoke with Jonathan almost daily, and we continued to look for other places to rehab. I picked Jonathan up for the weekend and he spent most of it with Tiffany.

Monday January 25

Mike to Terri, Michael and Kristin

Well, don't know what to think of this but Jonathan just tested positive for cocaine, meth, and benzos. He's po'd, punched a hole in the wall... update, he just called me, said he was assaulted by someone there (I find that hard to believe) told me to come and get him, I told him I wasn't, he said fine bitch (I think he meant bastard).

So, it's gonna be another fun day.

Terri to Michael, Mike and Kristin

We need to get to the bottom of this!!! I know we have to keep an open mind about Jonathan's honesty; however, there have been far too many weird situations and incompetency that has taken place over there. There is always a possibility that they made a mistake, too....so don't be too quick to judge. Also, if Jonathan's saying he was assaulted by someone, that should not be taken lightly...he may be telling the truth....and if so, he needs to report it to someone immediately, or call the police.

Michael to Mike, Kristin and Terri

Dad, don't let Jonathan screw up your job. Deal with it AFTER work. They've got to be tiring of his problems.

As for the drug test, who administered it and who gave you the results? What does Jonathan mean by assaulted?

Methamphetamines or methadone?

Mike to Michael, Terri and Kristin

Michael

Just listened to your voicemail. I haven't talked to anyone there, so thank you for checking into this. I will tell you that I asked Jonathan last night as I was driving him back to The Facility if he had taken anything. His behavior was a little off…not nearly what it had been, maybe 5% off, but enough that I sensed something. He assured me he hadn't taken anything.

A second test would be a good idea.

Good luck, let me know what you find out.

Michael to Mike, Terri and Kristin

Ok, I'll let everyone know. Larry couldn't talk just now, but said he'll call me back. We'll see.

During the next hour we received word that Jonathan's drug tests were in fact clean, no trace of anything in his body.

Terri to Michael, Mike and Kristin

I just got back from lunch. I texted Jonathan about an hour ago and asked him to call me and tell me what's going on. He texted me back and was obviously very angry…said one of the staff assaulted him and that you, Mike, would not help him, so he is leaving on his own and will just have to be homeless. Now that you found out he was, in fact, telling the truth, and that he was clean, after all, I feel very terrible about what he was accused of….I don't blame him one bit for being very angry after he has worked so hard at staying clean all this time and he has been having a horrible time there to begin with….he deserves to know that his feelings count, and that he will not be judged prematurely when he tries to tell us about a concern he has (though we know he can exaggerate, we still need to listen). I sincerely hope they apologized to Jonathan for treating him however they did that made him so upset and angry…I am sure (as we have all experience) Jonathan probably went ballistic on them trying to defend himself and his honor, probably got violent with them and who knows what might have happened. Still...I am going to try to text Jonathan again and see if he is still there. I DON'T WANT HIM TO LEAVE UNLESS WE HAVE SOMEWHERE ELSE FOR HIM TO GO.

He has come too far to quit now...but, though I know it is his choice to stay and continue to get well, I believe that everyone has their own limits as to how far they can be pushed emotionally and I am so tired of the situation there that seems to exist so much of the time. Jonathan should not have to be subjected to this day in and day out. I sincerely hope he has not left already. Has anyone got any further information since this last email?

Terri to Mike, Kristin and Michael

Jonathan just texted me and said he does not want to live anymore and he is saying goodbye.

What can we do? If he is thinking suicidal thoughts, we need to do something. He does not, after all, have a psychologist or a counselor there. I do not believe that Ed or Larry are qualified to handle a situation this severe, if in fact Jonathan is seriously contemplating this. Please, someone, tell me what your thoughts are. I am very worried.

Michael to Terri, Mike and Kristin

I just spoke to Jon, and he is fuming angry. Frankly he's being unreasonable...says he's leaving in 5 minutes. Says he's going to kill himself. Says he's doing it because Tiffany texted him that she's leaving him again. Jonathan is blaming Dad because he called her about the drugs. She is supposedly demanding a thorough drug test or she's going to leave him, blah, blah, blah. He's is incredibly irrational and overdramatic, but I do believe he might leave. He is making homicidal and suicidal threats. Ed won't answer his phone. Larry hasn't called back. Should I call the police? I don't know.

The thing about the assault is a guy named Melvin who works there apparently took swings at Jon. Who knows the truth?

While I was talking to Jon, Ed walked in and told Jonathan he doesn't care...just leave. What the?

Mike to Kristin, Terri and Michael

I've texted Tiffany today and she doesn't sound demanding to me...says she loves Jon. I do believe he's making this worse than it is, probably why Ed told him to leave. I just emailed Dr. Smith and filled him in. I'm not sure what they'll do.

Kristin to Michael, Mike and Terri

I agree with Mom I think someone needs to go over there if he is having suicidal thoughts. What's the latest news? Has he left the place? I texted him about an hour ago but he never responded back.

Terri to Michael, Kristin and Mike

I am so angry that Ed said that to Jon. If we do not step up in Jon's behalf, I am very afraid of what he might do. And, why did anyone think it necessary to call Tiffany and tell her Jonathan failed his drug test when we did not yet know the facts (as I mentioned in my first email...mistakes happen all the time in labs). Jonathan is way too fragile to be getting a text from Tiffany that even further questions his integrity when he is already fuming mad....I can't even get Jonathan to answer me anymore....he seems to have given up on every one of us now because he thinks no one cares about him. We need to keep in mind that, despite Jon's negativity, he HAS been detoxing for over a month and has gone through hell and still is! He is not like the rest of us, thinking like a rational person....his depression and anxiety issues are very severe to begin with...things like this can take him over the edge and I fear this might be happening. He needs us to be advocates for him....It does not appear that anyone at The Facility is trying to help the situation.

Mike, please don't expect Jonathan to "will" himself into being well... he is doing the best he can and has a long ways to go. He needs help and he needs help right now. If I sound overdramatic, I do not believe I am...I am being brutally realistic. Mental illness is very real...whatever happened to waiting things out and finding out the real truth first before jumping to conclusions? Jonathan needs someone to listen....and care....and yes, I'm sure he did act out in a very bad way...but remember he is not emotionally stable right now....he probably was extremely angry and hurt to have been accused of taking drugs when he did not, especially after all he has gone through while being there.

I want Dad's money to be refunded under the grounds that the relationship there is not in Jon's best interest for his mental wellbeing and we need to move him somewhere else. They have no right to keep the money and we can get him into a place that is actually professionally operated. For the moment, though, I am very concerned to the point that I am about ready to get in my car and head to Georgia. Is anyone going to go over there? That psychiatrist may be the only hope we have right now, but he needs an urgent phone call, as who knows how long it might be before he reads email? Jonathan may be gone even now.

Tuesday January 26

Terri to Michael, Mike and Kristin

I was up very late talking to Jonathan and Scott. I just called into work that I will not be in this morning. I am going to be calling the place in Clearwater and see what can be done to get Jonathan there. Meanwhile, I think I was able to calm Jonathan down enough to get him convinced that he should not do anything rash and just walk out of there. I told him to trust me, that I will do everything I can, as quickly as I can, but that I am going to get him out of there. For the moment, he needs to be the bigger person, keep to himself if necessary, do what he has been doing every day, and be the "perfect patient" in their eyes.

I told Jonathan that while he is sitting there today, I want him to write down in his own words, a list of all of the different situations that have occurred while he has been there that he feels have caused him to be unable to receive the "help" and healing that is necessary as I may need documentation describing everything that has happened.

I told Jonathan all about this place in Clearwater. They DO NOT take anyone who is not completely detoxed or is exhibiting even a slight amount of withdrawal symptoms. So, I told Jonathan he needs to stay where he is and continue the last 3 days of his medical detox, and that he needs to stay strong, have hope, and know that I am trying everything I can to help him.

Jonathan was very upset that Tiffany is not feeling comfortable with the truth of his drug test results, and she is insisting that Jonathan get a blood test to have his drug levels tested. Jonathan was crying and said that things were so wonderful with he and Tiffany, they had a beautiful weekend together and talked about their future, Jonathan had made a promise to Tiffany that he is finished with drugs for good, and Jonathan was full of hope for the future of their relationship. He insists that Tiffany has been supportive to Jonathan in his withdrawal period, and that he specifically had asked everyone in our family to NOT call Tiffany to discuss him or his treatment with her. He is very hurt and angry that Dad called her yesterday and told her that Jonathan failed his drug test and that Michael called Tiffany last night when Jonathan specifically asked him not to call her for any reason. He feels that these phone calls have served to make Tiffany now question Jonathan's sobriety and it has changed her attitude towards him because she doesn't feel comfortable trusting the situation. This is all causing Jonathan even more depression and anxiety than he was already feeling.

When I talked to him last night, he told me that before Ed drove him back to the apartment last night, someone had gone into his room and tore through it like a tornado went through there; clothes thrown out of the closet, his meditation shrine was knocked over, and his bed covers were ripped off the bed. He figures they did all of this contemplating kicking him out of there, and probably were looking for hidden drugs or something. Even after it was all said and done, he has not received a single apology from anyone.

Jonathan fully admits that he was very angry and acted aggressively in his reaction to their accusations but he never touched anyone. That staff person started getting in Jonathan's face and Jonathan told him to back off. The staff person continued, pushing Jonathan and then shoving him into a wall. Jonathan felt that they were intentionally trying to set him off enough to have an excuse to call the cops on him and Jonathan was not about to let that happen.

Anyway, Jonathan was packing all of his belongings last night and said he is leaving for sure, whether we are willing to help him get out of there or not. He says he cannot stay there, he is only asking for someone to get him out of there before he goes crazy from the stress. He is not at all saying that he does not want to go to rehab, just not there. He is beyond his tolerance level and has bypassed his emotional threshold. He was about to leave last night, even if he has to start walking and live in the woods, and he is very upset that dad won't come and get him now, even after the way he was treated yesterday. All in all, Jonathan is a very upset person right now, as you already know.

Scott has contacted the credit card companies and disputed the charges. I explained to Jonathan that these things take time, and asked him to hang in there and trust that I will be doing everything I can as quickly as possible. Meanwhile, every additional detox day he can get will help him to get into the other program faster. Jonathan said he only has a couple of days left anyway until he is completely off all meds and he feels well enough that even now he could stop taking the Suboxone and that any discomfort would be tolerable enough to get through it.

Jonathan sounded so hopeful and calmed down when we hung up and I got the feeling that he is hanging on to his last ray of hope to get the help he needs. He expressed to me that it is very important to him to have a counselor or psychologist to talk to, that his depression and anxiety is the worst right now that it has ever been and that being at The Facility has actually made him feel worse than when he first went in there. He is grateful that he has been detoxed from the drugs, but he wants proper psychological counseling/treatment and he, too, believes that he needs more intense treatment in this area.

I told Jonathan to be the "perfect patient", don't make any waves, get upset at anyone, just lay low and keep doing what he does every day. I told Jonathan not to raise any red flags whatsoever. He told me that Ed and Larry are both being complete jerks to him, all of his roommates have been kicked out, and he is VERY uncomfortable being there at all.

Right now he is staying there only at my request, as he was getting ready to leave last night. But, he will not be there long, I have no doubt about that, and I am trying to make things happen but have no idea how long this is going to take. Meanwhile, if anyone has any ideas or comments, please email me at this email, or call me on my cell phone. And, please, if anyone hears anything from Jonathan or the folks at The Facility, call me right away.

Mike to Terri, Michael and Kristin

Good job and good luck today.

Michael to Terri, Mike and Kristin

I have to say I'm really torn about helping Jonathan AT ALL. He no longer deserves it, especially from Dad.

When I spoke to Jonathan yesterday, and throughout multiple conversations I've had with him during the past several months, he has spoken angrily, with the highest level of hostility, and without a single breath of appreciation, towards Dad. Dad has done more than anyone to help Jonathan, and if Jonathan is willing to say and feel these things about Dad, then frankly I have neither the love nor obligation that a good brother should. Given the choice between a healthy and emotionally stable father or an extremely sick brother who betrays everyone he knows despite, and at the detriment of, his father, then I must choose my father alone.

As for Jonathan being angry at me about calling Tiffany yesterday, too bad. Take the blood test and prove everyone wrong. I WILL NOT give him the benefit of the doubt until/unless he deserves it. Because he's against the blood test, and because he's exhibited these exact same reactions of "insult and astonishment" that anyone would question his integrity, and because he lied about it previously (over and over), I consider him a liar and a cheat. As far as I'm concerned he is on some type of drug until he takes his blood test. Tiffany is right. Period. Imagine that...someone actually offering the tough love Jonathans desperately needs. It seems she's the only one he really cares about anyway, so hopefully he'll be a good boy and do the blood work. Besides I was calling Tiffany to ensure the situation wasn't as bad as Jonathan indicated, and sure enough it wasn't. He didn't want me calling her because he knew the truth was that he was exaggerating and lying. And no I never promised not to call her....I was actually attempting to help Jonathan yesterday because he seemed so distraught, but alas he was lying again.

I am an inch away from completely "disowning" Jonathan as my brother, and being entirely comfortable with not ever speaking to, or knowing of, him again. THAT is what Jonathan deserves. The one and only thing that keeps me from doing just that is Jesus Christ, and for Him I am humbled and ashamed about my feelings towards my despicable, detestable, ungrateful, unworthy, hateful, lying, cheating, lazy, unbrotherly, utterly embarrassing excuse of a man that is my brother.

I don't disagree that Jonathan should be removed from The Facility; however Jonathan has made it perfectly clear to both Dad and me that in his heart he'll feel 100% rehabilitated once his detox is complete in the coming days. He's told us both he doesn't need the counseling. He's telling you what you want to hear right now to help get him out of there. Don't be surprised if he attempts to trick you into staying with you at your home and tries not to enter the Clearwater program at all. Jonathan thinks he's fine. He needs involuntary lockdown because he's in denial. Still he continues to lie to us all about his real feelings. Jonathan thinks he's fine.

By the way, you'll need to consider his probation before committing to anything out of state. I hope you fully realize the box you're preparing to open. You may be the best answer for Jonathan right now, but trust me...he'll do everything in his power to pull you down to his level, including destroy your home, your relationships, your employment, your finances...whatever it takes for the enemy inside him to take control. And believe me...the enemy, a demon, Satan, whatever you want to call it is inside Jonathan. He is easy prey. And Mom please don't take this the wrong way, but your vulnerability and love for Jonathan makes you easy prey, too. Be extremely conscious and careful of this if/when Jonathan goes to Florida.

Kristin to Michael, Mike and Terri

I do agree that Jonathan should get out of this place, but I also agree with Michael about the fact that Jonathan has lied to us in the past just to get what he wants. I am afraid that he will take advantage of you, Mom, if he goes to the Clearwater place.

What will you do if you bring him to Florida and he turns on you and tries to convince you to stay with you or something?

I am just concerned. I don't know what we should do. I do believe that the place he is at right now though is no good for him. This place has done a lot of things that have been unprofessional.

Terri to Michael, Mike and Kristin

Thank you all for your responses. I have been on the phone all morning, and just hung up from my lawyer friend who specializes in fraud recovery.

After explaining the story, Terri's friend stated that it sounded like fraud.

So, I have not talked to Jonathan today, don't know if any of you have, and I am about to call the place in Clearwater and see if I can go over there and talk to them today. I do understand your concerns that Jonathan might be trying to "use" me, but I will make it quite clear to him that if he comes here he will not be staying with me but will be going into a facility to get the continuation of his road to recovery, hopefully in a professional place. The director at this program was very familiar with The Facility program. He has nothing good to say about them or their practices and said that regardless of where Jonathan goes, he needs to get out of The Facility asap.

Despite Jon's anger and hurt at all of us for not, in his eyes, standing behind him and basing our judgments on the past....he does love his family. All I can do is try my best....please support me in my efforts, if you can.

Michael to Terri, Kristin and Mike

You have my full support in this endeavor; however please understand I will not pander to Jonathan any longer. I don't wish to speak with him again until/unless he's physically and emotionally well, has taken responsibility for all his previous actions, acknowledges the efforts everyone has made on his behalf, offers appreciation for those efforts, apologizes to everyone in the family, especially you, Dad, Kristin, Laura, and Cherie, and makes strides towards becoming an independent man and a good father to his son. I mean this wholeheartedly. In fact I made the decision last night if Jonathan cowardly and selfishly took his own life; I would not attend his funeral. Jonathan, as I knew him, is dead to me already. I don't say that cruelly, but as a statement of fact.

On the other hand, I will help you with this as much as possible if you need me. Just let me know.

Kristin to Michael, Terri and Mike

I believe Jonathan is sick. He is not in his right mind. These are the drugs doing this to him and all I want is for him to get better. I support you mom, 100%. Jonathan is my brother and I hate the fact that we are not as close as two siblings should be. Michael and I don't talk very much because of our busy lives, but I still have a relationship with him. It meant so much to me to have Michael here for my birthday. I had the best brother/sister day when Michael and I went to LEGOLAND on my birthday. I hope one day that the both of us can have that kind of relationship with Jonathan again. Jonathan has been and continually will be in my prayers. I pray that he will find happiness someday and that he will be drug-free. Let me know if I can do anything. I love you all!!

Michael to Kristin, Mike and Terri

Kristin, you are the purest and most precious thing I know. Your heart is amazing. You are an inspiration. God bless you, my sister.

Mike to Kristin, Michael and Terri

It looks like I'll be picking up Jonathan tonight to get him out of there. I'm not sure if he'll stay with me or go to Tiffany's or I get him a hotel. He is desperate, certainly not the first time, and as we seem to agree, this is not the right place for him. I just spoke with Mom and she agrees he needs to get out of there pronto.

She is looking at the place in Clearwater and they have a bed open 2/2. The only issue is coming up with the initial $4900 they require, followed by the balance of $4900 within 2 weeks. I'm not sure how that will pan out.

He told me he would go over to the place in Hiram tomorrow (211) and hang out until they can help him. We'll see.

I have a couple of meetings this afternoon so I will be limited in my responses as well as limiting the amount of time I spend on the phone.

Michael to Mike, Kristin and Terri

He doesn't appreciate your help, and in fact expresses resentment towards you. Tell him to walk, then maybe he'll start to realize what alone really feels like. Maybe pick him up and drop him at a shelter...I don't know. He doesn't deserve to stay at your home. Maybe put him on a Greyhound destined for Clearwater rather than spend that same money on a hotel room. Remind him of the sentiments he expressed to me about you time and time again when he complains about not staying with you...maybe he'll start to get it. Let him know his bridge to me is crumbled. Tell him what I said. He STILL hasn't been broken to his foundation...I know it feels wrong, but this is yet another form of enabling him. He'll never grow up if he continues being babied. He must walk before he can run...in this case, literally. A child, he is.

Kristin to Michael, Mike and Terri

Thank you so much for saying that Michael. That really means a lot to me. I agree that if Jonathan ends up going to the Clearwater facility that the best way to get him there would be taking the Greyhound.

Mike to Michael, Kristin and Terri

I love you all dearly; all 3 of our children are wonderful, although one of them has a funny way of showing it and is still learning.

Jonathan just called and they want him out of there tonight to continue his detox. He can call back in a week to see if he's ready to return to the program. I wonder if they've gotten financial wind as to what's going on. Anyway, I like your idea about Greyhound Michael, I was just checking departure and arrivals to Clearwater. Terri, this may be the best, cheapest, and most convenient way to get him there.

Ironically enough, I had spoken with Jonathan earlier in the day and agreed to pick him up after work. Early that afternoon and after Jonathan and I had made pick-up arrangements, the Director and Ed called Jonathan into the office and demanded that he call me to come and pick him up. I'm not certain what kind of reaction they were expecting, but Jonathan told me later that when I said "Sure, I'll be there about 5:00 PM", Ed and the Director just looked at each other. Confused, surprised, or grateful they didn't have to argue with me, I'm not sure.

Post Rehab

Wednesday January 27

Terri to Mike
Have you talked to Jonathan today? What's going on? What's the plan? I texted him earlier but he didn't respond. Is everything working out ok so far? Are you concerned about him in any way as far as his stability at the moment?

She described some payment alternatives for admission into the Clearwater facility.

Mike to Terri
I just spoke with him. He got up late as he stayed up late cleaning his room. He talked with Ed and apologized as well as told him of the drug users. Ed appreciated it and said he was going to throw them out. Jonathan also said this is the first morning he's awakened and felt fine....no chest pain, headache, etc. Hasn't even taken Suboxone yet.

He's about to call Allstate to give his statement about the accident he had on 10/31. The person he hit, although fine after it happened, has decided to file an injury claim.

He's then going to call 211 to find out what his options are there.

I'm not at all concerned about him right now. We stayed up late (at least for me) after midnight, and had a nice long talk.

If I talk with him later, I'll tell him to check his email to check out Florida.

No idea about money or how to get another $10000.

Terri to Mike, Michael and Kristin; Mike's responses in bold
Terri: Did he call Ed or did Ed call him?
Mike: He called Ed

Terri: What is Jonathan apologizing about?
Mike: Yesterday's incident....he was being man enough to let him know he had some responsibility for what happened.

Terri: Seems more that Ed should be the one apologizing to Jon. Is Jonathan going to call the police and file a report on the guy that was pushing him around?
Mike: Don't know, forgot to ask him

Terri: I don't remember which accident was on 10/31 (one of several)…was this when he was driving your car?
Mike: Last of the accidents after he had received his methadone dose and had the mix of that and the over use of Klonopin.

Terri: I don't think I emailed the Florida info to Jon, since he usually never checks his emails. Did you forward it to him?
Mike: I have it at home

Terri: You might want to do that, if you haven't done so. Glad that Jonathan seems ok to you…I am really concerned that we don't get too complacent because he is very emotionally vulnerable. Remember, it was only two days ago that he was threatening suicide. His emotions are very unstable, and I worry the next time Tiffany and he argue again that he might go into crazy mode again, which could be disastrous…he REALLY needs to go to a good rehab program now with a positive attitude and a mind free of drugs, learn all the skills to avoid relapse, etc.

She identified other means for potentially borrowing money.

But, most importantly, this is all a moot point if Jonathan is not truly interested and wanting to attend the program. If he doesn't really care or is not acting enthused as he should be, then there is no sense in us spending the money. Obviously, any money spent will be a waste if he doesn't invest himself totally into the program. Negativity in any program, or just "going through the motions" because he is forced to be there, ultimately will not help him as designed to do. This seems to me to be a very important discussion needed with him as soon as possible.

Oh, also, you mentioned Jon's Suboxone…I was under the impression he was done with that as of today.

Mike: He actually has 2 more days and is supposed to see the doctor on Friday. He's not going to that appointment

Terri: Did he come home with more?
Mike: Yes

Michael to Terri, Mike and Kristin

Jonathan has exhibited in the past that his current proactive behavior will only last a few days, then he'll start getting lazy again and start blaming the world for his inability to improve his life. Previously that's when the particularly bad drug abuse has occurred. He will be fine today and tomorrow, maybe even Friday, but after that we'll need to be very concerned. If he's going to be admitted into a program, it must be soon because, despite his assurances to the contrary, I fully believe he will find more drugs when he begins feeling abnormally high levels of anxiety or when he perceives life isn't worth living. And seeing as he felt that way only 2 days ago, it could happen again any time. Remember, for years Jonathan has defeated his anxiety with one thing...drugs. And Jonathan believes drugs will cure anything. Be very watchful Dad, Jonathan will find drugs if he goes downhill. Your threats to kick him out won't sway him in finding and using them...they will only force him to be sneakier...don't forget the drugs are controlling his mind. Jonathan is lying when he says he has no way to get any drugs.

Michael outlined his stance on borrowing more money, and he was against it.

Look at it another way. If Jonathan truly...I mean with absolute, 100% resolve...wanted to get beyond all this and really believed he needing healing, he would be seeking all the "free" help he could possibly get...through in-patient clinics run by the state or other charitable organizations. This is how Jonathan does things...he works his TAIL off when he wants/needs something (ie: seeking church money, stealing thousands of dollars in merchandise, manipulating his friends/family into giving him money that he "swears" to pay back, etc.). This is the type of effort I want to see from him before I believe we'll see progressive and measurable progress. The fact he isn't doing this proves he's only trying to pacify us, especially Dad.

Please make Jonathan help himself. Don't do it for him. And don't ask anybody else to do it for him. He has to want it. Currently not only does he not want the inconvenience, he still thinks he's invincible and mentally strong enough to beat anything. Still the boy hasn't hit bottom because we won't let him.

Sorry for having to be the "bad" brother/son. I love you all. I don't want anybody else hurt.

Terri to Michael, Kristin and Mike

Jonathan just called me and we talked for quite a while. He is doing ok (not ready to run any marathons, he said) physically, but he said he is getting very depressed because he is just sitting there and has been trying all afternoon to request an urgent appointment to see the psychologist in the 211 program.

Contrary to the concerns you expressed, Michael, Jonathan is starting to get very anxious and more depressed over the fact that they are NOT able to see him. They said the earliest appointment time they had was on Feb 18. He explained to them that he just got out of a rehab place yesterday and that he really needs to get into a program immediately and that it can't wait for three weeks. They apologized and offered him to place his name on the cancellation list, which he did. He said he was feeling so desperate, and didn't want to take no for an answer, that he got Zack to drive him over there so he could talk to them in person. Looks like he just has to wait.

Meanwhile, I just found out from Jonathan that he has not finished the proper wean down from the Suboxone. Obviously the doctor doesn't even know that Jonathan is not at The Facility anymore. So, Jonathan only has enough medication to get him through tomorrow. HOWEVER, I thought he was down to a very minimal dose right now. He is NOT...he is still taking ¾ of a tablet (8 mg tablets) twice a day. Remember, that the total of 16 mgs a day that he was put on in the first place was at least twice as much as they give to other patients. So, he really hasn't weaned down that much at all yet. He was supposed to be weaned once again on Friday. I am very concerned, and so is Jon, that he is supposed to wean from this properly and, though he feels tolerable right now, there's no telling what would happen if he just stopped it all cold turkey. He is under medical detox orders...meaning that he is supposed to be detoxing under strict medical supervision! I am very angry to realize this now.

The longer he sits at Dad's, the more detrimental things could become. I would give anything if I could get him into this place here in Florida. However, now that I realize what he just told me about this Suboxone situation, he can't even get in there without being completely detoxed. I am just shocked to find this out. Now I am very concerned that The Facility just dropped the ball on him when he was not truly "almost finished" after all.

I am going to try to call this Dr. Smith and explain to him what is going on with Jonathan and find out what his plan was regarding Jon's wean down process. If he says it is very important for Jonathan to continue taking it at whatever dosage he thinks necessary, then we need to make sure Jonathan gets the medicine. I will see if Dr. Smith can call him in a prescription. Also, Jon's blood pressure is still not normal, and he is going to run out of that medicine too. I fear now that his detox is not as far along as we thought.

I hate to say this, but I heard a difference in Jon's voice, a little more depressed sounding, and more anxiety than I am feeling comfortable hearing. I am worried that time is of the essence to get him properly taken care of...Jonathan is afraid that Dr Smith when finding out he is not at The Facility anymore will want him admitted to the psychiatric hospital to finish his detox, and Jonathan does NOT want to do this. I can hear the fear in Jon's voice. I am sure Dad's not at work anymore to read this but I'm going to try to reach him as soon as I get off work.

Jonathan does want the help...in fact, he is desperately trying to find it....I think maybe, he, too, may be worried that he might fall backwards and he does not want to relapse any more than we want him to.....

We need to take this very seriously, in my opinion.

Thursday January 28

Michael to Terri, Mike and Kristin

I'll repeat here what I told you on the phone last night, Mom, just so Dad and Kristin know my feelings.

I touched on this very behavior in my previous email, and though I believe Jonathan wants help, he wants it ONLY if it's comfortable and acceptable to him...to hell with any alternatives (ie: the psychiatric hospital you mention below). This is the arrogance and denial I speak of. If he really wants help... REALLY WANTS HELP...he will go wherever necessary, including the least comfortable of all places. Think about it...he's going to be discussing previously ugly life experiences as well as current ones...nowhere is going to be comfortable. Personally I think the lockdown psychiatric hospital is the best place for him until/unless he is willing/able to enter a more cushy place, such as the one in Clearwater. He will get his medicine there, I presume, and he will receive therapy (both group and individual, if I remember correctly), though it's entirely up to him to make the most of it. If you let Jonathan tell it, The Facility was the absolute worst possible place he could have ever gone, so anywhere will be an improvement, right? Well...let's hold Jonathan to that and stop babying him. He needs to be a man, and humble himself enough to go wherever help is available, despite any imperfections (of which there will be many ANYWHERE he goes...we're dealing with unhealthy people, after all).

Terri to Michael, Kristin and Mike

For Michael and Kristin's knowledge (Dad and I talked last night), Jonathan was able finally to get an appointment at 211 today. Dad and I also discussed the fact that I found it extremely weird that Jonathan felt the need to call Ed yesterday and apologize to him after all that has happened there over the last few weeks. Jon's explanation was that he just wanted to do the right and noble thing, forgive, etc. since his behavior was not admirable either and he was "feeling bad" about the situation. Ok....so perhaps that is the case. However, when talking to him yesterday afternoon and asking him why he felt the need to ever have any dealings with any of them again and expressed that I was shocked that he called Ed, he further told me that he, while still at The Facility and after the last confrontation with Ed, had gone to Ed and offered his hand and apologized to him then and that Ed accepted his apology at that time. So, now I have to REALLY wonder, since he already did this, why he felt this strong need to call Ed again yesterday.

In the same conversation, Jonathan referred to situations which make him believe those people can do anything, have the power to put someone away, and he was appearing somewhat paranoid. He was seeming to get agitated just discussing it, and told me that we need to just put it in the past, not pursue The Facility or press charges against them, that there is over $10,000 at stake here. Jonathan tried to justify even that, by rattling off what the cost was for every time he went to the psychiatrist office, the high cost of the medications, the room and board, food costs, etc. and that he probably already got $10,000 worth of services anyway for the time he was there.

Bottom line Jonathan seems afraid of them. Thinking back to the confrontation with Ed when he told Jonathan he better not attempt to sue them, or he would have Jonathan put away for the rest of his life. That is a very aggressive and bold threat to Jonathan that should not be taken lightly. There has got to be a reason why, when most of us would be incensed over that threat, Jonathan feels some kind of need to be back in Ed's good graces for whatever reasons. All of this is very concerning to me.

I spent a lot of time thinking about it last night and trying to come up with a reason that makes any sense. Perhaps there is nothing Jonathan did wrong but it is possibly just downright paranoia on his part. But, my gut instinct tells me there is something major missing from this whole story. It does not all add up and it sounds suspicious. I am not trying to be cynical, just realistic. Dad said he was going to talk to Jonathan about it, and I don't know if he has or not, but Dad also said that Jonathan called him when he was out last night after visiting Remy and then at the book store, and said that he had come up with a good idea. Since Ed had told Jonathan he was kicking out those people Jonathan ratted to him about on the phone yesterday, and now that things are ok between he and Ed again, maybe Jonathan would like to consider going back to The Facility on an outpatient basis, Jon's logic being that if he did that, he would not have to stay there or put up with the drugs around him all the time, etc., etc. and he could just go there from 10 to 5 every day as an out-patient and still be able to get help from the program.

Also, Jonathan is certain that we will never get the money back anyway so he might as well use their services. This does not sit well with me at all and I don't trust Ed (or anyone there) as far as I can throw him. In thinking back to the sudden urgency when they called Jonathan in late in the afternoon to meet with Ed and the director, they ordered Jonathan to call Dad right in front of them so they could be sure he was actually calling him, demanding that Dad had to pick them up THAT NIGHT, etc., it really makes me wonder just exactly what the conversation was that took place in that room, other than what Jonathan told us about them saying his detox is taking too long, too expensive for the program to fit the bill, etc., etc. I wonder if there was something more to that whole thing, otherwise why would it be so urgent that Jonathan leave THAT NIGHT...what if Dad wasn't able to get him that quickly? They gave no 24 hour notice, nothing...just that he had to leave immediately. Of course, we all know that Dad was coming to get him anyway, but they didn't know that. The whole thing is fishy.

Any way you look at it, they basically kicked Jonathan out of the program when he was still in the midst of medical detox and was supposed to be under the supervised care of a doctor, in a controlled environment so that his health and possible medication issues could be observed at all times by a professional. What a joke! There are no professionals there! There are no employees who even have any medical background. I am willing to bet anything Ed said to Jonathan during the "apology phone call" was said to "appease" Jonathan since they probably now have gotten wind of the fact that we might cause trouble for them. They do not care about Jonathan at all! He couldn't get out of there fast enough and now all of a sudden he has a complete change of heart??

Jonathan called me this morning on my way to work...I strongly expressed my opinions and concerns about all of this, and I came right out and told Jonathan that my intuition is telling me there is something more that Jonathan is not telling us. I told him I will do everything I can to keep him from going back there, I DO NOT want him there, they are crooked, liars, deceitful, unprofessional, and I will not have someone in my family there. I also told him what the doctor at the Clearwater facility said; that we should get Jonathan out of there immediately, and that it is actually dangerous for him to be there. I tried my best to impress on Jonathan that if there is anything he is not telling us, regardless of what it is, even if he did something wrong, anything at all, I need to know the facts because if we end up having to pursue this in court, and an investigation takes place, Jonathan can't leave us sitting there with knowledge that is left out or we won't be armed to defend him if something comes up that we are not aware of. We don't need any surprises.

I assured Jonathan that if he did make a mistake, bad judgment error, even if he sold drugs, took drugs, whatever it is, it is in the past, just tell us, and we can move on…but we need to know everything. Jonathan was agitated even having the conversation at all, didn't want to talk about it, said he was getting stressed out, asked me to hold on and I waited, then he never came back to the phone. I tried to call him back and he didn't answer and I have not heard back from him. Clearly, my "pressure" or whatever way he interpreted it, was making him very uncomfortable. I do not want to cause him more stress, but at the same time I felt a strong need to speak my mind to him, as this is a very serious matter, and we may have a big fight on our hands with The Facility, and I tried everything possible to get him to tell me what's going on. He insisted there is nothing to tell. He also repeated several times that we just need to drop it, leave it alone, forget about all of it and not pursue it at all. This does not sound like something anyone would say who has experienced what Jonathan has over the last month.

I also feel very strongly that Jon, though he may seem fine to Dad (remember, Jonathan is a very good manipulator), should not be out alone at night under any circumstances, especially with Dad's car, and DEFINITELY not after Dad's in bed asleep. He needs to be monitored, he needs to be accountable constantly, especially now. He should have some very strict house rules set down, he should stop anything he is doing immediately and answer his phone when me or Dad attempt to reach him. We have every right to be concerned or worried about his whereabouts, his actions, etc. Jonathan is much too emotionally unstable. All he would need to set him off and possibly cause him to do something stupid would be a simple unpleasant conversation with Tiffany. I would suggest that if Jonathan wants to go somewhere, someone should go with him, to see Remy, to go to the store, whatever the case. Jonathan is known to make very bad judgments when his emotions are out of control, he is on probation as it is, and when he starts feeling desperate he does stupid things. He has not completed any program, had a single day of counseling or therapy of any kind, AND he is on Suboxone, which is a narcotic. Jonathan could get stopped for speeding, and once they realized he was on probation, they could really give him some problems. If they ordered a sobriety test in the form of a blood test and narcotics show up in the blood work, he could be arrested and thrown in jail for a DUI. And, God forbid, he might attempt shoplifting again. After all, he has no money. He is not well, far from it…the journey to his recovery has only barely begun. We have the right to his accountability, and he should honor and respect that and comply with ANYTHING asked from him from Dad or any of us who are helping him.

If anything I've said here sounds too harsh or judgmental, I apologize. This is not my intention. However, I spent another almost sleepless night again last night with a very bad feeling in my gut that there is a very real potential of something horrible happening at any time. I do not want to be negative in any way, just brutally realistic. There is far too much at stake to take any chances. Jonathan is too vulnerable, and in a very precarious position emotionally. He could easily get a drug craving and make a huge mistake that could cause disastrous consequences. Please keep in mind that he is ill and his rational thinking mind is not normal. Even in my conversation with Jonathan this morning, I could see his defensive and agitated ways coming out, though I will admit I was on the verge of "lecturing" to get my points about The Facility to Jon, loud and clear. I told him it would be a cold day in hell before I would EVER allow anyone I love to step foot in there or even entertain the idea. Jonathan finally said, "fine, I won't go there" but, of course, he was getting mad at me by then. I'm sure he has no desire to talk to me anymore about the subject and that is why he put me on hold and never called back. That's ok…let him think about all I said to him. I want it to sink in. I also am praying that if there is something else to this story (which I feel sure there is), Jonathan will fess up (assuming he did something wrong that he is too afraid to admit to us) and tell the whole truth rather than carry it around inside, which is not healthy for him and could be detrimental to our case against The Facility if it comes down to having to go down that avenue.

I am curious about something. Mike, when you picked up Jon, was Ed or Larry there? Was there any conversation that took place with either of them after you arrived? Just wondering, due to all the urgency of them wanting Jonathan picked up so quickly, if something major was brought up to Jonathan in that meeting they had with him, I'm curious as to whether they may have offered Jonathan that they would keep quiet about something in exchange for him leaving the premises…just a thought. However, as angry as they all were, knowing Jonathan is on probation, I would think they would have called you immediately to report something serious, or call the cops. So, I'm just thinking about this whole situation from many perspectives, playing "devil's advocate", if you will. I want with all my heart to believe that this is not really as suspicious as it seems, but I don't feel good about any of this, and I am also very concerned about Jonathan having too much freedom to drive around on his own, putting him back into a "normal" mode which he is not capable of handling. He needs to understand that, after all that has happened, he does not get to control things…if he is going to be at your house, he needs to be accountable in his every move and every action, even his every thought if he is feeling even slightly negative or feels his depression/anxiety is getting worse. He owes it to you, at least while he is there, as you are now the "caretaker" and someone needs to be responsible for keeping Jon's life in check, and Jonathan should have NO problem with this. If he does, then that attitude alone would make me question all of this, including Jon's intentions, even more. I am just saying…. don't be too naïve or trusting. He has not earned that right yet, though I want everyone to give him as much benefit of the doubt as possible, stay supportive and encouraging to his positive actions, but always one step ahead of Jonathans he is not the one in control (and as long as he is being treated with love and respect, he should have no problem understanding that we are looking out for his safety and his best interest). He should not be allowed to be anywhere but at home, especially after everyone is in bed. He can entertain himself there… he does not need to be out driving around, etc.

Sorry for the long email. As you can see, I am VERY concerned. What are everyone's thoughts or ideas?

Mike to Terri, Kristin and Michael

Larry was there. They hugged and Larry commented this isn't necessarily good-bye, that maybe they would see him in a week.

I'm about over this.

Michael to Terri, Mike and Kristin

I certainly agree with your major points, Mom. I don't think anything is necessarily fishy with Jon/The Facility, but it's definitely strange. But hey, Jon's irrational, so nothing should surprise us.

Yes, Jonathan should be accountable for every minute he's outside Dad's home. Every minute.

No, Jonathan shouldn't be allowed access to the car. C'mon Dad... Jonathan CANNOT drive...he's a crasher! Don't put yourself in that situation again. Make him ride his bike. Too bad if it's cold or rainy or far. Tell him to grow up. I had to ride my bicycle about 5 miles to/from Publix almost every day after school when Mom was up here for Kristin's first transplant. It's not so bad. Plus he needs exercise...it'll be good for him.

This is possibly unfair, but Jonathan shouldn't be allowed access to Remy. It's not good for Remy, potentially unsafe, and Jonathan hasn't earned that privilege yet. Jonathan doesn't exude anything positive, therefore Remy can only absorb various levels of negativity from him...incessant swearing, smoking, nervous behavior, etc. Remy will remember these things, and he'll be affected by them. It's unhealthy. Not to mention he's under the influence of narcotics, albeit small dosage.

Yes, strict...**STRICT**...rules should be in place. Bed time should be set. Chores...lots of chores (to keep his mind occupied). Phone access should be limited to waking hours only. (Take his phone from him.) Also Dad should be permitted to view his calls and text messages. It's intrusive yes, but Jonathan hasn't earned trust yet, and it must be assumed that he's hiding things. He is. He is.

Yes, it's VERY conceivable Jonathan will steal again if given the opportunity. He can't help himself. Really, he can't. Don't forget he swore on Remy's life, his own life, and God that he would never steal again...then he did. He's a liar. Don't forget that.

Let me say that again. He's a liar. Don't trust him. Make him prove things. If he doesn't like it, live on the street.

He's a child again, guys. A child. And he must be treated like one until he grows up, so to speak.

Terri to Mike, Michael and Kristin

Mike: What do you mean "you are about over this"? Are you referring to the stress of the whole situation with Jon's problems? We all have this, unfortunately, to deal with...this is a family disease. Are you referring to having a responsibility to monitor Jonathan or be the "caretaker" while he is at your house? I'm not clear on what your comment means specifically. You did not respond back with any comments or suggestions to the lengthy email I sent or the concerns I addressed. I truly do want to hear feedback. We are all struggling with this, and we are all trying to put in our comments and concerns out of love and a strong desire to help Jonathan get well. There is no finger pointing going on here…just suggestions to try to avoid potential disastrous consequences for Jonathan or anyone else concerned. I am very concerned for you, Michael, and Kristin's wellbeing, too. Believe me, I know how stressful this is, as I am dealing with it in a big way, too.

Perhaps my suspicions are just that, with no validity or any real situation that Jonathan is purposely leaving out. Be that as it may, I am sure our entire family is now in agreement that The Facility is not the place to give Jonathan the help he needs, particularly when we all realize he needs intense psychotherapy with real mental health specialist, counselors, etc. and this does not exist at there, unbeknownst to us when he entered their program. Glad to hear Jon's appt went well this morning and that they can see him more often. When you talked to Jon, how is he feeling and what did he have to say? Did he say he was mad at me? I hope not. I am trying so hard to help him and all of us.

Michael: I don't agree that Jonathan should not have access to spend time with Remy. On the contrary, I think Jonathan needs to spend much more time with Remy, as much as possible. I do agree, though, that Jonathan needs to keep his bad language in check when he is around Remy, but now that Jonathan is not a walking zombie anymore, I am not at all concerned about him scaring Remy with any weird behaviors. On the contrary, it is my understanding from Dad that Jonathan is talking to him as our grown son, for the first time ever. I actually think any time Jonathan and Remy can spend together can only serve to remind Jonathan that he has a very important reason to live and to be a healthy and responsible person and that his love and positive influence on Remy's life is profoundly important. Also, it will help renew Jon's once good relationship with Ashley, as this is important to both of them to have their friendship back (Ashley told me Jonathan was one of her best friends before all this happened and she wants him to be well so they can be close again), not to mention how important it is to Remy's emotional wellbeing to have parents who are loving and supportive to each other.

I also do not agree that Dad should take away Jon's cell phone at a certain time. Jonathan is a grown man. If he wants to make phone calls late at night, this is his prerogative. He many times stays up late and has trouble getting to sleep. Jonathan does not need his bedtime to be monitored, we just want to make sure he is safe and sober, and in the house for the rest of the night after checking in with Dad. Out of respect for Dad, who goes to bed early, Jonathan needs to be respectful to be home by the time Dad goes to bed, so that Dad knows he is home for the evening, and so that everyone can feel secure in knowing he is not out wandering around all night long. Regarding checking his cell phone call history, ONLY if absolutely necessary, only for the purpose of staying informed of potential bad situations and ONLY if strongly indicated due to irrational behaviors or obvious changes in Jonathan that warrant concern. Otherwise, I believe that taking control of his phone or checking his phone calls without due cause would be invasion of privacy.

Otherwise, I agree with the comments and suggestions and hope we are all in agreement that we just need to be cautious, not cruel or inhumane or completely untrusting with Jon…he still needs to be respected as a human being and he is trying, he just has a long way to go…for this reason, I simply believe we need to keep a tight control on his accountability and make sure that he is not put into a position of assuming too much responsibility for making important decisions, and definitely that he needs to be home, safe and sound, for everyone's peace of mind, after Dad's bedtime. That is not asking too much in my opinion, and should also serve to help Dad sleep more peacefully not having to wonder where he is….this is assuming Dad still feels comfortable about Jonathan driving in his car. That's up to Dad to decide. But, I would caution Jonathan to stay under the speed limit and don't do anything that might prompt him to be stopped by the police as it would probably open up a whole can of worms unnecessarily. I would suggest limiting Jon's use of the car to a couple of hours, with him checking in regularly as to his plans and whereabouts, etc.

Just my thoughts…I don't have all the answers….I'm just a mom doing the best I can.

Michael to Terri, Kristin and Mike

You're treating him like a trustworthy man. He's not. He's a boy in a man's body. He's never been a man. Never. Nor has he ever proven trustworthy. Never.

Surely you haven't forgotten all the tantrums in recent weeks. <u>HE IS A CHILD</u>, an emotionally insecure one at that.

And a deceiver. He was angry, in fact hateful, towards Dad because Dad called Tiffany following the recent positive drug test. Then he told you he was angry with me for doing the same later that day. Why? Because he didn't want her to know the truth. DECEIPT!

And he fully respects nobody. NOBODY!!! Not his father, mother, brother, sister, caretakers at The Facility, law enforcement, Ashley, not even Tiffany, who is "his only reason for living." That's why he can't be trusted with Dad's belongings. I expect he will abuse the privilege in short time. He just left you hanging on the phone mere hours ago...he respects nobody. How many times has he told each of us in recent days/weeks that he'd call us back, then never did it? The fact he felt obliged to apologize to Ed about something further proves his spontaneous immaturity and lack of respect at some level.

Treat him like a man at your own peril, because he will return the favor with the behavior of a child. UNTIL HE PROVES OTHERWISE!!!

These are the very reasons Remy shouldn't be around him. I'm sure it's great for Jon's soul to spend time with his son. That's beautiful...but it's not worth corrupting Remy's young, impressionable mind with deceit, laziness, anger, intolerance, disrespect, and more. It's hard for me to make that suggestion, but I truly believe it's in Remy's best interest or I wouldn't say it. Remy is at the age where he will try to be exactly like his father. If Remy observes negative behavior, trust me, negative behavior is what he'll recreate. Please trust me on this. Remy looks up to me, and I see him copying many of the things I do, right down to hand gestures and speech. And I am nothing to him compared to Jonathan. Remy is STARVING for his father's leadership. Remy talks to me about it all the time. He adores his father, and Jonathan is Remy's role model more so than anybody. This is the age he'll begin doing everything Jonathan does. Jonathan still needs parenting himself, yet you feel comfortable allowing him to parent...?

I'm sorry I have to say this, but those concerns don't even begin to address the legitimate fear I have that Jonathan will lose his mind at some point and kidnap Remy. I wouldn't put anything past Jon, and I suspect the idea has occurred to him and that he's probably given it brief consideration. Jonathan is nothing if not selfish and self-righteous...he can/will justify it in his own mind. Hopefully never, but don't dismiss the notion.

Always remember when making decisions about Jon...he is extremely sick. So much so that many doctors would consider him having a psychotic disorder. Put him before the right doctor while he's in one of his "moods" and Jon's gonna' get thrown into a strait jacket. That very well could be where he belongs, though none of us would likely have the courage or heart to suggest he be in one. Let's see...in the past few months he's been suicidal, homicidal, hateful, crazed, delusional, irrational, verbally abusive/disrespectful, self-righteous...and many, many more things that one can easily perceive as "insane" ALL AT THE SAME TIME!!! Now think about THAT person with Remy. Do you still think it's a good idea? I sure don't.

Terri to Michael, Mike and Kristin

Then, let's all work diligently towards the goal of getting him the psychiatric help he needs before too much time is wasted. That's the whole answer. Jonathan wants the help, too. Let's all not be complacent as one day rolls into the next. Let's all try our best to find somewhere he can go and get help. I have exhausted myself to death researching and calling for several weeks now, off and on. There are plenty of places, but everything costs money, something I don't have a lot of....we are truly in a dilemma regarding the financial part of this. I think we all agree Jonathan needs an inpatient, intensive treatment program...going to the free outpatient state run place is at least some counseling for the moment but it is definitely not going to cover most or all of Jon's psychiatric disorders. We all need to be researching. It is a big job and we all have limited time available to do it and try to hold down our jobs, too. I'm open to suggestions, and I'm sure you will all agree, I haven't held back a single sentence in giving MY two cents....sorry if I have been long winded too often. It's just me....a part of my sparkling personality.

The day after he left The Facility we all had our own thoughts and ideas as to how to approach the next day, week, month, or more accurately, the next moment. We didn't know what to expect.

I can say I didn't disagree with anything Michael or Terri was stating. Points and concerns were valid and came from their hearts and souls as to what needed to happen in order to get Jonathan well.

I responded in one of Terri's emails "I'm about over this." I never replied back to her question about what I meant by this, and I don't remember what I was referring to. I'm sure it was out of anger or frustration that I was feeling at the time. I certainly did have these feelings from time to time, but I found that I was able to release them and not let them linger.

As we experienced the ups and downs of this period, I did my best to practice some of the lessons that A Course In Miracles was teaching me. I didn't respond with these thoughts or express my opinions; rather I would meditate and focus on these ideas.

My inner peace is most important to me.

I am responsible for everything I see and I choose the feelings I experience and I decide upon the goal I would achieve. In other words, my perception was up to me. I could be sad, angry, or disappointed and I had no one to blame but myself.

In order for me to remain in this state, what must I remember?

Anger is never justified.
How can I have true inner peace if I am going to hold onto anger?

Don't judge.
If I judge, I must therefore be passing blame.
If I pass blame, how is that showing love?

Love
One of Jonathan's favorites from the Bible, and one you may be familiar with is:

> Love is patient and kind; love is not jealous, or conceited, or proud; love is not ill-mannered, or selfish, or irritable; love does not keep a record of wrongs; love is not happy with evil, but is happy with truth. Love never gives up: its faith, hope, and patience never fail.

Was what Jonathan doing or had become, evil? If so, go back to "Don't judge." Otherwise, proceed to "Love never gives up."

"its faith, hope, and patience never fail."

In this line I substitute trust for hope. To rephrase, I had learned that by trusting Jonathan and by having patience, the faith that the Holy Spirit would guide him down his chosen path would BE, despite my need to intervene. So my thought process was:

> Turn everything over to the Holy Spirit. I will try not to be arrogant and think that I know how he should live his life in order to make <u>ME</u> happy. I will try not to interfere with his path, as I haven't a clue as to what that is. I will

not intentionally support him harming others, but I will trust and send any doubting of his words to the Holy Spirit. I know absolutely nothing about what should, could, or would happen. I know I am to maintain my inner peace through love and trust.

I will lie down with you, Jonathan, when you are at your lowest and try not to judge you or your behavior. I will encourage you to follow your path and do my best to give you love, patience, and kindness; and trust you at the word you give to me.

February

On the evening of January 30 Jonathan borrowed my car so he could drive to Rome to visit with Tiffany. At 8:00 PM I received a call from him.

"Dad, don't get mad but I've had an accident."

Not again was the first thought that went through my mind.

"But it wasn't my fault!!!" he continued with excitement and relief in his voice. He explained that he was in a convenient store and a woman pulling into the parking space next to my car had hit and dented the front panel. Jonathan received the insurance information from the woman and he assured me that he would take care of making the arrangements to get the car repaired. Early the next week Jonathan made a February 10 appointment with the body shop.

Monday February 1

Michael to Mike and Terri
How's Jonathan?

Mike to Michael and Terri
He's feeling rough due to limited Suboxone this weekend. He saw the shrink today and she increased his dosage for withdrawing. He's also depressed and anxious and laden with guilt about what this is costing, among other things I'm sure. I'm also concerned that he may be deceiving or hiding things from me, I don't know for sure.

Michael to Mike and Terri
Given his history it is, indeed, likely he's hiding something if there is something "worth" hiding. What do you think that could be? I understand he still doesn't want you to participate in psychiatric discussions with his doctor. In my opinion you should insist upon it or make him find his own

way there. If he's not going to be 100% forthcoming, you shouldn't be accommodating to his needs.

Keep me posted, please.

Tuesday February 2

Mike to Terri and Michael

After he got his Suboxone in him, he was much better. I spent about 2-3 hours with him last night going over his history at The Facility to try and capture all the incidents that went on. I'll be calling Terry (the attorney friend of Terri and me) today to get his advice as to how to format the dispute letter, and then get the rough draft written tonight. If all goes well, please be ready to read first thing Monday morning so that it can be finalized and given to Scott.

For the next week, Jonathan and I continued working on the letter and gathering information to get the money back from The Facility.

Michael to Mike and Terri

He just tried calling me, for what I don't know. As I said before I don't intend to speak with him again until/unless he shows accountability for his previous actions, recognizes and appreciates the efforts everyone has made on his behalf, sincerely apologizes to everyone who has helped him, and makes measurable strides towards becoming a responsible man and a good father.

Ironically my bible study touched upon this very thing last night.

Terri to Michael and Mike

Though I understand your feelings, Michael, Jonathan is trying his best, as far as we know, despite the fact that he does not have a program to be in anymore. Please try, if you can, to give him at least the ability to speak to you. I'm sure he misses his brother, and, as Dad said, he is carrying a lot of guilt around with him as it is. Everything I have read or researched on the subject says the same thing...that it is vitally important, in order for someone to be successful in their attempt at sobriety, that family members are loving and supportive and try to be forgiving, as best we can, through this difficult recovery process. Obviously, this does not mean putting up with blatant disrespect or bad behavior, but as long as Jon's conversation with any of us is his way of reaching out to his family, I believe being hard on him is not the answer for anyone.

Terri then explained how hard it is on everyone and that it is the disease that is affecting him.

Michael to Terri and Mike

I understand your opinion, and I don't necessarily disagree. It seems love and forgiveness and turning the cheek would be the best thing for him. But Mom, that's how we've all "handled" Jonathan for the past decade, and what has it done? Nothing, that's what. Blame it on disease, drugs, whatever you want. The real blame lies with Jonathan alone. He made all those decisions. It's up to everyone else not to make excuses for him or accept the ones he tries offering, which you are effectively doing every time you tell him, "It's ok, Jon, we're all here for you, we love you, etc." It's easier said than done, but it's time to let Jonathan lie in the extremely uncomfortable bed he's made for himself; and by refusing to listen to his lying, complaining, hating, excuses, crying, etc., that is exactly what I'm doing.

I received your voice mail this morning when I woke up. If Jonathan is suicidal again, so be it. By talking to him you're not changing anything...just pandering to his emotional needs. Frankly I think his being able to bitch and moan about things is another "addiction" of his, and if there is nobody to listen, then maybe he'll grow up. Don't get me wrong. I will feel horrible if Jonathan ever kills himself. But like everything else, it's his decision alone. I'll have no part of it. I tried to help Jonathan, but he refused it.

If you want to remind him of the eternal spiritual condemnation he'll be in, tell him to read this. Very intriguing, and even if untrue, it's at least something to think about before he pulls the trigger or swallows the bottle. Terrifying!

(Michael attached a link to an article about a Christian man who had an out of body experience and went to hell for 23 minutes)

All that said, Dad, did he make it through the night without incident as far as you're aware?

Wednesday February 3

After I got home from work, I evaluated Jonathan and he seemed OK. He had an appointment with his counselor, so I let him drive. I received a call about an hour later from the counselor's assistant informing me that they wouldn't let Jonathan drive as he appeared intoxicated. A police officer picked him up and drove him home. I sat with the officer and explained to her what had been going on with Jonathan. She left offering words of encouragement for Jonathan, not threatening what might happen, but pointing out the benefits of seeking the help he needed.

Thursday February 4

I was at work when I received a call from Laura. She explained that as she was walking out of the bedroom and into the kitchen, Jonathan was standing in the hallway and collapsed. For a brief moment, she thought he had dropped dead. She ran over to check on him, saw he was still breathing, got him to wake up, and helped him back into his bed.

Mike to Michael, Terri and Kristin

Laura just called me and said Jonathan fell this morning. She's helped him back to bed and he's back asleep.

I think I know what has happened, and Terri, we briefly talked about this last week. When he left The Facility, he was down to 1 pill twice a day. That pill was a 2 mg pill. His refill from the FIS psychiatrist is for 2 8 mg pills. This would explain his drunken behavior. Whether intentional deceit or not, I don't know. I'll address when I get home tonight, or I get an emergency call.

I missed work yesterday so I can't be running out to address this. Also, I'll call the psychiatrist this morning.

Terri to Mike, Kristin and Michael

I am positive that Jonathan told me his last wean-down dose before leaving The Facility was ¾ of an 8mg tablet twice a day.

This is why I had asked you to verify the dosage he was given by the psychiatrist at FIS.

Terri further explained the effects of Suboxone and how one is weaned off of it.

I definitely think this should be looked at more closely, especially if he is taking Vistaril now, too, which also will make him drowsy. The blood pressure medication, since he accidentally took an additional one yesterday and it made his BP dangerously low, should definitely be administered by someone other than Jon. He is obviously too drowsy to make rational decisions and he definitely should be observed and should not be driving at all. How was his BP last night when you checked it later on? The cop yesterday said that, had he even started the car, he could have been arrested for a DUI. That is not a chance that needs to be taken again.

Mike, can you call the doctor and find out why Jon's dosage is so high? Maybe she misunderstood Jon, or maybe Jonathan didn't tell her the truth regarding the dosage he had been weaned down, in order to get more?

Is Laura home all day today? I'm concerned about Jonathan being alone now. Someone should be with him. Is Chris home, if Laura isn't? Was Jonathan hurt when he fell?

Mike to Terri, Michael and Kristin

Already called. He's not on Vistaril as I didn't fill the prescription. I do believe looking at the medicine chart from The Facility that it said 2 mg. I'll check today when I get home and I'll call Matt and Chris and ask them to keep an eye on Jon.

If Jonathan was hurt, he probably doesn't know it. Depending on how he is when I get home, I may call 911 and have him admitted.

Michael to Mike, Terri and Kristin

I think I've been a bit out of the loop. I'm assuming you're considering having him admitted because of the severe depression/suicidal thoughts? What is Jon's basic opinion of the place in Cedartown?

Mike to Michael, Terri and Kristin

He's not impressed and if his stupor state doesn't get any better, I may call because I'm concerned about his ability to function and given the amount he's taking, breathe. I just got off the phone with him and suggested he not take any more meds until I get home so we can evaluate. He got defensive and argumentative, so what he'll do I don't know. I reiterated we would talk about it when I get home, he got frustrated and hung up.

Oh well, not the first time.

Michael to Mike, Terri and Kristin

The fact he is still arguing about coming off the drugs means he is still very much an addict regardless of his intentions, however genuine they may be. Once again for the record, I am 100% in favor of locking him up in a place that will force complete detox. The psychological aspect can be addressed afterward if he's unable/unwilling to make strides there. Sounds like he's still in denial, as expected, and will likely remain so until his hand is forced.

Terri to Michael, Mike and Kristin

He does not react well to anything that sounds like an accusation that he just wants more drugs. On the other hand, if it is explained to him that he is acting too drowsy and that we are just concerned for him and wondering about his dosage possibly needing adjustment, he might be more willing to talk about it. I'll try to call and see if he answers. I doubt he will, though.

Monday February 8

It had been Super Bowl weekend, and I emailed Michael to see how the little side bets he made in Las Vegas had paid off. We exchanged good natured emails and I brought him up to date about Jonathan.

Mike to Michael

Jonathan seems OK....not great, but not bad. He's still not thinking real clearly, but that's a side effect of the Suboxone and his sleeping meds. I'm trying to encourage him to cut back on the sleeping meds a little at a time because he almost always looks tired. He told me his BP was up to 160/90 when he was at the hospital for his tooth on Saturday, but that's to be expected when you're in a lot of pain. He's also stopped taking the BP meds on Sunday because his BP was in the 85/45 range.

He sees the doctor again today, is actually done by now I would guess and getting his Suboxone refilled. I hope she cuts him back another tablet so he'll be back to where he was when he left The Facility.

Michael to Mike

Is Jonathan still exhibiting motivation to get better, or does he seem to be getting comfortable again? I have to say...this stand I've taken about not speaking with him until/unless he gets better, apologizes, etc. is tearing me up. And the fact he doesn't seem to care makes it worse. I really miss my relationship with him, as we all do. How's he doing with Tiffany?

Mike to Michael

His relationship with Tiffany remains as it always is. Good days, bad days, and horrible it's the end of the world days. She contacted him after last week's blowout and they seem to have made up.

I wouldn't say he's comfortable, but he is motivated to get off all the drugs it seems. Unfortunately, that's only the first half of the battle and I don't know that 211 offers enough therapy to get him where he wants/needs to be.

I do see progress in many areas, but some he seems to maintain. His anger is better, but his bitterness towards everyone doesn't seem to be getting any better. I wouldn't say Jonathan doesn't care, because he does. This entire thing makes him uncomfortable as I'm probably riding him harder than I ever have. I'm not sure how this thing will end up……jail, mental institution, homeless, state run place to dry out completely, I just don't know. I do know if he has another emotional blowout like he has had each of the last 2 weeks, it will be time for us to go and get the court ordered mandate to have him locked up and evaluated. I hope it doesn't come to that.

And try not to let this tear you up. You need to do what you have to do. Easier said than done.

Jonathan had gone to the hospital the previous weekend due to the extreme tooth pain he was having. Terri was making calls trying to locate a dentist in the area that offered a sliding payment scale based on income. She was having no luck. In the meantime Jonathan's phone was damaged and he was trying to get that repaired. He also had several errands to run.

Tuesday February 9

Terri found a dentist that could see him on an emergency basis and she provided me with that information.

Mike to Terri

Tooth is bothering him quite a bit. I just tried calling to let him know but no answer. His phone number is working, although I don't think it's his phone. He's got a lot he wants to do today, so I'm guessing he's in the middle of something. I'll get this info to him as soon as he calls me back.

Thank you for the info.

Mike to Terri

I just got off the phone with him again and he's applying for free medical (he just saw them about his tooth) and dental care in Rome, as well as renewing his food stamp card. He sounds good but very defensive and I suppose my reactions to his behavior over the last few weeks are why. I apologized and realize I need to remain at peace at all times if he's going to have any chance at having the slightest bit of peace.

He does have an appointment Thursday with Jessie (not sure what her role is) from 211. She's coming to the house.

We're going to sit down tonight and go over his schedule for the next 10 days. He admits to being overwhelmed with all the thoughts and things he has to or thinks he has to do. Guess I'll try to help him make it manageable.

He's supposed to pick me up at 3:30, so if anything else comes up, I'll let you know.

Terri to Mike, Mike's responses in bold

Terri: What is he defensive about? Your reactions to his behavior, meaning what? As far as I know, you have basically allowed him to do whatever he chooses to do about everything, showing nothing but love. What on earth does he have to be defensive about? All you have done is help him! What is he talking about?
Mike: I have been impatient at times and not very loving. I've also laid an unintentional guilt trip on him many times I figure. These are the reactions I must stop if I'm to help him get better.

Terri: I'm glad he is looking into medical/dental...hope they don't put it through a time consuming red tape ordeal, as those usually are....he could be waiting for a long time for an appointment, if that's the case, unless they will see him on an emergency basis. He didn't respond to my text message.
Mike: He hadn't received it at the time I spoke with him.

Terri: What schedule for ten days does he have?
Mike: Overall "things to do"....he gets overwhelmed when he thinks about getting car fixed, get a job, 211, seeing Remy and Tiffany, etc... Nothing the person in control with their mind can't handle. It'll be an attempt to settle him down and put him in control over his mind.

Terri: You mean his appointments at 211? Maybe this person, Jessie, will be able to coordinate a regular schedule for him at the clinic, including the psychologist, who he desperately needs to see regularly.
Mike: Yes, let's hope so. I did tell him today that he needs to step up his therapy or I would get involved and he wouldn't like that. I didn't say it but that would mean Michael and I arranging to get the form 1021 (or whatever it is) completed.

Terri to Mike

Well, we should all be apologetic when we lose patience or react to situations in ways that are not always the best. However, this is also one of the lessons Jon, himself, needs to be learning. Forgiveness, appreciation for all you have done for him, accepting others' faults, and realizing and accepting his own less than thoughtful ways. He has no right whatsoever to be defensive about anything. He's so fortunate he has a family who hasn't thrown him under the bus already, and it's time he recognizes the value in this. Don't be overly apologetic...your heart is in the right place and he knows this. Don't let him manipulate you into feeling guilty about anything.

Is Jessie going to be coming to the house while you are there? I really feel strongly that Jonathan needs to include you and me on the list of people who can talk to his caregivers about his situation, even if for the fact that in an emergency, we need to be able to do this. If Jonathan has nothing to hide, he should not have a problem with this. I'd love for you to be present when Jessie is there, especially since Jon's thinking is erratic these days. With your guidance and input, perhaps this might be the appointment that could coordinate some true regularly scheduled therapy sessions.

I am not sure Jonathan is even capable of holding down a job right now. Maybe if he is made to understand that the therapy is the most important thing in his life, he will recognize that, without it, he will fall back into the same frustrations, anxiety, and depression that he has had all along. The job situation, though he truly does need income, should not be his highest priority or everything else might fall by the wayside. I feel he is still in a state of denial about how much he needs psychiatric help. He will try to avoid it and try to assume the position of living a "normal" life, then will feel like a failure once again when things start falling apart around him, which will inevitably happen without him having the life tools to help him through coping every day in a not so perfect world. This is why I feel so strongly about having a serious conversation about this therapy and the importance of it, with no more leaving it all up to him....he will always take the easy way without someone pushing him to do what he needs to do. I am very glad you told him he needs to step up the therapy....he needs to hear that, especially from you. He can't stay for a "free ride" forever.

When does he see the psychiatrist again? Any idea when she is planning to start some more weaning?

Wednesday February 10

Mike to Terri, Kristin and Michael
Anyone hear from him?
I don't want to cause worry, but he dropped me off at 6:30 and was going

to go home to get ready to take my car in to the shop for a 9:00 appointment. He said he was going to go a little early to talk to one of the guys he knows.

Talked to Laura and she said the car wasn't there when she left and she didn't see or hear Jonathan getting ready.

Talked to Chris at 11:00 and he hadn't heard from him.

I left a voice and text for Tiffany, no word back, but I think she's working today.

I called both the Cobb and Paulding County sheriff's departments and he's not in jail there and they didn't have any accident on record.

When he left me today he was a little tired though perfectly coherent sounding.

I'll let you know if I hear anything and please do the same.

Michael to Mike, Kristin and Terri

Haven't heard from him. Did the shop confirm if he made it in or not?

Is Jonathan legally allowed to remove Remy from school? I hate to think the worst about everything, so please forgive me, but we need to be mindful of the possibility Jonathan might kidnap Remy. Please forgive me for saying such a thing...it's a horrible thought...but Jon's a desperate and unreasonable man.

Mike to Michael, Terri and Kristin

He's in Smyrna jail for "DUI". He appeared to fail the field sobriety test but passed the extensive test he was given at the jail so I'm not sure what the deal is. We're going to have a talk when we get home about a new set of rules. Gotta go to try and get him out.

I called the police department and got no information other than the car had been impounded and where I needed to go to pick it up. I called Chris and Laura to meet me so that we could get the car. After that, I went to see a bondsman to arrange bail. I drove to the jail to await his release, picked him up and returned to the bondsman to complete the paperwork.

As we drove from the jail, Jonathan explained what had happened. He had pulled off the side of the road to make a note in his journal. He dozed off, and the next thing he remembered were 2 people knocking at his window. He thanked them and was about to head home when 4 police cars pulled up and blocked him in.

They made him take the field sobriety test and told him he didn't pass as he couldn't walk a straight line. Jonathan was dressed in his pajamas, the temperature was 17 degrees, the wind was blowing at 20 MPH, snow flurries fell....and he couldn't walk a straight line. The police also told Jonathan that they smelled beer on him, something he hadn't sampled in over 2 years. Jonathan was handcuffed and escorted to the jail where he was administered more extensive tests. He passed them all.

By now Jonathan had developed a dialogue with several of the officers and two of the officers stated that Jonathan should be released. Time slowly passed as Jonathan sat in the holding area awaiting a decision. Finally, the sergeant in charge of the case walked into the room and said "Book him."

Jonathan was given an option to sign a statement that he had been drinking, or refuse to sign and he wouldn't be allowed bail. He signed the paper knowing that I was prepared to pay the bail.

During the next couple of months we tried to obtain the court documents to find out what the charges were, but the files to his case seemed difficult for the court administration to locate. We never did discover the nature of the charges.

Thursday, February 11

Terri had been working with both Scott and the credit card companies to get a refund from The Facility. The CC companies were appalled at the story and how the loan approvals were obtained, yet in the end, only a small portion of the refund was granted. Terri and I continued our search for the right rehab facility, making calls and emailing around the country.

Michael to Mike and Terri

Since Jonathan has all day, every day to himself, he should be making all these calls. Plus he has the benefit of knowing everything that has happened better than any of us. And since he's able to manipulate things so easily, he should have no problem describing/fabricating the story for whoever needs to hear it.

I'd help, but I don't know enough...I'm too detached.

Terri to Michael and Mike

Very good point, Michael...Mike, can you talk to Jonathan and ask him to work on this? Michael is right; he could be making some phone calls, too. No reason he should not be involved in advocating for his own situation... every one of us has diligently tried our best on his behalf....seems that would not be too difficult for him to do.

Mike to Michael and Terri
Excellent point. I'll discuss with him tonight.

Friday, February 12

Terri to Mike, Michael and Kristin
Did Jonathan have his appointment with the person from 211 who was supposed to come to the house yesterday? Wondering how it went. How are things? Is Jonathan driving and are you administering his meds?

Mike to Terri, Michael and Kristin
I'm administering his meds. Appointment was rescheduled to next Tuesday I think. Jonathan drove last night as he was fine and hadn't taken anything all day. Amazing what sleep and no meds will do. He's willing to make whatever calls are necessary to get the ball rolling towards The Facility fraud activity. He's with the psychiatrist now. Chris is driving him this morning.

I got home from work at 12:30 PM and picked up Jonathan. He had an interview scheduled for 2:00 PM and we needed to stop at the drug store to get his prescriptions filled. He had applied for a job as a cook at a local restaurant, so we arrived early to have some lunch before the appointment. At 2:00 PM Jonathan met with the Restaurant Manager. The manager was so impressed with Jonathan and his credentials that he wanted Jonathan to consider taking the Kitchen Manager position that was also available. A second interview was scheduled for the following Friday as Jonathan would meet with the District Manager. After we left the restaurant, Jonathan told me that he only wanted to cook and that he wasn't confident or comfortable being hired as a Kitchen Manager.

Monday, February 15

Terri to Mike, Michael and Kristin
Mike, I guess you know that Jonathan called me last night and was very upset (and very upset with me, personally) and he wanted to know what I said to you that made you decide to make you so angry that you decided to "give up on him" (apparently, you had told him, in anger, "Mom told me everything you said" and then told him he was essentially cut off from any

further help from you, including use of the car or financial help, etc.). He was NOT happy with me, told me he thought he could trust me to keep conversations between him and his own mom confidential, that he didn't know he had to watch what he says when he talks to me, etc. and essentially that, thanks to me blowing things out of proportion, you were so angry with him that you wouldn't even talk to him any further, that you wanted to spend Valentine's day with Laura (completely understandable), and that you refused to allow him to use the car to go to Tiffany's for their V-Day time together.

I tried my best to calm him down and tried to be realistic with him, pointing out your frustration (and everyone's) with his seemingly lack of appreciation for all you and others have done for him, the fact that he consistently "throws us under the bus" (except Kristin, to my knowledge) depending on who he is talking to at the time. He said that he tells you every day that he loves you, says thank you often, writes you loving letters, etc. and truly did not seem to understand why anyone in our family would not know that he loves us. He said "of course I love all of you...you are my family". I told him that everyone has reached beyond their emotional capacities to continue trying to be patient and supportive to him, and that he might want to consider that maybe he doesn't show his appreciation often or in the correct ways. Also, I reminded him that he needs to give benefit of the doubt, and stop jumping to conclusions and assuming everyone else but him is always wrong.

I told Jonathan to give you time to calm down, and suggested that he sit down with you today and have a heart to heart conversation, express his feelings and concerns calmly and fairly, and allow you to express yours to him, with no anger or raised voices or name calling involved. (He was still upset about you saying "F*@# you" to him and telling him to "Get the hell out of my house")...he sincerely seemed to think this was not deserved under the circumstances (I don't know the whole story). Unfortunately, his first instinct seems to always be that of getting defensive, and I imagine some of this is a true belief on his part that he is being misunderstood and not appreciated or respected, and that he is treated like he is a child and that he has no intelligence. He can't stand to be told the same things over and over again, things he says he already knows...he doesn't want things constantly "thrown in his face."

In his mind, he seems genuinely hurt that everyone automatically assumes he is doing something wrong or "up to something" and that he is questioned unmercifully for simply asking to use the car to run an errand ("why do you need the car, where are you going, why is this necessary right now", etc.)...his perception is that he can't do anything right in our (especially yours) eyes. His thinking seems so skewed...depending on the day and what's going on at the time.

I hung up with Jonathan last night telling him that, as far as I know, there was nothing specifically that I said to Dad that made him angry, and that the issues we talked about were already in existence, and that Dad had already mentioned to me that Jonathan was going to be mad that he wouldn't be allowed to use the car on Tuesday (Jonathan blamed me for this decision, too). I tried to be honest, and explained to Jonathan that we all talk on a regular basis and discuss our concerns over situations as they happen and that no one is trying to kick him to the curb, as he perceives it. He did say thank you for all the time, research, and typing time I had put into the documents for The Facility fight, that he loves me very much, and that I am very appreciated, despite what I may think. (I hear these words so infrequently that I hung up the phone and spent the next half hour crying). I encouraged him to show his love, appreciation, and gratitude to everyone else, as well, as he said that he is very appreciative, and he thought that Dad, especially, knew this, and that he has just had so much on his plate maybe he doesn't always express it as he should...so, it seemed that at least he recognized the truth in what I was telling him. Hopefully, by now, or tonight, whenever you are able to talk with him, he will be more humble and appreciative of all your efforts.

Have you talked with him anymore since the blow up last night?

Mike to Terri, Michael and Kristin

I tried calling but no answer. I did receive a call from Matt as it looks like Matt drove him to the Dept. of Family Services and Jonathan needed some information from me.

Terri to Mike

Terri sent me an email stating she had spoken with Jonathan about the accuracy of the documents being filed against The Facility. Jonathan added a few details, and then Terri informed the attorney that the documents had been updated.

Jonathan sounded good when I talked to him, was very kind and truly showed his appreciation for efforts made in his behalf. Tiffany is on her way over there.

Jonathan said he had called the public defender's office this morning and was told that he does not get "assigned" a public defender...the way it works is that there is a public defender present for all court cases. They don't meet, like a regular attorney, in advance of the court date. Jonathan will request the assistance of the public defender and he will meet with Jonathan for just a couple of minutes prior to his meeting the judge. In other words, there really is no real preparation or "case building" time available when using a public defender.

Of course, Jonathan is very worried about Thursday's meeting with the probation officer. He did say the lady sounds nice over the phone but she did say that if any arrests happen for any reason, guilty or not, it would automatically cause the duration of one's probation to be spent in jail. So, I just don't know what to think.

Jonathan told me that he still has no idea whether he passed the field sobriety test or not (I was under the impression that he had failed it) because he said he kept asking the officers if he did ok and they wouldn't ever say whether he passed or failed. So, he doesn't know which part (if any) of the sobriety tests done on him were failed.

Please let me know if you hear any updates from Jon...I think he may have a much improved attitude today. Perhaps he did some soul searching last night. I hope so, for everyone's sake.

But, he did truly sound calm, rational, and appreciative during our phone conversation, and he called me, not the other way around, which, in itself, is unusual.

What are your thoughts today on things? I know you are at work and if you don't have time to write back, please give me a call on your way home.

Mike to Terri

I'm glad he sounds good. Is he planning on spending the night at Tiff's? He has a 10:00AM appointment tomorrow morning.

My thoughts are basically empty. Every day is different and I deal with it as I can and try not to linger in the thoughts of "yesterday".

Wednesday, February 17

Michael to Terri, Kristin and Mike

I did speak with Jonathan. Though I was very careful not to sound "negative," that is unfortunately all he heard. I was honest and frank with him about why I didn't want to speak with him.

I told him his hatred and anger towards other family members (you and Dad specifically) is intolerable. He responded with, "Haven't you ever said anything you didn't mean?" I suppose I have...but not something so venomous and certainly not with repetition over the duration of months.

He said "Obviously you know nothing about severe, clinical depression." I said depression has nothing to do with it...I respect the diagnosis of depression...but those statements are wrong and uncaring. Period. No excuses. He said that I just don't understand and offered no humility or apology. I understand just fine...excuses for outrageous behavior.

There were many other things I touched upon, but basically he was defensive about everything. Not one thing did he "man up" to. He just kept saying I was being negative and he didn't need to be reminded of all his past behaviors. Well how do you make corrections if you're going to ignore and deny the truth?

Towards the end of the call I told him part of the reason I chose not to speak with him was in hopes that my absence in his life would serve as motivation to get himself together as quickly as possible. I was consciously positive, reminding him of the healthy Jonathan that I loved and how much I look forward to his health when he and I can simply enjoy a meal together again. I told him I don't even know him anymore. Then he tries the guilt trip..."I would never turn my back on my family, blah, blah, blah." I didn't remind him of all the times he already has...I figured it would be "too negative."

In closing I told him if he didn't listen to anything else I told him, he needs to find God. I told him not to keep placing God in a little box, using him for his own devices, and creating expectations and praying for miracles for his own benefit. I told him he must fully humble himself before God, with all his heart, mind, and soul, before God will come to him. He sounded thoroughly annoyed (as usual when I try to speak about God to him), then basically blew it all off, said he had to go be with Tiffany before he goes to jail for 11 months, and hung up shortly thereafter with a sour tone.

Overall there was much defensiveness, denial, blaming, underlying annoyance, complaining, and utterly childish immaturity...all the things I fully expected when I called him.

Truthfully I hope Jonathan does go to jail on Thursday. And I hope he's there for 11 months. He needs jail. He doesn't need the real world because it's too much for him right now. And it always will be unless he grows up, which he has proven for years he will not do here. He will be FORCED to grow up in jail.

Dad, I know your patience has been tried repeatedly. Truly I admire your ability to forgive and forget. But I'll say this...in doing so Jonathan is allowed to remain a boy. Not to preach...but I will anyway. I'll use the example of the "Prodigal Son" again. The father was overjoyed when his son came home from his sinful, reckless life...but note the father did not try to attempt to restrain or withhold his son from those important, albeit dangerous, endeavors and life lessons. There is power and wisdom in that truth.

Like a plant must be pruned to blossom fruitfully, sometimes a man must also be.

Terri to Mike

Did Jonathan say anything to you about this conversation? This breaks my heart.

Mike to Terri

Yes, Jonathan was annoyed and declared how "Christian" Michael is. As long as Jonathan doesn't accept responsibility, he and Michael won't get along. Jail or a state institution for a period of time may be the answer. However he does seem to be trying to turn it up a notch with 211....we'll see.

Terri to Mike, Mike's response in bold

Terri: Did you say this to Jon?

Mike: Periodically over the last several weeks.....one of the reasons I tick him off.

Terri: Hopefully he has the ability to see this for himself, if only during his private soul searching moments. It seems he would want to be honest and humble at this stage of the game...I don't understand the continuous defensive attitude....could be the mixture of meds, most likely his inability to accept responsibility, hence the blaming or fault of others.

Mike to Michael, Terri and Kristin

I just spoke with Jonathan and he sounds anxious as he is mentally preparing himself to go to jail. 211 wouldn't give him any documents identifying when he attended groups or when he saw the psychiatrist. Only the group leader or the doctor tracks that I guess. The doc is out for another 5 days. Tiffany is staying with him until tomorrow....I'm not sure if she'll go with us or not. Perhaps they'll take her car separately. Anyway, they're sounding quite sad at the moment.

And as the prodigal son goes, the father let him in when he wanted to return. Jonathan wanted to return so I welcomed him back. This makes room for great debate in what Christianity teaches versus what A Course in Miracles teaches. And since I don't debate belief systems, I appreciate the point you are making.

Love to you all as everything will work out as it is supposed to……jail, a new job, marriage, living in the streets, a mental institution, a rehab facility, or anything else imaginable.

Tiffany, Jonathan and I went to see the Probation Officer that Thursday. We waited out in the lobby for 15 minutes as the tears dripped from Jonathan's eyes as he held his head down. Tiffany and I would pat him and hug him, and let him know that everything would be all right.

When his name was called, the three of us walked in together. The PO was as kind in person as she sounded on her voicemail. I explained to her that we were with Jonathan to let her know that Jonathan had a loving and supportive family behind him, and how we were all working together to find an in-patient facility for him. She listened and then commented that in her line of work, she didn't often see loving and supportive families behind her clientele.

She excused Tiffany and I and spoke confidentially at length with Jonathan. Jonathan walked outside 45 minutes later to where Tiffany and I waited. With a big smile on his face, Jonathan told us that he wasn't going to jail but he didn't need to be getting into anymore trouble either.

The next week Jonathan found a part time, temporary job working on a farm with his friends Zach and Dustin. As the family continued to look for rehab facilities and attempt to get a refund from The Facility, things were beginning to look up. At least Jonathan had some work.

March

Monday, March 01

Terri to Michael, Kristin and Mike
    Hi…any updates from the weekend? Mike, were you able to have your "talk" with Jonathan regarding his priorities and compliance with the "rules"? Did he work all weekend at the new job? How are things?

Terri explained the new job Jonathan had at the farm and that he had been offered a full time position the previous Friday. She also expressed concern over the rules the psychiatrist had set the previous week. She concluded her email…

    Anyhow…just wondering how the weekend went.
    I am having a breast biopsy this afternoon…they found something on my routine mammogram last Friday they want to check out further. So that's the procedure. I have it at 12:30 today. Kinda scary, but needs to be done to rule out anything ominous.

I asked Terri when she would have the results.

Terri to Mike, Mike's responses in bold
Terri: Don't know….the biopsied tissue samples will be sent to the pathologist to look at…guess it all depends on how busy he/she is….maybe I'll be able to get some preliminary results before I leave today, but I doubt it….my guess is that it will probably take a few days before I hear anything.
Mike: Let me know as soon as you hear anything. My thoughts and prayers are with you.

Terri: Glad Jonathan is loving his new job. I think it is a great thing for him to be doing! Did Jonathan work all weekend?
Mike: Yes, and thoroughly seemed to enjoy it.

Terri: I talked to Kristin last night and she said you had Remy with you yesterday.
Mike: Yes, we went and saw Avatar. He seemed to like it quite a bit. He was also over on Saturday.

Terri: Did Jonathan see him and spend time with him? I hope so.
Mike: Yes, they spent a lot of time together. Remy was complaining of a headache on Saturday, and Jonathan got him to sit quietly and did a meditation/prayer with him to get rid of it. Remy said it worked.

Terri: Are you going to Jon's psychiatrist appt with him on Wednesday?
Mike: Only if it doesn't interfere with work. I have to try and get through a week to 2 with no turmoil.

Terri to Mike

Thanks, I will let you know....thanks for the thoughts and prayers.

I am so glad Jonathan spent quality time with Remy this weekend. Another great step in the right direction. That makes me very happy.

I haven't seen Avatar yet...I've heard from many people that it is very good. Hope to see it one of these days.

The family was seeing some very positive changes with Jonathan's reaction to his new job. He looked forward to getting up each day and going to work. During his commute, he would listen to his spiritual CDs. He looked healthier and felt better. He loved being outdoors and with the animals. His outlook on life seemed to improve, and the anxiety and depression decreased.

For the next 9 days Jonathan worked every day. Some days lasted only a few hours while other days he might work 10 to 12 hours. He spent most of these evenings at our house and we would talk each night, sometimes only a few minutes, other times a couple of hours.

Terri found out that her biopsy results came back positive and that surgery would be required. Jonathan called and told her not to worry about losing her hair, "I'll shave my head and be bald with you." It seemed as though by working outdoors, his compassion and sense of humor were returning.

One day he was telling me about a goat that had been attacked by a couple of wild dogs. Jonathan pulled his knife and charged the dogs, chasing them away. The goat was crying and Jonathan picked it up in its arms. He began praying and within a few minutes, the pain and fear the goat was feeling stopped.

Jonathan was also the only one who was able to walk in to the fenced in area where the alpacas were kept. If others entered the alpacas would charge and spit, but Jonathan walked in and they would trot up to be petted and fed.

On March 10, Jonathan was informed that he and the other workers were being let go. The owners of the farm had family who were struggling financially. They were arriving from out of town the next day to begin helping them on the farm. Jonathan was heart-broken and pissed off. He decided to drive out to Rome to stay with Tiffany for the evening.

Thursday, March 11

Mike to Michael, Kristin and Terri

I've spoken with Mom so you can stop reading if you want to Terri.

I got an attempted collect call from the Floyd County prison at 1:30 this morning. Jonathan is in jail in Rome. I wasn't able to receive the collect call as something is malfunctioning in their phone system. I have spoken with Tiffany several times this morning (Jonathan was able to get through to her cell phone), and I also talked with the desk sergeant at the prison. Here's what's happened.

1) Jonathan was arrested for shoplifting Reese's peanut butter cups. This is what Jonathan told Tiffany.
2) He was prescribed 120 Klonopin yesterday. Tiffany found the bottle in his book bag and there were only 31 pills left.
3) The sergeant said he was really messed up when they brought him in.

And here's what's being done about it.

1) I told the sergeant we weren't bailing him out and that he has a drug problem. I told him what Jonathan apparently may have taken and he will notify the nurses to keep an eye on him.
2) The prison doctor comes in at 8:00. The sarge will let him know to check Jon. I will also call the doctor to see if he can commit him to a detox facility followed by a long term visit in a mental institution.

3) I'll call the psychiatrist at FIS to see if she can write the papers to have him committed to such facility.
4) If neither doctor can help, Michael, I'll check to see what we might be able to do about filling out that form that allows family members to have a loved one committed.

That's about all I know right now. I'll keep you posted as I speak with the doctors.

Michael responded immediately offering any help he could.

Cherie to Mike
So much love to you my kind hearted father-in-law. I understand that you are very busy. No worries, it can wait. I have been praying for you and for Jonathan. As much as I know you want the best for Jonathan and are trying to be the best dad possible, I hope you know that Jon's fate is not in your hands. There is hope for Jonathan but it is not from you or Terri. Jon's needs are much bigger than any of us right now and they are his own. I hope you don't mind my 2 cents. There is a principle that is not the gospel but it is the truth..."Water seeks its own level." As soon as we get out of the way and let Jonathan have his "personal" course, the sooner the resolve...whatever that may be. Jonathan will find his own way.

Mike to Cherie
Thank you. This is what has been what has been my biggest internal struggle. You speak as ACIM speaks in that I don't need to worry or try to handle his path. He's going to follow whatever path he is destined to follow. It can be difficult knowing he is trying, yet lying to me and others, and then not offering a hand and say "My son, try again." I will just step back and let this take its course.

Cherie to Mike
Whatever you do don't feel as though you have wasted your time. The love and patience you have shown Jonathan are now a part of him and he won't forget it. Your behavior reminds me of how God is patient with all of us and then one day he lets us have our way. Thankfully, His arms are wide open and we can go back if we choose. For some reason, it seems as though Jonathan has not developed or matured at the same pace as most his age but I believe that he will catch up. Maturity can be so personal. As much as my

mom tried to shape and mold me in the end what remains of her teaching is all the good she instilled in me. That coupled with all of my screw ups and my victories is the sum total of who I am today. I thank God for her everyday and then I thank Him for his mercy. :)

"When I was a child I spoke as a child I understood as a child I thought as a child; but when I became a man I put away childish things." I Cor. 13:11.

Love you!

Visiting hours were limited at the jail to Saturday mornings from 9:00 to 12:00. I drove up to visit Jonathan for the 45 minutes allotted. He was very tearful and regretful, but happy to see me. He begged me to bail him out, and I told him I wouldn't. It was already noticeable that he wasn't eating as he had lost a few pounds.

I asked him about mail and he let me know that there was a delivery every day. I told him that I'd begin to write him each day, and that I would put money on my phone card so that he could call me collect most evenings. I confirmed the address with the guards as I left, and they explained how to properly address each envelope. They also let me know that all mail was opened and examined prior to delivery, so no tricky stuff.

Monday March 15

Michael to Terri

Hey there. I spoke to Jonathan for about 10-15 minutes last night. He was crying a little bit, but mostly sounded ok. He was very apologetic about being "such a lousy brother." I told him I forgive him, but I want him to get better. Same old stuff, really. He asked me to please be gentle in telling Remy about everything, but I told him Ashley and Dad already did. When I spoke to Remy about it, he seemed maybe a little bit sad, but mostly just confused and therefore somewhat indifferent. He's very concerned about April 1... wants me to follow up with Dad to make sure nothing gets missed that forces him to be in even more trouble. He wants out of jail pretty badly...he hates it. But of course he's going to hate it.

He said, yet again, that he'll never do anything stupid again, etc. etc. Maybe not, but at this point he's proven otherwise, so he has to accept his punishment without anybody bailing him out. He said he wants to go to an in-patient facility, but of course he's just looking for any way out of jail that he can. If it's not forced upon him, it won't last. I'm still liking jail for him right now, though I was pretty sad when we hung up. I think he'll get better as long as he doesn't give up hope.

Terri to Michael
Terri started her email stating that Michael's assessment of Jonathan's attitude and behavior matched what I had previously described to Terri. She also spoke of alternatives for addressing the April 1 court date. She concluded with ....

Dad had to drive to the jail on Sunday just to bring Jon's blood pressure pills because his BP was very high and they wouldn't give him anything for it. Jonathan has been asking for 3 days to be put on the "list" for the nurse to see him, and no one had come to help him despite his many requests. He was really sobbing a few times when Dad talked to him, saying there were people getting beat up, stabbing, etc. and he was really severely depressed. Dad said when he went to see him on Saturday, he was sobbing his eyes out and Jonathan was begging for us to get him out of there...he said he didn't care where he had to go as long as it wasn't there. My biggest concern is that the atmosphere he is in will make him even worse than he was before he got there...he already has major anxiety and depression...this is only making things worse....and his addiction disease is not being addressed at all.

Terri to Mike and Michael
There is a toll free number I wanted someone to give to Jonathan. It is for the crisis help line if Jonathan feels that he wants or needs to talk to someone about anything mental health related. This information was given to me through the Behavioral Health link at the hospital I called Saturday. Not only can Jonathan call them anytime and there will always be someone he can talk to....they also send volunteers to the jail to visit with inmates who need their help or counseling. Jonathan has to be his own advocate, though, and I've found this out from everywhere I've checked....he must make his own requests for help, even to be admitted to the hospital. He is a grown man...none of us can do any of this for him. I asked them if someone could go and talk to Jonathan and they said yes, but HE has to call them and request it.

Tuesday March 16
I sent the address of the jail and how to address the envelope to get letters to Jonathan.

Michael to Mike, Terri and Kristin

Thanks. He tried calling me 4 times last night, but I was in my Bible study group, and we went longer than usual. (Three of the calls were prior to 8:30, which is when I said he could call.) Did anybody else speak with him yesterday?

If/when one of you speaks with Jon, will you please tell him I can't talk to him during the day? He tried calling about 4-5 times yesterday, but all before I left work. They frown on personal calls around here.

Dad, is everything straight with April 1? Do you need my help with anything?

Wednesday March 17

Mike to Michael, Terri and Kristin

I didn't talk with him last night. I have only a few minutes left so I'm guessing he is holding off until today or tomorrow to make another call. Then after I get paid on Saturday I'll get another $25 credit towards calls. Also, I'll visit him Saturday morning so if anyone wants to get a message to him, let me know.

I want to check with Jonathan about April 1 on Saturday to see if he wants a postponement or wants to get it over with. In any event, I have to go to the courthouse on the 25th to request the postponement, or to make the arrangements for him to be transported. They may automatically postpone as that's the impression I got.

If I don't hear back from the probation officer by Friday, I'll give her a call to see if she has any idea when Jonathan will see the judge.

Terri to Michael, Mike and Kristin

Jonathan must be very lonely since he is calling you so often, Michael. He knows Dad doesn't have many minutes left on his plan, so he probably just wants someone to talk to...Dad said they don't have clocks there so Jonathan never knows what time it is. Have you been taking his calls in the evenings? It sounds like he is feeling a bit desperate to talk to you, so he is calling over and over again, as he has done before when stressed out or anxious.

Well, if anyone does talk to Jon, will you please let me know how he is doing and let him know I said hello and I love him?

Friday March 19

Mike to Michael, Kristin and Terri

I want to let you know I spoke with Jonathan last night. It wasn't our most peaceful conversation as I informed him I was not bailing him out tomorrow. We had only 6 minutes and we got cut off as he was trying to persuade me to bail him out. He did call back 3 times to leave a message while Mr. Auto Operator was talking. Mr. AO starts out by saying "You have a collect call from" and then Jonathan states his name. Although instead of stating his name, the first time he said "I love you Dad" and the second time was "thank you for everything." The 3rd time he tried he was cut off so I wonder if someone upstairs figured out what he was doing.

I go to the rehab center in Bremen this afternoon at 1:00 to discuss their yearlong program and to tour their building. It's about 40 miles from the house. I'll let you know how this goes and what Jon's reaction to it is tomorrow after I tell him.

Terri to Mike

I do feel bad for him having to stay in jail. Does Jonathan understand why he is staying there? Or does he just think we are all against him? I am hoping he will recognize that we are trying to protect him from himself, his bad judgments, his temptation to use drugs, act irresponsibly, and doing things out of desperation that are detrimental to himself and others. I wish so much he would finally just recognize and admit that he knows he needs help and really embrace the concept of getting true help for himself to start his future and get his life back again. As long as he is just doing things to "appease" others or to bide his time, he won't really be trying to get anything out of any of it.

At least in this long term program, he won't really have much choice in the matter. I think, assuming your impressions are good, and all the answers to the questions are favorable, this might be a great opportunity for him. And, the bottom line is, would he rather be in jail or somewhere else where he can get his life back and get the help he needs?? He did say he'd go ANYWHERE, just to get out of there. If it is ordered by the court, he will pretty much have to embrace it in order to be settled in comfortably for so long. Hope it goes well. I am anxious to hear from you.

Mike to Terri

I really don't know what he's thinking as we just haven't had much time to talk. Hopefully tomorrow will be a productive conversation and we can share a lot of information. I'm about to wrap up now so I'll call you after I leave the Bremen Rehab Center.

I did ask about letter correspondence. He can write and receive letters after 60 days. All the letters are screened.

He'll have to be off of all drugs and through most of the detox before he can get into the program. They don't have a nurse to deal with medical issues. They do have the psychologist pastor I was telling you about and they also have a Life Coach who is relatively new that comes in once a week to work with each person individually.

I left work at 11:30 AM and drove to the rehabilitation center in Bremen. The building itself was an abandoned elementary school. As I was given the tour, the curriculum was described to me. The program was nicknamed "Bible Boot Camp." It was a 12 step program with a Christian emphasis, and was operated with a sense of military discipline. Days were regimented, the rooms were spotless, and every item from cooking pans to individual's socks was in its place. I was impressed and remembered a time when Jonathan was in his early 20's that he would have fit in well in this environment. Now I wasn't sure.

During the next five days emails about Jonathan were quiet. Michael and I visited Jonathan on Saturday, and Jonathan did tell me that he was caught stealing engine supplements rather than candy. The logic was that without a job and a car that was having problems, he needed these to help preserve his engine.

Terri had her surgery to remove the tumor. Kristin was making arrangements to fly down to FL to visit while Terri recuperated and to be with Terri on her birthday. Kristin let us know she was a finalist for a position she had applied for with an insurance company. Also, the Relay for Life was taking place on the weekend of April 3. Terri, originally a sponsor and participant of this event, was now a cancer survivor too.

Thursday March 25

Mike to Kristin and Michael

I also spoke with Jonathan last night and he's trying to get himself out. Apparently there is some paperwork you can fill out and request a release from jail as long as you stay in the area. You can do this after you've been in for awhile, which I guess Jonathan has. He's still saying he would never do this to me.....blah, blah, blah.

I'm going to call the psychiatrist to see if she'll write the papers to have him committed if it comes to that. He still wants to get his court date on the 1st over with. If he does get out, he'll want to get to the court to get his records. I'll keep you posted as to what's going on.

Michael to Mike and Kristin

Isn't the psychiatrist the one who said he belongs in jail? Sounds like she'd be the best one to get him put away if the judge asks why. If he gets out, where did he say he'll go? If you won't have him and I won't have him... and I don't think Tiffany will...where? Is he mad at you because "he'd never do this to you?" Did you happen to tell him why I'm unable to receive his calls? He's tried calling 1-2 times per day all week, but not yesterday. Are you planning to visit him again Saturday? Has Tiffany mentioned anything about going to see him?

Mike to Michael and Kristin

I'll be going Saturday as long as he's still in there. Will you be going too?

I've left a message for the shrink, so hopefully she'll call back today.

Tiffany only works Saturday and Sunday, so it would be hard for her to get away, especially since she's already almost been fired for lousy attendance.

He doesn't know exactly where he would go, hopefully to a rehab place. But he might think he needs to get a few things done before he goes in. My guess is that he'll stay with Tiffany for a day or 2, perhaps even longer if he gets out this week. He'll want to go to his court date before he goes to rehab.

I've told him you can't take his calls, maybe he's thinking you'll change your mind.

Yes, he sounds mad, but then he'll tell me he isn't.

Michael to Mike, Kristin and Terri
Michael voiced his opinion about keeping Jonathan in jail, and was all for it.

If you get the money back from the The Facility Folly, I suggest you don't waste it by throwing it at some place Jonathan is comfortable with. He can't be comfortable if he's going to grow up...he'll just play the system like he's always done at places he was comfortable in. Remember how much he hated Francis and Ariadne? They made it extremely uncomfortable for him, probably because they forced him to look in the mirror and held him accountable for his own actions. Jonathan will tell you now that was among the best growth experiences of his life even though he hated it at the time. Conversely if he goes to a hospital like environment where they view everyone as "patients," his addiction will be further fueled because they will likely convince him, as if he needs it, that he'll always need anti-depressants and/or anti-anxiety medications. Food for thought.

Mike to Michael and Kristin

I agree that jail is better than being on the outside, but I also believe he needs help that jail can't provide. He's got to want the help, and at this point I'm not sure how the judicial system is going to view this. The probation office hasn't called me back yet, so I'll give her another call this afternoon if I don't hear from her.

Mike to Terri, Michael and Kristin

I just returned from the courthouse only to find out that the court transportation system will only pick up in Cobb County. They tried postponing until 5/20 and I insisted no. If he doesn't make his 4/1 date, he'll need to bring his paperwork in to show he was in jail. If he still isn't out by 3/31, I'll go back down there to see if I can get it postponed until 5/20.

I also spoke with the nurse at 211. She has made the psychiatrist aware of the situation. She could do the Form 2013, but, since Jonathan has been in jail he has detoxed. And unless he appears to be at risk to himself or somebody else, she can't do anything about it. She did say she would see him as soon as he gets out though.

I did find a place in Decatur and I haven't talked with them yet. Here's the website if you want to check it out and see what you think.

Michael to Terri, Kristin and Mike

I agree that Jonathan needs help jail cannot provide, and that place in Decatur sounds nice, but I don't believe it's right for Jon. He continues displaying and vocalizing that he's not sick. He really believes he can overcome his drug problem by himself. And more importantly, he doesn't believe the anti-depressants and anti-anxiety medications are a problem. In his mind the only problem they present is they "make" him steal. He's said it over and over...I NEEEEED my medicine!!! He doesn't accept the fact he's been unable live a mildly normal life without the "need" for drugs as evidence of a problem...he's in denial. Therefore if he's in denial, that program, and any other that he can "play" the system within, is a complete waste of money, effort, and time, in my opinion.

Jon's supposed willingness to check himself in somewhere is nothing more than his attempt to satisfy our desires for him so he can move on with his life of addiction minus our intervention. I'm 100% convinced he has no real, genuine interest in getting healthy the right way...only HIS way...and until he reaches that point of realization, the point when he desires ANY kind of help because he actually feels helpless, everything we do for him is effectively meaningless. Staying in jail for a greater length of time may help him reach that point of desperation...but it seems we may have no choice in the matter anyway.

Let us all stop denying the truth. The real problem is Jon's spirit, not his mind. You can bring up Jon's history with depression as a child if you like, but any kid is going to show symptoms of depression when his parents are divorced and there seems to be nothing happy in life. I was depressed, too... but I didn't cry and act out as a result. I held it inside and became contemptible, intolerant, and irritable, then later got over it. (Or did I...hmmm?) Fact is Jonathan was a remarkably strong (emotionally) and stable person as a young teenager. Cherie and I remember him that way. Do you? His youth didn't matter at that point. It was moving to Dallas and the introduction to drugs that began his downfall...and with the downfall, depression.

Forget the mind for a moment. Jonathan has had demons inside him... not skeletons in your closet kinda' demons...the kind people are scared of. The kind people kill themselves to escape. He has been possessed. Dad, your home had signs of evil spirits. Jonathan had to be physically restrained by several people when he was exorcised. Jonathan saw demons in his bedroom. Jonathan saw them in his car. Jonathan was scared to death. When Jonathan was living with me, I had to hold him as he cried himself asleep at night. He told me it was the only peaceful sleep he had, at the time.

I believe the Holy Spirit's presence within me kept evil at bay, at least temporarily. All this spiritual turmoil was because he was making real strides towards sobriety. What is that turmoil? Spiritual warfare! He actually made great progress while staying with me...at least so far as staying clean goes. Do you remember that? Do you remember he was offered the kitchen manager position, that's the third highest ranking job on the pecking order. When he moved away, his life turned upside-down again.

I'm not suggesting I'm the answer...I'm clearly not. But the evil was gone...at least temporarily.

The Bible says in Matthew 12:43-45, *"When the unclean spirit has gone out of a person, it passes through waterless places seeking rest, but finds none. Then it says, 'I will return to my house from which I came.' And when it comes, it finds the house empty, swept, and put in order. Then it goes and brings with it seven other spirits more evil than itself, and they enter and dwell there, and the last state of that person is worse than the first."*

I am afraid that is where Jonathan is now. I believe it's the reason for his mental drug dependency and I believe it's the reason for his significant spiritual confusion, and I also believe it's the reason that occasionally my presence causes him to say hateful, vengeful, and vulgar things and to become sometimes violent towards me. I think the same goes for his actions around you, Dad. The devil, enemy, Satan, whatever you want to call him, has saturated Jon's soul. Think about something...supposedly the devil wants to inhabit and destroy us, ultimately to own our souls, right?

One surefire way to control us is with drug abuse...that can't be argued. When Jonathan was at The Facility and was finally coming off the narcotics, he was more suicidal than ever! That's evil corrupting him and trying to bring him down entirely as an effort not to lose him!!! His discovery and rampant abuse of benzos upon leaving The Facility has quelled the appetite for self-destruction because it's keeping the enemy inside him satisfied.

More than any kind of doctor, Jonathan needs God. No doctor can cure or save his soul. Give it deep thought. Pray about it. Perhaps all of you will see it, too. I say it confidently, not arrogantly...I am right about this.

Love to you all...I'm glad you're getting better, Mom!

Friday March 26

Mike to Michael, Terri and Kristin

That's certainly one way to look at it. There is no doubt that there is something going on inside him. You are not aware of this, but he was seeing a psychologist and psychiatrist when Alicia and I were married and continued after we were divorced. Although not regularly, I think he was seeing someone even when the three of us lived together. He had horrible migraines back then, and that was probably the start of his addiction. I'm not sure where all of you stand on destiny, pre-destination, reincarnation, your Higher Self, or what each moment and every encounter or experience you have is meant to be for your own growth, but there is a line of thinking, primarily in the Eastern Religions, that suggests we come here to learn the lessons we need to learn in order to get back to God. (now, that's a run on sentence) Jonathan was going to do drugs. After he moved to Dallas, all of his Lawrenceville friends started doing them too. For that matter, one friend was kicked out of the marines for doing them and one of his friends died from an overdose. It is/was something he is/was destined to do, according to some religions.

I spoke with him last night. I don't know if you got my message Michael, but he said there is still $7 left on your account. Hopefully, you were able to talk to him. He was pleading to get out and start detox. Terri, he got your letter and unfortunately it came up late in the conversation so I don't know what he thought about it. It was however after this was brought up that he started pleading to be released. I got the impression he was very influenced by it. Whether that means he is considering Bremen program or was influenced by what the astrologer said or was simply touched by his Mother's kind and caring words, I don't know. Most likely a combination.

He told me that the Major is the one who makes the decision about who can be released under his own recognizance. When the bond is $1300 or less, which is what Jon's is, he usually releases them. (this is inmate rumor) He asked me to call The Major and talk to him. I will, but I'd like everyone's feedback, I still need to talk to his PO, and I'd like to see what he has to say tomorrow and to Michael last night. I will also call Tiffany today and let her know what is going on and ask what her involvement will be.

Let me know what you think.

Terri's letter encouraged Jonathan to enlist into the Bremen program. She also mentioned the importance of addressing his issues and to recognize that he had this disease for over 10 years. She described the affect it had on his psychological and emotional development. Even though Jonathan thought he could kick the addiction himself, she pointed out that it was a disease that he had and a team of counselors and doctors were needed to help him. Her letter continued.....

"I have some important information to share with you...you may not remember me telling you, but I had a session back in the beginning of January with a renowned Astrologer here. She has been doing this her entire lifetime and is extremely talented in her field. I won't bore you with all she had to say about me, but she had a LOT to say about "your middle child" (you). Keep in mind she did not know me at all, had no idea about my family, and knew nothing about me other than my first name, my birth date and the time of birth. She had very important information about you specifically that she wanted me to share with you. I am going to list things that she said right off the copy of my tape. Honestly, see if any of this does not affect you in a very recognizable and profound way, as it did me and Dad (I read it to him earlier today). We both think it is very important for you to hear, and I think you will relate to a lot of it. Here goes:

Jonathan is having serious issues and much confusion.

He does not feel strength.

He is easily led astray and the opportunity is there to drop off or not deal with life.

This is a VERY important time in Jonathan's life.

Planet Saturn return; Saturn has gone all the way around his chart and is back in the exact same place as his birth. This only occurs once every 30 years. This year (2010) will profoundly affect Jonathan's future. <u>What Jonathan does right now will follow him for the next 30 years.</u>

Jonathan must get his foot in the door of his future.

He can't take the easy way out. He must work very hard and apply himself now, more than ever before, THIS YEAR has profound effects. If he does not do this, he will continue current life pattern, constantly trying to make things work for him and spinning his wheels.

He is dealing with power struggles with authority. He does not want anyone telling him what to do.

He is quick tempered, and short. He is not calm in his life.

Right now, don't speed or he will get a ticket. Look over his shoulder as he is being watched by the "cosmic" cops.

This whole year for Jonathan is all about his home, health and family.

Don't give any authority figures any grief whatsoever or he can and will go to jail.

If he owes anyone money, or has problems with anyone, he must clear up or this will follow him for 30 years.

He will be mad about it; anger is necessary to let him know there is a problem.

Even though he is mad, he needs to recognize the need to suck it up, and just do what he needs to do and get it over with. He needs to just play out the year and do what is necessary regardless of whether he understands everything.

Jonathan must get something going on in physical fitness, and needs to work out to the point of exhaustion. This will help him get the stress out of his body.

This is a VERY SERIOUS and VERY IMPORTANT time in Jonathan's life. He must suck it up and work hard, and take orders; all year long he has to take care of his health, especially dental health, and skin, also bone structure. He needs to keep going in a forward direction; no going backward.

The egomaniac in his Aries sign is active; he wants it to always be about him. He expects other people to take care of it for him. He needs to work hard and get the help for himself. HE HAS to LET IT COME FROM INSIDE HIMSELF.

Jonathan is very strong, though he does not always recognize this. He has strong drive and strong initiative. Home, health, and family is important to him.

Extreme discipline is needed for Jonathan. He needs to learn to accept things. He needs to learn how to take disappointment, turn it around and say "this is what I have" and make the best of situations. He can't fly off the handle and be mad because he wants things his way.

JONATHAN MUST MAKE CHANGES NOW OR HE IS GOING to RUIN HIS LIFE. PERIOD. THERE IS NO SUGAR COATING HERE. THIS IS <u>VERY</u> IMPORTANT to JONATHAN'S FUTURE.

This is the time when he needs to find a place in a career and take off with it. 28-30 years from now it will be time to retire.

This year Jonathan needs to get real with society. He is going to be held accountable for everything in his life. That's what Saturn does. He MUST get through this and be VERY STRONG and then HE will be in charge. He will REALLY be in charge, not just thinking or expecting something he needs to be, for nothing. He will know how to be really in charge of himself and he will gain strength.

Planet Pluto is aspecting Jonathan's sun right now and will not aspect again for 40+ years! This does not happen often. THIS YEAR IS VERY LIFE CHANGING, EITHER WAY! It is up to Jonathan to choose which way it will go.

Jonathan's family must be strong and supportive without being enabling. It is up to Jonathan. He must stand on his own two feet and must work with authority figures. He needs to show the universe that he can stick it out and be strong.

People with addiction problems are feeding into the weakest parts of their personality, kind of giving up. Jonathan needs to stay strong and know that "Yes, I do have this part of me and I can turn it into something positive. IT IS THERE, BUT IT DOES NOT HAVE to RUIN MY LIFE!"

There you have it sweetie….I typed it word for word, exactly as she stated it all. Keep in mind she knew nothing about you prior to saying all this. In fact, she did not know you had an addiction problem. She figured it out just looking at your chart."

Terri concluded the letter and asked him to place his faith in God and to let Him lead. She offered words of love and encouragement.

"Happy Birthday, my precious son. Please know that I am with you in spirit, even though you can't see me. Just think of me and know that I am there with you, right by your side, today and always.
I love you very much!
Always and forever,
Mom"

Michael to Mike, Terri and Kristin

Actually I was aware of his psychiatric appointments, though admittedly I did forget about them. That doesn't change my opinion though. I still believe that time was a reflection of his hurt over "losing" his parents. Coupled with having no Mommy presence for the majority of his formative years probably led to his general disrespect for women and macho attitude, but I don't think any of that led to the depression he feels today. Certainly I could be wrong, but the depression is an umbrella excuse he uses for many different aspects in his life. Laziness, need for medicine, drug abuse, can't hold a job, stealing, etc...all of it can be easily excused (in his mind) by depression. As for Jon's friends being drug users, perhaps you're right...maybe he was simply on a path towards that. But you know what, so was I and every other kid I ever knew. I never did...not once...never even tempted, despite the fact almost all my friends (in Tampa, when I actually had friends) used them. I'm not saying he should be like me...but I am suggesting it was a choice he made. I don't buy the destiny argument. God gave us free will. That's all irrelevant now, I suppose.

I never heard from him last night. But the reason I can't talk is because of my cell minutes, not my balance on the credit card. If he calls tonight, I'll try to answer just to say hello, but I can't stay on the phone.

Regarding a release from jail, you can probably guess my feelings. Not unless the **COURT** mandates that he go to a proper treatment facility, and if we have any influence over that decision, it should be one akin to the Bremen program. I don't think a medical facility will do him much good...perhaps a little...but like I said, he'll play the system. Jail is better.

Kristin to Mike, Michael and Terri

I agree with Michael. I believe that Jonathan won't get the help he needs by himself. I believe that he needs to stay in jail or go into a place that he won't be able to leave until he gets the help he needs. I was wondering if he said anything to you about my letter to you Dad? I sent him a letter the same day Mom sent hers. I never knew that Jonathan was seeing someone when Dad and Alicia were married. I was still pretty young. One thing I do remember though is those headaches he got. Did Jonathan ever have those headaches before Mom and Dad got divorced? Maybe these headaches are drug related. When is the earliest someone can start drugs? I just hope he gets the help he needs. I told him that in the letter I sent him. I am with Michael on the drug thing. All my friends did drugs when I was a teenager, even Emily, my best friend had a time in her life when she did drugs, but I never once wanted to do them or even tried, not even a cigarette. It's not like I could with my medical history, but even if I had no medical problems at all, I really think that drugs wouldn't be for me.

I still haven't heard about the job. I will let you know what I find out, if I find out anything.

Saturday March 27 was Jonathan's 29th birthday. Michael and I met at the jail and waited to hear his name called so we could visit him for ½ hour. He looked like he had lost weight again, as he wasn't eating much and he confirmed the food was awful. The letters I had been sending had aroused interest with several of his cell mates, and as he told me later, a couple of the guards who reviewed each piece of mail before delivery were also curious. The cell mates wanted to meet me, and I met a couple of them through the security windows.

I had been writing him nearly every day since we had determined he wasn't going anywhere anytime soon. The first letter I sent him was on March 15, and within 2 days he had received it. The mail system and the jail delivery system turned out to be more efficient than we could have imagined.

In most cases, the topic of each letter would address the issue we had talked about the night before. On the night of Sunday March 21 he was asking why this was happening to him. He was crying and engaging in self-pity. He again pleaded with me to bail him out of jail, and I told him no. He reminded me that his birthday was coming up, and jail is no place to celebrate your birthday. "I can't Jon. It's not time yet," I told him this each time he asked.

I got up the next morning at 4:00, followed my daily routine which now included the extra step of getting the letter in the mail to Jonathan. On this morning I wrote to him,

> "My Dearest Son,
>
> I hope today finds you feeling better than yesterday. *(I began all the letters with this introduction)* There are times for all of us that we ask "why me?" I spoke with Uncle Joe last night and he described to me how his life is a circus. And to him it is as this is how he perceives it. He informed me that he just found out upon his return from vacation, he has a $20,000 medical bill that needs to be addressed for

his shoulder surgery several years back. He also said he is having issues with a new roommate that moved in several weeks ago. These events in his life have caused it to be a "circus."

I am reminded of something out of A Course In Miracles. "<u>I</u> am responsible for what I see, <u>I</u> choose the feelings I experience, and <u>decide</u> upon the <u>goal</u> I would achieve. And everything that <u>seems</u> to happen to me <u>I</u> ask for, and <u>receive</u> as <u>I have asked</u>."

This applies to all of us. During our journey it is necessary for us to experience certain things in order to rid ourselves of the hidden guilt we all carry. This may seem to be unfair and unlucky, but there is that part of us, the Higher Self, that knows. That's why it is so important that we accept this, and not blame others for our misfortune.

All of us need to go through the period of life where we learn to accept others, get along, pay our dues, start a career, learn how to deal with cranky bosses and other authorities. We all need to go through this, in one way or another, before we begin to recognize the inner growth potential that exist in us. In other words, we must <u>do</u> certain things before we can <u>know</u> other things.

I encourage you to embrace your situation, with understanding and love, accept what is happening, and prepare to move on.

I love you very much. Dad

My Journal March 28, 2010

Very little has been written over the past 5 months in this book. Much has happened with Jonathan that has brought to test all the lives of his loved ones. His drug addiction has seemingly peaked, although we can never say what the future may hold. He has been arrested three times, twice for shoplifting and once for a DUI. He has been in jail since the evening of March 9 for shoplifting and I haven't bailed him out yet. This is probably the first time in his life that I haven't paid the money, overlooked things, whatever to get him out of a jam, and it was tough for him to deal with at first, although he seems to accept it now.

I told him when he was arrested for his DUI in February that I wouldn't bail him out again. I think I also told him that last December, and I did anyway, though he did spend 3-4 days in jail just before I took him Facility.

As we are all each other's teachers and students, I've had to go within, reconfirm to myself what is most important to me, and find the lesson he is teaching me. After so many attempts at trying to teach me to let him walk his own path, perhaps I finally understand. I told him I cannot contribute to his addiction anymore. This means no more financial help if this is the path he chooses. I will lie down with him if he stumbles, but I must release myself from thinking that I need to save him.

One of my least favorite terms in the world is "tough love." Love is gentle and kind. It is non-judgmental. For me to take a tough love stance and say I am doing this for his good, is not what he is trying to teach me nor is it something he wants to learn, I think (that's my judgment, you see).

So I have concluded with the guidance of the Holy Spirit that I must allow him to walk his own path, and you know what, he'll walk it anyway. I have nothing to do with it. My role is to help as I can, and remain at peace with everything in the world of 5 senses. And more importantly, take the steps I need to take in order to get closer to God.

Monday March 29

Mike to Michael, Kristin and Terri

I just got off the phone with the Major. They will not allow Jonathan to leave on his own recognizance unless he has a medical problem, therefore, he's in there until his court date or until he's bailed out. Opinions please on whether to bail him out or not so he can get to his court date.

Terri to Mike, Michael and Kristin

He has a HUGE medical problem...he needs to be admitted somewhere for mental health issues. Did you remind the Major about the previous conversation I had with him when Jonathan first got there? He was the one who was going to hang up from me and go immediately to get the psychologist/psychiatrist to go see Jon. I don't know if this even happened. I wonder if he realizes or remembers specifically who Jonathan is? Also, besides Jon's obvious mental health issues (which IS a medical problem), he also has problems going on with his blood pressure and depression, correct? Did he offer ANY help at all?

The whole problem is that if Jonathan gets bailed out just to go to a court date...then he is OUT. We then have no options to get him court ordered and who knows what could happen with him between the time you got him out and the time he gets in front of a judge? Again, we must protect him from himself....this is the whole reason he has been there all this time....unless he is willing to have you pick him up and go directly to the boot camp (which we already know the court will go along with), I would not bail him out just to go to that other court date. Maybe this is the opportunity that is a blessing in disguise. Once you tell Jonathan that the Major won't let him out, then you have the ball in your court to make demands of Jonathan in exchange for bailing him out of jail. This is the chance to say "I will get you out as long as we go directly to admit you to the boot camp"...maybe he would change his feelings about everything then.

Michael to Terri, Mike and Kristin

All excellent points. What's this boot camp you speak of...Bremen? Whatever it is, it must be ensured that he's accepted prior to his bail out. Some of these places require a letter from the patient/student for admittance, then a mandatory waiting period for review. Also consider if Jonathan is truly sick in the head, which I maintain he is not, then he may not receive adequate treatment at a hip-hip-hooray type place.

I'm 100% for his bail out if, and only if, the court will back it. Otherwise I think he should take his lumps and hopefully want the opportunity when he's released.

Terri to Michael, Mike and Kristin

Yes, the Bremen program is nicknamed "Bible Boot Camp". As of Saturday, Dad said Jonathan had agreed he would go talk to them, at least. They don't appear to be a "hip hip hooray" place at all, according to what Dad saw....they are run very military like.....strict. Hard rules, no tolerance to violators. Might be just the ticket, as long as they are also loving and caring. Maybe you should go see it, Michael, and see if your opinion is the same as dads. I'm sure they would be happy to show you the place, too.

I don't understand why the probation officer won't return your calls.

Michael to Terri, Mike and Kristin

I suppose that sounded sarcastic...I don't know how else to categorize the place, because it's most definitely NOT medical. It is simply a morale boost type of place, of which I am fully in favor for Jonathan. The problem that exists with a place such as this is twofold...1) Jonathan is likely agreeing to see the place just to pacify us, he has no sincere interest, I assure you (unless

1 week made a 100% reversal difference in his world) <u>AND</u> 2) Jonathan thinks he has medical issues, which have obviously been overblown if the jail staff isn't addressing them, but they're not going to simply escape his mind as long as he keeps manifesting them.

My hope is that he'll visit this place and be encouraged to sign up. However he cannot visit without getting bailed out. Catch 22. If he decides he doesn't like it, then what? The only way is to ensure Jonathan this is why we're taking him out. He'll have the option to go there or go to a halfway house (or similar). No in-between. It cannot be allowed.

I do believe if he agrees to go there, his mind will eventually be eased of the "I NEEEEEED my medicine" issues. But he is a stubborn cuss, so he could be a problem child for a while.

Most importantly, let's be sure this place is well researched this time around. I'll look into it, and ask around here among people "in the know," but this cannot turn into another The Facilty obviously or he may lose all hope and faith in EVER getting better. This is absolutely IMPERATIVE to his mental health, of this I'm certain.

And Dad, let's think about the place in Cumming/Alpharetta also. They are structured much the same as Bremen it seems, but they may cost less. I, for one, feel confident they are a good program or my pastor wouldn't put his name to it.

Mike to Michael, Kristin and Terri

I left Mom a voice mail, but I'll address it here to get all of your opinions. Since Jonathan won't make it to his court date, would it make sense for me to go to see if I can get the judge to put him somewhere? Also, maybe I can find out what the charges actually are. Thoughts?

Michael to Mike, Terri and Kristin

Could be worth a try, but it stands to reason they'll just tell you to go away since Jonathan is 29 and you no longer have any "right" to speak for/about him with the judge. But then again, it worked when you got him the probation. An official postponement may not even get his name called… you'll probably have to work your way to the judge via the public defender again.

Terri to Michael, Kristin and Mike

You would, however, have the right to speak in Jon's behalf (and make decisions in his behalf) if Jonathan would be willing to sign a Power of

Attorney over to you. Maybe he would be willing to do that if it means getting out of jail.

I got your voicemail, Mike, but haven't had a chance to call you. I was at lunch when you called and had my cell phone at my desk. Sorry.

I wonder if the pastor in Bremen you met with would be willing to go pay Jonathan a visit in jail to tell him more about the program? Worth a call to ask him his opinion or thoughts since he seems to have an "in" with the courts.

Tuesday March 30

Mike to Terri, Kristin and Michael

I just got off the phone with Bremen to get a little more information, specifically costs of the program to see if it's even feasible. There is a one-time $850 entry fee. Then it is $650 a month for the next 12 months. So, if we get the refund from The Facility, it sounds affordable. Speaking of The Facility, Cindy, the woman I spoke with, said she had heard on the news that they are under investigation.

Terri to Mike, Michael and Kristin; Mike's responses in bold

Terri: That sounds reasonable, price wise. Seems 60 days is the magic cutoff time for any contact with the outside world. Didn't you also say the limited phone and visitation rights start then, as well? Or was it 90 days?
Mike: 60 it is.

Terri: I just tried doing a search for local Atlanta news, as well as the Atlanta Constitution, and can't find anything regarding the Facility investigation. I would be interested to see what they are saying. I wonder what news station she heard it on? Did she say?
Mike: No.

Terri: Did you talk to Jonathan last night?
Mike: Yes

Terri: If so, what did he have to say when you told him about the phone call with the major?
Mike: He expected the news. He spoke with a guard yesterday who told him the same thing the major told me. Then the guard sang to him...."Have yourself a Merry Christmas." Nice guy.

Terri: Any more conversation with him about going to the boot camp?
Mike: Yes, he said he'd check it out.

Terri: He shouldn't have any problem getting into the program if he goes straight there. He isn't taking anything now, right?
Mike: I'm not exactly sure. I think he's getting Lexapro.

Terri: Is he still taking BP medicine?
Mike: Yes and no. They take his BP sometimes.

Terri: He shouldn't be taking that unless his bp is being monitored every day. It is not safe for him to take it unless his BP truly is too high. Otherwise, he can make it too low and cause him to pass out.

If you don't hear from Kevin (our contact at the Facility who was investigating our refund request) soon, maybe you can reach him by phone. Did you try calling Dan (a former Facility employee who was consulting us) last night to see if he had talked to him recently?
Mike: No.

Terri: Did Jonathan sound at all enthusiastic about checking out the boot camp?
Mike: Somewhat, he just wants to get out and start rehab somewhere.

Terri: Also, what did he say about the court date situation; did you ask him about signing a power of attorney to you?
Mike: Yes, and he said it takes days to get something processed. I just went and postponed it until 5/20.

Jonathan and I continued to talk almost every evening. Some of our conversations were peaceful and positive exchanges, while others were angry and confrontational. However, at the end of each conversation, he would ask me, "Will you come and bail me out?" And each evening I would reply, "It's not time yet."

My Journal March 30

As I was meditating and contemplating this evening, a voice from my inner self kept quietly telling me, "It's time." During my conversation with Jonathan this evening, I agreed to bail him out of jail this weekend. He tells me he wants to get on with his life and face the consequences ahead of him. I've said I'll be there for him and not lift him up. Putting up the money, in my mind, is not lifting him up. If he is sincere in his desire to face his truth and get the help he needs, he will immediately address it. I look at this as walking with him to the crossroad. The choices are his, not mine, nor any of the rest of his family.

I'm not sure what kind of guidelines will be established in order for him to stay here. The emphasis will be on him to get well. He does need to get his DUI record, see his probation officer, and call some help lines to see what is available.

He made mention to me last night that each time he goes to a place, he thinks it's the worse place he's ever been. From his ups and downs with Tiffany, to jail, to The Facility, and to jail again. Each time it's worse. I wonder if he asks himself why?

My Journal March 31

It is not surprising to me how the family reacted when I told them I was bailing Jonathan out on Friday.

Wednesday March 31

Mike to Kristin, Terri and Michael

I'm going to bail Jonathan out on Friday so that he can address the issues he needs to address. These include getting his DUI records, seeing his probation officer and finding out what will be done there, and visiting Bremen, Alpharetta, or finding another place to go to get well.

He'll be calling you from my phone after he gets out. He says he loves you all and he can't wait to talk with you.

Michael to Mike, Terri and Kristin

I thought we'd all pretty much agreed Jon's future treatments were best left within the court system...? If you're going to bail him out, it is imperative that you stand your ground and not allow him to EVER stay with you again, not one night, if he doesn't complete/graduate whatever program we agree upon as a family. You MUST make this clear to him. If you don't he will very likely play the game again...history tells us so. If any part of the reason for getting him out is based upon fixing his legal mess, why are you helping him do this? He should take his lumps like a man and deal with it when he gets out... like a man. I'm afraid it will all serve as a distraction and contribute towards him not concentrating on fixing himself personally because he tends to focus on these little things and won't stop until he's satisfied with the outcome, a characteristic that I don't think he'll apply towards his "psychological" needs because he's made it very clear he doesn't think he's that messed up. Are you allowing Jonathan to play you, Dad? Please be honest with yourself and don't be a victim of deception, perhaps a spirit that Jonathan isn't even controlling. Also if you're going to get him out, wouldn't Friday be the worst time? The courts will be closed Saturday and Sunday obviously. Will the well-care places be open and available for appointments? Sitting at home will make him happy, but his cravings will begin immediately, and he cannot be trusted. CANNOT be trusted...especially for more than a day. You must set a very specific, short timeline for Jonathan to get everything done before he goes into rehab. And if he hasn't completed whatever it may be by that time, too bad, he's going to rehab. If he refuses because he needs more time or because he doesn't like any of the places, you gotta' kick him out, Dad. I don't know your mindset right now...pray and be strong!!!

Ephesians 6:10-18

"Be strong in the Lord and in his mighty power. Put on the full armor of God so that you can take your stand against the devil's schemes. For our struggle is not against flesh and blood, but against the rulers, against the authorities, against the powers of this dark world and against the spiritual forces of evil in the heavenly realms. Therefore put on the full armor of God, so that when the day of evil comes, you may be able to stand your ground, and after you have done everything, to stand. Stand firm then, with the belt of truth buckled around your waist, with the breastplate of righteousness in place, and with your feet fitted with the readiness that comes from the gospel of peace. In addition to all this, take up the shield of faith, with which you can extinguish all the flaming arrows of the evil one. Take the helmet of salvation and the sword of the Spirit, which is the word of God. And pray in the Spirit on all occasions with all kinds of prayers and requests. With this in mind, be alert and always keep on praying for all the saints."

Terri to Mike, Michael and Kristin

I don't understand, if you are going to bail him out (which I understood you were not going to do at this time) in order to deal with the court stuff, then why wait until AFTER his court date? You might as well get him out today so he can go to his court appearance tomorrow. I know you already postponed it, as of yesterday, but if you call them they will probably put him back on the schedule for tomorrow's docket.

I agree with Michael regarding the concerns about him having the whole weekend with no way to get any of the things accomplished, and two days for him to possibly get comfortable about being out of jail which may take away any sense of urgency or desperation feelings that might have swayed him towards agreeing to go straight to a rehab place as an ALTERNATIVE to jail time. I, too, am concerned that once he is back home again, he will procrastinate going anywhere for help, and since he doesn't truly feel he needs help, and he knows that ultimately it is his decision and none of us can force the help for him once he is bailed out, he may very well just be telling you what he thinks will be what you need to hear to just get him out of there…after that, you will no longer have any control over the situation. As much as I hate to say it, as Michael said, and unfortunately it is true, Jonathan has proven himself over and over again that his "good intentions" won't last for long.

As I mentioned previously, I think your ability to hold jail over his head may be the ONLY way to force the help to finally happen, as Jonathan can then choose to go for help or choose to stay where he is…going to your house should not be an option, at least in my opinion. There are other ways for him to take care of his legal issues. He does not have to be bailed out to do that stuff. Plenty of other people in jail have to deal with their legal issues, also. Also, the power of attorney I suggested would be a good way for you to get the records for Jon, if you are willing to do that…Jonathan told you it takes a few days….that's not very long, unless you had been trying to get things done before the court date. Well, now you have already postponed it, so there is not a big rush anymore.

I'm sorry, but I just don't think Jonathan merely agreeing to go check out the rehab place is enough…when he gets over there and decides he doesn't want to go there, then what are you going to do? If you bring him home now, Mike, you have no choices left once he is out. I hope you have considered everything here…I don't know everything, maybe. This scares me, though. This might be our only opportunity to get him to get help, since he wants out of jail so badly…waiting for the probation officer to call you back and seeing what might be able to be done through the court mandate system seemed a better idea to me. I do realize the process is taking longer than we'd like, but Jon's rehab is too important not to consider doing it however way is necessary to ensure that he will agree to go to somewhere long term to get his life together. He is not capable of doing this on his own.

Please consider everything before you go and get him out of there. Your hands will be tied then.

Kristin to Mike, Michael and Terri

Dad, I am going to have to agree with Michael and Mom. I think you would be in the exact same boat that you were in before if you go and bail him out, especially on a Friday, where he wouldn't be able to do anything until the very earliest Monday. I do agree that Jonathan wants the help right this second, because he is sick of being in jail. He wants you to come get him so he can check that place out. I also think that once he gets out he will procrastinate. He will maybe agree to go check the place out, but as long as he doesn't agree right now that he will let you admit him in the place, I wouldn't bail him out. Michael and Mom are right. He will screw you once again, I think. Plus, won't you be at work next week? If everyone is at work and he is at your house, who knows what he would do. I support whatever you think is the right thing to do, but please be careful. Jonathan may be "nice" today, tomorrow, next week, but there will come a day where he will jump out again and not be the same Jonathan we know and love. Not until he gets the help he needs.

Mike to Kristin, Michael and Terri

I expected this reaction, and I point out to you that I look at things from an entirely different perspective.

First, let's look at the tangible, that is, the world of 5 senses. I talk with him every day. You don't have the chance to listen to him and talk about things, I do. Nor do you write to him every day. I do. I point out the things of your concern and we discuss these issues in the evening. The one thing we have in common here is that we all pray for him every day, but we very likely may pray differently and for different results.

There seems to be a common concern about the weekend. I'm waiting until Friday so that I can spend a couple of days with him. And I'm taking Monday off so that we can see his PO and get the DUI records. If he gets comfortable, so what? I hope he comes home and feels the love and the safety of being at home. He's spent 3 ½ weeks there, and like I pointed out earlier,

I talk with him every day. It's time for him to get out and deal with what he has to deal with. One of those first things is to call the HELP lines. With me being there on the weekend, we can immediately head off to a facility if need be. These places can accept people 24/7, depending on the urgency. So if we need to go on Saturday, we will. Or we can wait until he talks with his PO, gets his records, and proceed after that. Sunday there are churches in session. My guess is that we will head off to the church by the house and speak with Tom, the person I introduced to you several months ago who was very interested in Jonathan.

He's not going to any pay facility as long as The Facility credit is still up in the air. The first payment is due 4/6. Which reminds me Terri, did you or Scott find out if there is a way to appeal?

This means a freebee. And as a freebee, he'll need to meet whatever criteria they have. And if he meets it on Saturday, off we'll go.

As far as Jonathan proving to everyone that he can do it with the right help, we'll have to see. He may be in and out for the next 30 years. Regarding the court mandate, it will be conducted regardless. If he's going to jail, let him go on Monday instead of waiting until he's released from Floyd County. Regarding the conditions set forth by me bailing him out, he can tell you.

Now let's look at the intangible. There are many spiritual paths to follow, and I can pretty much guarantee that I follow one that none of you are familiar with or at best, know very little about. This makes it neither right nor wrong, it's just different. Without going into a lot of detail, the basic differences are that it teaches unconditional love for everyone, forgiveness (not the kind you are familiar with), and non-judgment. Although it isn't called this in ACIM, Buddhism uses a term called loving-kindness as a behavior to model oneself after. It also stresses that we don't know the role everyone on this planet is to play and to think we do is arrogant. The Holy Spirit knows. For me to interfere with someone's chosen path only hinders my growth as well as theirs. It teaches the Oneness in all of Us, and not the separation that this world would have us believe. It is quite different than Christianity, Judaism, and Islam; all of which are very similar.

"Pray and be strong!!!" Son, I get up at 4:00 AM every morning and dedicate my first hour to God. This includes prayer, meditation, reading, contemplating, studying, and reflection. It all depends on the day and the circumstances. I get to work each day by 6:15 and spend the next few minutes praying to be guided through my work day and to give thanks for EVERYTHING in my life, including all those lessons that can be painful to learn. I get home at 4:30 PM and I go about the same morning ritual, although

I do get a lot of phone calls during this time, so it is often interrupted. Prayer is how I came to this next step in my relationship with Jon.

Rest assured, all will work out as it is supposed to, even if you don't like how it ends up. Have faith and give only love.

I love you all.

Dad/Mike

Michael to Mike, Terri and Kristin

The following may sound harsh, but with all due respect, Dad, you spoke with Jonathan every day for a dozen+ years and nothing you did or said stopped him from getting into this mess, potentially quite the opposite. Let me be sure I understand this from a simpler perspective. Are you going to simply allow Jonathan to run all over you (and the rest of the family) for however long he so chooses because you think he has a destiny? You are choosing to love blindly, and that is admirable; but to love blindly, or unconditionally, does not mean you should love without caution! Solomon, who history says is one of the wisest men the earth has ever seen, said, "Above all else, guard your heart..." Jonathan is not treading respectfully and cautiously near your heart, and you would be wise not to allow him to step all over it again. And how do you know his destiny is not jail? You accept destiny as a matter of faith, but by bailing him out, you are changing his course. You see, this can be viewed many different ways.

You say your spiritual path focuses on unconditional love, forgiveness, and non-judgment. So does Christianity. You and I are not so different in that respect.

You said Jonathan can tell us the conditions you've set forth. We need to know them from you. Jonathan cannot be trusted to tell us the truth, and he rarely fills everybody in on details. Please tell us so we can hold him accountable also.

I don't understand why you've taken this position without speaking with all of us about it. You're alone on the other side of the fence. It isn't right to disregard our positions, which by the way, are based upon hard evidence and history, not a spirit of hope and faith that can be manipulated on a whim and desire.

I am adamantly opposed to his release from prison without proper safeguards set forth. If he falls back again, don't chalk it up to destiny because you will have had a tremendous hand in contributing by enabling him.

I love you dearly. I think you know this. Please don't let this guise of help you're preparing be another step down a stairwell of despair. Please, Dad. Listen to us. Or at least be <u>EXTREMELY</u> rigid with him.

Cherie to Mike, Michael, Terri and Kristin

Well...I have tried to keep my 2 cents in my pocket but I feel that if nothing else, I should share my experiences with you. I have no suggestions or promises to make one way or another only facts. Having stood by 3 different family members through drug addiction, incarceration, and total self-destruction, this is what I have observed.

Drugs are not what we feel, believe, hope or know about a person. They are a chemical. A chemical that in spite of what we feel, believe, hope or know, has the power to completely control the victim that they ensnare. Chemicals have no compassion and no regard for how much you love your child or dearest brother. Chemicals work as they were scientifically compounded to. Chemicals have no spirit or religion. You have no power that can come against them. They will just sit there, a substance, until used or cast aside. They are not something you think out because they don't respond to reason. They are what they are apart from your intervention.

This is not to say that some have not broken free against these incredible odds but, research (as well as my personal experience), shows that <u>time</u>, determination and very tough love on the part of those closest to the user are the keys to success. Please know that as much as we all love our family member or friend, when they fall under the power of drugs, we must first deal with the drug and then the individual. The best way to do this is to get rid of them. Once you do this, you win only because they are gone.

Please understand that the medical facilities and counselors are businesses. The craving for these substances are difficult to tame because the satisfaction of feeding the craving itself is the <u>true addiction</u>...and that is why it is so very hard to stop. This satisfaction is so complete to the drug addict that it trumps everything. Its pleasure is more "satisfactory" to the user than the love of a child, parent, sibling or even God himself. It trumps hope for your future because satisfying the craving is your future as long as you are still in "addiction mode." Perfectly straight men have been known to sell their own bodies to feed this addiction. I reference this only because I am trying to make a point...there is no hitting rock bottom. If he could get a fix for his soul he would sell that too.

But the saying, time heals everything is especially true for the addict. You must get rid of the drug (as much as is biologically and physically possible. The cravings will begin to lessen and it eventually becomes possible to get a handle on your own life again. That is when the user can truly hear and not just listen to counseling.

We have all been praying for Jonathan to be free from drugs. Three weeks of incarceration will only render him panting, craving and hunting down his "satisfaction" when he gets out. The torment he feels is not something you pick up on in conversation or by just observing his behaviors. It is in his blood and brain but unbelievably tormenting just the same. Transition to another program is a good intention. It is also, in light of the magnitude of what the drug addict is attempting to overcome, a huge set up. He will find a high. The chemicals will work exactly as they are compounded to do. He can't help it. He will probably tell himself he is only going to do it once or maybe that is not going to do it at all. He will believe, with all his heart, that he is going to do it...this time. But he won't.

Time is the greatest help for the craving. Counseling should follow but initially <u>time</u> trumps the clear thinking drug abusers craving. I promise. I love you all and will be praying for the outcome. One last thing...please don't allow this to become about what <u>you</u> want. Chemicals don't have the ability to care what you want. They will still function like a drug. Don't allow the pride of doing things your way to govern your actions. After all this is totally about Jonathan and whatever you do, don't fall prey to the manipulation of the drug.

So Sincerely and so full of love for you and Jon,
Cherie

Cherie to Michael, Mike, Terri and Kristin

Oops. I made a promise and a suggestion after I said I wouldn't. Sorry. I forgot to mention that I have also seen the evil that comes as a result of drugs and it is a force that will try to destroy us. Destroy our relationships with each other, with me, and certainly with Jon. We can't ever, ever let that happen. Keep the focus on Jon. Pray for him without ceasing. Love again,
Cherie

Terri to Cherie, Michael, Kristin and Mike

Thank you, Cherie. Your input is so very caring, loving, and valuable, and it is very appreciated, too.

Love you,
Terri

My Journal March 31 (continued)

Their concern is of course for Jon's best interest. And perhaps it is a mistake to get him, although an extra 30-120 days in jail isn't going to make a difference. He wants to face his truth, so it's time.

I did struggle emotionally after I read Michael's first email. I went outside, took a couple of deep breaths, appealed to the Holy Spirit, and was back in spirit. I'm learning not to push my beliefs on anyone. If they ask, I'll tell them. If they wonder why I feel a certain way, I tell them. I tend to share my beliefs with Jonathan because that appears to be his interest, and he's very good at throwing them back at me. And to this I give thanks. I wonder if a civil war is being created? Jonathan says he is ready to tackle and pay for the mistakes he's made. Time will tell.

I made this list for Jonathan and gave it to him after I bailed him out on Friday.

Get Well
Phone calls Saturday or Monday
Get list of possible rehabs
Locate homeless shelter
Locate half-way houses, churches, FIS
Off all meds
See probation officer
What is/will be punishment?
Get DUI charge and determine legal action
Truth
Anything needing to be cleared?
No more lies to anyone
See FIS if minimal luck Saturday
N/A meetings and sponsor

Consequences of lies

Drop car insurance
Kicked out of house
No phone calls from jail
No storage payment
$0 financial aid

You are free to choose to walk the path you've chosen.

April

On Thursday April 1, the email conversations were quiet. The only correspondence was from Terri to let us know that Kristin had arrived in Tampa to spend time with her during her rehabilitation.

Each morning Dean, a spiritual friend of mine at work, comes in early to share a lesson from Oswald Chambers. Chambers originally shared these thoughts as lectures at the Bible Training College in Clapham, England, from 1911 to 1915, and as devotional talks while serving with the Young Men's Christian Association from 1915 to 1917. The YMCA had appointed him to serve in Egypt with the Australian and New Zealand troops who were guarding the Suez Canal during World War I. These lectures and talks were later compiled by Chambers' wife and published in book form in England in 1927 and in the United States in 1935.

On this day Michael and I received this lesson from Dean.

> Looking Back on Life, by Oswald Chambers
>
> A person may plan his own journey, but the Lord directs his steps. (Pr 16:9)
>
> No one sees the hand of God working in his life more clearly than when he reflects back on the years of his life. Augustine said that if a person had a choice of either dying or reliving his life over again, he would certainly choose death because of all the danger and evil he so narrowly escaped. In one sense, this statement is certainly true.
>
> Looking back, a person can see how much he has accomplished and suffered without trying or thinking about it, even against his wishes and will. He gave such little thought to what he was doing before it occurred or when it was happening. Now, after everything has been

carried out, he is amazed and says, "Why did these things happen to me when I never thought about them or thought something completely different would happen?" So Pr 16:9 is true, "A person may plan his own journey, but the Lord directs his steps," even against his plan and will. So we must agree that our own cleverness and foresight don't guide our life and actions. Instead, God's wonderful power, wisdom, and goodness guide us. Only as we look back do we fully recognize how often God was with us when we neither saw his hand nor felt his presence at the time it was happening. Accordingly, Peter said, "He cares for you" (1Pe 5:7).

Even if there were no books or sermons to tell us about God, simply looking back on our own lives would prove that he tenderly carries us in his arms. When we look back on how God has led and brought us through so much evil, adversity, and danger, we can clearly see the ever-present goodness of God, which is far above our thoughts, mind, and perception.

Friday April 02

Michael to Mike

Dad,

I love you. This email from Dean is God "speaking" directly to you in response to our conversation last night. He loves you and will continue speaking to you through me (and others) to give you all the information and inspiration you need to soften your heart and turn you from the false teachings you are currently following so that you know Him personally!!! The reason I know this is God speaking is because this is a direct answer to a prayer I had after we hung up last night. God is faithful and ever-loving...I pray you'll find it in your heart to accept Him as your Father.

Dad, we may have our differences of opinion, but neither of us should be so arrogant as to assume this a matter of coincidence. Jesus said, "For judgment I have come into this world, so that the blind will see and those who see will become blind." John 9:39

I love you, Dad.
Your son,
Michael

Monday April 05

Mike to Michael

I love you too. For the time being, let's just agree that our spiritual paths are different. Yes, God is faithful and ever-loving to his Son, who is all of Us. I do know God personally, as I've been to Heaven's Gate about 10 times during my prayers and meditations. Let me tell you, it is unlike anything you have ever experienced. Until you read or at least try to understand the basics of A Course in Miracles, I encourage you not to judge my path or anyone else's. I'm not telling you anything you don't know, but it's judgments like this that led to the Inquisition, Holy Wars, Witch Trials, and the separation of religions who think to know that they know what God means in either Judaism, Christianity, Islam, Buddhism, or Hinduism. This is how the different sects form. That's why there is the Catholic, Baptist, Lutheran, Methodist, etc, etc. All forms of Christianity and all stating they know what God means.

A Course in Miracles

T-13.in.1 – If you did not feel guilty you could not attack, for condemnation is the root of attack. It is the judgment of one mind by another as unworthy of love and deserving of punishment. But herein lies the split. For the mind that judges sees itself separate from the mind being judged, believing that by punishing another, it will escape punishment. All this is but the delusional attempt of the mind to deny itself, and escape the penalty of denial. It is not an attempt to relinquish denial, but to hold onto it. For it is guilt that has obscured the Father to you, and it is guilt that has driven you insane.

The Bible

Romans 1,2 – God's Judgment – Do you, my friend, pass judgment on others? You have no excuse at all, whoever you are. For when you judge others, but do the same things they do, you condemn yourself.

And Son, I have been told by many people, that I'm one of the kindest, loving, and most compassionate men they have ever met; and they believe I have a very soft heart. This is your perception, another great teaching within the Course, but one I won't go into now. I've tried to get out of the judging business and encourage you to do the same. The Golden Rule says "Do unto others as you would have them do unto you." Would you have me judge your path, or anyone else's?

And I agree that this is not a coincidence. All things happen for a reason; and for all of us, it's a chance to learn.

The blind are all of us who are not enlightened. We look on darkness and refuse to let the light in. Those who see, like Jesus, want us to become blind to this world, as he was. He came to teach us to be like him. Again, I encourage you to at least glance at ACIM before you judge me or anyone else. This is the only thing I've read that has made any sense to me and explains why the world is as we perceive it.

I love you more than you can possibly know.
Dad

On Monday April 5, I worked from home for a few hours in the morning. Jonathan spent the previous weekend appreciating many of the things we take for granted; sunshine, a comfortable bed, good food, and loving family. He helped me around the house and truly seemed to embrace his freedom.

It was time now to leave the house and make a few visits to get Jonathan started on his road to recovery. The first stop was at 211. We were informed that their policies had changed. Jonathan would be starting off as a new patient, and the sliding payment scale that had existed before, had been eliminated. We stopped at his storage facility so he could grab a couple of things he needed while in rehab. The last stop was the Police Department to pick up the documents that defined what he was being charged with from the DUI he received in February. The documents were not there and we were told to contact someone else in another building. We did, and those people didn't have anything either. I wondered, he was arrested for drinking, yet he hadn't had a drop in over 2 years. The morning during his arrest, he looked like he had just gotten up, which he had. They can't seem to locate the charging documents, and no one takes responsibility for them. My poor kid needs help, and this is the crap they are putting him through.....I continued wondering as I put my arms around him while he cried out of frustration in the parking lot.

Wednesday April 07

Terri to Mike and Michael
Just wondering what the plan is for Jonathan? If he does not have transportation to go and check out rehab places, what is the plan? Is he

just sitting at home? I am really concerned that he is falling into further depression/anxiety issues by doing nothing and having no plan in action.

Terri asked for updates regarding the police records, potential refund from The Facility, and rehab center information.

I also think Jonathan should go in person (though I know it is far away) to the probation office since she is not returning phone calls. He is a nervous wreck not knowing where he stands. I truly am afraid this is working against him and that time is of the essence to get him into some kind of established plan before he starts going backwards again. I am worried about him. He sounds really down to me. What about him, at least for now, going to meetings and back to the outpatient place again? Maybe the psychiatrist can help now that he is available to see her again. What does everyone else think? I don't feel good about this limbo status. Not that I have any big ideas...just thinking out loud.

Michael to Mike and Terri

I think we all agree idle time does Jonathan no good. It's up to him to start making headway now, and when we spoke Monday night, he said there were no plans. My observation was that he didn't sound enthusiastic about moving forward. Was still making excuses...he's too tired, the free counselors are too far away, he doesn't have a car, he has no money...same as before, unfortunately. He may soon become despondent again, and with that comes lack of care about anyone or anything, just the determination to escape (drugs). I hope he's being watched closely. Dad, how have you observed his attitude to be?

Mike to Michael and Terri

Sorry, just got back to my desk and saw these. All these things are being addressed or are in the process of being addressed. Left message for The Facility. I called the place I told you about and they are in West Palm Beach and $12,500 for 4 weeks. So much for sliding scale. The sliding scale kicks in after 4 weeks. Jonathan has been kind of quiet and we will talk about the next step this PM. Also, if no word from PO we're driving out there on Friday. At this point, he won't turn to benzos. Jail is still fresh in mind and being homeless sounds worse. If he hasn't called anyone today, he'll start tomorrow as he should be caught up from sleep. Also called places in GA today...one is for teens and I need to call the other back. Also came across good website listing many places in GA as well as around the country. Here's the link.

Thursday, April 08

Mike to Michael and Terri

Jonathan is making some calls today. We looked at 8 websites last night and these are the people he will be calling. He's also eating, cutting the grass, and he even watched most of the Cubs game with me last night. He is very coherent, the first time I've seen him like this for any extended period. Although he has a bit of depression, he is seemingly at some peace. We'll be going to see the Probation Officer tomorrow if we hear no word today.

Terri to Mike and Michael

Terri expressed her concerns about the near future.

Tiffany has been emailing me. She says she hasn't heard from Jonathan and she feels left out in the cold, and that she thinks about him every day and misses him. She also gave me a message to give to him the next time I talk to him. She said she doesn't know what to think when her whole life was focused around the two of them being together for the future....all her plans were made, etc. I just simply emailed her back and told her that Jonathan is trying very hard to focus on getting his life together right now and thanked her in advance for her understanding. I told her I'd give Jonathan the message from her, and that she should not take it too personally that Jonathan is not contacting her, as he is not really calling anyone right now and he needs the time necessary to do what he needs to do to take care of himself.

I'm glad he seems more peaceful to you.

Mike to Michael and Terri

Jonathan wants to stay away because I think he realizes that he needs to get his life right before he can continue the relationship.

Friday, April 09

Mike to Michael and Terri

I have a busy day ahead so let me catch you up quickly. After a long discussion last night, I agreed to let Jonathan go to Tiffany's and get his stuff. He got home right after I got up this morning and he said it went as well as one can expect. He let her know that he needed to get to an inpatient facility and he wasn't sure how long he would be out of commission. She said she wants to wait for him.

He got a hold of 6 of the places yesterday, and most were half way house type facilities as opposed to medical rehab place. He liked the one I talked to in West Palm Beach, the one that cost only $12,500 per month. He left a message for the place in Decatur, and they will hopefully call back. They have medical staff and are dual diagnosis. I'm hoping they offer the same services for a cheaper price....we'll see.

He's going through some withdrawal as is evidenced by his high BP. It was 150/108 last night after he had taken his meds.

We spoke of some of the consequences should he go back to narcotics. I let him know that if that's his choice, I would take him to the hospital, drop him off, and he's on his own after that. I let him know that my reason for this action would be that he is telling me to get out of his way and let him be.

We plan on going to the PO today and possibly 211 or to a state run inpatient facility. He's out of BP meds and should get some more.

I'll call Kevin again to see if any decision has been made about our refund.

Terri to Mike and Michael

Benzos are also narcotics. I had a conversation with Jonathan about benzos and he seemed resigned to the fact that they had a very bad effect on his life...I don't think he wants to take benzos anymore...he honestly sounds like he wants to get well...the jail thing really scared him. He told me there is nothing, no matter how bad cravings get, that would be worth going back to jail...he said those 3 weeks were horrible and really showed him just how much he doesn't want to be there ever again. I believe he means this wholeheartedly....but we all know that drug cravings if they get too bad have a way of taking over one's rational thinking....this is why time is of the essence to get him somewhere as quickly as possible.

After work on Friday I picked Jonathan up and we went to the doctor for his BP medicines, no benzos. We decided not to see the Probation Officer. She hadn't called back and we were leery about what might be in store for Jonathan. We agreed to wait until she contacted us by phone. Jonathan spent most of the weekend with Tiffany as they worked on patching up their relationship.

Tuesday April 13

Mike to Terri, Michael and Kristin

I just got a message from the Probation Officer. There is a warrant out for Jon's arrest. Her message was that if he is out of Floyd County, he needs to turn himself into Paulding County. So far, I haven't been able to get a hold of Jonathan or the PO as I've tried to call her back.

I'll keep you posted.

Within 10 minutes Terri and Michael had seen the email and responded with their concerns, wondering if I had been able to get in touch with anyone in the family.

Mike to Terri, Michael and Kristin

I've tried home, Tiff, Matt and Chris' phones. It's still early, they're probably sleeping. Won't be time for breakfast until 2:00.

There was a good reason we hadn't heard from either of them. While we were emailing, they were getting married.

Tiffany had spent the last few nights at the house to be with Jonathan and to help him with some of the issues he was facing. Sleeping in Jonathan's lumpy bed, she said she had never slept better in her life. The night before, Jonathan asked her, "What are we doing tomorrow?"

"I don't know. I don't know how I'll feel when I get up." This was a typical answer as she gets up in the morning in a funk. It usually takes her a couple of hours to get going in the morning.

They went to sleep that night and when she awoke in the morning, she felt great....no funk, almost pure bliss. He lie beside her very close, squished in the little bed, and she thought, "Today is the day, definitely this is it."

She felt it, and knew it was supposed to be that day. The night before, he had tried to get her to commit to getting married the next day, but she hesitated not knowing how she would feel. Little did she know she would feel blissful.

She got up, left him in bed with the thought of surprising him when he woke up. She went downstairs to search the internet for a county and location that would do the ceremony on the same day. After several failed calls, she found a county only a half hour away that would perform the ceremony.

She walked back into his room and said, "Wake up."

"What?" he grunted.

"Wake up!! You're getting married today!!"

They quickly got dressed in their everyday clothes and drove to their destination. Before the ceremony, Jonathan excused himself to go to the bathroom and fix his hair. In all the excitement, he left the house with "bed head hair," and had to fix that at the church before they stood at the altar.

After they were married, they stopped at the store and picked up some snack foods and rented the movie 2012, one that he had wanted to see since its original release. They arrived at home and she quickly posted her new last name on a social media network. This is how most of the friends and family were informed, and to most it came as a shock.

They danced their first song to their song, The Scientist. That was followed by some more slow music, until Jonathan put on "Boot Scootin Boogie." He broke into dance, grabbed her hands, and said, "Follow my lead!!" She admired his ability to get down and boogie. They danced a little while longer before it was time to watch the movie.

After the movie finished she reminded him that he had forgotten to carry her over the threshold. He picked her up, not getting a very good grip, and dropped her on the floor. She banged her leg on the fireplace and he apologized profusely. They laughed as she said, "You tried, and that's all that matters." He picked her up again and carried her to the other room.

For the next 12 days, we saw Jonathan on several occasions, but for the most part he stayed at home with Tiffany. He was experiencing bouts of depression, and they became more severe whenever Tiffany had to work. When she was at home, they would hang-out together. They talked about going to Concord for their honeymoon, but it would have to wait until finances improved. So in the meantime, he would rub her feet, and as Tiffany said while we interviewed, "These feet really miss you!!" and the tears came to her eyes.

The more Jonathan thought about going to rehab, the worse his depression and anxiety became. He frightened Tiffany when he would complain of not feeling well and feeling suicidal. She had taken too much time off of work so she couldn't call in without a valid reason. Her first day back to work after their wedding, she immediately put him on her health insurance plan.

Terri had located a dual diagnostic rehab facility in Tennessee and Tiffany confirmed that this program was covered under her policy. We found a place that could help Jonathan!!!

Thursday April 15

Terri to Mike

Hi...haven't heard from anyone...what's going on? I still never got a call from Jon, nor did Michael or Kristin. You gave him messages to call me and Tiffany also promised he would call when I spoke to her the night you talked to him. He didn't call that night or yesterday or today...I really want to talk to him. Do you know what his plan is? Have you talked to him again?

Mike to Terri

I spoke with him for a few minutes yesterday. He is stressing over going back into jail. He started crying for a moment before he recomposed himself. He told me he'd try the place in Decatur today but I don't know if he will. I'll try calling him when I get off of work.

Terri to Mike

I'm sure he is...this is one of the reasons I want to talk to him. I want to be his mom and I can't even get a hold of him. How are you reaching him? Or is he calling you?

Mike to Terri

I called him yesterday on Tiffany's phone and he called me back later in the day. I don't know if Tiffany left the phone with him today or not, guessing she did as Jonathan had some calls to make.

Terri to Mike

Has he tried any further to get his records from the evidence place? What will happen regarding that court date? Will he get penalized further for not appearing in court? Didn't you say they only allow one postponement? Did he try to get a hold of his P.O.? Maybe she can help the situation. I'm surprised you have not gotten another call from her if she wants to find him so badly. She has no way of knowing whether you even talked to him (or got her message). It seems it might be easier for Jonathan with not so much "unknown"...if he has the facts and knows exactly what to expect, maybe he might be able to sort it through a little better emotionally. Has he told you anything about his intentions?

At 4:00 AM the next morning, Chris awoke to the most real and disturbing nightmare he'd ever had, startled and crying. He dreamt that Jonathan died. The dream seemed very real to him and it scared him. Knowing Jonathan's schedule, Chris called him. Jonathan answered and Chris told him of the horrible dream he just had. Jonathan did his best to comfort him, yet there was a tone in Jonathan's voice that implied he knew it was going to happen. Jonathan told Chris, "We need to put it in God's hands."

Jonathan and I spoke several times a day for the next few days. Most of the conversations were pleasant and encouraging as I urged him to admit himself to the rehabilitation center in Tennessee. As each day passed, Jonathan's fear of the arrest warrant and its consequences, and the potential long term stay in TN added to his anxiety.

On Monday April 19, Tiffany drove Jonathan to my house so he could use my car and go and say his good-byes before leaving for TN on Tuesday morning.

Tuesday April 20

Terri to Mike, Michael and Kristin

Is Jonathan still going to Tennessee today? Did you talk to him anymore last night or this morning? I left a message for him to call me but he never did call me back.

Mike to Terri, Michael and Kristin

He left my house last night about 1:00 AM. He told me that he was still planning on going today. I've sent a text to have him call me when he's able to.

He packed up all the things he needs for the rehab place, spent some time with Remy, we spent a lot of time talking, and I know he spoke with Michael last night. It sounded like he cut you off Michael, but at that point Matt was going to take him home and Matt was ready to leave. Chris got home shortly after you got off the phone with him and took him instead.

When Chris arrived at home late in the evening on the 19th, Jonathan was sitting at the kitchen table writing a letter to Tiffany. After Jonathan finished the letter, they both went to Jonathan's room to gather his duffle bags to put into the car. Before leaving the room, Jonathan took 1 ½ Oxycontin 80s (enough to be fatal to a non-opiate user).

The hour drive to Rome was unlike any of their previous drives together. They didn't turn on the radio. They didn't plug in a CD. They just talked. They spoke of Jonathan leaving for the rehab center in Tennessee, though Jonathan spoke mostly about his love for Tiffany.

They got out of the car after they arrived and moved Jonathan's belongings into the house. As they said their good-byes, they hugged and Jonathan said, "I love you. Be good, I won't see you again soon, but I will see you again."

As Chris drove off, he thought that Jonathan's good-bye was odd. Chris thought that he may have been lovey because of all the Oxys he'd just taken. Or maybe because he was leaving for Tennessee and he'd be rehabbing for quite a while. Then Chris remembered the dream he'd had a few nights before.

Terri to Michael, Mike and Kristin

I'm glad he came by to see you before he went home. If you spent a long time talking, what did he have to say? I'm very hopeful about his state of mind going into this. Does he seem like he really wants the help? Has his arrogant attitude gone away? Any idea what time he is planning to leave today? I hope he will call me back before he gets there so I can say goodbye before he gets too involved to talk to me at all. Is he still seeming very depressed? And, did you address again the idea that he was taking something (meds)?

Mike to Terri, Michael and Kristin

He apologized as soon as he got to the house, and there didn't seem to be a hint of any drugs in him. He was very coherent. Absolutely no arrogance and we did discuss his recent behavior. I reminded him of the benefits of addressing his issues rather than procrastinating.

He was very depressed and talked of suicide, not that he said he would do it but that he is feeling worthless. He didn't say what time he would be leaving today, I'm guessing sometime late morning or early afternoon.

Terri to Mike, Michael and Kristin; Mike's responses in bold

Terri: I'm glad he apologized for his earlier behavior. The sooner he gets there, the better. Do you think he does truly recognize that he needs psychiatric help?
Mike: Yes, without a doubt.

Terri: Did he say specifically what he is depressed about?

Mike: Not working, being a failure in general, no car, having no money, etc.

Terri: Is he depressed about going to rehab?
Mike: I don't think so, although the time element (length of time) can overwhelm him. In some ways, he's looking forward to it, particularly since he can bring his Wayne Dyer materials with him. He spoke with Matt, the Program Director of the inpatient clinic, several times yesterday and the only thing he was hesitant about is the first step of the 12 Step Program, that being that he is powerless over his addiction. I pointed out to him that at this point he is powerless, but he still thinks he can control it and it looks like he just doesn't want to admit he is powerless over anything, I don't exactly know. There are smoking privileges, good visiting hours, phone availability, nothing really major to turn him away from the program.

Terri: Or, depressed about the legal stuff and not knowing what will happen?
Mike: That's bothering him, but I don't think that's foremost on his mind.

Terri: How's Tiffany's attitude with him?
Mike: She has been supportive. He said she was a little cranky when he spoke with her last night but that was while she was still at work and very well may have been Jon's perception. I pointed out to him last night that although he doesn't realize it, he is very demanding and self-centered, and that compassion is a skill/habit he'll develop as he goes through rehab.

As it turned out, Jonathan had tried calling 4-5 times while Tiffany was with a very sick patient. With the time she had missed, she had to be very efficient and focus on her job.

Kristin to Michael, Terri and Mike

I called Tiffany's number yesterday and it went straight to voicemail so I haven't talked to Jonathan at all. If someone talks to him will you please let him know that I tried calling him on Tiffany's phone yesterday but there was no answer. I left them a message though so maybe he got it.

I hope everyone is doing well. I will talk to you soon. Also, Michael called me last night and he and Cherie are in California. He was calling me to tell me that he just passed Mel's Diner. I was pretty jealous. :) I really want to go to California!!! I think he said that they were coming back today.

Wednesday April 21

Michael to Mike, Terri and Kristin
Got home and to bed last night around 2:00. Did Jonathan check himself in?

Ashley called me yesterday before my flight left LAX. She was very concerned about what might be happening.

Kristin to Michael, Mike and Terri
I don't know what's going on with Jon. I still haven't heard from him. I saw on Facebook that today is Tiffany's birthday. On Jon's Facebook page he put that he is spending the day with his beautiful wife, so I guess that means he hasn't checked himself in yet. He put that up about 45 minutes ago.

Terri to Mike
Michael sent this paragraph in an email to me today. Did you know about this? I thought you told me everything was a wonderful visit between Jonathan and Remy and Ashley. Did Jonathan say anything to you about any of this?

See below:

> "Ashley was calling because Jonathan apparently went to her house on Monday night to say "goodbye" to Remy and ask Ashley and Ben to take good care of him "no matter what happens." Jonathan told Ashley he was suicidal and homicidal, and she was thoroughly unnerved because of it. Jonathan got Remy very upset, and Ashley doesn't want it to happen again, so she was hoping I knew more about what's going on."

Mike to Terri:
First I've heard of it and Friday I'm told is the plan.

Terri to Mike
And, what was his reason for waiting again this time? If he's not careful, the cops are going to show up at her house and arrest him...then he'll really have a problem.

Even when I told him that I had had a particularly upsetting day due to some scary news I received yesterday from a phone call from my doctor, he didn't even once ask about me or what the doctor said....no big deal, I guess, but I don't deserve this treatment from anyone. I am just being a concerned mom who is worried about our son and regardless of your accusing me of being judgmental, I think everyone in this family has every right to be concerned and every right to continue our attempts at getting him treatment.

I don't buy it for one minute that one of them never woke up at all for the entire day, when they both KNEW we were all waiting on word regarding whether he was admitted or not. Call me judgmental if you wish, but it was inconsiderate and rude of Jon, as well as Tiffany, and, even especially to you, as well...it seems you are not being consistent with your feelings, Mike... just the day before yesterday you told me how angry you were with Jonathan and the huge argument you had with him regarding his irresponsibility and arrogant attitudes...then, suddenly, yesterday you didn't think we had the right to receiving information from him anymore. You made it seem as though I was completely out of line and rude to even be concerned about "their business"...I am not concerned about THEIR business...I am concerned about MY SON...that's all.

When the word suicide is mentioned regarding my son, I take that very seriously. Were you not even the slightest bit surprised or upset that no one bothered to contact you, either, when he left it with you the night before that he was leaving for the hospital yesterday morning and he knew you were waiting for his call? I'm sorry if I was reactive and defensive with you last night, but I am entitled as a mom to know if my son is safe....this is a very serious situation.

This is NOT the time that I'm worrying about how much romantic time he is spending with his wife. Right now, his health is the priority, at least where I am concerned. His life and what happens with him right now are the biggest priority in my life...yes, I want to stay informed, as I should be. That goes for both of us and the rest of this family, as well. And, as far as Tiffany, no, I do not consider her to be acting responsibly either. She will go along with whatever Jonathan tells her, obviously....and that, in this particular situation, is not safe for Jon's wellbeing. It is only a matter of time before something else bad is going to happen. Even now, you said you are concerned about possible drug use again.

I will hope to hear updates from you. I doubt I will hear from Jon, and if that's the way he wants it, I guess that is up to him. I don't know what else to do. It is hard to put this aside and not worry, being a mom, but I am going to do everything I can to do so. Even my docs are saying I need to avoid stress at all costs, especially now. I did not talk to him for long, and told him I loved him and asked him the plan and he said he didn't know.

So…..whatever happens will happen, I guess. I have done my best at trying to stay in touch with him, be loving, encouraging, and wishing him well…trying to lovingly convince him to go on over there and start his life in a forward motion so he will have a happy life to look forward to when he is well. Nothing I have ever said or done regarding Jonathan has been derived from anything but true love and concern for his life.

I don't know what in the world you said to him but he certainly had the impression that I was a horrible person, that YOU are the only person who has repeatedly saved his life and shown him love….and of course, "dad doesn't lie"…never mind the fact that I have always been there to the best of my ability, too.

Anyway….hope we can move forward from this…the whole situation has been stressful and life-changing for all of us…we should all stick together, not be at odds. All I have ever wanted was to be included in being part of the parenting process…whether he is 29 or not, you and I both know he is not mature enough or stable enough from one day to the next for us not to be involved to whatever extent we are able.

Now that I hear what happened at Ashley's, that is very disturbing to me, as well. I wonder if Jonathan has a plan that neither of us know about…I don't trust blindly anymore that all will be ok….he is putting this off more and more all the time. I have a bad feeling in my gut…maybe that's why I am trying so hard to stay on top of things.

By the way, below is another comment from Michael's last email when I further questioned him about Ashley's conversation with him:

> *"I'm surprised drug use hasn't surfaced…just a matter of time. I was thinking his suicidal thoughts may have revolved around feeling like he failed because he may have taken something…don't know…never asked. By the way, when I said earlier Jonathan was calling to say his goodbyes, his plan was to kill himself that night. That's what he told me. That's what he told Ashley. The only reason I didn't call the cops to come and get him was because if it ever came back to me as the person who turned him in, I don't trust he wouldn't retaliate. He is crazy, Mom. Really, he's out of his mind. Brainwashed."*

This is all very upsetting and disturbing to me, and obviously to our other children. Please try to be understanding and patient regarding my feelings, too. I don't want to be upset with anyone, nor do I want anyone in this family to be upset...period. We all have quite enough emotions to deal with as it is....this has not been easy on anyone, especially you....perhaps you don't realize still all the credit I have given to you for your efforts.

On the other hand, I believe it is time to be firm with Jon. You bailed him out with the understanding he would go right away to a rehab place and he is procrastinating more and more every day. You may be the only person he listens to....please, I'm begging you....don't be so "accepting". He needs help, and quickly....before another tragedy happens.

My apologies for my part last night.

Thursday April 22

Mike to Terri

My apologies for the other night too.

I didn't talk with him yesterday, so I don't have an update.

And try to do the best you can to relieve your stress. This can't be helping you. What did the doctor say?

I have a lot to do today, so I'm not sure how often or when I'll be available. Hopefully he will go in to the hospital tomorrow.

Tiffany awoke in the middle of the night and wrote this to Jonathan.

My Wonderful Husband

It's about 3:00AM and I'm smoking a cigarette waiting for that awful "I just woke up" feeling to pass so that I can go back to bed and sleep. You looked like you'd been crying when you came to bed. I can't imagine how you must be feeling right now. Every time I do let myself see it through your eyes or imagine what you are about to go through, I just feel sick at heart and cry. I'm afraid to leave you alone to go to work. Please my angel, my soul mate, don't harm yourself. I don't want to have to wait until we meet again in another life to make this work. I've waited so long to find you. Please grant me this selfish wish – don't take away my heart and soul, for that is what you are. I know it now more than ever before. You are my life. You are the missing piece that has made me whole. We are meant to live this life together. I took you for better, for worse and right now we are going through a "worse" period, but we have <u>so</u> much that is wonderful waiting for us. I will be here every step of the way through this. I will write you every day if you want. They may be silly, mundane letters, but at least you'll know my thoughts are with you.

And I have a feeling this is going to turn out to be not half as bad as you are imagining. You have a whole team of us working for you. As your wife, I will be able to do much more and have more influence than as your fiancé. That I chose to marry you in the midst of all this chaos should speak volumes for your character.

I know you are not made to be incarcerated. But, baby, this time you can and will be able to face it. I <u>know</u> this. You can do anything you set your mind to. I believe in you.

So please, as I said before, please don't take away my Love, my Life, my You. I need you. My life is incomplete without you in it. We have a beautiful life to live. Let's get this last bit of the past out of the way and leave it behind us. Please don't think that I am overlooking the magnitude of what you are experiencing. I am not, by any means. I'm just trying to help my teammate, my best friend, my lover, my reason for living.

I love you truly, deeply, eternally. There's been a shift inside me, a good shift. I've felt it since the night you came over last week, but especially since that second day at your house. My eyes have been opened to the wonder of ever even having found you, much less getting to spend my life with you.

Put it in God's hands, baby. You'll feel a tremendous burden lifted off your shoulders. So, good morning, my Love. My thoughts are with you throughout the day.

Love
Tiffany Dacy

Friday April 23

Michael to Mike, Terri and Kristin
Hi Dad,
Any word from Jonathan about his supposed intentions to check in to rehab today?

Mike to Michael, Terri and Kristin
I spoke with him briefly last night and he said he didn't know. He said it might be Monday.

Kristin to Michael, Terri and Mike
I can't believe he is thinking about not going in today. He is going to get in more trouble than he is already in. Did anyone get his Facebook email this morning? He wrote it at like 4:30am this morning. I have copied it below. Let me know if you hear anything more. Love to you all!!

> *I finally created a Facebook profile after all these years of tribulation, and look, you guys can't even shoot me an e-mail or leave comments on the pictures of my beautiful wife and family :) Oh, yeah, I'm married now, I'll be expecting my wedding gifts in the mail soon, LOL. I love you all so much and will be looking forward to hearing from you soon. With all my love- Jonathan Dacy*

Terri to Mike, Michael and Kristin
Has he given any reason at all as to why he is not going?

Mike to Terri, Kristin and Michael
I remind him of the potential trouble he can be in every time I talk with him.

Michael to Terri, Kristin and Mike
I just left an encouraging (hopefully) message in his Facebook inbox. I will never stop reminding him of his blessings despite all his misgivings.

Terri to Michael, Mike and Kristin
That was nice. I will be leaving him a message, as well, tonight when I get home. I can't access FB from here. What did you say?

Michael to Terri, Mike and Kristin

Basically that I love him and encourage him to take full advantage of his immediate opportunities, because they may not always be so easily attainable, however difficult they may seem to be at this time.

Terri to Michael, Kristin and Mike

That is true....the thought crossed my mind that he would be without the ability to go to the treatment place if something were to happen to Tiffany's job and they lost insurance. It appeared on FB last night that she was having some kind of possible trouble with her boss at work.

April 24 and 25

On the 24th, I celebrated my 57th birthday as we typically do. Mike and Cherie, Jonathan and Tiffany, Ben, Ashley and Remy all came over in mid-afternoon to eat burgers off the grill. At one point before we were to eat, we noticed that Jonathan and Tiffany were missing. I went to Jonathan's room, knocked on the door, and was granted entrance. She was lying on Jonathan, who was quietly weeping. I asked what was wrong and he said his depression was really bad this day. I made my efforts to console and love him, and it seemed to have a positive effect for the rest of the time they spent with us. He and Tiffany joined the company a few minutes later and all appeared to be OK.

After dinner I opened my cards and gifts. I received some beautiful homemade heartfelt cards from Tiffany, Chris, and Remy. Jonathan presented me with one that I will cherish the rest of my life. It said:

> **To My Beloved Father**
>
> **Father,**
> There are few words I could say to express my gratitude for signing up to be your son. You have taught me things I'm not sure any man could have directed me with. I believe we are spiritual soul mates – and it would be hard to find anything with more honor than that. You have saved me in virtually more ways than are even possible – I am in your debt forever. My love for you reaches the stars, where all things are possible. Let's always remember, my best friend, love is all that matters, and all that will ever matter. And, my dear

father, my angel, my savior, I love you more than the words of my mouth are capable of describing.

"And now abide faith, hope, love, these three; but the greatest of these is <u>love.</u>"
1 Corinthians 13:13

Have a wonderful birthday – you deserve nothing less.

"Do not go where the path may lead, go instead where there is no path and leave a trail."
Ralph Waldo Emerson

Go and make your path, Dad. You are capable of so much more than you realize.
True love conquers <u>all.</u>
With all the love I possess,
Jonathan

I also received a couple of videos, a beautiful picture of Jonathan and Tiffany, a plaque, a bookmark on happiness, and a special rock from Remy.

We continued to visit and eat cake. Jonathan, Tiffany, and Remy went bowling and to play some games and take some pictures. After they returned we ended up playing Beatles Rock Band until midnight. It was a wonderful day that was filled with love, fun, and laughter.

Jonathan and Tiffany left that night with the understanding that they would leave for Tennessee the next day to get Jonathan admitted to the rehab facility.

During the night Tiffany wrote this to Jonathan.

Jonathan

Well, it's your last day at home and we seem to have opposite sleep schedules again. I'm sorry that I upset you by going through your things last night. I was afraid to go to sleep before I was sure you wouldn't hurt yourself with something you brought from home last night. I am worried about you. I tried to do something nice for you with the roses. I think it worked for a few minutes. I don't know whether to wake you or not. I don't want to argue all day, and lately we seem to be doing a lot of that. Neither of us is really happy right now because of the circumstances, and that's understandable. We have so much going on in our lives, our life. Life feels like a rollercoaster right now, up, down, unexpected highs and lows, twists and turns.

I love you Jonathan. I think you know this. You've been asking if I want a divorce a lot. No, I don't. Do I like what's going on? No, I don't. But I have to believe that things are going to get better. There is no way that we could have been so in love 2 weeks ago and for that to be gone now. I don't give up that easily.

Tomorrow we will take an important trip. I know it won't be an easy journey for you. Please, Baby, open up to these people. Really open up. Don't step around the real issues. I know how hard that can be but it is liberating. I spent time with a psychologist a while back who helped me get past some really difficult things from my past. It was embarrassing and very difficult until I realized that I was letting go of hurts, shame and guilt that had plagued me my whole life. Yes, I still get depressed, but those feelings are gone for the most part.

Well, you are up now, so I'll just close by saying I love you and believe that if you use this time to your advantage instead of seeing it as a sentence that it can be the best thing to happen to you – for you.

I will write every day and visit often. You will be in my thoughts and prayers always. You are not alone. I love you and will be waiting to start our new, better, happier life when you get out.

All my love, Tiffany

I got up Sunday morning, the 25th, watched Avatar for about the 8th time, did a few things around the house, and received a call from Jonathan in mid-afternoon asking if he could borrow some money to take Tiffany out to dinner. They were planning to go to rehab the next morning and wanted to have a nice dinner before leaving. He was not in a good mood, as he was arguing with Tiffany as we talked. When they arrived, they continued arguing. Jonathan threatened suicide often and Tiffany was getting sick of hearing it. He finally pushed me too far and I said "Let's call 911." At that point Jonathan said "You want to play hard ball!!" and he marched down the stairs to the garage. I followed him down the stairs.

As I entered the garage and saw him pulling a rifle out of a case, hundreds of thoughts seemed to go through my head.

"Do I be gentle?"

"Should I try to reason?"

"How do I handle this peacefully?"

"Holy Spirit, what do I do?"

"Is this going to be a homicide/suicide?"

"What the f*@#!!??!"

I yelled "Call 9-1-1!!" I ran around the work table, jumped on his back, and tripped him to the ground. He was face down on the ground and I lay on top of him trying to keep him from getting up. Matt, Laura and Tiffany came racing downstairs to see what was happening.

"Take the gun!!" I yelled and Matt ran off with it.

"Dad, get off of me!!" Jonathan pleaded.

"No Jon, I love you!!" I yelled back.

"Dad, get off of me!!" Jonathan pleaded.

"No Jon, I love you!!" I yelled back.

I was trying my best to force my weight on him as he tried to lift up and get away.

"Dad, get off of me!!" Jonathan pleaded.

"No Jon, I love you!!" I yelled back.

This conversation repeated itself probably 20 times (seemed like 100, might have been 10). In the meantime, Tiffany came over to help and to try and restrain him. Laura called 911. As this was going on, I realized Jonathan could have easily punched my face or bitten my arm. But he didn't, he didn't do anything to try and physically hurt me.

Since I wasn't letting him up, he began banging his head on the garage floor. I tried to hold his head up without letting go, and Tiffany was doing her best to hold his head and lessen the blows to the cement. By the 5th time he'd hit his head a bruise was forming and blood was coming out of a cut that was made.

After he'd banged his head on the ground for the 8th time, I let him up and held him against the wall. He then started banging his head against an old console TV that was being stored in the garage. My strength was giving out and I finally released my grip. He stormed off and grabbed the car keys.

"Go do whatever it is you are going to do! We all love you! Go and get some help!" I yelled.

Tiffany insisted that she drive and Jonathan handed the keys to her. They got in the car and drove off before the police got there, probably passing each other as they exited the neighborhood.

When the police showed up they seemed more concerned about my bleeding and the "assault" on me. I finally, after about 2 minutes, mentioned that my son needs help...."Do you think you might want to track him down?" One of the officers got on the radio and the questioning changed from me to where they may be headed. We suggested the local hospital or towards their home driving down SR278.

As it turned out they headed back to Rome where they were going to pack Jonathan's belongings and head to the rehab clinic in TN.

After getting packed, Tiffany got in the driver's seat and Jonathan got into the back seat, which was highly unusual. After a few minutes on the road, he announced he was going to kill himself and appeared to swallow 3 ½ bottles worth of blood pressure and anti-anxiety medicine.

They happened to be within a few blocks of the hospital where Tiffany was employed and she did a U-turn and headed to the emergency room. She pulled up to the emergency entrance and Jonathan opened the back door, grabbed one of his bags, and sprinted around the building. That's the last time that any of us saw him.

In August 2009 Jonathan wrote from the Bible, Matthew 7:13-14; "<u>THE NARROW AND WIDE GATES:</u> Enter through the narrow gate. For wide is the gate and broad is the road that leads to destruction, and many enter through it. But small is the gate and narrow the road that leads to life, and only a few find it."

And so Jonathan left Tiffany knowing he couldn't go through with the traditional rehabilitation approach. He wasn't going through the Wide Gates.

Everyone has their dark side; where we hide our hidden guilt, fears, and shame. We might feel guilt for something we did or didn't do for someone; or shame for having hurt another and then not doing anything about it to correct it. At what point does one quantify the injustices he has done to another and feel he needs to run from his life because he can't take anymore? At what point does one feel so guilty that he can't forgive himself? At what point are society's demands so great that one can't bear facing the consequences? At what point is fear so overwhelming that it's terrifying to think about the next day?

Perhaps Jonathan's relationship with God had gotten to the point where he could truly turn it over to Him. As Jonathan told each of us, he would go and find God when it was time for him to heal. Jonathan was looking for the Narrow Gate.

The Search

Tiffany told the doctors what she thought Jonathan had taken, and they said he wouldn't get more than 100 yards from the hospital before the medicines would kill him. The police arrived at the hospital, and after being informed of the situation, an APB was issued. Shortly thereafter, there was a report that someone fitting Jonathan's description was seen running through a restaurant parking lot not too far from the hospital. A second car was sent to patrol that area, but they were unable to locate him. Meanwhile, the first police units on the scene spent the next hour combing the woods that surrounded the hospital. It was after 9:00 PM when they finished, and they assured Tiffany that they would inform her if Jonathan was located.

After Tiffany got home at 9:45 PM, she called me to explain what had happened and I told her that I would be there in an hour. While driving out there I called Terri, Michael and Kristin to let them know what had happened. I arrived at Jonathan and Tiffany's home about 11:00 PM.

We stayed up and talked until 3:30. We planned the next day and how we would search the woods around the hospital. We talked of the possible scenarios; where he might be, what he might be doing. We also prayed that he was OK and to come home to us. Tiffany wrote a letter to place on the front door encouraging Jonathan to come in and to let him know that we all love him.

Monday April 26

Tiffany and I left the house at 8:30 to begin our search for Jonathan. We arrived at the hospital parking lot and spoke with security personnel to see if they had heard or seen anything. They were aware of what had happened the previous night but didn't have any additional information to share with us. We let them know that our plan was to walk through the woods to look for him. They offered assistance in any way it might be needed. We searched the immediate vicinity for about an hour and then left for police headquarters to speak with the detective in charge of the case.

We explained to the detective the sensitive state that Jonathan was in. The detective was cordial and understanding, and gave us his opinions. He was confident Jonathan would show up. His thoughts were that Jonathan would head to Florida to be with his mother and to escape what was happening in Georgia. The detective explained to us that there was a train track a couple of miles from headquarters that transients used to travel south. He reminded us that an APB was out for him and they were looking for him. We emphasized the need for him to be admitted to a hospital first and not be placed into custody. He told us he would see what he could do, but we didn't feel comfortable with his sincerity.

Michael met us in the early afternoon and we went back to the woods to search further. After completing a search of about a 1 mile radius around the hospital, we went to Berry College to talk with the security people. Berry College is a beautifully wooded campus only a couple of miles from where Jonathan and Tiffany lived. There are hundreds of wooded acres on the campus and the surrounding area, and someone with Jonathan's expertise in living off the land could have hidden indefinitely. The security staff was very understanding and cooperative. They took a handful of flyers Tiffany had made and posted them around campus.

After that we headed to a church not too far from Jonathan and Tiffany's home. Jonathan loved large gothic styled churches, and we thought he might stop there to pray. We entered the church and were greeted by the Reverend and a member of his staff. They told us that they hadn't seen him, but they offered compassion, love, and prayer to the three of us. They were given some flyers and they assured us we would hear from them if they saw Jonathan.

The next stop was to go to some of the places that Jonathan and Tiffany had frequented. Michael suggested that as sentimental as Jonathan was, he may go back to one of these places and reminisce. We checked along the river, a couple of stores, and some restaurants. As we looked we would stop people who were bike riding or taking a stroll and ask if they had seen Jonathan. No information.

It was dusk and I had to get home so I could get some sleep and go to work the next morning. Tiffany went home and called Terri to update her on what had happened during the day.

Tuesday April 27

Tiffany and Terri stayed up late the evening before discussing other options and how to enlist the help of others. They came across a website that offered Dog Team Search and Rescue services. When Tiffany awoke the next morning, she contacted the Search and Rescue Hotline.

The rest of us were back at work so we continued our email correspondence.

Michael to Terri, Mike and Kristin

Just checking. Last I heard was Tiffany/Mom trying to arrange search/rescue dogs.

Terri to Michael, Mike and Kristin

That's all I know. I talked to Tiffany a long time last night. She is trying to blame herself for not being more forceful with Jonathan over the last week when he was manipulating her and she was trying to keep the peace and allowing him to postpone going to the rehab place.

She said she never realized just how mentally ill Jonathan is....she is now realizing what she has gotten into with marrying him and we talked about his long history of drug abuse, depression, and all...she seemed to have no idea of the extent, severity, and the length of time his problems have existed.

She was scared and worried and had been searching some more on her own last night. She is going to the police dept. this morning to ask them to help to enlist the help of the free search and rescue dogs. She said she'd let me know what happens.

Michael to Terri, Kristin and Mike

What a surprise...Jonathan didn't tell her the whole truth. Thanks for the update.

Mike to Michael, Terri and Kristin

I spoke with the detective this morning. Jonathan is officially listed as a missing person. I also informed him as to what we got done yesterday afternoon. He mentioned a couple of the homeless shelters in Rome and suggested we go down there and look around/hand out pictures/etc.

I then spoke with Tiffany and she informed me of the dog rescue teams and she is going to call the detective. She also....update, I just got off the phone with her and there will be a search tomorrow. She doesn't know what time and she'll let me know when she finds out. I guess they wait for all the people/dogs to show up, then call Tiffany, and then meet out at the hospital. Michael, let me know if you want to go out there. I may come into work for a few hours, or wait to hear from Tiffany, and then get there in 45 minutes.

Michael to Mike, Terri and Kristin

I'll need to know a fairly specific time frame before I can commit the time away from work, but I'm open to it. Candie (a longtime friend of the family) sent me a message this morning. She was planning to go out today...I'll touch base with her about tomorrow maybe instead.

Terri to Mike, Michael and Kristin

I am so glad they arranged the search dogs. I am trying very hard to stay busy at work but I am a wreck. The homeless shelters are a good place to check, but I am not sure he would go there for fear the cops would look there, too. I am very surprised and worried that Dad would not have heard from him by now, as he always calls for him when he calms down and is all alone and scared. It makes me fear the worst and I'm trying desperately not to go there in my mind. Thank you for the update. Let me know if you hear anything, please.

Mike to Terri

Please do whatever you can do to get the stuff out of your mind. Remember, try to stay in the present moment and don't think of the future or dwell on the past. And I'm not surprised he hasn't contacted me. We've never been down this road. I was the one who said call 911 and my last words to him were get help, and I may have sounded angry when I said it. I think he'll contact Tiffany first.

Terri to Mike

I thought he would call her, as well, or even be hiding out waiting for no one to be home so he could sneak in the house to get things he needs. But, Tiffany said she could tell he had not been there and nothing was missing. I have a feeling he is either in bad shape close by or is very far away.

Tiffany to Terri

Just wanted to let you know that the search and rescue squad are coming out tomorrow morning at 9 am. Pray for NO RAIN! I'll keep you posted if I hear anything new. Candie- I guess you know her family- is going to come out then also. Hope you are holding up and were able to get some sleep.

Terri to Tiffany, Mike, Michael, Kristin and Cheryl (Terri's sister)

Thanks for the update, Tiffany. I am forwarding your email to everybody else, too. This is how we all stay informed together so when you have anything in the way of news, please "reply to all" so we can all see it. It makes communication much easier for everyone.

Hope you got sleep, too. Take care of yourself and stay strong. Yes, I know Candie and her family... so nice of them to come and help.

I am so glad the police were cooperative in getting the rescue dogs. Did it take much persuading? I just wish it were today.

Take care... talk to you later.

Love,

Terri

Tiffany to All

They were not really hard to persuade. I just told them I knew the service was available and free and that all they had to do was call. I actually spoke with a captain about it because I got the detective's vm when I called. But it's set up and the detective did call me back after the captain did to tell me what time. Candie has a few lawyer connections and they may be of some help in getting things done. She said she's going to start pulling some strings, so that's a real blessing. I'll update when I hear anything. Everyone keep me in the loop as well :) Love and prayers- Tiffany

Michael to All

I will do my best to be there, though it may not be possible. I'll let you know.

Terri to All

I just received a call back from my oncology doctor's office stating that my genetic testing (tumor markers, dna analysis, etc.), which determines the percentage of probability of recurrence, results came back today and I am at a very low risk of recurrence, 7% and score of 10 out of 100. This means that this does not point towards metastatic disease (cancer that spreads to other areas of the body), which is excellent news and seals the deal for me that I will not have to have chemotherapy treatments. Thought you would all like to know some good news. So, now my radiation treatments will likely be scheduled to start very quickly in the next few days. They don't want to put it off any longer, as we were just waiting for this test to come back to determine if I needed chemo since it has to be done first before radiation (if it is needed, which in my case is now not an issue). Thank God.

Love to all of you...

We all replied in separate emails sending our love and thanks to God for this outcome.

Michael to All

Unfortunately I won't be able to make it tomorrow morning. My workload will not permit it due to my recent time away and the half-day yesterday. Hopefully there will be a surplus of help and I won't be missed.

Tiffany to All

I'm so scared of tomorrow. You guys just please be praying for him, which I KNOW you are, and please pray for me, because I am literally terrified of what is going to happen in the morning. I have a friend who will meet us there.

Wednesday April 28

Laura and I got up early to get ready and drive to Rome to meet the Rescue Team. We picked up Tiffany, and then met her friend in the hospital parking lot. We drove around the parking lot and found the Rescue Team. We met the captain who explained that it was his job to manage the search. He described how he and the teams would proceed and showed us a map of the area. The area was divided into 30 small sections that needed to be explored. The three S&R Teams would cover that land. The Captain would remain at Mission Control to direct the teams as they phoned in announcing completion of their assigned section. The Captain would then direct them to the next section to investigate. Also meeting us was the detective in charge of Jonathan's case as he accompanied one of the S&R teams.

The Captain was very friendly, and he told light hearted stories about himself and how so many times people were found alive and returned to family. He also answered our many questions, and took time to make us feel as comfortable and optimistic as possible.

As we chatted we would often be interrupted as the team members called in to report their findings. Each time that phone went off, I felt a wave of fear or nausea come over me. Everyone else had those same feelings as we dreaded a call saying they had found Jonathan's body. Fortunately, for the next six hours, the teams came up empty.

After the S&R teams were finished, we gave our thanks to the captain, the teams, and the dogs. The detective stayed with the family for awhile to discuss our next steps. He again stated that he thought Jonathan was on a train to Florida to find Terri. While that was certainly a possibility, the family considered it a long shot as we thought Jonathan would stay in the area. We again emphasized the extremely fragile state that Jonathan was in, and, if the police did find him, to be as gentle as they could and take him to a hospital rather than to jail. The detective suggested we go to City Hall and have a form 1025 filled out. It was nearly 5:00PM, so Tiffany and I decided we would go on Thursday.

While Laura, Tiffany and I were working with the S&R teams, Terri was busy trying to find ways to help. She had heard of a renowned psychic who specializes in finding missing persons. After Terri explained the situation, the psychic agreed to meet Terri at as soon as she could get there.

Michael and Tiffany also developed a plan to get the police involved without alerting Jonathan should he show up at the house. As Jonathan was terrified of being arrested and thrown in jail, Tiffany didn't want to scare him if she were to pick up the phone and call the police. She set her speed dial for Michael's cell phone and would hold the phone in her pocket and call Michael if Jonathan surfaced. If Michael received a call and she wasn't talking, Michael would call the police and the police would send a car quietly to escort Jonathan to the hospital. Both Tiffany and Michael spoke with the detective to make sure the plan was agreeable with the police force. Both Michael and Tiffany were assured that the police would cooperate.

That evening Terri met with Linda, the psychic. Linda told Terri that we needed to search further west, perhaps 20 miles. 20, Linda told Terri, was a significant number she was seeing. She told Terri that Jonathan was by two huge towers (Linda couldn't identify what the towers were), lots of smelly water, and in a heavily wooded area. She also told Terri that the family would have our answers on Thursday and that it was critical to find him by then.

Terri called Michael as soon as she got home to let him know what she had been told. Michael got on a website that showed a geographical map. Following Linda's instruction, Michael searched. After a short time, he located 2 high towers that were very prominent on the map. What this brought to our searching attempt was amazing. On State Route 20 (not 20 miles west, 8 miles west of where we were concentrating our search) is a paper mill company. There were 2 huge smoke stacks pointing toward the sky and a foul smelling lake (we would discover later) that appeared to store liquefied pulp and other waste. As it turned out, Linda was the first of several Godsends to come into our life over the next few days.

Thursday April 29

I got up early to get to work ahead of schedule. Terri had left me a message the night before about her meeting with Linda, so I called her on my way into work and got the full story. I knew exactly where Linda was referring to as I had driven through this area many times with the kids when we would drive to Huntsville to visit my parents. And yes, I recalled, it smelled awful at times.

After I got to work Dean came into my office to check on me. I explained what was going on and he sat down and said a prayer for the entire family. We spoke for a few minutes and he offered any help that he or anyone in the company could provide.

I settled into my office, turned on my computer, and there was a message from Michael.

Michael to Terri and Mike

Let me be careful with this. You both know I'm a Christian, and the Bible actually forbids entertaining soothsayers and the like. I do not care to invite what could be a negative spirit into my life...I apologize if you don't understand this, but it's complicated. There may be credence to what the psychic said, and if you feel it's prudent to follow up with her comments, please do so without my participation. I must refrain from entertaining these spirits...I am sorry.

> Leviticus 19:31
> Give no regard to mediums and familiar spirits; do not seek after them, to be defiled by them.

Mom, please talk to Dad about what we said if you feel it's right. Instead I choose to trust God entirely.

> Proverbs 3:5
> Trust in the Lord with all your heart and lean not on your own understanding.

I believe this psychic intervention to be a possible trick, a deception. This event does not expel the spiritual warfare that exists among us. Please be careful and consider the repercussions. I love you both with all my heart.

Mike to Michael and Terri

I certainly respect everything you say. I love you very much too.
Dad

Tiffany spent the morning working on a new flyer to hand out. She emailed me a copy of it to make sure I was comfortable with it. I forwarded the email to the family.

Mike to Terri, Michael and Kristin
This about broke my heart.

MISSING
29 YEAR OLD MALE
6'1"   170LBS   BLUE EYES   BROWN HAIR
LAST SEEN ON 4/25/10
BROWN PANTS
NAVY LONG SLEEVED THERMAL
NAVY/GREY T-SHIRT OVER THERMAL
BLACK AND WHITE ADIDAS SNEAKERS
BLACK BACKPACK
SILVER WEDDING BAND
CALL 706-555-1234 OR 678-555-6789
PLEASE CALL IMMEDIATELY!
THANK YOU! GOD BLESS!!

Michael to Mike, Terri and Kristin

It is a blessing that Tiffany has been so diligent. She has been a very good wife, and I feel shame for the occasional feelings of irritation or anger or blame towards her. Mom, I hope you also realize her devotion to Jonathan. Tiffany is proving a very good woman, and she is most worthy of the love of our entire family.

Terri to Mike, Michael and Kristin

Yes, my thoughts or doubts about Tiffany are no longer there. She and I have had lengthy conversations over the last few days, talked in depth about Jonathan and his issues and problems, and she was blown away and did not realize how severe and how long Jon's problems have been with him. She, after all, has only known him one year. She just thought he was going through a bad time in his life, and now she realizes what she's gotten into. In spite of all of it, she loves Jonathan with all her heart. She shared with me some beautiful things that are meaningful and sentimental and described a true soul connection with Jon, though she is anxious for him to get the help he needs. She recognizes how talented, bright, and how much he has to offer to the world. She wants, as we all do, for him to believe in and love himself and feel worthy to be here. My feelings about Tiffany are nothing but good and I feel very sorry for her for her worries and suffering.

She is really praying hard and having many others do the same.

I hope today will prove to be revealing.

Tiffany had a doctor's appointment at 1:00 PM. I left work at the same time as I was to pick her up after her appointment and we would go to the area that the psychic told us to look. While driving to Rome, I received a call from Michael. He told me he had just received a call from Tiffany, and she wasn't talking. He told me he was going to call the police, and I agreed he should proceed.

In Michael's own words, here's how the call evolved:

> "I recall shaking nervously as I called the police department to inform them. The butterflies in my stomach were overwhelming, and I remember feeling a lack of bodily control (shaking, stuttered speaking when talking to the police dept., extreme adrenaline rush)…it's the only time in my life I can remember feeling out of control other than

drunkenness. I recall being very frustrated with the police department because they were completely unprepared for my call...despite our several discussions with them about Jonathan and that this call might be coming their way, they had no idea what I was talking about when I requested they send a squad car immediately though an "emergency" was not in progress. What should have been a 30 second "go get him" call turned into a several minute explanation of what was happening while they seemingly looked around the room at each other, bewildered about who knew what. I imagine those emotions are the stuff ulcers and heart attacks are made of. It was very intense for me."

While Tiffany was with the doctor, the speed dial was accidently activated. She didn't know that the number had been dialed. After her appointment, she left to go home. As she turned onto her street to get to the house, she saw seven police cars with lights flashing. She was terrified!! What was happening!?!? Had they found Jonathan!?!? Why were there so many cars?!? Didn't they remember they were to arrive quietly and use their compassion genes?!?!

Tiffany rushed out of the car to speak with the officer in charge. He told her that they had received an emergency call to pick up a missing person. He knew nothing about coming quietly or proceeding with care. If Jonathan had been there, he would have been off in a flash.

I arrived shortly thereafter to pick her up. She had already talked with Michael, and they decided against using that plan again.

Tiffany and I packed up the flyers and proceeded to our first stop, City Hall. When we went to file form 1025 as the detective suggested we do, we were bounced around a couple of times before we found the correct clerk to speak with. We explained the situation and she asked,

"Have you observed any unusual behavior in the last 24 hours?"

Tiffany replied, "He faked an overdose, jumped out of the car, and ran away a couple of days ago."

The clerk apologized, but the observation had to have been in the last 24 hours.

"But he ran away? Isn't that unusual behavior?" I asked.

"But it hasn't been within the last 24 hours," she stated.

This "negotiation" went on for a few minutes without any compromise.

"So if we had come here the next day, we could have filed this?" Tiffany asked.

"As long as it had been within 24 hours."

"But the detective said we need this form in order to have Jonathan taken directly to a hospital instead of custody," I pleaded.

"The detectives don't always know the proper procedures."

I asked "What form is available to cover what we need to happen?"

"There isn't one."

We felt like we were in an Abbott and Costello movie.

We got into the car and proceeded to Coosa where the two towers were located. Our first stop was at a flea market where we met John, our second Godsend. John told us he had seen Jonathan a few hours earlier that day. He told us that Jonathan was walking with his head down and that he didn't look well at all. Later that evening, John helped with the search. After the flea market closed for the day, a friend of John's, a bounty hunter, picked John up and they left to look for Jonathan.

Tiffany and I spoke with other people who had tables set up, and they confirmed that they had seen Jonathan yesterday as well. One commented that she talked to him briefly as he was looking at baby clothes. She mentioned that he had been quiet, but very polite.

Driving around the immediate vicinity, Tiffany and I stopped often to hand out flyers to local merchants and people along the road. One of the merchants at a convenient store remembered Jonathan and commented on how polite he had been. The merchant also remembered that Jonathan had purchased a Dr. Pepper. We stopped at a church along the road and spoke with the custodian briefly. He let us post a flyer on the front door.

We then drove back into Rome to speak with the detective about where Jonathan had been sited. We were honest and told him we got our "leads" from a psychic who specializes in locating missing people. The detective shared his opinions about psychics, they never work.

I asked him "You've had no luck in finding him. Yet we've met several people who have seen him. Can't you look in the area?"

"And these people work at a flea market? And a merchant in the area claims to have seen him? Flea market?" he asked, questioning the integrity of our sources.

"We have cars that patrol the area regularly. We'll keep a look out."

"Why not a search party?" Tiffany asked.

"Because psychics never work," the detective insisted.

I understood that the lack of manpower could be an issue, and he stated this reason as his final determination for not coordinating a search party.

"By the way, how often have you used a psychic?" I asked.

"Never," was the answer.

Tiffany and I turned to leave and I scratched my head……..hmmmm, psychics never work and you've never tried using one. I thought we were back in the Abbott and Costello movie.

It was about 6:00 PM, and I called Terri to let her know how the day's events unraveled. She was very concerned about one of the things Linda had told her. We needed to find Jonathan by Thursday evening. I let her know that we were doing our best. She suggested I call the police and arrange for a helicopter search. After my recent conversation with the detective, I wasn't confident that there would be agreement to issue a helicopter search. I called the police department and explained the situation (left out the part about the psychic) to the officer on duty. He told me he would need approval and that this usually took time. I emphasized Jonathan had been without his heart medications and that he was very sick. I asked him to see if he could make the arrangements and that I would call him back in 20 minutes. While I waited, I walked around the downtown area handing out flyers and talking with people. I called back 20 minutes later and I was told there was nothing that could be done. If I wanted to, I could come back in the morning and speak with one of the superiors.

After we finished in Rome, we went back to Coosa and parked in the flea market parking lot. Tiffany and I walked down to the smelly lake to see if Jonathan might have set up camp around there. We arrived at dusk and thought we saw a fire going in the distance. As we approached what we thought was the fire, we saw that is was merely a reflection of the setting sun on the lake. As we retreated back to the car, Tiffany received a call from John about what he and his friend discovered during their search.

John met a man in a neighborhood a mile from the flea market who had taken Jonathan to the hospital at 7:00PM that evening. According to this man, Jonathan didn't look well. The man offered Jonathan both food and drink, Jonathan accepting only the drink. As Jonathan accompanied the man to the hospital, Jonathan repeatedly told him, "I want to go home."

After hearing this story, John and his friend drove to the hospital. They spoke with an employee who was leaving the hospital as her shift had just ended. She confirmed seeing Jonathan, but he had been there only a few moments. She noticed that Jonathan drank some water and abruptly left.

With this information, John told Tiffany that they would continue looking around the woods by the hospital, and they continued until 2:30AM.

I dropped Tiffany off at her house and then went to the hospital to talk with security to see if they might be able to help. No luck, they hadn't seen him so they rewound some of their surveillance film to see if they could find him on camera. Nothing was detected. I left a few flyers which they posted by the entrances and returned to Tiffany's house. We spoke of the day's events, thanked God for the people He had sent into our lives, and called it a night. I went down the street and stayed at a hotel so I could get an early start the next morning. I wrote a few thoughts in my journal.

> "As each day starts, Tiffany's optimism is an inspiration to us all. I've been able to know Tiffany over this past year, but the rest of the side of Jon's family has only seen turbulence for the majority of the time. Her love, her strong belief, her optimism results in just that: love, belief and optimism about finding Jonathan. She extends her love, not only for Jonathan, but for life in general, and all of us notice this. If there were any doubts or questions about the relationship Jonathan and Tiffany share, the "in-law" opinion has been shattered. Her grace through the turmoil only endears her to Jonathan's side of the family.
>
> As we meet people along the way during our search for Jonathan, she expresses a loving call for help....an innocence...a pure love extending out to someone else, a perfect stranger, and she receives it in return."

Friday April 30

I got up early, ate breakfast and left to search the woods around the medical center. The sun was rising and I prayed for guidance as to where to take me to look. I stopped several times to get out of the car and explore the area, but found no trace of Jonathan. At 8:30 I returned to Tiffany's house so we could plan our day.

We decided that we would look within a 2 mile radius of the hospital. Based on the condition we assumed he was in, he wouldn't walk any further than that. I was to go to Shorter College, talk with security and check the woods around campus. Abby, a friend of Tiffany who would spend the upcoming weekend helping with the search, was to hand out flyers and talk with people on the street. She was to target Broad Street, the main street in downtown Rome. Tiffany would make more copies of the flyer, and then return to Coosa to talk with John about the previous night's events.

I left to handle my assignment at Shorter College. After finishing there, I stopped often to post flyers on trees along nature trails, and searched some of the surrounding woods. Feelings of hopelessness began to overcome me so I called Abby at 11:00 to see if she was having any luck. She told me that she talked with someone who thought that he might have seen Jonathan, but the description of the clothes that person was wearing didn't sound like anything Jonathan owned. Abby informed me that she was meeting Tiffany for lunch at a downtown restaurant, so I drove out there to meet them.

As I drove through downtown Rome, I noticed a church that I thought would appeal to Jonathan. I stopped and was greeted by the pastor and 4 people of his administrative staff as I entered the building. These people were wonderful as they supplied me with arms of information about the shelters and soup kitchens in the area. They made calls to people and organizations to alert them about Jonathan. As I prepared to leave, the pastor led a prayer, after which I received hugs and blessings from each of them. I left the church feeling that some of my inner peace had been restored.

As I was looking for one of the soup kitchens, I got a call from Abby telling me that Tiffany had received a call from a merchant in Coosa who had seen Jonathan earlier that morning. We dropped our lunch plans and I headed to Tiffany's house to pick up Abby. As we drove out to Coosa to meet Tiffany, Michael called me to let me know that he was taking the afternoon off. He would be in the area in an hour to help with the search.

While I was talking with Michael, Abby received a text from a high school friend who was an ex-cop and hunted missing persons for a living. He also had recently moved to Rome, and wanted to know if he could help. Another Godsend!! Of course he could help!! We met Tiffany in Coosa and returned to Rome to meet Mark, the ex-cop, and Michael.

We met Mark at his house and quickly got down to business. He asked questions and noted answers as he developed his plan. He then called his wife, who happened to have been born and raised in Coosa. She knew many people in Coosa, so she called family and friends to enlist their help. Between Mark and his wife, they proceeded to get much community involvement in the search as they organized people to knock on doors, and examine the empty trailers, mobile homes, and buildings in the area.

While they were conducting their search, Michael and I spent some great father/son time together as we searched the railroad tracks in the area Jonathan had been seen. We also drove through neighborhoods and handed out flyers. On a couple of occasions we met people who were aware of "some guy missing" and they had already spread the word. They let us know that their hopes and prayers were with us and that we would find him. Michael and I talked about the different possible outcomes and Michael reminded me that Jonathan had always said that when it's time to give up the medicines, his mind and God would do it. I also remember Jonathan telling me that more than once. I told Michael it wouldn't surprise me that if three months from now, Jonathan would walk out of the woods as an enlightened being.

At 10:00 PM many of the people who spent the afternoon and evening searching for Jonathan met at a truck stop in Coosa. There was one more lead Mark wanted to follow up on before we concluded the search for the evening. We waited to see if we needed to visit the home of a reputed drug dealer. Mark had determined that if Jonathan was looking for medicines, this would be a likely place to turn. Mark also knew the person living next door to the drug house, and this person was also an ex-cop who said he'd keep an eye open for Jonathan. Another Godsend! He confirmed to Mark that after scouting the area around the drug house, no one was there. As the day ended, our entire family realized that we had eyes and ears everywhere in the area.

Saturday May 1

Tiffany was up early Saturday morning and left the house to hand out flyers and look for Jonathan. She was becoming known around town as the woman looking for her husband. As the day wound down, she drove to a wooded area that looked like a place Jonathan might camp. She plugged in a Sublime CD (Jonathan's favorite music group), turned up the volume, and called Jonathan's name. She let him know she loved him, and wanted to help him.

Terri met with Linda, who saw this in her vision.

> "He's close, not harmed, talking, nosing around place to place....he spent one night on a bus bench, sleeps a few hours at a time.....he's comfortable, the area feels familiar....he's not as dehydrated, his shirt has changed, he didn't steal it, not flannel, it's blue and gray.....he will be found on Tuesday, don't question hard, he thinks nothing is wrong, he feels like he's lost....he's not afraid, he's finding his way around and has a sense of belonging..... he hasn't noticed the posters, in his own world, severe

mental health issues.....needs a hospital, ticks, for physical reasons.....he'll be surprised, not going to fight, he'll be calm.....he doesn't remember family, feels like he's lost, he feels safe, going home is not in his thought process.....no prescriptions, he must be protected from himself.....he has a dog, brown with white spots, medium size, wiry hair, the dog is with him, they'll see the dog..... everyone recognizes him, he talks to lots of people, very likable.....shoes are worn down, problem with his foot, finding things, dumping his own stuff.....during day, he can hear people....Dad will be the one to talk to him, no ultimatums, don't scare, calm, soothing, "I'm glad to see you. I found my friend again," let him feel safe, relax for next few days.....he moves, doesn't sleep in same place, in old building not boarded up....candles are important.... has buddy he just met, long hair, shaggy, Viet Nam vet, very kind to Jon....homeless, comes out during day, not bothering anyone, little place, small town, Coosa, had a breakdown, sees this as his home.....something mental has been inherited and has been there since he was born, has gone without oxygen a few times in his life, combination of mental issues, bi-polar......someone will be talking to him and another will call Dad.....amnesia, own congregation in town, feels like walking in sleep and body surging, what's keeping him going....his mind is not right....very spiritual, talented, intelligent....he likes area he was living in....works with his hands.....by Tuesday Dad will get call.....no buses or trucks, is there a bus station?.....wandering from place to place, talking with different people, doesn't like people to be mad at him.....no police, call as back up only.....will be shocked when he sees Dad....mind has snapped, problem for a long time, crossed threshold....needs to be monitored at all times, no control, medicines by a professional, will take a long time, it's his last chance.....if he gets help he won't go to jail, as long as he gets the help he needs.....it will take a couple of hours to bring him in, be gentle and calm, give him time.....he's not angry, much calmer, he's terrified of confinement, keep him calm, say nothing to scare him, reassure him he's not going to jail if he goes with Dad, will be later in the afternoon.....he has little money, he's not stolen anything, is safe in his own world, not going further, not coming home on his own, state of amnesia, there's a friend who won't tell him where he's at......today and tomorrow, take it easy, much calmer by Tuesday..... will naturally happen, will go in for help without a fight, don't scare, patience, take home for a couple of hours..... he's calm, not seeing posters, breathing is not as bad..... here for a special reason, not supposed to die....blood pressure is high, not in stroke zone.....stability will take time.....he fears getting help and not being able to continue his spirituality as he knows it.....he is a good, loving person, sensitive.....everyone understands how sick he is....will feel like he's in a dream....he is fragile.

Sunday May 2

It was a quiet day. I spoke with Tiffany and let her know I wasn't feeling well, and would be out there again on Tuesday as I needed to catch up with work on Monday.

Tiffany continued her search. She went out to Coosa and checked in with those who now viewed her as a regular. She was on a quest and would continue searching until she found her soul mate.

My Journal – May 1 and May 2

I've spoken with many people over the last few days; many concerned about my wellbeing. I've also seen and heard a lot of crying and much upset about what is going on. Terri's added stress from these events to go along with her cancer, Tiffany working so hard to deal through these times, Laura's upset and fear, Michael's anxiety or feelings of hopelessness and deep concern, Kristin's fear and knowing there's nothing she can do to help from afar.

This weekend I felt ill.......chest pains, body aches, feelings of fear about Jonathan, a sense of listlessness. My meditation and prayer didn't connect, yet this is a period of time when I need it most. I don't know what it was. My brother Joe pointed out that he's heard the stress and anxiety in my voice over the last week or so, and it's true.

Love to us All

Monday May 3

Michael to All
Given the rainy conditions, it is conceivable Jonathan might head towards a free shelter to stay dry, especially if he has no tent and no "friends" to help him out. Have all the area shelters been thoroughly plastered with flyers? Also, has anyone given thought to maybe altering the flyers to say "REWARD with info leading to recovery"? Nobody needs to know what the reward is...we'll just give $50 or something...we can all chip in a little bit.

Terri to All
I went back to Linda on Saturday and she gave me a lot more information regarding Jon. I will be happy to share it with you on the phone if you want to call me tonight when you have time. It is too much to put in an email.

I don't think Jonathan will head to a shelter (i.e. homeless shelter) as there are, from my understanding, many abandoned buildings, trailers, even an abandoned elementary school in the area...I think he is taking shelter right where he is.

The reward is a good idea, but if what Linda told me is accurate, he will be found by no later than Tuesday.

Tiffany to All
Terri, my phone battery is totally drained (now charging) and I just got my internet back up, so sorry about earlier today. Michael, the reward idea is good. I am thinking about doing another flyer with updated info and those little tabs that people can pull off so they can take the numbers with them so if they spot him they will have the numbers WITH them instead of having to go back to look at a flyer. Several people have taken flyers to distribute in their neighborhoods. One lady even took one to work and made copies to give out. She called me tonight just to see if we have heard any news. She said she woke up in the middle of the night when it was raining and immediately he came to mind, and she decided to help out. Apparently there is a hiking trail where people camp near her house and she is sending her son to look tomorrow after school. Any ideas for a new flyer if we make one? The people definitely know his face. My friend told me her coworker's husband saw the flyer at one of the two factories that Mike and I went to. Hoping we have him safe by tomorrow and won't need it, but just in case, let me know. Kristin, so glad you like your new job. Terri, can you e-mail any rehabs you have found? I can check on insurance. Love to you all- Tiffany

Tuesday May 4

Terri to All

Mike, Michael: do either of you still have any of the information from any of the rehab places we looked at months ago when we were looking? I discarded them due to no insurance and the cost involved. However, there were some good ones out there, and now with insurance we have a much better selection to choose from. I will do some more research. The flyer idea sounds great. I am praying he will surface again today.

Michael to All

Like you, I have deleted them. Have we been guaranteed they won't throw Jonathan in jail upon being apprehended? Beyond what the officer said, I mean? And if the county or state intends to maintain control of Jonathan, a private rehab facility may not be an option anyway. I know lots of things have been said about how the courts will honor his admittance into a private facility, but given his recent track record, it's realistic their mindset may be different now.

Terri to All

No, there is no guarantee, but the plan is to try to avoid involving the police unless absolutely necessary and to take him directly to a hospital. Depending on his condition, they may or may not deem it necessary to keep him, and therein lies a problem if Jonathan does not want to stay voluntarily. At that point, we may have to involve the police in order to get a court order. Of course, if he is not already admitted for treatment, it is possible the cops could decide to take him elsewhere. That would be horrible if they did that, but I'm not sure what will happen. I do know, though, or have been told, that once he is in treatment (admitted), it would be illegal for police to try to come in and remove him (besides it is private property) until he has been released from doctor's care. It would be up to the doctor to decide.

Michael to All

Ok, let's hope it's that easy. But it's worth repeating, yet again, that Jonathan has shown absolutely no indication that he's truly willing to surrender himself voluntarily to a rehabilitation facility. Obviously having gone so far as to run away and threaten/attempt suicide to avoid it should be enough to pretty much guarantee any initial promise he may make about checking in won't stick. And no, it doesn't have anything to do with him trying to avoid jail...he is avoiding incarceration/lockdown/hospitalization/whatever you want to call it, period...any place that will not permit him 100% freedom to do as he pleases. In his heart of hearts, I believe Jonathan desires help. But in his mind and spirit, both of which are wild and free (since he was a child), there is no interest. In fact he has consistently exhibited a bitter defiance. And let's face reality...Jon's mind and spirit rule him, despite the regular conflict he has with his heart. Surely Tiffany can attest to that better than any of us.

Remember all the times we talked about Jonathan needing to hit "rock bottom" before he can make real progress? Maybe this is that point for him...? Maybe this is what he needs above all else...? Maybe this is God's will...? Maybe we are running interference with His will...? Maybe your psychic is a devil's advocate who is leading us to catch Jonathan before God has revealed Himself...before Jonathan is saved! Maybe not...it's a very difficult conclusion to draw, of course, one that likely none of us is spiritually equipped or wise enough to answer confidently. As I said before, let us be very careful with this. Scripture is very specific.

> Leviticus 19:31
> Give no regard to mediums and familiar spirits; do not seek after them, to be defiled by them.
>
> 2 Corinthians 11:14-15
> ...for Satan himself is transformed into an angel of light. Therefore it is no great thing if his ministers also be transformed as the ministers of righteousness; whose end shall be according to their works.
>
> Deuteronomy 18:10-12
> Let no one be found among you who...practices divination or sorcery, interprets omens, engages in witchcraft, or casts spells, or who is a medium or spiritist or who consults the dead. Anyone who does these things is detestable to the Lord...
>
> 2 Thessalonians 2:9
> The coming of the lawless one will be in accordance with the work of Satan displayed in all kinds of counterfeit miracles, signs and wonders...

I could go on. Indeed scripture also warns us specifically about those who speak in the name of the Lord, but who require payment for the service. (Micah 3:5-12, specifically verse 11) Seek real wisdom and understanding with the answers quoted below.

> *Proverbs 3:5*
> *Trust in the Lord with all your heart and lean not on your own understanding.*
>
> *Jeremiah 17:7*
> *Most blessed is the man who believes in, trusts in, and relies on the Lord, and whose hope and confidence the Lord is.*
>
> *Psalm 118:8*
> *It is better to trust and take refuge in the Lord than to put confidence in man.*
>
> *Jeremiah 17:5-7*
> *This is what the Lord says: Cursed is the one who trusts in man, who depends on flesh for his strength and whose heart turns away from the Lord. He will be like a bush in the wastelands; he will not see prosperity when it comes. He will dwell in the parched places of the desert, in a salt land where no one lives. But blessed is the man who trusts in the Lord, whose confidence is in him.*

Dad and I receive the same daily devotional from a God loving man with whom Dad works. This is today's (below), excerpts derived from writings by Oswald Chambers. Can we all learn something from this? Is this coincidence or divine intervention? Tread wisely and have faith...I believe wholeheartedly that is all we can really do. Sorry to ramble...my love to you all...

> *"Willing to Let Go*
> *The Lord has given, and the Lord has taken away! May the name of the Lord be praised. (Job 1:21)*

Isn't it true that your money, property, body, spouse, children, and friends are good things created and given to you by God himself? Ultimately, they all belong to God and not to you. What if he were to test your loyalty by taking them away from you? What if he wanted to learn whether you were willing to let go of them for his sake? What if he wanted to see whether you would hold tighter to him or to his gifts? What if you became separated from your loved ones? Do you think you would have the right to rant and rave, forcibly attempt to get them back, or sulk until they were returned to you? But if you argue that these are God's good gifts to you and that you want to get them back no matter what the cost, then you would be making a big mistake.

If you want to do the right thing, don't rush ahead without thinking. You must fear God and say, "Dear Lord, the people and things you have given me are good, as you have said in Scripture. Yet, I don't know whether you will let me keep them. If I knew that you didn't want me have them, I wouldn't even try to get them back. However, if I knew that you wanted me to have them; I would do what you want by taking them back. But I don't know what you want me to do. All I can see now is that you have allowed them to be taken away from me. So I'll turn the whole matter over to you. I'll wait until I know what to do. I'm ready to live either with them or without them." Oswald Chambers

Terri to All

Bottom line....Jonathan is very ill...he has had a mental breakdown. He needs help desperately. He has been without his blood pressure medication for a week and his BP is probably through the roof by now. I want him found, however means it takes to do so. We have to get him to a place where he can be treated before it's too late. Everyone's personal beliefs are respected. But, Linda was completely accurate with her previous information that led us to the area where Jonathan was sited. Her reading on Saturday was even more informative and specific as to the extreme mental breakdown he has suffered. I was going to tell you the information last night when you called but you didn't ask and I didn't bring it up because I don't want to offend you or talk to you about it if you are uncomfortable with it. Out of respect for your concerns, I didn't want to do that.

No matter what anyone believes, Jonathan needs to be found. No matter what...someone who attempts suicide is mentally ill...period. He needs to be found, and fast.

Based on what Linda had told Terri Saturday night, I decided to go to work on Monday and Tuesday, and leave a little early on Tuesday so I would be in Rome during the time Linda predicted Jonathan would be located. I explained this to my boss, David, and he just gave me a quizzical look. I reminded him that the psychic had correctly directed us to the area Jonathan was staying. Like David, I found this was hard to grasp but Linda had pointed us in the right direction. There was no reason for me to doubt her now.

As I was driving to Rome, I received a frantic call from Tiffany.

"They found a man's body down by the railroad tracks!! I called the police and they won't tell me anything!!" she cried. Tiffany had heard the report coming over a police radio as she was shopping for some batteries to use in her flashlight later that evening. She called me as she was driving to the location where the body had been found. I tried to calm her down and not to jump to any conclusions as I silently told myself the same thing. We got off the phone and Tiffany arrived at the scene a few minutes later. There was only a police car and two of Tiffany's best friends (who had overheard the same report and knew Tiffany would be there). The policeman told Tiffany that the body had been taken to the coroner's and no information would be available until tomorrow. Tiffany begged for some kind of clue, but the officer was very close lipped. Her 2 friends accompanied Tiffany back to her house and waited for me to get there.

I called Michael first to let him know what was going on. By the time we got off the phone I arrived at Tiffany's. She was terrified to think about what we might find out. I then called Terri to let her know what was happening. She listened and started to cry, not knowing what to think. We hung up and I left a message with the detective telling him to call me and let me know what was going on.

"You're a detective for Christ's sake," I stated to his voicemail, "and you know a lot more than you're telling Tiffany. You can't put this family through a night of hell not telling us what you know."

After I left that message I received a call from Cherie. They had just gotten off the phone with Terri, and Cherie told me that Terri was beside herself. She pleaded with me, "Don't tell Terri anything. Let us do it. She'll never make it up here if she knows that it's Jonathan." I thanked her and readily agreed.

The detective called me back within 10 minutes. He was hesitant at first to volunteer any information, but I asked for some specific details and he finally told me they were 98% sure it was Jonathan. The back pack identified next to the body was Jonathan's and the clothes matched what Jonathan was wearing.

I slowly went back to the porch to let Tiffany know what I had just found out. Tiffany was in the bathroom, so I let her friends and Mother, who had just arrived, know what the detective had said. Tiffany received the news and broke down. It was by the grace of God that Tiffany's two dearest friends had heard the same police report, dropped what they were doing, and rushed to meet her. Between the two of them and her Mother, they were able to provide the immediate support Tiffany needed.

In the meantime, Terri was trying to get through to me, but I'd been on the phone or was waiting to inform Michael and Cherie first. I got through to them and I gave them the news. Terri finally got a hold of me and I just told her that I have no word yet, but she should get up here regardless. If it's not Jonathan, then she could help in finding him. She got off the phone and began making arrangements to get to Georgia, fearing the worst.

The detective had given me the name and number of the coroner, so I called him next. He informed me that to make a 100% positive identification would take some testing as the body was not in a state for viewing as he had passed several days earlier. The coroner asked me if there was anything on Jonathan's body that might help identify him. I let him know about the tattoos he had, Integrity on the underside of his forearm and the Chinese symbol on his chest. He said he would call me back within the hour to let me know what he had discovered.

I called Laura to let her know. She began crying and asked about my wellbeing. I let her know I was okay and that I'd wait to hear back from the coroner and spend some time with Tiffany before I headed home.

I called Kristin to break the news to her. She began sobbing as I tried to comfort her the best way I could, and I knew that Matthew and his family were there to help her through her sorrow.

Joe was next and I asked him to call the rest of our siblings.

I called David and asked that he let the work crew know, and that I would let him know when the funeral arrangements had been made.

Michael called me to let me know that he didn't think he could break the news to Terri. I told him to just be there and I would let Terri know after she landed.

The coroner called back to inform me they were 99.9% sure it was Jonathan, but they still needed to run the battery of tests to be 100% certain. I thanked him and let him know that I would call the next day to set up a meeting with him.

I made some more calls and let Tiffany know that they were now 99.9% sure it was Jonathan. I stood out on the sidewalk by myself for a while and just stared into space. I wondered if the reason I felt so out of sorts over the weekend was because something in me knew that Jonathan had already passed.

Michael and Cherie drove to the airport to pick up Terri. As Terri got off the plane and looked into Michael's eyes, she knew the body that had been found was Jonathan. The three of them just hugged each other and cried.

I was on my way home when Terri called me. I picked up the phone and she was sobbing, "OUR BABY'S DEAD!"

You Are At Peace

Terri and I spoke for another 20 minutes. We reminded and reassured ourselves that Jonathan was now in a better place and without any of the pain that he suffered on this earthly plane.

As I continued home my brothers and sisters called to give their love and condolences. I thanked them, let them know that I was OK, and told them that I would call with the funeral arrangements as soon as the plans were made.

As I pulled into the driveway, Laura was there to meet me at the door. She gave me a hug and looked at me to see how I was feeling. I assured her that I was holding up. We sat down at the kitchen table and talked for the next several hours about Jonathan, about the plans that needed to be made, and about telling Chris.

Matt was at his computer when Laura returned home from work, and she informed him of Jonathan's passing.

Chris was scheduled to work until 10:00 PM, and we decided to let him finish his shift. By 11:00 PM, Chris hadn't arrived so Laura called him to inform him that she needed to talk with him. After that conversation, Chris knew something had happened. When he walked into the kitchen a half hour later and saw both Laura and me sitting there, he knew. The words were no sooner out of Laura's mouth before Chris burst into tears.

Wednesday May 5 – Friday May 7

The next three days were a blur and the events and preparation seemed surreal. As each of us tried to get over the shock of the news and grieved in our own way, we knew that we only had a few days to make the funeral arrangements. I called Tiffany early Wednesday morning to ask her how she wanted to proceed with the plans, and she asked that Laura, Terri, and I carry on without her. She trusted our judgment completely, and she was too distraught to think about this.

Laura and I continued our conversation from the night before, and we agreed that beginning with a local funeral home would be the best place to start with the arrangements. We waited for Terri to arrive at our house as she had spent the night with Michael and Cherie.

After meeting with the funeral home representatives, we understood what we needed to do in order to be ready for Saturday's service. The rest of Wednesday and Thursday were booked with appointments with the coroner, several cemeteries, and the pastor at a local church. These meetings resulted in research calls that needed to be made in order to answer legal questions. Friday was left open for last minute decisions and to cover anything that may have been overlooked.

Ashley was informed of Jonathan's passing while she was out of town working. She made it clear to all of us that she wanted to be with Remy and be the one to tell him that Jonathan had passed. She made arrangements to get back to town as soon as possible. She got home on Thursday, called Remy into the room and told him about what had happened to his Daddy. They hugged and cried. After a few moments, Remy informed her that he needed to go write a letter.

> **"Dear Dad,**
> **I love you, and I hope you feel better. And don't forget we all love you and we will never forget you. Me, Mom, Ben, Gramba, we all hope you We will never forget you. I hope you have fun and make friends. I will miss you now and I will see you in 70 years."**

Along with many of Jonathan's personal treasures, this letter was placed in his coffin to be with him in eternity.

Matt and Kristin flew in early from Chicago to help. Laura's parents, David and Frances drove down from Tennessee to support in any way they could.

While we were busy making these preparations, Matt and Chris, Matthew and Kristin, Ben and Ashley, Michael and Cherie, and Tiffany all worked diligently gathering pictures to be displayed at the service. They created a beautiful tribute to his life. Chris and Tiffany also composed a CD with Jonathan's favorite music that would be played throughout the visitation period of the service.

The Funeral

Saturday May 8

After Reverend Frank finished his sermon, I accompanied Tiffany up to the podium. She was the first to speak.

> "The first time I met Jonathan I knew he was the man I would marry. We had an instant connection that we both felt. I prayed for many years that God would bring the right man into my life. And I knew then and there that my prayers had been answered. He was everything I prayed for and so much more. He was the most beautiful soul I'd ever met. He restored my faith in love and life. He taught me that love is the only thing that matters. He taught me so many things in living a life in service of others. Compassion, forgiveness, faith, hope, and belief. I feel so blessed to have met him and spent a beautiful year with my soul mate. I have so many wonderful memories to carry with me and the day I became his wife was the happiest day of my life. I'm proud to carry his name and will carry him in my heart forever, because soul mates are forever.
>
> I love you to the moon and stars Jonathan. Always.
> I close with his favorite verse from the Bible.
> And now these three remain: faith, hope, and love. But the greatest of these is love. 1 Corinthians 13:13"

I was the next to speak.

> "When Laura, Terri, and I started looking at the variety of verses available for the prayer card, I saw the title "I am Free" popping out at me on one of the sheets. I immediately

grabbed it, got half way through it, choked up, handed it over to Terri and Laura and said "This is the one."

They read it, nodded, and we continued looking at the different options. In the end we all agreed unanimously that this was the most fitting.

I'd like to take a moment, in case you haven't read it, to read what it says as this could easily have come from Jonathan's hand.

I am Free

Don't grieve for me now, for now I'm free
I am following the path God laid for me.
I took his hand when I heard him call,
I turned my back and left it all.
I could not stay another day
to laugh, to love, to work or play.
Tasks left undone must stay that way.
I found that peace at the close of the day.
If my parting has left a void,
then fill it with remembered joy.
A friendship shared, a laugh, a kiss,
Ah, these things, I, too, will miss.
Be not burdened with time of sorrow,
I wish for you the sunshine of tomorrow.
My life's been full, I savored much.
Good friends, good times, a loved one touched.
Perhaps my time seemed all too brief
don't lengthen it now with undue grief.
Lift up your heart and share with me.
God wanted me now; He set me free."(Author Unknown)

Tiffany and I returned to our seats as Kristin and Terri walked to the podium. Terri had written a letter to Jonathan that she proceeded to read.

"My beautiful son,
Mere words cannot express the immeasurable love that I have for you.
From the moment I held you in my arms for the very

first time, I knew depths of love I didn't know were possible. Although we have lived miles apart, I pray that you have always known how very much I love you, and how much everyone loves you.

My heart breaks that you were never able to reach your fullest potential, and I know that you were filled with many hopes and dreams for the future. God had a very special plan for you.

Your beautiful blue eyes gave us a window to your sensitive and loving heart, soulful insight, and deep love for your family, friends, and for the world around you. You have entertained us and inspired us with your amazing talents, your beautiful music, incredible artwork and profound writings. I will always remember all the fun and special times we had together laughing, singing, and creating music together.

My heart is breaking at the thought of never holding you in my arms again, but I know that you will be forever with me, right here in my heart. Please know how very much you are loved and how incredibly your far too short time with us has inspired and impacted our lives in ways we never imagined possible.

May you rest in peace, my angel, in a place where pain, heartache and sadness are no longer possible. When you were a little boy, and I tucked you into bed at night, I always said "Good night, Jon Boy". So, I will say to you again..... Good Night, Jon Boy, my precious son. I will miss you so very much and I will think of you every day of my life, and I will always remember all of our memories and happy times until we are together again.

All my love forever,
Mom"

Kristin gathered her notes and approached the podium to speak about her brother.

"Jonathan wasn't just my brother, he was my friend. Although we didn't talk every day, I knew that he was always there for me whenever I needed him. I have many fond memories of my brother but one in particular is a time when we were younger. He always liked to tease his baby sister, like big brothers do. He would make me come out of my bedroom and walk into whatever room he happened to be in and make me get him a coke or whatever he wanted. He would make me so mad. He would always say "Kristin, if you don't get it for me, I'll take away your prizes, tickets, and tokens the next time we go to Chuck E. Cheese" and then laugh. I look back at that memory now and can't help but smile. He was just being a big brother teasing his little sister.

Another fond memory I have of my brother was when we were a bit older. One of Jon's best friends, Derek, was living with us at the time. I woke up for school one morning and on the kitchen table was a note that said "Thank you for being such a great sister" along with my favorite movie at the time, Titanic. Both Jonathan and Derek know how much I enjoy that movie and really wanted it. I still hold that note to this day. I have it in a special place. I will cherish it for the rest of my life.

I remember when my husband Matt asked me to marry him on a cruise we were on. When we got back home, Matt and I drove to Jon's work and I told him that his baby sister is engaged. He came up to me and said that I look happy. I said that I am. He gave me a great big hug and told us congratulations.

I have many beautiful memories that I have shared with Jonathan. I will love him for the rest of my life. He will be truly deeply missed by his friends and family.

Rest in Peace, Jonathan. We love you."

Michael spoke next, and after he finished, Chris went to the podium to deliver his eulogy.

"I cannot put into words how I am feeling at this moment. Jonathan was my brother, my best friend, and a huge inspiration to me. Even though Jonathan is legally my step-brother, he and I grew a very special and tight bond so many years ago that runs as thick as blood and is just as unconditional. Jonathan was the kind of brother who would have done anything and everything within his power to take care of me and protect me, no matter what he had going on, he was always more than happy to take the time to be with me. Jonathan had a brilliant mind and a never ending thirst for knowledge. He loved to learn new things and he could not wait to find me to share his knowledge. I have learned so much from my brother over the years and I am so grateful for that. He has taught me more in the 12 years we were together than most people could hope to learn in a lifetime. He has lived a very full life and still had so much living to do.

My brother, Jon, still is and will always be one of the most important and cherished people in my life. I love him with all my heart and soul and I am so proud to call him my brother. Jonathan meant the world to me and I feel like a huge piece of me died along with my brother. There is and always will be a huge hole left in my heart that no one or nothing could ever fill. A very smart girl once told me, "Although that hole will never go away nor will it get any smaller. Instead your heart will grow so much bigger so that the permanent hole seems smaller, and that will make you a better person with time."

Even though my brother was with us for such a short time, he has still accomplished so many things that I know he was proud of. Jonathan was such a great musician and music was one of his greatest passions. Most people know that he was a great drummer, but not everyone knows what a good singer he was. Jonathan just naturally had a great ear for music, because he was so passionate about it that he devoted himself to it entirely. Jonathan was also a brilliant writer. He truly enjoyed writing and he took great pride in everything he wrote. He had a way with words that most people could only dream to have. Jonathan was the best story teller, he had so many stories and he knew I loved hearing them....I could listen to his stories all day.

Chris was beginning to choke up. He cleared his throat and continued.

> But all of his talents aside, my brother's greatest accomplishment is how great a father he was to his pride and joy....his son Remy. He was always so proud of Remy and he loved him more than anything in this world. Even though Jonathan is gone, I know he will be watching us. He will still see Remy grow up while guiding him and protecting him forever.
>
> The thing I will probably remember most about my brother is his passion for music. He loved everything about it and loved to share this passion with his friends and family. Music was so important to him and it always brought him peace and joy. And he loved to share that joy. Jonathan recently spoke to me and said, "Don't die with your music still in you." I will never forget these words as long as I live because....

Chris began crying and Michael walked up to the podium and put his arm around him for support.

> ...sadly I know my brother still had so much music inside of him to give to the world.
>
> Even though I am here today speaking at his funeral, I still can't believe my brother is gone and never coming back. I still cannot believe that he is never going to walk through my bedroom door with that huge smile on his face ever again. I still cannot believe that I will never get to talk to him again....and there are still so many things I wanted to say. But I take comfort in the fact that the one thing that I never needed to tell him was that I love him with all my heart and that he means everything to me.....because he already knew exactly how much he means to me. He knows the unbelievable love and respect I have for him is 100% unconditional.
>
> I am going to miss my brother so much more than any words could ever describe.

By now, Chris' voice was cracking and the heartbroken emotions he was feeling were flowing freely.

I am forever going to miss the way that only he could make me smile. But I especially am going to miss all the good times that were still to come and all the unfinished plans we had together.

I love you Jonathan, from the bottom of my heart....I will always love you. Goodbye brother....you will never be forgotten, I promise....I will make sure you are never forgotten. We will be together again."

After Chris had finished, he and Michael went back to their seats. There wasn't a dry eye in the house.

The Aftermath
Healing

As we returned to the routine of our daily lives, each of us sought remedies to bring us inner peace. The frantic and desperate emails we exchanged only weeks before changed tone and focused on concern for each other's wellbeing. While we fully supported each other with encouragement and love, each of us looked for resolution in different ways to the solitary questions that crept into our minds. Some of the answers came quicker than others, and as the answers came, they were shared among the family.

Kristin

Wednesday May 12

Michael to All

This is from a friend of Jonathan on Facebook. I promised to forward the message to everyone.

> "You don't know me but I actually made this Facebook page for Jonathan while he was in The Facility. My name is Nick. This is very upsetting news and I can't imagine what you, his family is going through. I will miss knowing that he is not around to take care of his son who I met once with Jonathan's father while they were visiting at The Facility. I don't know who I'm writing this to, but whoever is on the receiving end please accept my sympathies. Any way I can help with the coping please do not hesitate to contact me via Facebook, or Phone... 813-555-1234."

Terri to All

That was very nice. Thank you.

How is everyone doing? I am back to work today and it has been very hard for me, as I knew it would be. There was much love and support here awaiting my return, and they gave me a beautiful card signed by everyone.

Hope you are all hanging in there. I love you all.

Michael to All

Just hanging in there, praying for peace for his soul. Every day is easier to cope, but the emptiness hasn't faded...probably never will.

Kristin to All

That is such a sweet message. Tell him thank you for me. I am hanging in there. It's the hardest when I am thinking about different occasions that Jonathan and I shared together. Work is helping a lot. I am keeping busy so I don't think about it much. I still have a cry at night though but Matt and his family are being so great. I also have gotten some sweet cards in the mail, so I am going to send out thank you cards this week. I miss you all and love you very much!!! I am at work so I gotta get but I will be online tonight.

Kristin and Matthew were living with Matthew's parents during this time. Kristin was able to find the immediate support she needed not only through Matthew, but from her loving and compassionate in-laws. The grieving period lessened as time passed, but she was always able to find solace knowing that there was always a shoulder to lean on whenever she needed.

Thursday May 13

Mike to All

Emptiness best describes my feelings. I'm back at work today and I thought it might help me get my mind off of things……not working. David asked that I do a couple of my planning things and then take the rest of the week off. I believe I need to do that.

Terri to All

Mike, I can completely relate to what you are saying. I came back to work yesterday and just mechanically went about everything here. It is very difficult to concentrate and focus, and it definitely does not take my mind off things. I'm glad you are taking more time off from work. I would be doing the same if I could. I'm just taking things minute by minute.

Michael, Kristin, Tiffany: I love you and hope you are feeling better. One day at a time is the best any of us can hope for.

My arms are around all of you always.

Michael

Tuesday May 18

Tiffany to All

Hi everyone. I am glad to see that you are all getting through this, each in your own way. I am struggling very hard right now. I feel so lost, I just don't know what to do. Please keep me in your prayers. You are all in mine, of course. I miss him so much. I love you all- Tiffany

Michael to All

Tiffany, sorry you're still struggling. Feel free to call me any time you may want/need to talk.

Last night I spent about an hour with my bible study group. The conversation was very healing. Are you familiar with the Bible story of "The Prodigal Son?" It is one of the most popular stories in the Bible, and it's been my favorite since I became a Christian because it always gave me hope in regards to Jonathan. One of the guys presented it to me last night in a way I never thought about. Go read it, then finish reading this email. (Luke 15:11-32)

The Parable of the Lost Son

[11] Jesus continued: "There was a man who had two sons. [12] The younger one said to his father, 'Father, give me my share of the estate.' So he divided his property between them.

[13] "Not long after that, the younger son got together all he had, set off for a distant country and there squandered his wealth in wild living. [14] After he had spent everything, there was a severe famine in that whole country, and he began to be in need. [15] So he went and hired himself out to a citizen of that country, who sent him to his fields to feed pigs. [16] He longed to fill his stomach with the pods that the pigs were eating, but no one gave him anything.

¹⁷ "When he came to his senses, he said, 'How many of my father's hired servants have food to spare, and here I am starving to death! ¹⁸ I will set out and go back to my father and say to him: Father, I have sinned against heaven and against you. ¹⁹ I am no longer worthy to be called your son; make me like one of your hired servants.' ²⁰ So he got up and went to his father.

"But while he was still a long way off, his father saw him and was filled with compassion for him; he ran to his son, threw his arms around him and kissed him.

²¹ "The son said to him, 'Father, I have sinned against heaven and against you. I am no longer worthy to be called your son.'

²² "But the father said to his servants, 'Quick! Bring the best robe and put it on him. Put a ring on his finger and sandals on his feet. ²³ Bring the fattened calf and kill it. Let's have a feast and celebrate. ²⁴ For this son of mine was dead and is alive again; he was lost and is found.' So they began to celebrate.

²⁵ "Meanwhile, the older son was in the field. When he came near the house, he heard music and dancing. ²⁶ So he called one of the servants and asked him what was going on. ²⁷ 'Your brother has come,' he replied, 'and your father has killed the fattened calf because he has him back safe and sound.'

²⁸ "The older brother became angry and refused to go in. So his father went out and pleaded with him. ²⁹ But he answered his father, 'Look! All these years I've been slaving for you and never disobeyed your orders. Yet you never gave me even a young goat so I could celebrate with my friends. ³⁰ But when this son of yours who has squandered your property with prostitutes comes home, you kill the fattened calf for him!'

³¹ "'My son,' the father said, 'you are always with me, and everything I have is yours. ³² But we had to celebrate and be glad, because this brother of yours was dead and is alive again; he was lost and is found.'"

From a human perspective, we can easily understand how beautiful it would have been to see Jonathan humbled and awakened like the man in the story. It is truly inspiring.

Now go read the story again, but this time, insert God as the father in the story and Jonathan as the lost son. Amazing!!! The idea that Jonathan is not only in Heaven, but is being CELEBRATED there by God himself, is overwhelmingly emotional. It fills my spirit with joy and I can more easily get beyond my selfish desires to have Jonathan in my life. The idea lightens my heart and helps with the grief because, ultimately, I care so much more about Jonathan's eternal soul than I do my own earthly body. Perhaps you, too, can find solace in the passage.

> "He who deals wisely and heeds God's word and counsel shall find good, and whoever leans on, trusts in, and is confident in the Lord - happy, blessed, and fortunate is he." (Proverbs 16:20)

Like Kristin, Michael was able to depend on the loving support from his spouse, Cherie. Although Michael misses and thinks about Jonathan every day, Michael finds great comfort in his faith in God and knowing Jonathan's eternal soul is with Him.

Terri and Tiffany

Friday May 28

Terri to Mike, Michael and Kristin

Tiffany just sent me a text message saying "I am having a really bad morning. Please say a prayer for me. I can't stop crying. I don't know what to do without him. I love you."

I am worried about her. I texted her back and suggested she jump in the car and start driving to Florida. She is probably spending too much time alone with too much time to think….not working or having any distractions much. We could be good company for each other. I told her if she leaves soon, she could be here by dinnertime. I have a 3 day holiday weekend….it would be good for her. And, she is planning to come anyway…if any of you have a minute to call or text her, please try to talk her into coming today so she doesn't spend the holiday weekend being sad.

I feel so bad for her. She is just lost right now.

Mike to Terri, Michael and Kristin

I just left her a voicemail suggesting that she either drive down there or come over to our house. I told her to give me a call if she feels like talking.

Michael to Mike, Terri and Kristin

It's good and important to grieve; as well as it is to have people in your corner. She will make it through this…both through her own reflections and through the love of others. Offering her space as equally as human comfort is the right thing…I'm glad to see you are both supporting her wholeheartedly.

Terri to Michael, Mike and Kristin

Was there any doubt that we wouldn't? I think the world of her, and, as far as I know, everyone else does, too. She is family now. And, as far as I'm concerned, she will always be in my life. I think we all got to know her in a whole different way during the last month. Unfortunately, we all didn't know her well enough back when we were concerned her presence in Jon's life was making him worse. Interestingly, in our long conversation the other night, she was talking about how Jonathan withdrew from everyone and never wanted to call anybody and he didn't want her to either. She always felt bad that we didn't really get a chance to get to know her... she was trying to abide by Jon's wishes of it just being "the two of them".

I now know what an ongoing living hell she went through practically all by herself. My heart goes out to her and I am trying to do whatever I can to help her.

While Terri and I tried to convince Tiffany to drive to Florida to spend some time with Terri, Terri continued to look for other means to help relieve her heartache. She began reading books about heaven and the afterlife. She attended support group meetings that specialized in grief counseling for people who have lost family members. She also made a third appointment to see Linda, the psychic who helped us locate Jonathan. The following Wednesday Terri met with Linda whose vision brought immediate comfort, as Terri was able to make sense of much of what Linda explained.

"He passed directly into the arms of his grandmother.
She is standing on his right side.
She is very short. **(describes my mother)**
He is totally healed in his head.
He was heading home. He collapsed. Fell down on knees, then forward, and sideways. **(this was how he was found)**
He did not suffer one bit. His soul was taken beyond a split second.
Nothing was in his stomach (**autopsy revealed this**); his brain was telling him he was not hungry. He did not want food. He was only drinking.
He loved the woman he married. It is very hard for her to understand.
Father and mother understand him.
He was always chasing or running – fast on his feet.
His mind, at times, told him "go, go".
He was on the right path. God made up his mind with him.

He has always loved you. He is your guardian.

Seeing his brain – he had such enormous mental pain. It is all healed now.

Was it hot when they found him? He seems very dehydrated and his lips are parched.

He never looked back to see his body – went straight forward to his grandmother; she was hugging him like a little child.

His heart stopped when he collapsed.

There was an unbelievable amount of people trying to find him, and he is very thankful.

It was a beautiful funeral. He was there, definitely, looking down. His soul was there. He loved the service and was very happy. He had so much peace.

What did he like to fumble with/in his hands? **(he regularly held his rosary beads)** He is showing me his hands, fumbling with something.

Not much longer for autopsy results and you will get your answers.

Just before his soul left, he saw the most gorgeous angel, like scooping him up. He got healed instantly.

His wife gets signs with electricity (inside and outside lights, etc.). **(Tiffany stated that this happened quite often)** He is trying to let her know he is ok and is around. He is scared for her. He knows his father and mother are strong.

He is a very spiritual person. He did everything to try to heal himself. He had the will but couldn't do it. He tried everything. He couldn't understand it. Spiritually, he thought he could heal himself. **(As mentioned earlier, Jonathan told all of us that when it was time to get well he would go to God and do it)**

He never liked people crying. It upset him. He did not know how to handle other people's tears. He did not like goodbyes; they sometimes tore him apart.

He was ahead of people in this world. He didn't feel like he fit in. If he was born 25 years before or after, he would have felt that he belonged more.

This is not goodbye. You will rejoin him. Jonathan and I (mom) had a past life together. Dad is not doing good; he wants people to think he is ok but he is not. Needs to share his feelings to others, needs to allow grief for healing. Takes time. You will feel better once he has talked to you.

Jonathan is a happy soul. Many times they have to go through mourning periods, are discontented at first, when crossing over, but not Jonathan. He is very happy.

He had a great sense of humor. He was very talented.

When walking, he would look at clouds and see people's faces. He was not imagining this.

He needed drugs to balance himself mentally, even though they did bad things. His mental health issues were very severe – no one understands the depth of this. But, he knew this because he was so spiritually connected and he knew his destiny. He was hoping he could go to the rehab place but deep down he knew he couldn't. He did not like being closed in; that would be like jail to him. He knew he could not be helped.

He was walking his journey, seeing things he'd never seen before. Walking through town, amongst people, and he was more together than you could imagine.

He was trying to get home. So close, yet so far away, when he collapsed.

Did he ever hum? He is humming a certain song. Something like "come to me" or "come for me"]? (**The Scientist, Jonathan and Tiffany's song, begins "Come up to meet you..."**)

He was not sad. He saw so many lights. He knew he was leaving.

Down on his knees, he could feel his soul leaving his body and it was very beautiful to him. He was happy. He knew his destiny path. He went with a lot of pride and graciousness. His body just couldn't take any more.

His wife is wondering what was the purpose of getting together and then losing it so quickly. The answer is that it made both of them happy, even if only a short time.

He didn't want anyone worrying about him anymore. He was strictly with God.

Grandmother received him in Heaven. Many people were there to join him.

Did he have a dog? (**Sammy**) There is a dog playing at his feet. Also, younger ones (children) (**Cullen and Terri's brother Dalmond, who passed at the age of 3**) are around him, too. He knows everybody. No one is a stranger to him, not at all. Joy (**grandmother, Terri's mother**) is with him. They are all having a grand reunion. Their family in the spirit world is bigger. It is a celebration. They were prepared to receive Jonathan. They already knew what to do.

He never doubted your love. He always tried to protect you from knowing and worrying. He wanted to protect you from the drugs. He didn't want you to see the effects of drugs on him. He didn't want anyone else in trouble because of what he was doing. He knew you loved him and he loved you very much.

You (mom) understood much more what was going on with him. Dad didn't always realize or understand.

He had severe emotional struggling. Extreme guilt. He could never get rid of the guilt. A very low percentage of heavy drug abusers are ever able to get off. He wanted everyone to be proud of him. There was nothing else that could have been done for him, as he knew he could do no more. Severe addiction causes chemical poisoning. The least little thing would trigger him back. Rehab would not work for him. He knew this. Now he is not judged.

When Jonathan left, he didn't think he was coming back home, in the mental state he was in. He never bothered anyone. He always wanted something to drink everywhere he went. He did not scare anybody. He was very calm and polite.

As days went by, he started realizing he was walking a destiny. In the beginning, he didn't even know what time it was. One day went into the next. Things cleared up after a few days. He was trying to make peace. He had a lifting feeling like in astro-projection (out of body feelings) as a warning to him that he was going to go.

He had said goodbyes before he left. He couldn't say goodbye to mom. The one we love the most becomes the fear that we run from. You will get so much from him spiritually. He is with you. You will feel him brushing across neck, right shoulder, hair.

Everyone is sad here, but he is so very happy. He knows how much he was loved. He is beautiful. He has a lot to do with many lives. Remy will follow the same spiritual path.

His passing occurred three days before he was found. It was because of the heat that he was not recognizable.

He is smiling, happy, and peaceful."

Terri shared the reading with me and Tiffany the next day. Terri also informed Tiffany that a renowned medium, a person who regularly assisted law enforcement agencies with investigations for missing persons, would be in Florida in a couple of weeks. Terri suggested to Tiffany that she come and stay with her for a few weeks, and together they would see the medium. Tiffany was convinced that a change of scenery would do her good, and on Friday morning, left her house to visit with Terri.

Monday June 07

Mike to Terri

Are you and Tiffany having a good time? Are you guys doing OK? I assume she eventually made it down there.

Remy spent much of the weekend with us. He seems to be handling everything very well. He went to storage with me and helped me go through some of Jon's things, and actually he was in his room going through things by himself. He asked some questions like "what do you think Dad's doing right now?" He also wanted to know if I had any of Jon's cigarette butts left because he thought I should keep one. He spent a lot of time in the workshop coloring and just talking about stuff. He's a great kid.

Terri to Mike

Yes, Tiffany got here finally around 11 on Friday night. We stayed out on the balcony talking until 4:30am! It really helps both of us to talk about everything in Jonathan's life, including the dark side, because, even as sad as it is, it helps to make sense out of things better, and lends itself to having more closure and understanding as to WHY.

Interestingly, when I went to my appt to see the oncologist (cancer doc) on Friday, I was sitting in the waiting room reading a magazine and who walks up to bring me back to the exam room but Tiff! She is working there at the cancer center, doing her last 4 weeks internship before she earns her medical assistant certification, for which she has been going to school for nearly two years. As it turned out, we talked for a good 45 minutes or more and I will tell you it was a very profound type of conversation. She told me things about Jonathan and his past, her experiences with him, and she seems anxious to get together and talk about all of it (things she could have never told a soul while Jonathan was still with us).

I got the feeling she has been somewhat tortured holding so much information inside of her for so long. She offered several times, in fact, requested it, to get together while Tiffany is here, to be able to talk to her, too, hopefully to help her not to feel guilty that she could have changed the outcome of things, as Tiff too, has been through so many of those types of feelings when it came to Jonathan. She told me it took her until just a little less than a year ago before she was finally able to get rid of a lot of the guilt and heartache she carried with her that had to do with Jon. Also, she said she has worried about him every day of her life, even since they broke off their relationship, and that she has never stopped loving him and will always love him...the only reason she had to leave him was because she couldn't bear to watch himself destruct any longer. She always knew (even he had basically indicated it to her) that the end result would be what did eventually happen. There was a lot she wanted to say to me, almost like she wanted to cleanse herself, but we ran out of time. I will call her to get together some night this week, as Tiffany wants to meet with her, too.

I wonder if you have information about things that have happened in Jon's past that he shared with you in confidence and you never wanted anyone else to know? Tiffany has opened up, too, and started talking about things Jonathan told her about his past that were the reasons for the demons and guilt he carried with him for so many years. She said that Jonathan was so ashamed, but that it was all in his past, and he was a completely changed person by the time she got together with him. But, he made it very clear that he would NEVER be able to forgive himself. He always did tell me that he had done some very, very bad things, and even told me some of them, but NEVER to the extent of what I have learned this weekend. It seems both Tiffany and Tiff are needing to talk about these "secrets" in order for all of us to finally know and understand our deepest fears of the unknown for so many years.

It has been an emotional, yet eye-opening weekend. I showed Tiffany lots of old pictures of Jonathan and we laughed a lot, also talked a lot about his problems and the reasons for them. She had a couple of short "melt downs" this weekend, but not when we were talking...always when she was alone thinking and looking at his picture. I do the same thing off and on, but all in all, we both agree that talking about everything is very healing. She is doing much better than she was...she is now talking of being able to sleep in their bed again...something she was completely unable to think about until the day before she got here.

She is such a beautiful person, Mike....and she clearly loved Jonathan very deeply and I do believe they were true soul mates. She brought a huge box full of the most beautiful and inspiring letters Jonathan has written to her (and she wrote to him)....beautiful, all of them. She misses him so terribly. And, Jonathan clearly loved her the same way.

Remy is such a beautiful little legacy of our sweet Jonathan. I am so glad he is doing ok....but we definitely need to keep an eye on him, as children always tend to withhold their feelings. He is undoubtedly affected much more than what he shows to everyone else.

What did you answer when he asked what you thought his daddy was doing right now? What a sweetheart.

Mike to Terri

I'm glad. It sounds like this is being very therapeutic for both of you. Both Tiff and Tiffany are lovely people. Perhaps the 3 of you can bring the closure to Jon's death that you seek. I can't remember anything specifically that Jonathan told me about what he did; only that he did some bad things. Our conversations would focus on forgiving himself, and he admitted having a hard time doing this.

I told Remy that his Dad was at perfect peace and that he was smiling very lovingly on both of us as he loves us very much.

Terri to Mike

Knowing what I now know, albeit only a fraction of the whole story, I completely understand why Jonathan felt he could never forgive himself. It breaks my heart to think of how tortured he was every single day of his life, and how very hard he tried to fix himself. Tiffany had a lot of input about all of that, too. He spoke about his feelings to both Tiff and Tiffany, with some very difficult things to hear. They listened, as I am now, with no judgment and all love and sympathy/understanding for how much Jonathan was trying to get rid of the demons and fix himself for the future.

That was a great answer you gave to Remy.

Mike to Terri

In terms of rebirthing, Remy is a very old soul. There is a sense around him that makes me believe he will grow up to be a very spiritual being. He's very interested in many of the knick knacks in the workshop. He asks what they are for. We talked about Reiki yesterday and the ability to heal the body through loving energy. We also talked about the power of the mind, and how Jonathan would reinforce that to him often. He's quite a person.

Terri to Mike

He sure is…and I completely agree…he is a very old soul, indeed. And, he learned a lot from his Daddy. Jonathan, even though all the trials and tribulations, spent a lot of his time with Remy teaching him about what is truly important in life. He is quite a person, indeed. I, too, feel that spiritual sense around him. I am so thankful for the time he spends with you and I treasure my time with him, as well.

I just talked to Tiff…she got up at 12:30 (good for her, she needed the rest)…she's going over to the beach to hang out by the pool across the street and read. So glad she is doing better now. She seems much more peaceful now.

Tiffany and Terri spent the next 10 days laughing, crying, and doing their best to heal. On Wednesday evening, June 16, they met with the medium, Pat.

Tiffany sat with Pat first and waited for Jonathan's arrival. All of sudden a smile came to Pat's face.

"He has a colorful vocabulary! He uses some prime words!"

Tiffany laughed and confirmed that Jonathan used a lot of four letter words.

Pat then told Tiffany that his first words were "I DID NOT F*@#ING COMMIT SUICIDE!!!!"

Pat continued with the reading.

"He was a very bold man and he was a cusser. He was an awesome man. He tells me that he walked in this world differently than everybody else. He is adamant and, as a rule, I've never thought they were wrong when they are this adamant...that he DID NOT commit suicide!

When I searched to look for murder, he says "What the hell, I just didn't commit suicide!" He is trying to calm himself down. He is showing me other times that he has done things. He played Russian roulette with a hand pistol one time. He had done little things like that all through his life, never intending to end his life. He just walked differently than anybody else.

He passed at nighttime, not daytime. He is showing me night time.

He is saying "I love you, Tiffany."

He shows me how much his head hurt. He was in a very upset mood that night. But not out to kill himself. He says his head was bursting and he felt like he might be having a stroke or something and he took several blood pressure pills. He says the bottle wasn't full and he took some antidepressants and combined them with the blood pressure pills, something he had done many times in the past. He just meant for his headache to go away and he wanted to calm down and then he says he was going to go back and have a talk with you once he was calmer. He just felt like he needed that time, and by the time he got to where he was, his head was just "popping" (boom, boom, boom). He mixed them and mixed too many at one time. He just needed quick results. So instead of taking two of something, he took 4 or 5 of something.

He went and checked. There was not a full bottle in either one. There were not 30 in either bottle. But, just enough, without him thinking, with the interaction, that it could stop his heart. But, he definitely did not commit suicide.

He says to tell Chris, "I'm ok". Tell him "It's ok. I'm ok". He is repeating it several times.

He loves you very much, with every ounce, and he says that you're afraid that you had caused his death. He says he was going back the next day.

He keeps saying "Tell her I love her" (repeatedly). He is a very impatient man! He keeps saying, "Did you tell her?" He wants to make sure you know he loves you. He says, "We had fun. We had fun. There were bad times for us, but there were many good times for us." He is trying to recall the good times and not any bad ones.

He had his moments when he was in high school. He is saying he found life very difficult but he was not wishing death on himself, ever. He was afraid he had made mistakes and hurt you. So, that night he thought "maybe I made a mistake...I don't want to hurt her...maybe she is better off...." He couldn't handle a lot of stressful things. He always had to get away from it. All he was doing that night was needing to get away from the stress and when he calmed down he was going back. He was going back to tell you he needed to get out for a while so he could get well.

I don't see that he went to anyone's house. He keeps showing me a car, but I don't think he was in a car. But he is doing this over and over."

Perhaps the car that Jonathan was referring to in his reading with Pat is best described in an experience that Terri shared with me nearly two years after Jonathan passed.

The Car

> *I no sooner returned home after Jonathan's funeral and was driving to work one morning when I was amazed to see a car that looked exactly like Jonathan's parked off to the side of the main road that runs in front of my home. This would not be so unusual if it were just any car but one like Jonathan's car was not one we would see every day and it really took me by surprise. It was the same exact car model, color, etc. as Jonathan's car*

and it was parked in the closest parking space to the building where I live.

I drove right past it every day. A few weeks later, I spoke to Tiff who brought it up to me, as she drove that same route every day, too, and she was profoundly affected by it, too, especially when we had both noticed the car had remained there in the same spot and had not moved for all those weeks. Every time we drove by it we both thought of Jonathan.

Finally one day I actually pulled over and looked into the windows of the car and the inside looked like Jonathan's car too, including miscellaneous snack wrappers, soda cans, and cigarette packs! It was just amazing to me, like the car was there as a message to remind me he was still near me. That car remained in that exact spot for exactly one year! Surprisingly, it was never towed away as would usually be the case in this area if a vehicle appeared to be abandoned. I actually felt happiness every time I drove by it each day and then suddenly one day it was just gone, as quickly as it had appeared one year earlier!

Pat continued her session with Tiffany.

"He says, "I wrote a lot of notes" and he did not leave a suicide note that night because he was not planning to kill himself. He says he wrote lots of notes and says loudly "was there a suicide note??" He is being sarcastic and is making a point so we know for sure. He is angry because they wrote it up that way. "It kept her from getting something". Life insurance? Not sure how to interpret this. But, he is really angry over that. "Go tell them how many pills could have been left in the bottle from the time it was filled." If he was going to commit suicide he would have taken full bottles of pills. They are assuming he took whole bottles just because they were empty. They had asked if he had ever attempted it before and he hadn't in the way they were talking about. He did do that gun thing. He showed it to me. He was a lot younger then.

He was on antidepressants but half the world is on antidepressants and they are not suicidal; they just need balancing. They need their anxieties taken care of...

He was not worried about money. He never had a lot of it, he is showing me. He is pulling his empty pockets out and putting them back in. But, he wasn't worried because he felt he could always earn money.

He is loving his family. He was closer to his dad and said "I love you very much". But, he is saying to Mom, "We love each other very much, too". We did not always think exactly alike. He is loving Tiffany and his son, Remy. Again, he repeats adamantly that he did not commit suicide and to please let everybody know this! Let everybody know that he loved them and he would give a big group hug if he was here!

He is saying "What about the watch? What are we going to do with the watch?" He says it is one he gave to somebody. It was a gift.

He has brought up the military several times. I know he was not in the military and I do not see him in a uniform, but he keeps bringing it up and it seems important to him. Was his dad in the military?

He was very bright, smart, and intelligent. He could have taken entrance tests to get in the military but he probably didn't know the rules have changed since he first checked his eligibility. He talks about the military over and over again.

He had depression, but he was not manic. This probably led to headaches and emotional upset that he took medication to bring him down. He took blood pressure medication anyway, prescribed for him. He was not taking someone else's medication.

He keeps showing the numbers 3 6 (36?). Not sure what this means. Was this his age?

There were good times. We saw him fulfill everything important to him in his life. He had a child who he loved and a marriage...everything but the military. He got to do more than some of us do. Some people will never see our dreams come true. He is saying, "Don't worry, don't worry. I am ok." No one caused his death. It was his time."

That concluded the session with Tiffany and Terri's reading began. Pat continued:

"He is quieter with you than in Tiffany's reading. This is common when the information is the same and the readings are so close together. Often, they will not repeat details and they come through in broken sentences that are difficult to interpret. But, he comes through in both readings adamant that he did not kill himself.

He is saying "I love you, Mom".

You favor him a lot except you have different eyes. He roams through the house every once in a while. He looks at a new picture of him and wonders if he really looked like that in the physical. He was a very handsome man. He was always worried about his weight. He did not want to get heavy. It made him self-conscious. I don't know if he was an exerciser, but he is telling me he liked to keep himself slim. You will always see Jonathan in Remy.

He will come to you in dreams. This is the first way he will communicate. He is trying to come but he is having trouble....some kind of blockage preventing it. He says to make it crystal clear..."I will come through." But, it won't be all the time. It may be months in between. He says "I always believed in the hereafter and think of me as a veteran."

He wants Dad to know how much he loves him. He hasn't gotten all the way through to his father. Father has felt him, but not yet seen him.

You think that you never got to say goodbye. He is saying, "Yes, you did, Mom. You told me goodbye at the funeral."

He would go to his room at age 15. This is when his addiction started. He would get "dark", then get "light". He says he had spinning games, then spin back in. (Highs and lows?) He never intended ever to kill himself.

He is saying "tough love would not have worked"...not with him and his type of personality. But, he would not have gone to get the help of others on the 29th year of his life. He would have gone by the 32nd year of his life, though, and he would have gone all the way through the program. He had a big fear of being without his medications. He felt he needed pills to feel well and normal. It was all too scary for him. He had a weakened heart. The pills combined with dehydration and other factors stopped his heart. By age 32, he would have been straight. There are so many different types of addictions. He got ahold of those that helped him to escape because he did not handle stress at all well. School, friendships, whatever ups and downs in his life, took a toll on him. That night he just was trying to escape for a while, but not to kill himself. He just wanted to calm down.

He was driven to the emergency room by a stranger, he is showing me. But, he did not stay. He left and walked away. At this time, he was very confused and he was just trying to go back home. He had a psychotic break. If we could have gotten to him in time, he would have recovered. All medications were not in his stomach at one time. Not taken all at once. If not for the combination of all the conditions and circumstances, he would have come back. Dehydration caused kidneys to stop flushing and even small amount of pills were not being metabolized properly. He is showing me the number of pills he took. He says it was not that many.

He says he is stressed because we are all stressed. He will be at peace when we all are at peace. He says he is in a good place. His grandfather met him. He is laughing. He is saying "I wasn't wandering in the wilderness,

Mom. I was wandering in society." He is saying "I thought I heard God many times but, until I got here, it was not God I was hearing there.." He realizes now that he could not have healed himself on his own. He is saying "The awesomeness of God vibrates you". While here, he talked to God but didn't realize he wasn't feeling the full force of Him. God can heal with complete faith. He thought if he walked around in the wilderness and talked to God he could heal himself. He was confused and lost and could not handle any more stress. The more stress that came, the harder it was for him.

He says "Mom and I understood each other. You are a good mom. Nothing you could have done would have changed anything". He says that I knew how he thought and felt...more than his dad did. He and his dad were like buddies.

You and his father support each other. Sometimes he listens to your conversations and he is saying that our memories are not always correct!

He liked sports when he was young, but he didn't feel like he was good at it. He didn't feel like he fit in there. He was always a loner, of sorts.

He is ok. One day he will come in a dream when it is acceptable and he will hug you and you will definitely feel it. You will feel hugged. Not all the time, though.

He is mostly with his grandfather. There is a cousin there, also a grandmother (broken, but seems to have a word that starts with MA sound... could be first name, middle name?). Also, Ann (first or middle name of a grandmother?). He walks with five angels. He and his grandfather sit on the bank a lot. He has seen Charlotte but she is not with him right now. He was with a child briefly...one who passed away before him. Has seen him but only for a short time. He is in a different place/level...a different Heavenly place. But, he visited with him.

He says it's a better place. If not for everyone here hurting, things would be perfect! He loves everybody and wants us to know this.

Message to Remy:
He is very proud of him.
They will always be buddies.
I wish I could be with him as he grows.
I will always be standing by him.
I am proud of my little man and the strength he has. (He calls him a man, not a boy, because he is handling everything like a man)
Always stand tall.

Message to Kristin:
She is trying to move on.
Tell her not to try to look for answers and to know he loves her.
Tell her that her nose is still too big for her face!
He is showing chocolate bars (not sure of significance – trying to give Kristin candy?)
He is showing me a baby with Kristin. Don't name anyone after him. Everyone needs their own name.
Tell Kristin she is not coming here to Heaven anytime soon. She will be healthy and happy for a long time. He is watching over his sister!

Message to Michael:
Michael is the rock and tries to keep everyone together.
He has no addictions.
He is proud of his brother.
He says he is sorry he couldn't be, but he did the best he could and tried very hard."

Tiffany stayed with Terri a few more days before returning to Georgia. Together they both found solace in sharing and talking about Jonathan's life, reliving his past and trying to understand what had happened during his life. They also found reassurance from both Pat and Linda who were accurately able to describe much of Jonathan's past, and then describe how his spirit is sending messages to us that sound like the Jonathan who loves us, and who we all love.

With this knowledge and the love and compassion Terri received from her family, friends, and support groups; the pain, although it will never go away completely, has subsided. Terri has learned to take one day at a time and to never take life for granted.

For the next year Tiffany struggled. She was close to being offered several nursing positions as she was in the final three for a position several times. Each time though she lost the offer to someone with more experience. She started her own photography business, and this helped to make ends meet, but the work was inconsistent and unpredictable.

In June of 2011, she accompanied me, Laura and Remy to a family reunion in Chicago. She was able to spend quality time with Remy, and got to know some of Jonathan's cousins, aunts, and uncles. While vacationing, she continued looking for a nursing position and received positive feedback from a summer camp facility that was looking for a full-time nurse for July and August.

Upon returning from vacation, she had several phone interviews and was offered the job. The camp was located in Pennsylvania, and leaving the Georgia area for a new experience turned out to be exactly what was needed. She made some good friends while doing what she really loved to do, work with kids. She communicated regularly with the family to let them know she was having a good time. When the camp ended she decided to do some vacationing in the place where she and Jonathan had talked about honeymooning.

Thursday August 25, 2011

Tiffany to Mike

Hi! I am in Massachusetts right now. I went to Concord yesterday. I don't know if Jonathan ever said anything to you about us going there to Concord for our honeymoon, but I know he was with me. I visited a church where Wayne Dyer was during a DVD that Jonathan and I were listening to right after our wedding. I believe it is the oldest church in the country, and a very spiritual place. I met the minister of the First Parish church there and she was wonderful. After I told her my story and reason for being there, she opened the doors to the sanctuary and said I could stay as long as I wanted. She said that my walking through those doors was no accident.

I saw all of the homes of Thoreau, the Alcott's, and Hawthorne. I saw their burial sites at Sleepy Hollow Cemetery. I am going back today to tour Emerson's home and see Walden Pond. I also saw the Concord School of Philosophy! There is a great feeling in the air there. I felt Jonathan's presence the entire time and know he would have absolutely loved it! I had a feeling of peace and contentment while there; it felt like a miracle occurred.

I am getting to a place of peace. I know that Jonathan is asking this of me, needing me to move forward in my life and be happy. I remember one of his plaques, "Go confidently in the direction of your dreams, live the life you want to live". Thoreau

I will always miss him, but I was so blessed to have him in my life for even a brief time. Not many people can say they met and married their soul mate, and know that it is true. I am truly grateful for my time with him and know that we will meet again, where neither of us has any problems.

They say time heals all wounds. I don't know that any of us will feel the healing of missing Jonathan, but time brought Tiffany the experiences needed to feel contentment as she moves forward with her life.

Chris

As Chris placed the last shovel full of dirt on Jonathan's grave, he thought to himself, "I'm sick and tired of not being able to think of anything else. It's time to go and celebrate his life." Chris returned to the house and visited with the friends and family who had gathered after the service. Later that evening, he, Zach, Dustin, and a few other friends headed to the gravesite with guitars in hand. They sang, jammed, and told Jonathan stories for hours. They laughed together and cried together.

They continued to do this often. I spoke with the owner of the cemetery about it, and he welcomed and encouraged it. He told me that if it helps them with their grieving, the more they should do it.

A few months after Jonathan passed away, Chris and Zach drove out to Rome to see if they could find the location that Jonathan's body had been found. They knew the general vicinity, so they parked the car in a nearby parking lot and started searching the area. They found a tent that looked like it had been abandoned, but the clothes hanging on a nearby tree didn't look like anything Jonathan would have worn. They also found some old Marlboro packs crumpled on the ground and wondered if these might have been Jonathan's. As they continued investigating, Chris suddenly felt as though Jonathan was with him. Chris felt directed to a certain spot. As Chris stood there, he called the coroner. The coroner described to Chris where Jonathan's body had been found. Chris was standing where he felt Jonathan's spirit had guided him, and exactly where the coroner told Chris his body had been found.

This gave Chris some closure, but the feelings of sadness and despair continued.

Almost a year later on March 27, 2011, Chris made arrangements with a group of friends to go to the gravesite to celebrate Jonathan's 30th birthday. Yet when the time to meet arrived, Chris couldn't bring himself to go to the cemetery. Instead, he waited until 11:30 PM and drove to Jonathan's grave by himself. He looked at the beautiful headstone. In the four corners are etched symbols that represented Jonathan's life. In one corner is a stack of 8 spiritual books that reflect his beliefs and studies. In another corner is the yin-yang symbol to identify the balance he was trying to attain. There is a pair of drumsticks in the third corner that characterize his love of music. The last corner is a set of praying hands to show his love of prayer and to symbolize one of his favorite drawings to sketch. In the center of the stone is an etched picture of Jonathan.

Jonathan's gravestone

As Chris stood there and reflected, sending his love to Jonathan, he noticed a light drizzle in the air. No rain falling to the ground, just a very light mist. All of a sudden, a single raindrop fell on the gravestone on the tear duct of Jonathan's etched eye. Chris stared at it in bewilderment, trying to receive the message from Jonathan. "I am crying too," Jonathan said. "I don't want you to feel pain anymore. I am here with you."

A sudden realization hit Chris. "When he ran off that night in April, there was nothing I could have done or nothing any of us could do. But he is here with me now."

Chris, too, needed time to heal. With the help of his friends and with his own solitary intuitions, he was finally able to sense serenity in losing his brother.

Mike

Laura's willingness to listen and talk whenever I needed to helped me tremendously as I grieved in my own way. After he passed, I spent the next several months gathering and sorting his belongings. I bought several books with topics about the afterlife, near death experiences, and Heaven as I wanted to know as much as possible about the last few days of Jonathan's life and the state of his present spirit. I also continued my daily routine of getting up at 4:00 AM. I would study my spiritual lesson for the day and follow that with meditation, contemplation, and prayer.

Six weeks after Jonathan had passed, the alarm sounded at 4:00 AM, and I rose to get out of bed and begin my daily routine. I did something I never do; I hit the snooze button and laid down into bed. For the next 8 minutes I had an extraordinary dream. I was on a surf board on the ocean without any waves. I was coasting along the sea. Jonathan's presence was with me. He told me that he was fine and without any pain. Where he was now there existed only love and total peace. He told me not to worry about him and that he loved us all very much.

The alarm sounded again and I awakened Laura to tell her about the dream and what I was feeling. I was startled, amazed, at total peace, in joy, and comforted. Jonathan had just visited me to let me know that he was happier than he ever was during his life with us.

We received the coroner's report on August 10, 2010. The following morning I experienced another visit from Jonathan. After it happened, I awoke Laura to tell her of my experience and then got ready for work. A little later that morning, I sent Terri an email.

Wednesday, August 11

Mike to Terri

I was about 5 – 7 minutes into my meditation and all of a sudden I heard breathing. I wasn't sure what it was as the air conditioner had just kicked in so I thought it might be a noise from that. It continued for another couple of minutes so I opened my eyes and looked at the love seat (that's where it sounded like it was coming from). But as soon as I opened my eyes, I stopped hearing it. I waited for a few seconds, closed my eyes and resumed the meditation for the day. As soon as I closed my eyes, the breathing started again. I tried communicating with Jonathan and mentally asked "Jon, is that you?" I didn't feel a response, only heard the continuous breathing. I continued then to apply today's lesson and combine it with Jonathan being One with me and that we are all God's Son. I meditated for another 10 minutes or so, focusing on these ideas as the breathing continued throughout. I opened my eyes when the clock chimed 4:45AM, and asked out loud, "Jon, is that you?" All of a sudden I felt as though a wave of spirit (I don't know how else to describe this) run through my body and a feeling of total peace and joy engulfed me. I smiled and told him I love him. Next, I went to the kitchen and sat down and started my final prayers and contemplation before getting ready for work. About 5 minutes later, I heard the door from the house to the garage close (not slam, but I could definitely tell it was this door as it is a distinct sound). I got up and went downstairs. All the lights were off, so I turned on the garage light and went into the workshop and called Jon's name. I didn't see or hear anything. I went back upstairs and finished what I was doing and got ready for work.

I'll let you know if something happens tonight or tomorrow.

The "spirit hug" that I received from Jonathan that morning was the most incredible feeling of pureness, love, peace, and joy that I have ever experienced. I knew he was with me.

He left his mark on something else that morning. The clock that chimed at 4:45 AM is set to chime every 15 minutes throughout the day. For the next several months before it was time to change the clocks back to Eastern Standard Time, the clock didn't chime between 4:00 AM and 6:00 AM. He was telling me not to worry about the time and to spend whatever period was necessary to look within to find my tranquility.

It has been two years since Jonathan passed away and during that time all of us have healed to an extent. What were "bad Jonathan days" have turned into "bad Jonathan moments." Time has helped us to heal, but each of us had other means to heal as well. Whether it was depending on friends and family, following our faith in God, turning to people who could communicate with the spirit world, being in solitude and following our intuition, or looking within ourselves; responses to our fears or questions appeared in unique ways.

As the Spirit of Jonathan wants for all of us, be at inner peace.

Facts, Thoughts and Thanks

Facts

On August 10, 2010 Terri received the copy of the coroner's report. What was stated was what we feared the most; that Jonathan had committed suicide.

Scientific evidence. Fact. Undisputable truths. Lethal, toxic, and normal amounts of six different medicines were found in his body. Revealed was a lethal amount of one of Jonathan's anti-depressants; toxic amounts of an anti-anxiety medicine; two blood pressure medicines, one with an elevated amount in his system and the other at a normal level; a normal amount of another anti-depressant; and an elevated amount of an allergy medicine.

The amount of medicine found in his body and the fact that Jonathan had spoken of suicide recently resulted in the coroner's findings. Terri spoke with the coroner after receiving the report and pointed out that Jonathan had been self-medicating for years. She let him know that the amount of medicines he took was often enough to put him in a toxic or lethal state, but he had never been affected. She also pointed out that one of the side effects of the anti-depressants was suicidal thoughts, and he had spoken of these feelings on and off over the last 8 months. As convincing an argument that Terri tried to make, the coroner stayed with his conclusion.

As often as Jonathan spoke of suicide, he spoke equally of going to the woods to find God and put his addiction problems into His Hands. That is exactly what Jonathan did. He didn't leave Tiffany the evening of April 25th with the intent of ending his life, nor did he get up on his final day with that idea. He knew he had to change the direction of his life. He was searching for the narrow gate.

> "When great thinkers talk about union with God, there's this theme that comes through. It is silence. When everyone else is asleep, and there are no distractions, you feel yourself alone

with Source. I have experienced this many times in the past 5-6 years. It explains why I always feel so great real late at night when it's just me, my studies, and God. This is the time you are closest to Source. Being alone with Source is not just about feeling good, it's about my own awareness of my divinity and what it's capable of achieving. It's all about returning back to the place where you came from. T.S. Eliot has a great quote…"We shall not seize from exploration. At the end of our exploring will be to arrive where we started, and know the place for the first time." Jonathan Dalmond Dacy, October 15, 2009

Thoughts

April 26 – May 4

As the days passed, Jonathan routinely took his medicines as he needed. He also began experiencing new but familiar feelings. He was connecting with his Truest Essence.

He walked around town with his mind going in and out of the present moment. He occasionally thought of his family, but for the most part he was in the NOW. While in this state of being, he found himself smiling and being drawn to new faces. The love and joy he was feeling was overwhelming him and he demonstrated this through his kindness and politeness. This uncommon behavior was reciprocated by the people he met. They were drawn to his innocence, and the love they felt coming from his being. Jonathan walked around his new home with a feeling of serenity.

All of the affirmations he repeated to himself hundreds of times; the quotes of the philosophers and spiritual leaders that had been his focus of many meditations; and the essays and thoughts he had written as reminders to himself; were overtaking Jonathan's mind and soul.

Yet as he returned to the woods each evening, thoughts of his family and his responsibilities would cover his mind. He began missing Tiffany and Remy, and he knew he needed to get home. He would self-medicate, taking what he thought he needed to rid him of pain and to get some rest.

Did he intend to end his life on his final day? I think not.

He awoke from his last earthly sleep with a thought he had written six months ago buried deep into his subconscious mind.

> "Those were the days I dreamed of the likes of everyone, but today is the day I dream of the sun."

He was in physical pain. He had gone days with little to drink and less than that to eat. He took his normal dosage of medicines which would be toxic for most people. As he walked his final steps to fulfill his destiny, the 11 years of medicines had taken its final toll on his body. Although his body didn't look well, his mind was flowing with light.

Clinically, perhaps he was losing his mind.

Spiritually, perhaps he was finding it.

He had a deathbed vision. He looked up at the sky and saw a light shining through that he had never seen before.

And he let all his guilt go.
And the vengeance.
And the hate.
And the fear.

Then the unconditional love of God entered.

And the joy.
And the peace.
And as he fell onto his right knee, there was only the light.

Thanks

May 4, 2012

My Dearest Son,

I know today finds you at perfect peace and joy. By sharing your life with us, you have presented us with many gifts for which we will be forever grateful.

You presented us with love. The unconditional love that you displayed toward Remy is a model for love that any parent can follow. The patience and kindness you demonstrated toward your son makes your mother and father very proud. You pointed out love to us on a much grander scale. Through your studies you concluded that the Love of God can be found in many belief systems. Whether God is found in organized religion, spiritual studies, poetry, or philosophy; it doesn't matter. You said it best when you wrote that one evening in the autumn of 2007:

"Where there is life, there should also be love."

Your life has also given a gift to people dealing with their own addictions. They have been able to look at your life, and realize how difficult it is to stop. You demonstrated the extreme behavioral effects of self-medicating, and how this can hurt relationships and lead to trouble with the law. You also showed us the means you went through to obtain your medications. There were times you worked hard to earn your paychecks, yet there were the times you needed to lie, manipulate, or steal in order to satisfy your cravings. Your experiences are accepted with thanks by people who share similar life situations, as you have influenced how they will lead their lives in the future.

During The Rollercoaster time period, you taught us what families face during these times of crisis. Your family felt the fear, frustration, anger, and helplessness that comes with watching a loved one experience what you were dealing with. You taught us that the options to assist you were plentiful, yet the answers were all unpredictable. Even through these events, despite the disagreements, angry words, and critical viewpoints; it was love that pulled your family through the toughest times. "Where there is life, there should also be love." You showed your family, and now other families facing comparable circumstances, how to do that.

To someone not familiar with addiction, you give to them the knowledge of addiction's effects. They might now be a bit more compassionate and understanding toward people or families trying to overcome the consequences of addiction. An employer might say, "Take the day off and take care of your family." A neighbor may state, "Let me know how I can help." The gift of loving-kindness has been received and is now more prevalent in their thinking.

The gift of your story has presented us with options as to how to handle our own addiction problems; provided families with a variety of perceptions and options available as they attempt to help an addicted loved one; and taught a lesson to people who are unaware of the seriousness of addiction. From the friends you have made who have read your story, they send their love and give great thanks.

The impact the gift of your life has on your family has been received by all of us, and each of us has a special thanks for you.

Chris was taught to be polite and respectful to others by his mother from the time he was old enough to comprehend these behaviors. You reemphasized these characteristics, yet how to be "cool" at the same time. Whether you were dressed in camouflage, black, or suit and tie, he noticed how you were always polite and how you respected the existence of others.

He will never forget this. You taught him how to live life and how to be a better man. He took his "life notes" watching your actions and learning both the positive or direct, and the negative or indirect. He's been influenced forever by your gifts, and he will never forget you.

Little sister + Big brother = Best Friends

Kristin appreciates the big brother – little sister relationship you shared. When you were younger, you helped her to develop her wonderful sense of humor with your good natured pranks. When you periodically lived together during your teenage and early adulthood years, she remembers the best friend relationship you shared. Watching you protect your baby sister taught

Kristin the gift of loyalty. By making light of your addiction situations even as you were going through some of your toughest times, she learned how to laugh at herself. She remembers when she awoke after her second heart transplant, and you were there to listen and to do whatever she needed to feel better and to heal. She recognizes this gift from you as the reason she is compassionate and an attentive listener. She thanks you from the bottom of her heart for these gifts.

Your big brother has hundreds of memories he thought about sharing in these closing pages but ultimately he chose these few because, to him, they're all that really matter any longer. Michael loved you like nothing and nobody else in his life. From childhood to adulthood, you defined and represented all the positive qualities of the word BROTHER, and your mutual love for each other was unique and special. Michael adored you. Unlike most brothers, you never fought and you ALWAYS loved one another without compromise despite very different personalities and life choices. Together you shared a love and bond that Michael has never experienced elsewhere in his life. You were devoted to each other during life's warm, easy seasons, but also during the cold and difficult ones. You were more than brothers... more than friends...you were kindred spirits, and you lived in Michael, and he in you. With you, Michael never felt safer during any circumstance in his life because he knew your love was protective and true and whole, and he knows you felt the same. You esteemed each other higher than anyone else in the world, including your own family members, and Michael vividly recalls times he'd defend you, blindly confronting family and foe alike without knowing if you were right or wrong...he simply had your back...and broken hearted, he always will. He thanks you for forever being part of his life.

I spent some time with Remy a few days ago. We were sitting in the workshop and he, like always, was looking at your memorial wall, asking questions, and talking about you. I asked him what he missed most about not seeing you. He immediately reminded me that you are with him in spirit all of the time. He told me that when he talks to you, he feels you with him. He let me know that he says goodnight to you every night, and he can hear you saying goodnight to him. When he talks to you about his problems, he senses you there with him.

Remy remembers your sense of humor. He started laughing when he imitated you being pregnant with a "basketball baby." He remembered when Tiffany was searching for a lighter, and you pulled out your 5" X 8" oversized Zippo. "I've got a light, Baby" you said, and the three of you burst out laughing. He misses you showing off; doing flips on the beach and spinning and screeching your tires. He also mentioned that he misses watching and listening to you while playing the drums. Since he'll be eligible for band soon, he may follow in your footsteps.

I asked him what he thanks you for and he had a hard time coming up with an answer for that. I rephrased the question and asked him what you showed him that he will do with his kids. The answers flowed. You were always nice to kids. He'll never forget your Halloween dates and how the two of you would be the last ones to finish up with trick or treating. He'll always remember how you taught him to sit still so that his headaches would go away. He blurted out "He was a good listener!" No examples, but a gift given and one received. He spoke of your patience with him; how you taught him how to shoot a B-B gun and how to balance himself on a skateboard.

Although he couldn't answer the specific question "For what do you thank your Dad?" the answers are there. He'll always remember the love, kindness, sense of humor, and patience that you, as his father, demonstrated. These are gifts he will take with him, and share them with others and his own children as he follows his path.

Tiffany sent me an email about 6 months ago stating that she had just read a line in an Agatha Christie novel that grabbed her attention and screamed JONATHAN at her.

"Confidence radiated from him like captured sunlight."

It made her think of the man she loves, her soul mate.

She will be forever grateful that you chose her to be your wife; for opening her eyes to what TRUE LOVE really is; and for bringing her closer to God. She gives everlasting thanks for having known you, if only for a year, as being her greatest teacher.

Every now and then, you and Mom would have heart to heart conversations, and talk about the spiritual bond that the two of you share. Perhaps it's because your birthdays are so close together; or maybe it's the past lives the two of you shared. The two of you are alike in so many ways.

One of your common interests was watching live performances. Whether it was a magician, concert, or play, the two of you loved attending these shows.

Many times these events were in areas of town where homeless people resided. What you taught her is something she'll never forget. You seemed to have a spare dollar or coin to give to these people. When you didn't, you stopped to talk, to share a "God bless you" with them.

On your shrine is a copy of something you wrote that defines a sage.

> "A sage has no fixed mind. He is always aware of the needs of others. He understands that salvation lies within, yet he just as well knows we are all One. To serve another is to serve yourself. Separation does not exist."

Mom watched as you behaved like a sage with the homeless people and this has created a profound change in her thinking. Her life path has changed. She moves with clarity and purpose wanting to make a difference by helping others. She's more conscious and observant, and less judgmental.

I asked her what she meant, and she responded this way:

> "Rely on love, faith, and a sense of humor to get through life's tribulations. Open your heart to others and help those in need. Never judge a book by its cover as we never know what pain and turmoil a perfect stranger may be carrying inside their heart. A simple gesture or smile can make an enormous difference in the life of someone else. Show love and compassion at every opportunity. Life can be cut short in an instant. Live every day filled with love and gratitude. The love you give will fill your heart and soul with joy and happiness in ways you never imagined."

She is overcome with love for you and thanks you for the gift of guiding her down her new path.

Over the years we spent hundreds of hours in the workshop discussing life's problems, relationships, work, and issues with your addiction. The one topic though that seemed to interest us most was the subject of spirituality. On many occasions you told me that I was your greatest teacher and you would thank me for the insight I brought to your future contemplation.

You've influenced my life and taught me more things than you will ever know. You are deeply thanked and loved for this.

Just as you thanked me for being your greatest teacher, I thank you for being mine.

Just as you thanked me for loving you unconditionally, I thank you for loving me the same.

Just as you thanked me for always being there for you, I thank you for putting me in a position to extend my love.

Mike Dacy

Just as you thanked me for the money spent to help with your expenses, I thank you for teaching me that there is much more to life than materialism.

Just as you thanked me for being non-judgmental and holding opinionated comments to myself, I thank you for presenting me with situations that enabled me to practice tolerance and true forgiveness.

Just as you thanked me for rarely getting angry, I thank you for allowing me to realize that anger is never justified.

Just as you thanked me for my patience, I thank you for helping me understand that everything that happens is a helpful learning lesson.

Just as you thanked me for signing up to be your dad in this lifetime, I thank you for being my son.

And as you thanked me for helping you through this life and dealing with its ups and downs, I thank you for helping me know that we all have a better place to go, where we will be together again in perfect peace, love, joy, and happiness.

I love you always,
Dad

"Where there is life, there should also be love."
Jonathan Dalmond Dacy, September 19, 2007

Appendix
A Mother's Everlasting Love and Inspirations

As we worked to complete Jonathan Behind Blue Eyes, many letters, thoughts, and inspirations were shared by family members. Some of these written before Jonathan passed, while others were noted afterward. Terri wrote a letter to Jonathan while he sat in jail on his 29th birthday. The thoughts behind the letter are included through the email exchanges in The Rollercoaster, but this is so beautifully written, Terri and I thought it should be included in the book.

March 27, 2010

To my dear Jonathan:

I was told I am not able to send you any correspondence other than typewritten or handwritten, and no pictures are allowed, either, so I am writing you a letter instead of a card to wish you a happy 29th birthday! I know being where you are right now is not anyone's idea of a happy birthday, but the remembrance and recognition of your birth and your existence and importance in this world is **extremely** worth celebrating and acknowledging, regardless of where you are today or where your life's path has taken you for now.

Dad has given me your messages, and I hope he has also relayed my messages to you. I love you and miss you very much. I am very sad about the situation you are in right now, and, of course, I was very shocked to hear that you were there in the first place. However, until you are able to get the help and rehabilitation you truly need to conquer your addiction disease once and for all, unfortunately these types of negative and heartbreaking situations seem to happen over and over again.

I know you are a grown man and, ultimately, the choices of what you decide to do with your life are in your hands, but please know that our entire family wants nothing more for you than to see you happy and healthy, free of the curse of addiction, and able to stand and survive on your own two feet, independently, confidently, and filled with hopes, dreams, and goals for your future. Perhaps you are unable to see how much it hurts us, too, to see you suffering for so long, and I'm not sure you realize the reasons for everything, but I sincerely hope you know that everything we have done and continue to do is out of nothing other than complete and total love for you, and with a never ending persistence and desire to help you through this dark time of your life and to do our best to try to hold your hand through the process of the journey, to catch you when you fall, and to encourage you to keep trying, be strong, and never give up.

It may seem that no one wants to bail you out because we don't care about your feelings. This is absolutely not true. As much as you hate being where you are, we hate it equally as much from the perspective of seeing someone we love so dearly having to live your life this way. It especially breaks my heart, as your mother, as this is not at all what any parent wants for their children. My maternal instinct is to love and protect you, and yet I feel so helpless when I know that I don't have the power within me to fix the situation. If I could, I certainly would.

My hands feel tied, and yet I believe in you so strongly, and I know you can do this if you'll just recognize yourself what everyone else already sees – that you really can't do this alone and that the addiction disease is bigger than you, despite all your attempts at trying to fight it by yourself. As you know, addiction takes a very strong hold on anyone and particularly someone like you who has been in a drug dependency situation since you were just a young teenager. Your very ability to grow, mature, and learn life lessons to the fullest extent, including being self-confident, independent, and possessing the tools you need to move forward in a positive direction, focus and achieve your dreams, plan your future, and simply follow the "natural" course of life's learning through ups and downs, learning to deal with crisis events as they occur in the natural course of our lives, dealing with heartache and disappointments in a healthy way, etc. – all of these important aspects of anyone's life that are just part of life's realities – this has all been somewhat halted or "incomplete" from the very time you became dependent on drugs to get you through life. When you consider this, your whole mental and emotional health growth process was severely interrupted at a very young age, and you deserve the chance to catch up and learn all that you missed through the years, as there are so many things you don't realize that could profoundly affect your life, yet you would have no way of knowing if you had not had the opportunity to experience them with a clear head, without the negative effects of drugs clouding your ability to comprehend, learn, and experience life to the fullest extent.

If you would really think about the value of putting yourself out there and completely embracing a Christian program, just delving into it all the way, and allow others who hold great resources to help you to do so, and just concentrate on nothing else at all but **you**....I know you will get through anything it takes, regardless of whether it means some inconvenience to your normal routine, or not spending as much time seeing or talking to family and friends for some time. Just remember, it would only be temporary, and the experience, if you put forth the greatest efforts you possess, and pour your heart and soul into helping yourself, it could very well change your life completely in a very real, positive, and powerful way.

The seemingly "strict" rules at Bremen are designed for the purpose of allowing YOU to focus only on yourself and the job that is in front of you to accomplish in order to save your own life and build your future, without distraction from outside interference or worries about family, job, etc. The military style regiment is why the program is referred to as "Bible boot camp". It is run by pastors, there are many

Bible study classes (which you already study on your own anyway), they keep you very busy from the time you get up in the morning until bedtime, you work at a job all day long every day (different ones depending on the week) – this particular week everyone is working on a construction site. Last week it was working at a car auction, I believe. There are about 8 different churches they attend on Sundays (for variety and personal preferences).

There are only 12 people there at any given time, and they all become close to one another, comrades, and all there for the same reasons and to help each other succeed. Dad said the director (pastor/counselor) was very nice and so was his wife who he had first talked to on the phone before he went there.

Anyhow, I spoke with Dan, who you met while he worked at The Facility, and he wanted to know how you are doing. He moved back to Minnesota after quitting his job at The Facility, and he was very upset to hear of your present situation and that you had never had the opportunity to complete a rehab program after you left. He, again, reiterated that NO ONE can do drug rehab alone…. it is impossible. He, himself, went through 12 tries before finally forcing himself to give it all of his efforts and finding the ability to truly embrace a program and finally absorbing the help that was being offered to him.

He said the program at Bremen is very intense but VERY good and has one of the highest success rates of any programs out there…over 86%. You would stay very busy, go to work each day, go to school, get your GED, learn other job skills of your choosing, and go to Bible study classes. They keep everyone very busy all the time. They don't have time for phone calls, etc. and don't allow phone calls for the first 60 days. However, though this may sound harsh, you have to remember the reason for this…no distractions, putting your whole being into the program and concentrating only on yourself and your purpose for being there. After 60 days, they start allowing some phone and some visitation, and as time goes on, students are allowed offsite passes (like weekend passes, etc.).

Also, Dan told me about a program in Minnesota near him that he says is also very good…another Christian based program where you go to school, get your GED there, get help with all kinds of life skills, etc. and it doesn't last as long, but you'd have to come to Minnesota for a few months. He personally knows the director there very well, and said he was certain he could give him a call and he'd accept you to the program if you would be interested in going there. They, too, help you with learning job skills and job assistance, etc.

Anyway, as I said before, the choice has to be yours, Jonathan, but we are all trying our best to help you find a way towards getting the much needed help that is waiting for you whenever you are ready. Meanwhile, we all want you to be "safe from yourself", not left in a position to become weak and fall backwards, relapse, get into trouble, make poor choices and judgment errors that you will regret or that would cause you to suffer severe consequences because of them. You have seen enough of this already, as we all have. This pattern of destruction has nearly destroyed you, and all of us, and we can't let this happen to you again. I know it seems a strange way of showing it, but please know that our whole family is operating completely out of love and trying our best to protect you from further troubles. Please try to understand how much we love you and only want the best for you.

We are trying our very best to be loving and supportive, but we cannot enable you to continue on a disaster course any longer. PLEASE try to think about this from another perspective….it is not your fault, and no one is blaming you…this is why you need to go get the help, so that you can get your life back again. There are steps you need to take to get well, and if you will have faith in programs that work with people who are experienced in addiction disease, you will have a good chance for full recovery. You have come so far already, now that you are completely detoxed from the wicked hold of the drugs you were so dependent on for so long. Now, you just need the rehabilitation and counseling to help you to learn the proper way to move forward in dealing with life without drugs as a crutch.

I know you truly believe you know how to do this on your own, but sometimes in matters this serious we just have to trust that we don't know it all and put our faith in others and allow experts and those who are experienced to guide us in the right direction. Without getting the help you need, you will continue in the same dysfunctional path, and I know you don't want to do that. Despite how much you truly believe you are fine on your own, I hope you now realize that this is simply not true and that you truly do need help and support from professionals and fellow comrades who can all be there for one another, and I know you can do this with hard work and an honest, strong desire to see a positive change in your life course.

I have no doubt that you will be a happy and productive person someday, as you have so very much to offer to this world. You are bright, intelligent, creative, soulful, and talented in so many ways. I have always known that you have a very special purpose in this world, Jonathan, and once you have a clear head, free of all the demons and fears that have seemed to haunt you for so long, and inner peace and happiness with yourself, you will move forward into a wonderful place that you have never really experienced before in your life. Above all, you have a sweet, precious little son who worships you and loves you with all his heart. He is patiently waiting for his daddy to "feel better". He misses you, as we all do. The wonderful thing about children….they love their parents unconditionally, and no matter how long it may take, he will always love you and will wait patiently for you to come home to him. When you do, you will be the wonderful father you have always wanted to be, and who Remy deserves to have in his life.

I have some important information to share with you…you may not remember me telling you, but I had a session back in the beginning of January with a renowned Astrologer here. She has been doing this her entire lifetime and is extremely talented in her field. I won't bore you with all she had to say about me, but she had a LOT to say about "your middle child" (you). Keep in mind, she did not know me at all, had no idea about my family, and knew nothing about me other than my first name, my birth date and the time of birth. She had a very intricate birth chart mapping all of the planetary alignments, etc. throughout my lifetime, and she was able to also see my parents, as well as my children, and other aspects of my stars and planetary interactions and pathways. It was all very intricate and mostly over my head, but extremely interesting.

Anyway, she had very important information about you specifically that she wanted me to share with you. I went back today and listened to the entire tape again and wrote it all down so that I can share it with you, as I do believe it is information that you need to know as it will affect your life profoundly and you need to pay it heed. I am not going to go into any paragraphs here…I am going to just list things she said that I took right off the tape. Honestly, see if any of this does not affect you in a very recognizable and profound way, as it did me and Dad (I read it to him earlier today). We both think it is very important for you to hear, and I think you will relate to a lot of it. Here goes:

Jonathan is having serious issues and much confusion.

He does not feel strength.

He is easily led astray and the opportunity is there to drop off or not deal with life.

This is a VERY important time in Jonathan's life.

Planet Saturn return; Saturn has gone all the way around his chart and is back in the exact same place as his birth. This only occurs once every 30 years. This year (2010) will profoundly affect Jonathan's future. What Jonathan does right now will follow him for the next 30 years!!

Jonathan must get his foot in the door of his future.

He can't take the easy way out. He must work very hard and apply himself now, more than ever before, THIS YEAR has profound effects. If he does not do this, he will continue current life pattern, constantly trying to make things work for him and spinning his wheels.

He is dealing with power struggles with authority. He does not want anyone telling him what to do.

He is quick tempered, and short. He is not calm in his life.

Right now, don't speed or he will get a ticket. Look over his shoulder as he is being watched by "cosmic" cops.

This whole year for Jonathan is all about his home, health, and family.

Don't give any authority figures any grief whatsoever or he can and will go to jail.

If he owes anyone money, or has problems with anyone, he must clear up or this will follow him for 30 years.

He will be mad about it; anger is necessary to let him know there is a problem.

Even though he is mad, he needs to recognize the need to suck it up, and just do what he needs to do and get it over with. He needs to just play out the year and do what is necessary regardless of whether he understands everything.

Jonathan must get something going on in physical fitness, and needs to work out to the point of exhaustion. This will help him to get the stress out of his body.

This is a VERY SERIOUS and VERY IMPORTANT time in Jonathan's life. He must suck it up and work hard, and take orders; all year long he has to take care of his health, especially dental health, and skin, also bone structure (chiropractic?).

He needs to keep going in a forward direction; no going backward.

The egomaniac in his Aries sign is active: he wants it to always be all about him…he expects other people to take care of it for him. He needs to work hard and get the help for himself. HE HAS to LET IT COME FROM INSIDE HIMSELF.

Jonathan is very strong, though he does not always realize this. He has strong drive and strong initiative. Home, health and family is important to him.

Extreme discipline is needed for Jonathan. He needs to learn to accept things.

He needs to learn how to take disappointment, turn it around and say "this is what I have" and make the best of situations. He can't fly off the handle and be mad because he wants things his way.

Quote: "JONATHAN **MUST** MAKE CHANGES <u>NOW</u> OR HE IS GOING to RUIN HIS LIFE. PERIOD. THERE IS NO SUGAR COATING HERE. THIS IS <u>VERY</u> IMPORTANT to JONATHAN'S FUTURE."

These are HUGE planetary aspects that only happen once in MANY years. Saturn's return to place of Jonathan's birth only happens once every 28-30 years.

This is the time when he needs to find a place in a career and take off with it.

28-30 years from now it will be time to retire.

This year Jonathan needs to get real with society. He is going to be held accountable for everything in his life. That's what Saturn does. He MUST get through this and be VERY STRONG and then HE will be in charge. He will REALLY be in charge, not just thinking or expecting something he needs to be, for nothing. He will know how to be really in charge of himself and he will gain strength.

Planet Pluto is aspecting Jonathan's sun right now and will not aspect again for 40+ years! This does not happen often. THIS YEAR IS VERY, VERY LIFE CHANGING, EITHER WAY! It is up to Jonathan to choose which way it will go.

Jonathan's family must be strong and supportive without being enabling.

It is up to Jonathan. He must stand on his own two feet and must work with authority figures. He needs to show the universe that he can stick it out and be strong!

People with addiction problems are feeding into the weakest parts of their personality, kind of giving up. Jonathan needs to stay STRONG and know that "Yes, I do have this part of me and I can turn it into something positive. IT IS THERE, BUT IT DOES NOT HAVE to RUIN MY LIFE!"

There you have it, sweetie...I typed it word for word, exactly as she stated it all. Keep in mind she knew NOTHING about you prior to saying all of this. In fact, she did not know you had an addiction problem...she figured that out on her own just looking at your chart. It was profoundly amazing. She said she will be happy to do a birth chart specifically for you, if you'd like. I can tell you that everything she had to say about mine was spot on accurate. Amazing and interesting, to say the least. Kind of a profound experience for me, actually.

Anyway, I hope you will think about some of the things I've said here. I want to see you happy and healthy more than anything in the world. I think of you every day of my life, I pray for you, too, and I appreciate your message to me that you are thinking of me and praying for me, also. As you know, my surgery will be this Wednesday. Please continue to pray that all goes well for me. I must admit, I am a little scared, as anyone would be. But, I will be the strong person I always am, and do whatever I need to do. This is all any of us can ever do…keep on keeping on….make the best we can out of every day, and always remember that life is too short to waste a single day being unhappy. Shake off your troubles. Don't worry. Worrying never changed or fixed anything. Tomorrow is another day. The past does not matter anymore, other than the good memories.

We never know what is in store for us from one day to the next. I get through life's trials and tribulations by taking one day at a time, keeping a positive attitude, and relying on love, faith, and a sense of humor to get me through, along with putting my faith in God to direct my path. Please let Him hold your hand and lead you, too, Jon. Your peace will come to you when you can just let go of everything and accept the help that is waiting for you. Never underestimate your own strength and courage. You can do whatever you set your mind to do, as I have heard you say many times. If you set your mind to allowing God to take over, and to let others more experienced than you in to help you with this situation, you will be free of the burden you carry every single day of your life.

I wish so much that I could talk to you on the phone. All these medical bills have cost me the ability to pay all my bills this month, so I am unable to get that phone plan where you can call me. But, as soon as I am able, I will do that. Meanwhile, I want you to know how <u>very much</u> I love you, and I am sending lots of positive thoughts and energy your way. Please be strong for me, and know how much I believe in you.

Happy Birthday to you, Happy Birthday to you, Happy Birthday dear Jonathan; HAPPY BIRTHDAY to YOU!!!!!!!!!

May this year be the best year of your life! I wish you love, health, and happiness, and may all your dreams come true starting right now and continuing on through the rest of your lifetime. Be safe, be well, be strong, and find lightness in your heart and peace in your soul; rise up and move forward without fear; leave all past problems behind you and move on to your dreams. Reach for the stars! Do not be afraid of anything. God will light your path. There is much waiting for you and many who are counting on you! Believe in yourself and your divine purpose. Love yourself, as much as we all love you!

On this, your birthday, I will be remembering the day you were born, one of the most precious moments of my life...my sweet little baby Jonathan, so perfect and beautiful. No matter how old you are, you will always be my baby. I love you, with all my heart, and I always will.

Happy Birthday, my precious son. Please know that I am with you in spirit, even though you can't see me. Just think of me and know that I am there with you, right by your side, today and always.

I love you very much!

Always and forever,
Mom

Terri wrote this heartfelt letter as her eulogy to Jonathan.

May 8, 2011

My beautiful son,

Mere words cannot express the immeasurable love that I have for you.

From the first moment I held you in my arms for the the very first time, I knew depths of love I didn't know were possible. Although we have lived miles apart, I pray that you have always known how very much I love you, and how much everyone loves you.

My heart breaks that you were never able to reach your fullest potential, and I know that you were filled with many hopes and dreams for the future. God had a very special plan for you.

Your beautiful blue eyes gave us a window to your sensitive and loving heart, soulful insight, and deep love for your family, friends, and for the world around you. You have entertained us and inspired us with your amazing talents, your beautiful music, incredible artwork and profound writings. I will always remember all the fun and special times we had together laughing, singing, and creating music together.

My heart is breaking at the thought of never holding you in my arms again, but I know that you will be forever with me, right here in my heart. Please know how very much you are loved and how incredibly your far too short time with us has inspired and impacted our lives in ways we never imagined possible.

May you rest in peace, my angel, in a place where pain, heartache and sadness are no longer possible. When you were a little boy, and I tucked you into bed at night, I always said "Good night, Jon Boy". So, I will say to you again..... Good Night, Jon Boy, my precious son. I will miss you so very much and I will think of you every day of my life, and I will always remember all of our memories and happy times until we are together again.

All my love forever,
Mom

As the months went by after Jonathan passed, the family shared poetry that brought Jonathan to our minds. These are two of Terri's favorites.

Those We Have Loved Shine On

**We look at the night sky
in the quiet of darkness,
and they are never far.
Those we have loved and cherished,**

those who have changed our lives
in some small or profound way
are closer than we know,
because it is their light
that shines on our world.
It is the brilliance of their souls
that makes our night sky glow.

Author Unknown

I'm Still Here

Friend, please don't mourn for me
I'm still here, though you don't see.
I'm right by your side each night and day
and within your heart I long to stay.

My body is gone but I'm always near.
I'm everything you feel, see or hear.
My spirit is free, but I'll never depart
as long as you keep me alive in your heart.

I'll never wander out of your sight-
I'm the brightest star on a summer night.
I'll never be beyond your reach-
I'm the warm moist sand when you're at the beach.

I'm the colorful leaves when fall comes around
and the pure white snow that blankets the ground.
I'm the beautiful flowers of which you're so fond,
The clear cool water in a quiet pond.

I'm the first bright blossom you'll see in the spring,
The first warm raindrop that April will bring.
I'm the first ray of light when the sun starts to shine,
and you'll see that the face in the moon is mine.

When you start thinking there's no one to love you,
you can talk to me through the Lord above you.

I'll whisper my answer through the leaves on the trees,
and you'll feel my presence in the soft summer breeze.

I'm the hot salty tears that flow when you weep
and the beautiful dreams that come while you sleep.
I'm the smile you see on a baby's face.
Just look for me, friend, I'm everyplace!

Author Unknown

Framed, sitting next to a picture of Jonathan, is this comforting thought about our loved ones who have made their Heavenly journey.

Perhaps they are not stars but rather openings in heaven where the love of our lost ones pours down through and shines upon us to let us know they are happy.

As the year after Jonathan passed, each of us had events when we felt Jonathan's presence or we could feel that he was guiding us in a certain direction. Terri describes an experience she had.

Profound Experiences

It is difficult to believe that it has nearly been one year since I said goodbye to my youngest son.

The aching in my heart is still so deep, and I think of him and miss him every day of my life. But, as time moves forward, it has become increasingly evident just how much Jonathan's time with us has impacted my life, and the lives of many others, in the aspect of prioritizing and putting into prospective what truly is important in life.

The challenges faced by Jonathan and our family, which seemed almost insurmountable, have now, in retrospect, given rise to new realizations, greater goals and inspirations, and an overwhelming desire to honor his time here with us by carrying forward the love, human kindness, and charity that he so wanted to give to the world as a result of his tenacious efforts to heal himself in order to obtain this ultimate goal....the ability to make a positive difference in the lives of others, and to share spirituality, love, kindness, understanding, patience, forgiveness, passion, empathy, and integrity with as many people as possible, before our time here is finished. It is very important to me to honor Jonathan's legacy by living by these beliefs and philosophies to the best of my ability. Although his life here was cut short, as his body was unable to catch up with his best attempts and his spirituality, there is no doubt in my mind as to his good intentions. I believe that when God reached out His hand, Jonathan knew that his destiny path was already established, and he was to be finally at peace with allowing his faith to carry him forward and into the arms of God's grace, love, and glory.

    I have had many occasions in recent months where I felt an overwhelming desire to reach out to others, offer random acts of kindness, or making more concentrated efforts than I ever had in the past, towards taking notice of others, including perfect strangers, saying hello, or just simply smiling at them, recognizing that life on this earth can be very short, and we should never take a single day for granted. I have learned to live every day with the thought in mind that none of us ever truly know what turmoil may be in the hearts of those people we pass by every day of our lives, and what a difference the slightest gesture of kindness might make in their day.

    I had a very profound experience that took place just a short time after Jonathan's heavenly journey. In the depths of my own sorrow and grieving, I went to run an errand at a store where I had an item to return. As I was walking from the parking lot, I noticed a young man, about Jonathan's age, who was so pitiful, filthy dirty, obviously homeless, in tattered clothes and wearing old sneakers with his toes protruding out the front of his shoes. It was immediately evident to me that he was timid and embarrassed by his situation, and as I observed him, I saw that he was trying his best to rummage through a nearby garbage can, apparently looking for any small scrap of food, but he didn't want anyone to see him. Whenever anyone started walking in his direction, he quickly retreated until there was no one in sight, at which time he went back to the garbage can.

I watched in fascination, but I could feel my heart swelling with emotion and sympathy for this young man. When I got closer to him, I made a point to speak to him, and I asked him if he was alright. It was at this moment that I noticed the warmth and sorrow in his eyes, the hurt in his soul, and he, too, must have sensed that I was not just any ordinary person, of the many he had seen scurrying in and out of the store that day, immersed in their own thoughts and problems. He looked as though he felt "safe" to talk to me, and he then asked "Ma'am, I am so sorry to bother you, but, by any chance do you have eight cents?" I truly did not have any cash with me, but I opened my change purse and poured its contents into his hand, at which time he promptly tried to give it all back to me and said that all he needed was just the eight cents. He explained that he had not had anything to eat in two days and he had almost enough to get a hamburger at a nearby establishment on the other side of the parking lot. I insisted that he keep the money I had given him and apologized that I didn't have more to offer him. He had tears in his eyes, thanked me profusely, and said "God bless you, Ma'am" as I walked into the store.

While in the store, I could not stop thinking about this young man. I stood in line at the front of the store to wait my turn for the cashier, and the entire time I could not stop staring at my new friend through the large glass windows at the front of the store. I felt the urge to speak about him to the two women on either side of me in line, and stated how sorry I was for his misfortune. Immediately, one of the women said, "Well, you know he's just another one who is begging for everyone else's hard earned money, most likely so he can go buy some more beer or drugs". I was so saddened by this response that I responded with "If that is the case, then he would be most likely suffering from a terrible addiction disease, and God bless him if that's what he needs to do. Obviously, he has not had help available to him or he would not be standing here homeless right now.

I, for one, feel very sorry for his situation and I am worried about him".

Suddenly, the cynical woman got tears in her eyes and turned to me to say, "You are so right. I feel bad for him, too, and I should not have said that". Then, the second woman commented that with the current state of our economy, the young man's situation could easily be one of our own someday. It was a profound moment, but just the first of more to come. As I proceeded to the cashier, I received $28.00 in cash from the item I had returned.

I walked out of the store, and I didn't see my friend, so I went to my car to leave, assuming he had walked over to get his hamburger. I drove out of the parking lot, and proceeded to drive home, and suddenly, after making my way several miles down the road, I was overwhelmed with a desire to turn my car around and go back. I drove back to the store, and as I pulled into the parking lot, there he was, back on the sidewalk near the garbage can where I had originally seen him. Without any need for further thought, I drove right up to the curb, rolled down my window, and when he caught my eye, I motioned for him to come over to my car. He was hesitant at first, but then slowly walked over to me.

I handed him a twenty dollar bill and told him that, even though I knew it wasn't much, I hoped it might help him to get at least another meal or two. At that moment, he broke down in tears, and told me it was just too much and that he couldn't take that much money. After I insisted, he finally accepted my measly little contribution to his sad plight, and he seemed to have the need to explain to me that he hasn't always been this way....he said he had a job, was laid off, and he was also a musician in a band, but their services were no longer needed due to a lull in business at the venue where they had been performing. He had no family, no one to help him, and had been forced to live on the street. He had tried to make friends with the owner of the hamburger place, in hopes he could be hired there, but, so far, no luck.

Before I left him, I assured him that everything would

be alright, and to hang on to his faith. I wished him well, as tears welled up in my eyes again, and he told me that my gesture was the kindest thing anyone had ever done for him in his entire life. He said, "God bless you" once more, and I drove home, thinking of him all the way there.

This was, by far, the most well spent $20.00 of my life. Not a day goes by when I do not think of my "friend", and I wonder how he is doing and whether he has found abundance and love in his life by now. Perhaps he reminded me far too much of my own son who was frighteningly close to being in this exact same situation. Maybe the fact that he was a musician, also like my son. Perhaps it was the warmth in his eyes, the windows to his soul, that made me realize, without hesitation, what a special person he is, like my Jonathan always was, and always will be.

Most of all, I believe, with all my heart, that this experience was inspired by the love and inspiration left behind for my life by the legacy of my son, Jonathan, a beautiful soul, who I know is smiling down on me from Heaven, constantly nudging me forward with reminders of all that I can accomplish on his behalf and through his love.

Since the day I shared this story, it has become a regular routine in my life to give a small contribution to every homeless person I see. It may seem strange, but it has become more important than ever before in my lifetime to extend a "hand up" to others in need whenever these opportunities present themselves to me. It has added greater meaning and purpose to my life to "pay it forward" through simple gestures of human kindness, just as others have offered their love and assistance to me during my own times of feeling downtrodden and broken hearted. It is so important to me to help others, not only because I want to do it, but because there is a constant force always nudging me in that direction. I simply can no longer ignore someone in need, if it is within my power to help, if only to add a smile to their day.

I think of my precious Jonathan with each and every one of these experiences, and it truly adds so much joy and peace to my life. It always warms my heart, knowing that I am remembering and honoring my son and his legacy, continuing to do my part to carry forward the fulfillment of his dreams of making a positive difference in this world, and praying that his inspiration will encourage others to open their hearts and experience the most important reason for our existence...

TO LOVE,
AND BE LOVED, IN RETURN.

Terri Dacy

References

A Course in Miracles. Mill Valley: Foundation for Inner Peace, 1976.

The Bible

Bach, Richard. *Jonathan Livingston Seagull*. New York: SCRIBNER, 1970.

Berg, Michael. *Becoming Like God: Kabbalah and Our Ultimate Destiny*. Los Angeles: Kabbalah Centre International, 2004.

Brown, H. Jackson. *Life's Little Instruction Book, Vol. II*. Nashville: Rutledge Hill Press, 1993.

Byrne, Rhonda. *The Secret*. Hillsboro: Beyond Words Publishing, 2006.

Casey, Karen. *Change Your Mind and Your Life Will Follow*. San Francisco: Conari Press, 2005.

Casey, Karen. *Fearless Relationships*. Center City: Hazelden, 2003.

Chambers, Oswald. *My Upmost for His Highest*, edited by James Reimann. Grand Rapids: Discovery House, authorized by Oswald Chambers Publications Association, LTD, 1992.

Durant, Will. *The Story of Philosophy*. New York: Pocket Books, 1953.

Dyer, Wayne. *The Shift*. New York: Hay House, 2010.

Dyer, Wayne. *Excuses Begone!*. New York: Hay House, 2009.

Dyer, Wayne. *Change Your Thoughts-Change Your Life, Living the Wisdom of the Tao*. New York: Hay House, 2007.

Dyer, Wayne. *Inspiration*. New York: Hay House, 2006.

Dyer, Wayne. *The Power of Intention*. New York: Hay House, 2004.

Dyer, Wayne. *10 Secrets for Success and Inner Peace*. New York: Hay House, 2001.

Emerson, Ralph Waldo. *Nature*. Nashville: American Renaissance Books, 1836.

Feuerstein, Georg. *The Yoga-Sutra of Patanjali*. Rochester: Inner Traditions International, 1979.

Flach, MD, KHS, Frederic. *Faith, Healing, and Miracles*. Long Island City: Hatherleigh Press, 2000.

Gibran, Kahlil. *The Prophet.* New York: Borzoi Book published by Alfred A. Knopf, Inc, 1923.

Hicks, Esther and Jerry. *Money and the Law of Attraction.* New York: Hay House, 2008.

Hicks, Esther and Jerry. *A New Beginning I.* San Antonio: Abraham-Hicks Publications, 1988.

Howard, Thomas. *Dove Descending: A Journey into T.S. Eliots Four Quartets.* San Francisco: Ignatius Press, 2006.

Jampolsky, MD, Gerald. *Teach Only Love.* Hillsboro: Beyond Words Publishing, 2000.

McKeon, Richard. *Basic Works of Aristotle.* USA: Random House, 1941.

Millman, Dan. *The Way of the Peaceful Warrior.* Novato: Kramer Book and New World Library, 1980.

Moore, Thomas. *Soul Mates.* New York: Harper Collins, 1994.

Mundy, Jon. *Listening to Your Inner Guide.* New York: Crossroad Publishing, 1995.

Osteen, Joel. *Become a Better You.* New York: Free Press, 2007.

Osteen, Joel. *Your Best Life Now.* New York: Faith Words, 2004.

Osteen, Joel and Victoria. *Hope for Today Bible.* New York: Free Press, 1996.

Smith, Jean. *The Beginner's Guide to Zen Buddhism.* New York: Bell Tower, 2000.

Suzuki, Shunryo. *Zen Mind, Beginner's Mind.* New York: Weatherhill, 1970.

Thoureau, Henry David. *Everyman: Walden, edited by Christopher Bigsby.* N. Clarendon: Tuttle Publishing, 1992.

Tolle, Eckhart. *The Power of Now: A Guide to Spiritual Enlightenment.* Novato: New World Publishing and Namaste Publishing, 1999.

Warren, Rick. *The Purpose Driven Life.* Grand Rapids: Zondervan, 2002.

White, Ellen G. *Steps to Christ.* Altamont: Harvestime Books, 2000.

Wilson, Leslie. *Cliffnotes Thoreau, Emerson, and Transcendentalism.* Foster City: IDG Books Worldwide, 2000.

CPSIA information can be obtained
at www.ICGtesting.com
Printed in the USA
JSHW020514181122
33284JS00001B/2